SKIER'S DIGEST

2nd Edition

By Frank Covino

Follett Publishing Company / Chicago
T-0596

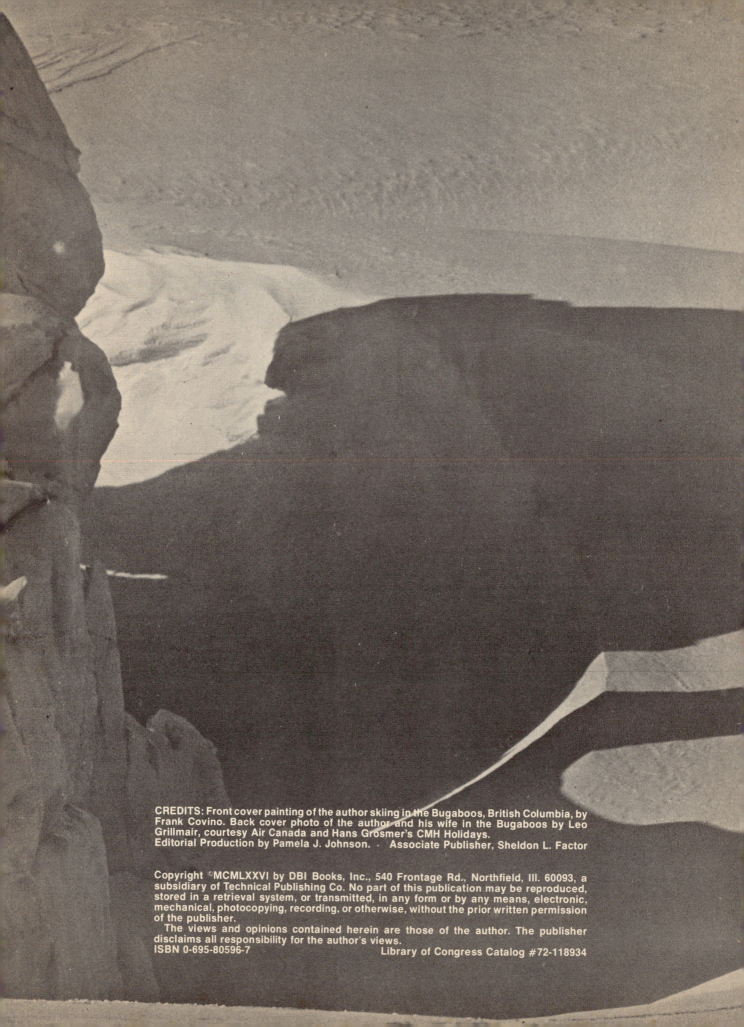

CREDITS: Front cover painting of the author skiing in the Bugaboos, British Columbia, by Frank Covino. Back cover photo of the author and his wife in the Bugaboos by Leo Grillmair, courtesy Air Canada and Hans Grosmer's CMH Holidays.
Editorial Production by Pamela J. Johnson. · Associate Publisher, Sheldon L. Factor

ISBN 0-695-80596-7   Library of Congress Catalog #72-118934

SKIING is not racing against a clock
not a triple inverted moebius flip
not the precise form of an expert technician
not a world of happy faces and well-shaped bodies
not a flight into unexplored territory and virgin snow
not a God-like feeling of control over natural elements

SKIING is all of these things...

Table of Contents

Dedication

*This book is dedicated to my beautiful wife, Marge,
without whom it could not have been created. F.C.*

Chapter 1
PREPARE YOURSELF

CHAPTER 1—PREPARE YOURSELF

I FIND IT CURIOUS that most of us spend weeks, months in some cases, prepping for the approaching new winter by reading last year's ski magazines, the new technical books published in the fall, by attending consumer ski conventions and ski club meetings, and by pacing a countless number of hours in the local ski shop buying the latest fashions, honing our edges and trying on new boots. Yes, skiing, for most of us, is obsessive and the passion, for many, is uncontrollable. This makes us fair game for the analysis of tongue-in-cheek psychologists. Freud related our compulsion to sex. Other psychologists have analyzed the motivation for participation in the challenging sport of skiing as an unconscious process related to "conquering the fear of castration"; we bring ourselves to the brink of disaster and then cheer ourselves in victory over successful conquest. That achievement varies with each level of the learning process. For a beginner, it might be no more than a successful basic turn; for a seasoned veteran the impending doom might be the anxiety of antici- pating a roaring avalanche or skiing into a bottomless crevasse, deep in the heart of the Bugaboos. Analysis of the unconscious motivation has led to a variety of conjectures, but most psychologists, who have had more than a few skiers on the couch, will agree that participation in skiing is certainly an ego trip. While the rich scald our eyes wearing the latest high fashion furs and colors and tickle our gonads by securing the tightest fits, the sub-culture freaks call attention to themselves by wearing the longest beards or frizzing their hair like a zulu and going out of their way to wear the oldest, loosest, non-commercial clothing they can find in the local tag sale. There are so many skiers "trip- ping" down the lift line with one ear open for praise shouted down from the chairlift that these trails invariably develop the most moguls. The hot shots wait below until they see an instructor's parka on a distant chair, and blast off just when he is close enough to be impressed by their first five turns. The intermediates spend most of their day on the novice hill, impressing the beginners, and even the beginners can't wait to return to their offices and boast of their skiing involvement to others who can't afford the sport or who simply are not in condition to participate. Skiers are masters of one-upman- ship.

What stirs my curiosity, in an objective observance of much of the skiing contingent, is that many of the ego bolstering practices which occupy their time are *superficial.* Take a good look at yourself. The most expensive and flashiest outfit is not going to help you ski better, nor does that beard or your old baggy clothes make you any less pretentious. And boogying down the lift line with your skis wide apart and your poles flailing above you impresses no one but the least oriented. If you really want to inflate that ego beyond the effect of surface manifestations, if you really want a feeling of *accomplishment,* take lessons to learn the

science behind your skis' descent and perfect your tech- nique, ski more challenging and exotic areas and begin your annual season's preparation with a tune-up of your *body*, the *foundation* beneath the facade.

Plato encouraged man to strive for the perfect form in body and intellect. Religious leaders added to that by advising us to search for a perfect spirit. The Renaissance man of da Vinci's vintage probably came closest to such complete life fulfillment. What do we have today? Spiritual involvement is ridiculed, the well-developed male body is mocked*, and the development of our minds is terminated by far too many on graduation day. While the ancient Greeks strived to get the *most* out of their natural potential, many of us today seem to be content with the *least*, as long as we can cover up our inadequacies with insignificant *surface* em- bellishments. The fancy or freaky clothes hide our wasted bodies, the television set has replaced our books, and, even in our esoteric world of skiing, too many of us are content to settle for less than mediocrity while we applaud the per- formers who color our skiing magazines. Why not strive to be the *best* skier you can possibly be; why not continue to develop your intellect after school; and, don't you think it's time to stop laughing at those well-developed bodies on the beach (the simplest cop-out in rationalizing your own fat or frailty) to see what you've been missing? Physical culture carries a hidden guarantee; it not only will develop a stronger and thus longer living body, but it will also awaken your *mind.* Your reflexes will improve. Your energy will be stoked. Your blood circulation will improve, and even your complexion will change for the better. Concomitant with the development of your muscles through progressive exercise must be a healthy diet, and surrender of destructive habits like smoking and excessive drinking, of course. If you think it's not worth the sacrifice, skip this chapter; you might do well to skip the *sport*, too.

First consideration should be for that of your *endurance.* The performance of an automobile is not totally dependent upon its horsepower; it is dependent upon how well the motor is *tuned.* A car's performance relies upon timing of its engine and the functional relationships of its motorized units. Your endurance is determined by the capacity of your lungs and the condition of your cardiovascular system. By now, the methods of improving one's pulse rate, (the timing of the cardiovascular system) developed by Dr. Lawrence Morehouse in the Human Performance Laboratory at UCLA, are legend. Dr. Morehouse's work has been quoted and publicized in more conditioning articles than any other, and not without merit. It is worth reviewing. He believes that you can prolong the time it takes your heart to reach its

---

*It is curious that the well-developed female body gets quite a different reaction.

maximum pulse rate by exercising vigorously 10 minutes a day, while maintaining a pulse rate of at least 120 during the exercise period. You probably know that a normal pulse rate beats between 60 and 80 per minute. A fast string of avalements down Al's Run at Taos could more than double that rate. That kind of skiing demands *preconditioning*. One sure road to heart failure is traveled by men and women who lead a relatively passive life, seldom increasing their pulse rate beyond the normal span, but who sporadically tax their hearts with an extreme overload like that run down Al's.

Determine your pulse rate by pressing the tips of your fingers between your throat and the sterno-cleido-mastoid muscle, just beneath your jaw. (Fig. 1-2) Compare the beat to the sweep of the second hand of a clock. My own pulse runs about 62 beats to the minute, while my wife Marge has a count of 72. My age is 44; she is 26. During a strenuous workout we both maintain a pulse rate of about 120. To find out what your *maximum* count should be, deduct your age from 220. It is doubtful that any sport will bring you close to that maximum count; if it does, you *have* got trouble, and it's time you had a *stress test*. Your doctor can tell you the condition of your cardiovascular system by taking mechanical measures of your pulse rate at various intervals while you are engaged in some form of exercise, like the pedaling of that bike in his office. His measurements are more exact than your finger test. While this stress test will determine the maximum count at which you should tax your heart, it does not necessarily mean that you have to settle for your present condition. Dr. Morehouse's recommendation of a daily 10-minute exercise program, maintaining a pulse rate of at least 120 will ameliorate your endurance and increase your capacity to endure a heavier load. Please don't surpass the recommended program unless exercise has been a regular part of your daily routine. The type of exercise you select is your prerogative, as long as participation will allow you to maintain that 120 pulse rate. My advice would be to select a form of exercise that relates to skiing, like running, bicycling, hiking, etc. If you are less adventurous, jumping jacks in your own living room would be sufficient. Outdoor exercise has the added benefit of flooding your lungs with clean air, but, if the air over your city is polluted, you had better stay inside until you can swing a trip to ski country. The beach is another environment conducive to lung and cardiovascular development. Don't follow the throngs who give it up after Labor Day; it's most beautiful between then and November, and even the Northeast has skiing *somewhere* on Thanksgiving. There probably is only one better off-season exercise for a skier than running on beach sand; hiking up and down the ski slopes at a fast pace. Both are cheap investments with rewarding returns.

Endurance alone will not enable you to chalk up 150,000 vertical feet of skiing through Hans Gmoser's Bugaboos in a week. Muscular development is essential. This does not mean that our male readers must look like Mr. America before boarding Hans' helicopter; nor must our female readers resemble bull dikes. It is possible to have strong muscles without appearing mesomorphic. It is *not* possible to ski most expert slopes without greater than average muscular development, however, so you had better learn a little about it if the total skiing experience is your goal. Muscular development is possible at just about any age through a system of progressive exercise and diet control.

FIG. 1-2: You can find your pulse rate by pressing your fingers in the space between your jaw and your sterno-cleido-mastoid muscle.

The first step in beginning a systematic program of progressive exercise is to find a compatible workout partner. Few of us enjoy exercising alone, and a workout or two alone, after years of no physical effort at all, is certain to result in boredom or lack of interest. Whether your partner is male or female is inconsequential; beneath all that pulchritude, your wife or girlfriend has the same basic muscular structure as you (so does your child, for that matter), and we can all profit from the exercises I intend to demonstrate. The movements have been selected specifically for their relationship to movements while skiing. The schedule I recommend is *daily* for those who should lose some fat, and three times a week for the rest of us, except for the abdominal exercises which should be done by everyone daily. Study the photographs and muscular analyses of my wife and me on pages 8 and 9 for a moment and learn the specific names for the muscles. This basic medical vocabulary will help me to describe exactly how an exercise affects a particular muscle group, and why it should benefit you as a skier.

A muscle is developed or made stronger by a periodic concentration of flexion and extension against a formidable resistance. Every part of our body has an extensor group of muscles which counteracts the flexor groups. Thus, when the biceps (on the arm or the leg) is contracted, the triceps on the other side is stretched (on the leg, the triceps would be represented by the vastus internus and externus, plus the rectus femoris); when the triceps is contracted, the biceps is stretched. If the contraction and/or the stretch is exercised against some form of substantial resistance, more blood

KNOW YOUR SKI MUSCLES

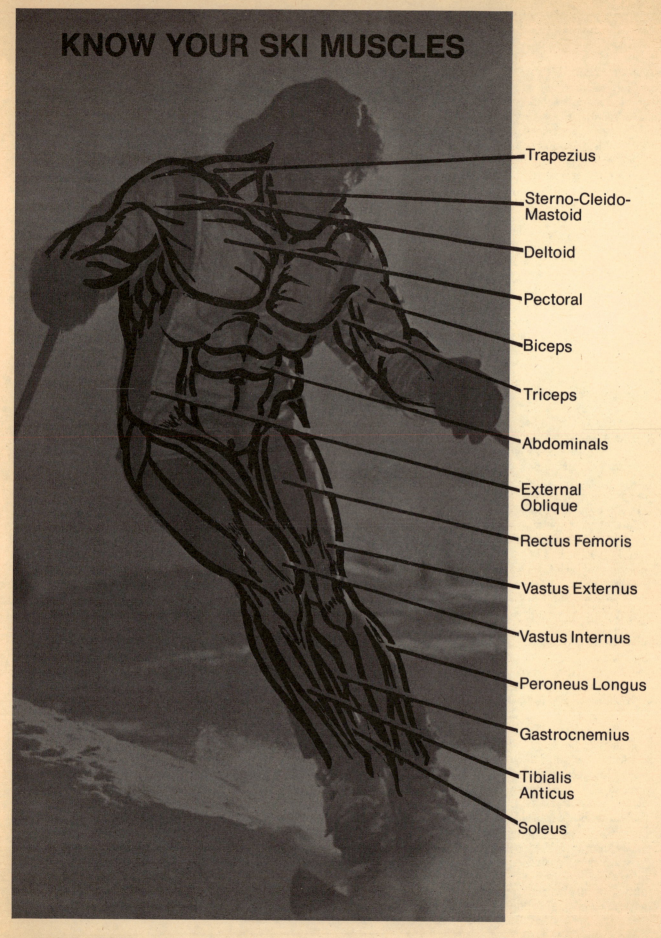

Trapezius

Sterno-Cleido-Mastoid

Deltoid

Pectoral

Biceps

Triceps

Abdominals

External Oblique

Rectus Femoris

Vastus Externus

Vastus Internus

Peroneus Longus

Gastrocnemius

Tibialis Anticus

Soleus

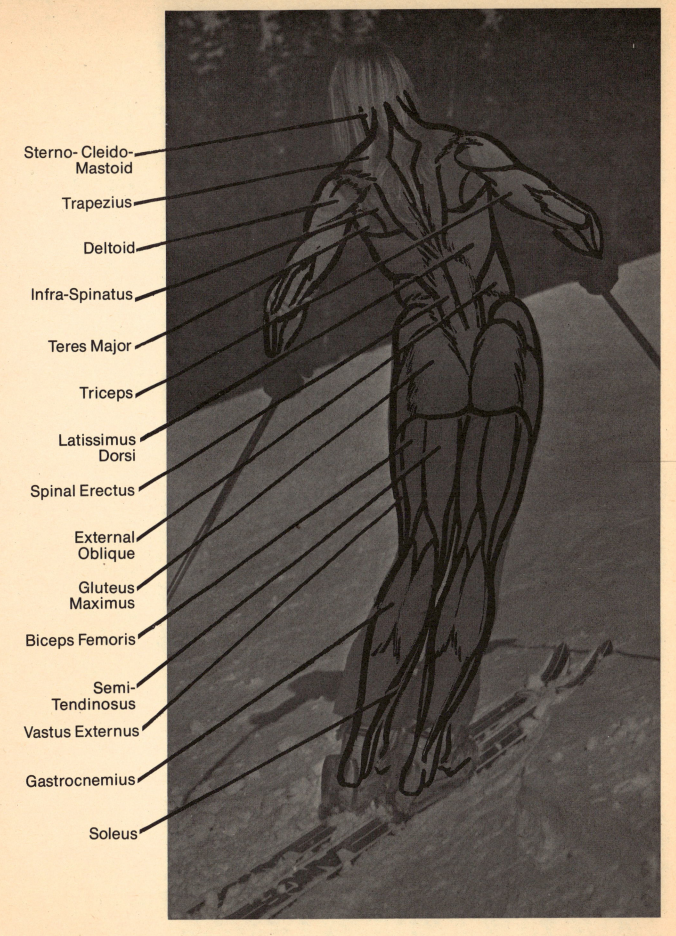

Sterno- Cleido-
Mastoid

Trapezius

Deltoid

Infra-Spinatus

Teres Major

Triceps

Latissimus
Dorsi

Spinal Erectus

External
Oblique

Gluteus
Maximus

Biceps Femoris

Semi-
Tendinosus

Vastus Externus

Gastrocnemius

Soleus

rushes to the struggling muscle and engorges it. The swelling subsides after a rest, but continued practice of the exercise will gradually enlarge the muscle more permanently and give it added *strength*. Many repetitions of the exercise toughen the muscles without increasing their size appreciably. Less repetitions and more sets of the exercise between rests tend to strengthen the muscles and increase their size. I prefer to keep the concentration of blood flowing in a logical direction; thus, I like to follow exercises for the lower leg with upper leg exercises, followed by hip exercises, stomach and side movements, back and chest activity, shoulder and neck work and finally, with exercises for the arms. For variation, the flow may be reversed.

The best type of "formidable resistance" used to exercise the contracted and extended muscles is arbitrary. Weights are ideal but often impractical. They might be substituted with your own body, as in push ups, with a workout partner, or with various domestic elements like that iron frying pan or your wife's steam iron. Some modern gymnasiums, YMCAs, etc., are equipped with "Universal" type weight lifting devices that are extremely practical for exercising all parts of your body in the shortest amount of time. The following demonstrations will utilize all the variations of resistance devices I have just mentioned.

Before we begin, I want to let all our women readers in on a well-kept secret: weight lifting exercises have been employed by movie stars, models and sports participants of both sexes for more years than you can imagine. One of my most memorable experiences some 20 odd years ago was pushing the iron around at Abe Goldberg's gym in New York City with a friend named Mickey and his girlfriend, Jayne Mansfield. I literally watched that girl add 6 inches to her chest inside of one year, and not a single ounce of it was fat. Abe's gym was a friendly place, with a health food and drink bar near the entrance, and a variety of physical culture enthusiasts spread from wall to wall, each doing their own thing. He was one of the innovators of the health spas that are currently so popular—there is probably one in your city. If you're shy, here are some exercises you can do in your own home.

Warmup Exercise: JUMPING JACKS (Fig. 1-5)

Purpose: This is your basic warmup exercise, with which most of us are familiar. Whoever invented it hit upon an excellent comprehensive movement which employs most of the major muscle groups from head to toe. In addition, Jumping Jacks function as an ignition to fire up your circulatory system and develop your endurance. If you did nothing but this exercise for about 10 minutes, daily, you would note a marked improvement in your stress capacity in a matter of a few weeks plus a beneficial reduction in your resting heart rate. Begin every exercise period with a set and start every day with Jumping Jacks, especially before skiing.

Description: The photos are self-explanatory. From the starting position, standing as erect as you can with your chin held high, leap up and land in the leg spread position clapping or crossing your hands; this is the count of *one*. Leap back to the first position, then continue with the advised number of repetitions and sets for your Class.

Frequency: For athletes, health freaks, day people and the physically superior, (*Class A*) begin your routine with *five*

Fig. 1-5: JUMPING JACKS. You can't beat Jumping Jacks as a thorough warm-up exercise, and you can do them almost anywhere.

sets of 60 repetitions, one minute rest in between each set, for 10 minutes daily. One set of 60 is sufficient just before an exercise period or a day of skiing.

For *Class B* readers, those of you who fall in between the two extremes, begin your Jumping Jacks with five sets of 30 repetitions, resting 2 minutes after each set, daily, as the others. One set of 30 is sufficient just before an exercise period or day of skiing. Try to work your way up to the *Class A* schedule. To run a decent slalom or giant slalom course at maximum efficiency, your heart should be able to maintain the stress of 60 rapid Jumping Jacks and settle to your normal pulse rate shortly after.

For smokers, heavy drinkers, night people and the physically inadequate, (to whom we will refer as *Class C* readers from now on), begin your routine with five sets of 15, 2 minutes rest in between each set, 10 minutes daily, especially just before an exercise period or a day of skiing

Exercise 1: ONE LEGGED HEEL RAISES (Fig. 1-6)

Purpose: To develop the *gastrocnemius*, (Fig. 1-6A), commonly called the calf, a vital muscle for the serious skier. This muscle is in a state of extension during most of your skiing but contracts every time you jump, dropping your ski tips, or when you extend on the downhill side of a mogul. With the modern high-heeled boot, many skiers feel a burning sensation in their "gastrocs" after the first day of skiing each season. Skiers who use longer skis use this muscle more since they must maintain their body weight on the balls of their feet; short ski advocates use it less, as they

ski mostly with their body weight distributed along the whole foot. We all use our gastrocs when we climb.

Description: Sit on the edge of a stool and prop your partner or some other form of weight resistance on one knee with the ball of your foot on a 2-inch board (or a fat book) and the heel of that foot on the ground. Now, push the weight resistance up by raising your heel off the floor and as high as you can. You will see the muscle contract. Then, lower, and continue for the repetitions and number of sets advised for your class.

Frequency: For *Class A* readers, four sets of 15 repetitions (each leg) three times a week, unless you are skiing every day. Get a heavier partner when it gets easy.

For *Class B* readers, three sets of ten repetitions (each leg) three times a week, unless you are skiing every day. Try to work up to the Class A schedule.

For *Class C* readers, three sets of ten repetitions (each leg) with no weight resistance, three times a week, unless you are skiing every day. Take a 2-minute rest between each of the following exercises. None of these exercises, beyond the warm-up Jumping Jacks, are necessary on days that you are skiing.

Exercise 2: SOLEUS GASTROC STRETCH (Fig. 1-7)

Purpose: While this exercise also stretches the upper attachment of the gastrocnemius, often shortened by women (and men!) who wear high-heeled shoes, it also strengthens the most important tendon a skier has: the *soleus* (Fig 1-7A).

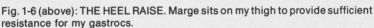

Fig. 1-6 (above): THE HEEL RAISE. Marge sits on my thigh to provide sufficient resistance for my gastrocs.
Fig. 1-6A (left): THE GASTROCNEMIUS. Commonly referred to as the *calf* muscle, this is one of a skier's most important muscles, and one that is usually least developed among less athletic individuals.
Fig. 1-7 (below): THE SOLEUS STRETCH. Walk away from the wall until you feel a good stretch in your soleus when you touch your heel to the ground.
Fig. 1-7A (right): THE SOLEUS. Beneath the gastrocnemius, but projecting like buttresses on either side, the soleus is the muscle most frequently damaged in a forward fall if it is underdeveloped.

Fig. 1-8 (above): THE BICEPS STRETCH. You'll feel a burning sensation in your leg biceps if the muscles aren't as long as they should be and you stretch them this way. Fig.1-8A (right): The BICEPS FEMORIS and SEMI-TENDINOSUS are the muscles which are connected to what is commonly referred to as your *hamstrings,* the two prominent vertical cords on either side of your popliteal. The cord on the outside is actually the tendon of your biceps femoris on its way to connection with the top of your *fibula* (the small bone of your lower leg). The cord on the inside is the tendon of your semi-tendinosus which passes across the inside of your knee joint and is connected to the shaft of your shin bone (tibia). Both muscles are used extensively in *avalement* type maneuvers when skiing.

Think of the soleus as the attachment of the *lever* (which is your body) to your skis. It is a tendon that is frequently ripped away from the tendon of Achilles in a forward fall, if the skier has not stretched it beyond its average extension by progressive exercise such as this.

Description: With your hands on a fence rail, door jamb or anything solid, walk away from your hands as far as you can until your heels just barely touch the floor. Then do alternate heel raises, raising and lowering your heel to the floor each time, in an effort to stretch each soleus tendon.

Frequency: For *Class A*, two sets of 100 repetitions (50 with each leg).

For *Class B*, two sets of 50 repetitions (25 with each leg).

For *Class C*, three sets of 20 repetitions (10 with each leg).

Exercise 3: BICEPS STRETCH (Fig. 1-8)

Purpose: Sorely neglected among many skiers is the muscle group on the back of the leg, the *biceps* and *semi-tendinosus* (Fig. 1-8A), sometimes referred to as the hamstrings. Most of us are short in this area from sitting too much and walking too little. Every time you retract your skis or swallow your knees, as in avalement, you are using this important part of your thighs. Develop your leg biceps and you will slither through the moguls like a snake!

Description: If a partner is unavailable, prop your foot against a wall while you sit on a bench. Reach for your ankle until you feel a burning sensation in the back of your outstretched thigh. Eventually, you will be able to stretch beyond your foot.

Frequency: Class A, three sets of 25 repetitions (each) with each leg.

Class B, two sets of 15 repetitions (each) with each leg.
Class C, two sets of ten repetitions (each) with each leg.

Exercise 4: LEG CURL (Fig. 1-9)

Purpose: A muscle develops strength and size when it is alternately extended (stretched) and contracted against a resistable force, over a systematic period of time. This exercise *contracts* the leg biceps (Fig. 1-9A) and should follow the Biceps Stretch exercise just experienced, for total development of that muscle group.

Description: You are out of luck if you don't have a partner for this one, unless you can find a leg curl "machine" at your local YMCA or physical fitness center. Lying prone, with your knees stationary, curl your heels back to your derriere while your partner offers resistance. Don't cheat. Only you can tell her whether to apply more or less resistance. Each repetition should be a maximum effort. If your partner isn't strong enough to provide sufficient resistance, do the exercise one leg at a time.

Frequency: Class A, three sets of 15 repetitions.

Class B, three sets of ten repetitions.

Class C, two sets of seven repetitions using your ski boots for weight resistance.

Exercise 5: SUMO SQUAT (Fig. 1-10)

Purpose: This important exercise, which reminds my wife of a Sumo wrestler position, is a great way to move the concentration of blood that you just summoned for the back of your leg to the front of your thighs for development of the quadriceps (Fig. 1-10A). This is the group of muscles you will use most while you are skiing, as they come into play with every up and down movement when you unweight your skis. Also strengthened is the "vital to skiing" biceps tendon that

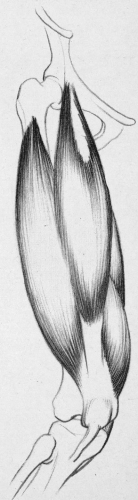

Fig. 1-9 (above left): THE LEG CURL. The biceps femoris is one of the least developed muscles in most inactive people.

Fig. 1-9A (left): *Flexed* BICEPS FEMORIS and SEMI-TENDINOSUS contract to form a rounded volume very similar to the form of a contracted biceps when the arm is flexed. My sketch here shows the connection of the biceps femoris to the head of the fibula or small bone of the lower leg. Excessive *rucklage* (sitting back) while skiing places a severe strain upon this vital connection.

Fig. 1-10 (above right): THE SUMO-SQUAT. Here's a fantastic exercise for building up your thigh muscles and strengthening your ligaments.

Fig. 1-10A (right): THE QUADRICEPS. Composed of the four major muscles on the front of your thigh, my reference to quadriceps includes the VASTUS EXTERNUS or muscle on the *outside* of your thigh, the RECTUS FEMORIS which runs right down the center, the VASTUS INTERNUS that tear-shaped muscle just above the inside of your knee, and the SARTORIUS, which you can barely see in this sketch, a long narrow muscle that has its origin at the iliac crest, stretches all the way down the inside of the thigh and is finally connected to the inner surface of the shin bone. These are your most important skiing muscles!

is attached to your tibia/fibula junction.

Description: The stance is wider than the grande plié in the second position of ballet; with your toes pointed outward, space your feet as far as is necessary to allow your lower legs to remain absolutely *vertical* throughout the exercise. With your hands on your hips, slowly lower your bottom until your thighs are parallel to the ground. Keep your back *vertical*, and thrust your hips forward as you *slowly* rise back to the starting position. Rest two minutes between sets.

Frequency: Class A, two sets of 50 slow repetitions deliberately tensing the thighs through the movement.

Class B, two sets of 25.

Class C, two sets of ten.

Exercise 6: SHALLOW KNEEBENDS (Fig. 1-11)

Purpose: While the old familiar "deep" knee bends have been rejected by most physical therapists as dangerous to the knees, those same knees can be strengthened and supported by powerful *quadriceps*, if knee bends are performed *part way* and some weight resistance is used to tax the muscle group. You still have time to build up your quadriceps (Fig. 1-10A), and lighten the burden of those heavy skis and boots!

Description: Place your heels on a 2-inch board or large book, legs spread about a shoulder width, toes pointed straight ahead, your partner on your shoulders. Marge uses my daughter Cameron for her weight resistance. Lower in the traditional deep-knee-bend manner, but stop your movement when your thighs are slightly above a position parallel with the floor. Then rise for a full count.

Frequency: Class A, three sets of 15 repetitions. If it gets too easy, find a heavier partner.

Fig. 1-11 (above): SHALLOW KNEE-BENDS. She's neater than a barbell. This exercise helps build up those quadriceps. (See Fig. 1-10A)

Fig. 1-12 (below): BOTTOMS UP. Pick something softer for her to kneel on than rough cement.
Fig. 1-12A (right): THE GLUTEUS MAXIMUS. Call it the "shoulder" of the lower body. We must use it a lot when skiing, as this seems to be the most well developed muscle among ski champions (and the first to turn to fat when you become less active). The protuberance to the right in my sketch is caused by the head of the *femur* bone. This bone of the thigh slants to a greater degree in most women and some men, causing the familiar *riding breeches* look. It also causes difficulty when skiers with that characteristic try to *edge* using only their knees. Body *angulation* would solve the problem.

Class B, three sets of ten repetitions.

Class C, three sets of 15 with no additional weight resistance.

Exercise 7: BOTTOMS UP (Fig. 1-12)

Purpose: Aside from too many of us having sagging bottoms or no bottom at all, this exercise will not only improve your appearance, but will also develop the strength of your *gluteus maximus* (Fig. 1-12A) beyond the capacity required for tireless skiing.

Description: From an animal position on one knee, straighten your other leg and lift it beyond a position parallel with the floor, while your partner offers sufficient resistance on your calf to make the movement difficult. It is important to keep the working leg straight throughout this exercise. The gluteus maximus powers the lifting of your leg in much the same way as your deltoid (shoulder muscle) powers the lifting of your arm.

Frequency: Class A, three sets of 15 repetitions (each leg).

Class B, three sets of ten repetitions (each leg).

Class C, three sets of 15 repetitions (each leg) with no partner resistance.

Exercise 8: JACKKNIFE (Fig. 1-13)

Purpose: One of the weakest pair of muscles in all non-athletic individuals and one of the first to atrophy with age is the *spinal erectus* (Fig. 1-13A) which forms a column of support on both sides of the spine or vertebrae. Curiously, this set of muscles can even be weak in athletes if their particular sport of concentration does not require them to bend at the waist

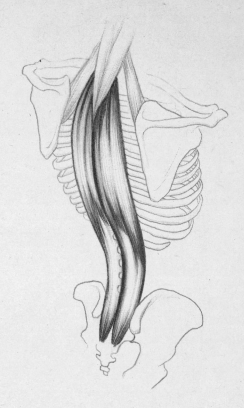

Fig. 1-13 (below): JACKKNIFE. If it's too tough with your hands behind your neck, try it holding your arms out and touching the ground.

Fig. 1-13A (above right): THE SPINAL ERECTUS. Bordering your spine like two healthy eels, these twin muscles come into play with every twisting or bending body motion. Hyper-development can give great support to skiers with disc problems (and be substantial preventive maintenance for skiers who are not yet afflicted!).

Fig. 1-13B (right): THE SARTORIUS. My sketch here is of the *inside* of the thigh. The sartorius is the long narrow muscle that I have darkened. Damage to it, at its terminal point inside the knee is quite common among skiers who "ski" in a wedge position, commonly called the *snowplow*. Keeping your thighs together will protect your sartorius, among other things.

Fig. 1-14 (above): SIDEBENDS. Provide just enough resistance for her to have some difficulty rising.
Fig. 1-14A (below): THE EXTERNAL OBLIQUE. You can't *angulate* without a good set of these. Neglect of the external obliques almost always results in the familiar *rubber tire!*

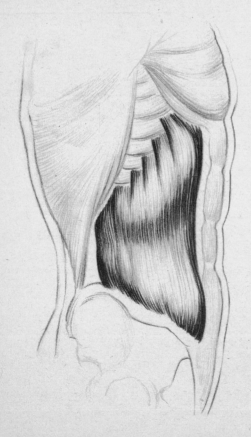

frequently. For skiers, the spinal erectus is taxed every time we angulate, or when we tip our upper bodies downhill in anticipation, or when we maintain an egg or bullet shape while racing downhill, or in all aerial flip maneuvers. It is worthwhile developing

Description: Alone, or with a partner, prop up one foot on a railing, couch or chair, high enough to prevent you from bending the other knee. With your hands clasped behind your head, bow forward as low as you can, then raise your torso upward as high as you can, for a count of one. Performed on one leg in this manner, the exercise will also stretch your sartorius, the long muscle on the inside of your thigh (Fig. 1-13B)

Frequency: Class A, three sets of 25 repetitions. If it gets too easy, have your partner apply resistance, clasping her hands over yours while she stands before you.

Class B, two sets of 15 repetitions.

Class C, two sets of ten repetitions, with a chair close by, in case you get dizzy.

Exercise 9: SIDEBENDS (Fig. 1-14)

Purpose: For optimum balance on a steep fast slope, your shoulders should be slanted parallel to the hill while traversing, while your hips swing uphill of your skis. A frequent instructor command to his students is, "Drop your downhill shoulder." This will be difficult, if not impossible, if your waist measurement is greater than the girth of your chest. That rubber tire on most people, but especially those in the Class C category, can usually be deflated by developing the muscle called *external oblique*, which spans both sides of your body like a corset holding it all together (Fig. 1-14A). Your control of your skis will improve in direct proportion to your capacity to angulate, unless you are fortunate enough to ski in deep powder every time, where a "banked" body posture is permissible.

Description: With your partner lying down to offer you resistance, spread your legs, place one hand behind your head for maximum stretch, hold his hand or forearm with the hand on your working side and bend sideways as far as you can, returning upright for a count of one. Should you be without a partner, use some kind of weight in his place; a heavy frying pan, steam iron or magazine basket will do, although you should work up to about 15 pounds of resistance, at least.

Frequency: Class A, three sets of 15 repetitions.

Class B, two sets of 15 repetitions.

Class C, three sets of ten repetitions.

Exercise 10: LEG RAISE OR BODY RAISE (Fig. 1-15)

Purpose: Many skiing movements require the upper or lower parts of our bodies to function as levers, using *the abdominals* (Fig. 1-15A) as a fulcrum. That familiar rubber tire around many waists is round. The *Jackknife* will take care of the rear portion of that tube, the *Sidebends* will whittle down the sides and *Leg or Body Raises* will shave off the front. Top expert skiers sport the same washboard abdominals as a well-conditioned fighter or gymnast.

Description: The leg raise is performed while lying outstretched, flat on your back, with your hands behind your head grasping an immovable object for support (that immovable object can be the board on which you are lying). Class C readers should then raise their knees to their chest and

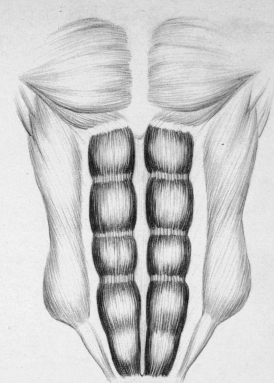

Fig. 1-15 (above): LEG RAISES. One of the best abdominal exercises, for skiers who find their skis heavy when they take to the air.
Fig. 1-15A (right): THE ABDOMINAL WALL. Among too many of us, this ''wall'' has crumbled. Build it up again before the muscle atrophies!

Fig. 1-16A (below): BODY RAISE 1. Start with your body as vertical as possible.

Fig. 1-16B (above): BODY RAISE 2. Lower to a horizontal position.
Fig. 1-16C (below): BODY RAISE 3. Touch your toes and return to the first position without touching your hips to the ground.

Fig. 1-17 (above): HALF LEVER SCIS-
SORS. Sit on the ground until you get
strong enough to do this one as I am
demonstrating.
Fig. 1-18 (right): SITUPS. They may be the
oldest known bodybuilding exercise, but
they are still the most effective for trim-
ming your waist.

return to the starting position for a count of one. Class B
readers should raise the entire legs with no bend at the knee
until the lower back just begins to raise from the floor; then
lower the legs to an inch or two above the floor for a count of
one, and repeat. Class A readers may want to try Lower
Body Raises in place of Leg Raises for greater stress upon
the abdominal group: From the same supinated position
raise your entire body until it is vertical and resting upon
your upper back (Fig. 1-16A); then slowly lower until your
body from the upper back down is *parallel to the floor* (Fig.
1-16B); then, touch your toes to the ground, with space
between the ground and your body (Fig. 1-16C), and return
to the starting vertical position for a count of one.

Frequency: Class A, (Lower Body Raises), three sets of ten
repetitions; less repetitions, if you find it difficult, until you
get stronger.

Class B, (Leg Raises), three sets of ten repetitions. As
your strength develops try for 15 repetitions, then try Lower
Body Raises.

Class C, (Knee Raises), three sets of ten repetitions. If
you get to the point where you can handle 15 repetitions, try
Leg Raises instead.

Exercise 11; HALF LEVER SCISSORS (Fig. 1-17)
Purpose: The abdominals are a stubborn wall of muscle that
demands at least two exercises for total development. The
Half Lever Scissors will toughen that wall and your *avalement* turns will be effortless.
Description: Marge shows the basic movement for Class B
readers while I show the variation for those in Class A.

Class C readers may find even Marge's less strenuous
movement tough; they should forget it and try sit-ups, (see
next exercise) instead, until their abdominal strength improves. For Class B, simply sit on the floor or on a board,
supporting your balance with your hands, either beside you
or above and behind your head grasping a door knob. Class
A readers should spread your fingers as shown and
straighten your arms until your hips are raised from the
floor. Both classes, now raise your feet off the floor, spread
your legs as wide as you can, and return for a count of one.
Continue for recommended repetitions without allowing the
feet to touch the ground.
Frequency: Class A, three sets of ten or more repetitions.
Progressive increase.

Class B, three sets of ten or more repetitions. Progressive
increase.

Exercise 12: SITUPS (Fig. 1-18)
Purpose: Readers with real problems in the middle can add
this exercise, which should be performed daily by everyone,
anyway, either to tear away fat, to build strength, or merely
as a precaution against the most common physical inadequacy, the *abdominal wall*.
Description: Most of us are familiar with the basic movement.
From a supinated position, with the feet hooked under a
strap or sofa bottom, and the *knees bent*, clasp your hands
behind your neck and raise your torso until you can kiss your
knees. For added stress the exercise can be performed on an
inclined board and the torso can be lowered SLOWLY.
Frequency: Like I said, we all need this one every day. Work
up to 100 repetitions per day and try to make it a habit.

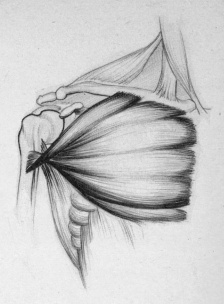

Fig. 1-19 (left): PEC POP-PER. This exercise can develop strong pectorals and a snappier pole plant! Fig. 1-19A (right): THE PECTORAL. The principal mass is called MAJOR and the small strand that I've sketched below it is called MINOR. Hyper-development will provide a natural bra for women and a formidable shelf for men to support their ski sweaters. Both will find their pole plants less tir-ing with well developed "pecs."

Exercise 13: PEC POPPER (Fig 1-19)

Purpose: The uninformed might suspect that the skier need only concern himself with development of his lower body, since the skis are worked mostly with the legs. Analysis of the physique of any racing or free-style champion will reveal solid chest, shoulder and back development, with strong arms and an iron grip. Analysis of your own aches and pains after the first few days of skiing will corroborate my opinion that more than lower body development is needed to master the vigorous sport of skiing. This exercise will develop the major chest muscle, the *pectoralis major*. (Fig. 1-19A). You use it when you climb on skis, with each pole plant, and, also, when you rise from a fall. The "pecs" are the easiest muscle in the body to build. Well developed, they will enhance your appearance, whether you are male or female, and make your pole plants less of an effort.

Description: Supinated on the floor or on a board, extend your arms laterally. With a partner applying resistance to your forearm, raise your fist and arm in an arc with your shoulder as the central axis. Bend your elbow only slightly

and keep your arm moving until its fist is above your opposite shoulder. If a partner is unavailable, hold some kind of weight in your hand for resistance. Do a set of the repetitions recommended for your class, then switch to your other arm.

Frequency: Class A, four sets of ten repetitions with max-imum effort.

Class B, three sets of ten repetitions with maximum ef-fort.

Class C, three sets of seven repetitions with maximum ef-fort.

Remember, only *you* can tell your partner whether or not to apply more pressure. Every repetition should be a con-centrated maximum effort!

Exercise 14: LATERAL RAISE (Fig. 1-20)

Purpose: The pectorals are capped by the all important *deltoids* (Fig. 1-20A) which are the fulcrums of our arms and thus are vital to any upper arm movement, as when we plant our poles or move in anticipation of the next direction of our

Fig. 1-20 (left): LATERAL RAISE. The shoulder muscle is used when you ski, more so than you realize.
Fig. 1-20A (right): The DELTOID. It gets its name from its delta shape. This shoulder muscle is used more than you might im-agine when skiing, and underdevelopment has caused many a case of bursitis among skiers.

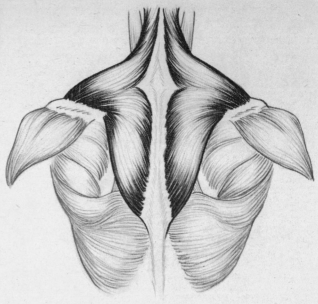

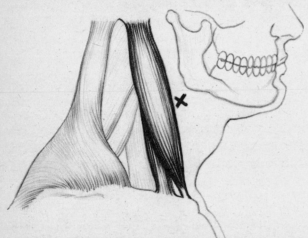

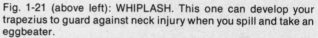

Fig. 1-21 (above left): WHIPLASH. This one can develop your trapezius to guard against neck injury when you spill and take an eggbeater.

Fig. 1-21A (above): THE TRAPEZIUS. This large kite-like shaped muscle is the major connection between your head and your body. Skiers frequently develop neck vertabrae problems (pinched nerves, etc.) because of underdeveloped "traps." The body can only tolerate so much bone grinding without muscular support, and every time you lift your head you are compressing your neck vertabrae!

Fig. 1-21B (left): THE STERNO-CLEIDO- MASTOID. Forming the two columns on either side of your throat, this muscle also is a vital connection between your head and your body. The *carotid artery* may be found where I have marked an "X" if you should want to check your pulse rate.

Fig. 1-21C (below left): THE TOWEL TRICK. A variation of the last exercise if you prefer to do a solo.

Fig. 1-21D (below): BETTER THAN ASPIRIN. Try this exercise next time you get a headache. It will also develop strong sterno-cleido-mastoid columns on the sides of your neck.

skis; the deltoids also help us to climb, to get up from a fall, to push out of a starting gate in a slalom, giant slalom or downhill race. The deltoids help to propel us from the kicker of a jump. Even if it is for no other reason than to give you strength to punch out a lift line crasher, you should work upon development of your deltoids.

Description: With a partner applying resistance to your forearm, slowly raise your fist to the side and up over your head with only a slight bend at your elbow. A hefty iron skillet in your hand could replace the "partner" and give you as much benefit if it weighs enough. Yes, girls, this exercise is for you, too. It will not make you look like a football player, but it will put some beef around your bony acromion process and possibly guard against destruction of your bursa next time you fall on your shoulder.

Frequency: *Class A*, three sets of ten with maximum effort, each arm.

Class B, two sets of ten with maximum effort, each arm.

Class C, two sets of ten with light weight resistance, like a heavy ash tray.

Exercise 15: WHIPLASH (Fig 1-21)

Purpose: The familiar automobile crash injury that occurs when the head snaps forward then back like the movement of a cracking whip is not unfamiliar to many skiers, whose neck muscle development was insufficient to prevent similar injury in their fall while skiing. The two major muscle groups that might save you from a broken neck are the upper portions of the trapezius (Fig. 1-21A) which are attached to the base of your skull at the rear, and the sterno-cleido-mastoid (Fig. 1-21B) columns which begin at the mastoid bone behind your ears and end where the sternum or central column of your chest meets your collar bone or clavicle. The trapezius is the muscle that pulls your head backwards; the sterno-cleido-mastoid works to pull your head forwards or to either side.

Description: For trapezius development, have your partner stand in front of you and apply pressure with her hands clasped on the back of your head as you bend it forward. Slowly press your head backward as she adjusts the pressure of her hands accordingly, to require your maximum effort. If you would rather do a solo, try creating similar resistance with a rolled up towel pulled over the back of your head. (Fig. 1-21C) You may do it seated for greater concentration of blood around the taxed trapezius.

For the sterno-cleido-mastoid exercise, your partner would have to stand behind you and clasp her hands over your forehead as you roll your head back as far as you can. Then, slowly, and with maximum effort, roll your head forward while she applies resistance (Fig. 1-21D). For a solo, simply place the palms of both your hands on your forehead with your head thrown back, and apply pressure from your arms as you slowly roll your head forward.

Frequency: *Class A*, three sets of ten repetitions, each exercise.

Class B, two sets of ten repetitions, each exercise.

Class C, two sets of ten, solo, each exercise.

(All with maximum effort).

As I mentioned earlier, many YMCA's and physical fitness centers offer the use of a Universal machine (Fig.1-22). At the Fairfield Y in Connecticut, where Marge and I

Fig. 1-22: Marge and I using only a small part of the Universal system at the Fairfield YMCA.

Fig. 1-23: DALIA VALLE. One of my favorite girls. Drop in to see her. You'll walk away revitalized!

work out during the "off" seasons, they call it a Marcy Gym. These "machines" are not to be confused with vibrator belts, motorized rowing or bicycling machines or any kind of massage unit (which all do nothing more than shake up your fat and loosen your skin). A Universal machine is a progressive weight lifting device that provides eight stations with bars and different pulley systems. This allows eight people to exercise at the same time in a concentrated area. Keys and slots eliminate the nuisance of changing plates and collars, and it is possible to exercise every muscle in your body on one of these machines in a

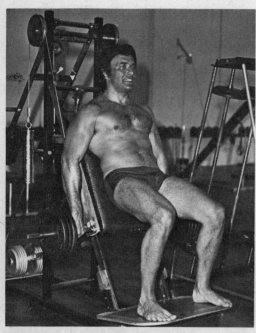

Fig. 1-24 (above): THIGH MACHINE. Not as soft as Marge, but the weights do provide more resistance.
Fig. 1-25 (below): LEG PRESS MACHINE. One of the best exercises for building strength in your thighs.

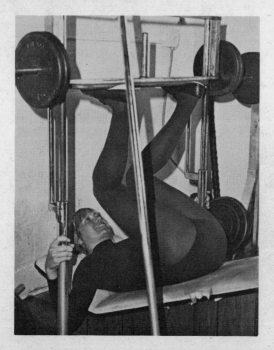

short amount of time. Complete instructions for the use of this equipment are usually posted on a wall near the Universal. Check it out; you might like it!

Modern gymnasiums are well equipped to help you isolate the development of any particular muscle group that you feel is deficient for skiing tolerance. One of my favorite gyms is run by a delightful woman in Miami Beach. Dalia Valle, four feet, eleven inches, wasp-waisted and bosomy is 59 with the life and vitality of a girl in her twenties (Fig 1-23). She has been in the business of physical culture for over 16 years, molding male and female bodies like a sculptress. Her medium is iron. The kind you push around. Hers is not the kind of spa where you are pampered with exotic perfumes, massaged and occasionally dropped into an automatic shaking machine. "There are no shortcuts to physical development or health maintenance," smiles Dalia. "It takes genuine work, sensible diet and self respect."

Study my exercising posture in Fig. 1-24 and relate it to the movement of your legs while skiing. By periodically increasing the weight resistance on such an exercise facilitator you could develop strength in your thighs comparable to an Olympic champion! Now, look at Marge, at work on the leg-press machine (Fig. 1-25). By keeping her feet spread apart and her toes pointed straight forward, Marge's knees are closer to her sagittal plane than her ankles, creating the same relationship as her outside knee to her outside ankle if she were carving a turn on skis. Aside from directly developing the thigh and lower leg muscles that she would use in such turns, this exercise also places stress upon the important medial and lateral collateral ligaments that brace the knees. Stress upon those ligaments naturally calls for additional assistance from muscles like the vastus internus and externus, the rectus femoris, and even the biceps femoris and semi-tendinosus on the back of the thigh. In the lower leg, the pre-leg-press movement contracts the tibialis anticus and peroneus longus which will pad your shin bone, and extends the important soleus muscles, which give you grief in the beginning of every season because you are not used to being locked into ski boots.

Skiing is a dynamic athletic activity. It demands strength and endurance, two potentials we fail to develop even to half capacity because of the automated world in which we "live." The truth is that many of us are not *living* but are merely existing. To *live* one must actively participate, mentally, spiritually and physically. Skiing is one activity that invites the expression of all three potentials, but if your body is in a state of near atrophy it would be wise to reawaken it with a systematic program of progressive exercise and sensible diet. Ponce de Leon was not too far off course. The Fountain of Youth is at Dalia Valles, 715 Washington Avenue, Miami Beach, and all over the country, at places like hers. Look for one in your community.

There it is; a prescription for tuning up your body before and during the ski season. It is also a prescription, barring accidents or destructive habits, for a long and healthy life. A well-tuned body is the generator for an alert mind. Just as the brain stagnates from lack of creative use, so your body will atrophy and decay from lack of exercise. Your workouts can become as perfunctory and habitual as eating or sleeping if you discipline yourself to follow a schedule religiously. Your body is your most important piece of skiing equipment. Now let's look at some of the other tools.

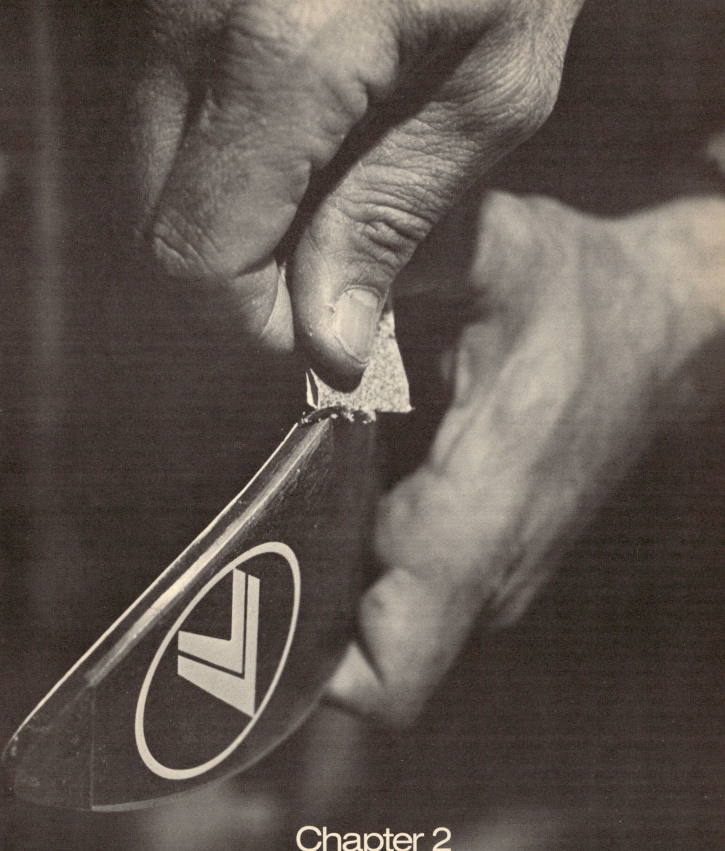

Chapter 2
KNOW YOUR EQUIPMENT

CHAPTER 2—KNOW YOUR EQUIPMENT

WRITING A CHAPTER such as this, any author is tempted to capitalize upon the opportunity to accept money and gratuities in exchange for eulogizing a few trade names. I think they call it soft-sell advertising. Rest assured that this particular piece is written with no commercial gain. I chose to expose the Lange plant for two reasons. First, it is a totally American enterprise, although its facilities are also employed by Oriental and European subsidiaries in deference to the quality of its production. Bob Lange of Dubuque, Iowa, innovated the substitution of synthetic material for leather boots in 1957. Call this chapter my humble offering in this Bicentennial year to the desperately needed "Buy American" program. At a time when the state of our economy has reached a precarious low, while our government continues to play the thankless role of benefactor to the world, I feel motivated to plug an American company which, in fact, happens to produce equipment comparable to any European product, but just hasn't had the promotional dollars to pay professional athletes for using their equipment, or to tell the world more about themselves via 12 page ads in the trade magazines. Secondly, I have used Lange boots since they first came upon the ski scene (they were the first synthetic buckle boot) and, for 3 years, have been faithfully using their skis which not only perform well, but are the most durable on the market. I would never plug a product that I didn't test and rate highly, first.

This, of course, does not mean that Lange boots and skis are for you. Nor does this article intend to underrate other competitors. For many years, I used Kneissl skis exclusively. They were the first skis to employ fiberglass in their construction. I still believe that they are a high quality product. No one can argue that Rossignol, Fischer, Kastle, Spalding, Blizzard, Dynamic, Atomic, Volkl, Olin, K2, Hexcel, Hart and Head, are also top quality ski manufacturers, as are a few other new brands that are unmentioned. My advice to the recreational skier is to try out as many different brands of skis that you can and choose for your own those that work best for you in the ski area that you frequent most; just be sure that they are constructed with durability as a qualification, as too many products today are designed with planned deterioration—such as American cars.

Boots are another problem. They must not only function well, but they should also be comfortable. Quite frankly, up until this year, Lange USA was so concerned with durability and performance, they paid less than adequate attention to the consumers' *comfort*. Either you had "a Lange foot," or you grew bunions and calluses and nursed frost bitten toes in sub-zero weather, *but at least the highly functional boots made your skis perform well*. The latest Lange models, designed with performance AND comfort, are the finest ski boots made. For me. And, they may be for you, but try them.

Any reputable ski shop will carry most of the top brands of boots. Try on all of them. Walk around in them for 10 minutes. Pick out the three that feel most comfortable. Then, talk to skiers who own the boots that you favor to find out about their performance. Above all don't buy any boots or skis just because they are touted by ski champions. They are probably paid to use them. It is no secret that downhill "amateur" racing champion Franz Klammer will earn a six figure salary this year for his use of Fischer equipment during his Olympic victory. Don't put him down for accepting the bread. Athletes have a high mortality rate. One year they are heroes, and, several years later, they are nearly forgotten. They have to make it when they can. Like the models and movie stars. Fischer makes a great line of skis, but the equipment requirements of an Olympic champion are certainly nowhere near the needs of a recreational skier. You will probably never reach the velocities at which he races, and, even if you buy the same *brand* of ski, you can bet that it is not quite the same product that he used in the contest. Every ski manufacturer has a special department which does nothing but research the peculiar needs of racers and develop *super* equipment for them that is several cuts above the skis and boots that are produced for the average consumer. They know that we are a society of hero worshipers, and heroes are the world's best salesmen.

Read all you can about equipment. Talk to skiers who use different brands. Visit factories, if you can. Then try several brands. Good ski shops will have "demo" skis that you may borrow for a day or two. You may be as lucky as I have been in finding the right combination for my pleasureable recreational skiing. Once you settle upon a brand, try to find out how their equipment is made. Here is what Marge and I found at the Lange USA plant in Colorado.

The clean white factory buildings of the Lange USA Company are silhouetted like a picture postcard against the rocky brown foothills which rise like a dam before the white majestic range between Mt. Evans and Long's Peak, protecting the flats of Denver from the spring thaw. (Fig. 2-2) A beautiful setting for one of the smallest but finest ski and boot manufacturers in the entire world.

Marketing director, George Page, greeted us, introduced us to an attractive secretary, and rapped a little about the new modifications in Lange equipment. Because skiing is still a relatively new sport in this country, subject to constant research and planning that is 5 years ahead of current production specifications, we consumer skiers must necessarily purchase equipment that we know will be obsolete in 5 years. *Caveat emptor*. It is a seller's market. This keeps the industry alive. It also produces better skiers, for, as much as the changes have put a quinquennial bite on our bankbooks, they also have made it a lot easier and safer to descend our challenging mountains. I really thought that Lange had put

Fig. 2-2: The Lange USA plant has the Rocky Mountains in its front yard.

together the best combination in last year's Banshee boot and FS ski. My own skiing proficiency took a great leap forward when I started using them (reassuring, at the age of 44), and the only gripes I had was that the top of the skis had vulnerable cosmetics, and my toes would freeze after a few hours of skiing in the sub-zero trials of January in Vermont. I had no disappointments with regard to performance.

George was quick to inform us that the Lange-flo material, used inside previous liners will be replaced with a substance called *Ultra-Fit* that no longer requires 20 minutes of wear to assume the shape of a skier's foot; that shape will be molded immediately. The new material is also *warmer* (Vermont skiers, take note), and the boot will be 1½ pounds *lighter*, a blessing for those who use heavy bindings like the Look Nevadas or the Burts. The shell, or outside of the Lange boot is still *Adiprene*, a Du Pont urethane elastomer material that has an incredible memory once it has been molded. Lange USA makes Adiprene shells for its foreign subsidiaries also, about 150,000 shells per year, and their distribution is worldwide. They are still a modest, relatively small company when compared to an outfit like Nordica which distributed over 280,000 pairs of boots in the United States alone last year. To appease my concern about cold feet, Page assured me that the new boot models will have an insulating foam foot bed under the liner, while the entire inner boot will be lined with a warm felt-like material. We looked over the prototypes, placed our order for two pair on a pro-form and asked George for a tour of the factory. He turned us over to Greg Stone, Manager of Public Relations and International Traffic, who gave Marge and me some protective goggles to wear in the expansive production room.

All Lange USA products are made totally "in house" right from the original raw material. The boot process begins with laminations of the liner material, die-cut by a machine that applies 60,000 pounds of pressure per square inch. The liners for all Lange boots are identical, except for color and height which differs for each of their boot models. The cut patterns are then stacked upon a staging rack. Color patches are stitched to the liner material to differentiate patterns for different boot models.

Volara foam is glued to the liner to form a heel hugger,

which guards against the possibility of heel slippage. (Fig. 2-3). It is most important, when you try on new boots, that you lock them into a pair of binding mounted skis and press your knees forward, as they would be if you were skiing steep fast terrain on skis taller than your height. If you feel your heels lifting appreciably off the sole of the boots in that effort, the brand you are testing was not designed for optimum performance. Try something else.

The new Ultra-Fit foam, called UCO, is attached to the liner, replacing the older *Lange-flo* substance, and the width

Fig. 2-3: Lange USA's heel hugger process insures no slippage while skiing.

Fig. 2-4: Specially designed triple stitch keeps base of inner boot flat.

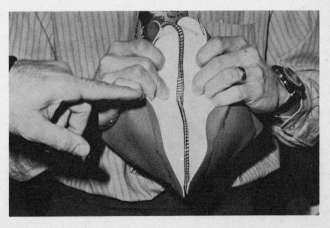

Fig. 2-5: This is the edge before it is sealed in the ski.

of the foot is then considered with one-sixteenth of an inch, (all around), marking the difference between a narrow, medium or wide width foot. Length variations are stretched by a heating process. There are 96 pieces in every Lange liner—Lange says it's the most expensive boot on the market, *to produce*!

A "surge-machine" next stitches the base of the liner with a triple stitch that flattens when the skier's foot is inserted. (Fig. 2-4) Be sure to check out the inner stitchwork of any ski boot that you intend to purchase, as a welt in a sensitive area can give you a lot of grief with extensive use. The final liner step is the attachment of the tongue. I must congratulate Lange for increasing the depth of the foam material in the new boot tongues. Pressure above your instep at the termination of the tibia can be severe if you use a boot with too thin of a tongue.

The high-heeled, forward-tilted Adiprene shells are cast by pouring the substance into an aluminum mold, which presses out the basic shape. A high-speed router is then used to trim off any excess. Next stop is the riveting area, where rivets adhere the metal buckles to the Adiprene shell. A polyurethane paint is then applied to the molded brand name. After inserting the liner into its mated shell, the Lange producers then subject their completed product to the scrutiny of a final quality control group, who must do a good job because less than one percent of the boots made by this conscientious company are returned for flaws. Lange USA provides an unconditional guarantee against manufacturer's fault, something

you should insist upon when you purchase *any* boot. Their service for repair is a 2-day turn around, with an added gratuity of a walk-in-and-wait service if you need an excuse to fly to Colorado!

Our curiosity about boot construction satisfied, Marge and I followed Greg into the ski production room. Every worker in the plant looked healthy and happy with their particular function. They were quite a variety, ranging, in the boot division, from shapely T-shirted packing girls barely out of their teens to wholesome pleasant grandmothers who are master craftsmen with a needle. The men dominated the ski production staff where a little muscle was required in addition to artistry. We were especially impressed with the sincere *care* that each employee seemed to exercise in the performance of his particular station.

First stop in the ski room was the bench where steel edges are adhered to a urethane tip protector. (Fig. 2-5) Greg claimed that Lange is the only company that takes this step, as a precaution against tip delamination. Because of this tip protector and the "wet-wrap" process which we will see shortly, it is virtually impossible to delaminate a Lange ski while you are skiing! Think about that next time you see some unfortunate soul walking down the mountain with a splintered ski over his shoulder.

There are two types of steel edges used on every top brand of ski, one-piece and cracked, with a running controversy over which type is more functional. My own experience has

Fig. 2-6: Sweden's Ingemar Stenmark finds an ideal course during Sun Valley's World Cup held on Baldy's Grey Hawk Run. Racers in his category are seldom on the flat part of their skis. (Sun Valley photo)

taught me that one-piece edges have a snappier bounce, which is especially useful when descending a steep slope with a sharply edged short swing. One-piece edges also will spring you higher off a kicker if you like to go for air. This characteristic *snap* also facilitates up-and-forward un-weighting if you ski with longer skis and pivot under their shovels. The cracked edges seem to allow skis to hug the terrain more tenaciously, torquing in conformance to the shape of the ground with no sudden snap back to their original shape. This permits a skier to *snake* his way down the trails more fluidly. Choose the type of edge that best suits your style of skiing.

The "base-assembly" proceeds by adhering the edges and tip-protector to a pre-cut *base* made of either P-Tex 1000, which is fastest and thus is used in the higher priced skis, or a "Special" P-Tex, which is used on lower priced models, since skiers using those skis are probably less concerned with speed. A top sub-assembly is then molded by adhering a material called ABS to poly-urethane *sidewalls*, making the sides of Lange skis almost as fast as their bases! If you don't think this is significant, take a good look at a racer in the middle of his turn: he has tilted his skis onto their inside edges so sharply that only their edges and their sidewalls are touching the snow! (Fig. 2-6)

A lamination of six layers of fiberglass is then constructed; directional, multidirectional, unidirectional, mesh, matte and chopped fibres form this part of the wrap.

The core is made of wood; one piece of Sitka Spruce imported from the state of Washington. The boards are shaped in-house with their tips formed by a heating process. This core is wrapped in fiberglass and cemented with epoxy resin. Greg assured us that the "wet wrap" process makes Lange skis the strongest on the market. Most other brands have sandwich-type constructions that are *not* wrapped, which makes them vulnerable and susceptible to the curse of delamination. In the process of wrapping, Lange uses 25 percent more epoxy resin than is needed. This excess is pressed out in a later stage of the construction process.

Before adhering the base assembly to the top sub-assembly, strips of urethane are laid down the full length of the ski's edges. This allows the metal to stick to the epoxy and has the added feature of dampening the skis to make them more quiet when performing.

The wet-wrapped sandwich is completed by placing the entire new unit into a mold that operates at 200 degrees Fahrenheit with 2,200 pounds of pressure, pressing the ski into its characteristic bottom camber and tip splay. There is a total saturation of epoxy resin because of the excess amount that was applied in the earlier stage of the ski's construction. This is followed by a cold press, and the ski is near completion. A trimmer slices off about a sixteenth of an inch on both sides of the top material which is then subjected to its characteristic cosmetic markings and coated with a gloss that is probably in the urethane family. Big Bill would not permit us to see this final process as Lange skis, this year, will be one of a few U.S. made skis with a high gloss finish, and that final production process is top secret. (Fig. 2-7)

The final quality control step is an important one which not every manufacturer takes the time to exercise: the *matching* of individual skis by their flex pattern. Each ski is

Fig. 2-7: Three stages of final construction.

hung from its center and weights are applied to its tip and its tail. The flex is measured and calibrated on a chart with a number for tail flex and one for tip flex, i.e. 53/42. When two skis come close to the same calibration, they are married and presumably will spend the rest of their lives together. A maximum variance of 2 is allowed.

But Lange is still not satisfied. They take still another step that many manufacturers skip. They test for warpage. Their testing table is a perfectly flat marble table. You may perform a similar test if you have a perfectly flat surface. Simply place each of your skis base down on the flat table. With one finger, press down on the right side of each tail, then again on the left side of each tail. If there is a warp, your ski will rock. It is probably too late to correct yours, but the newly constructed Lange ski is not completely cured yet. The total curing process takes 2 weeks. In an uncured state, the ski may still be *bent* into a straight shape by using a mortised wooden tool and a bit of muscle. Equal bottom camber is also checked at this *really* final stage, and a bar on the side of the marble warp testing table permits correction of any fault, so that every pair of Lange skis is perfectly matched.

Marge and I left the factory suitably impressed. Perhaps the reason why Lange USA takes such care in the produc-tion of their product, (one pair of skis takes a full week for its completion), is that they are a small company with a traditional respect for craft. They only turn out about 20,000 pair of skis per year. Compare that to the 970,000 pair that Rossignol averages annually or to the 750,000 pair that Fischer produces each year, and you may draw some of your own conclusions about quality control. But, as beauty lies in the eyes of the beholder, so will there never be ubiquitous agreement upon the best brand of ski. What works for Franz Klammer may be a bummer for you. What works for me may be a noodle for Franz Klammer. Suffice it to say that there are differences in construction, differences in performance and differences in durability. This article was only intended to supply you with a few guidelines for planning your next purchase.

CHOOSING EQUIPMENT

Skis

WITH REGARD to equipment designed for the beginner or advanced skier: There is such a thing as a ski designed for tyros, thanks to Clif Taylor, promoter of the short flat ski. New skiers today are generally taught to ski by skidding on the flat part of their skis, twisting their boards by axial motion, like propellers. It is true that some skis are designed for this type of motion, while other skis are not. For such a *skidded* turn, a wider, shorter, less cambered ski is most appropriate; for such turns, the groove running down the center of the base need not be appreciable, also. Advanced skiers, who ski on their edges most of the time, need a ski that will *carve*. Such a ski is more narrow, has more side camber (the waist of the ski) and good torque (the ability to twist in conformance to terrain changes and return to its original shape). Its tail should also be stiffer if you dig *wheelies* or ski the bumps with *avalement*, and its length had better be longer if you like the cruise of a Cadillac or shorter if you like the precise short turns of a sports car (mine, at 190cm, are somewhere in between). Slalom racers may prefer a stiffer shovel for carving their turns out of the fall line on their ski tips, whereas mogul lovers appreciate a more flexible shovel that will snake over the bumps instead of blasting through them.

Boots

While now practically extinct, the leather boot cannot be denied its rightful place in the history and evolution of skiing. It paved the way for the synthetic shells and custom-fitted liners we accept as commonplace today. The leather boot's metamorphosis—from a rather flimsy foot-covering that barely connected skier to ski to today's colorful, high-backed, high-performance boot—gives rise to our understanding of the ski boot as a tool that has added significantly to the pleasures and skills of skiing.

The advent of the steel-edged ski in the early thirties helped set the stage for the marriage between technology and skiing. While designed to protect the ski, it was soon learned that this thin steel strip made better control possible. The problem was finding a means of securing the boot to the ski in a way that would take advantage of this new-found control. This led to devices such as the Amstutz Spring and the Super Diagonal, a strap that wound around the upper boot and was attached behind the heel to the ski. Cable bindings, introduced in the mid-thirties, offered even better control, but often caused the boot sole to buckle. As a counter measure, a steel shank was fitted into the leather sole, and eventually more layers of leather were added to prevent buckling and twisting. Finally, a true ski boot emerged, not as we know it today, but it was a beginning.

For the next 10 years a series of handcrafted, hand-sewn boots appeared on the market replete with brass hooks, lace adjustments at the Achilles tendon and in varying degrees of stiffness and heights. A common denominator of all these boots was the necessity of breaking them in.

Breaking in boots meant more than just walking around in them for several hours. Achieving a sense of fit required patience, devotion and time. Boots were worn for hours in a tub of warm water, walked in until dried and conformed to the shape of the foot, baked in a slow oven, basted with paraffin and then buffed and polished. The result was a pair of boots that were comfortable and looked quite good. But, they withstood the rigors of skiing for only a short time. They soon lost their stiffness and shape and with it the sense of control required to guide precisely the long skis then in general use.

With the introduction of the metal sandwich ski, an easy flexing, wood-laminated ski which had virtually no twist, a new era of control on powder and on ice emerged. Improved boots were designed to compliment these skis. They were higher, several layers thicker, stiffer and some incorporated steel spring inserts.

Beginning in 1955, skiers were absorbed with wedeln and the American final form technique. The contortions which skiers went through to master these techniques were an outgrowth of the new skiing style as well as the equipment they used. Long, stiff skis were part of this equipment. To attain a direct connection between ankle and ski edge, many skiers used a long thong attached to a turntable on the ski. Through this device, the virtues of direct leverage control over the forepart of the ski began to be understood. The buckled boot, offering real time savings and a good tight fit, soon emerged, and eventually, boots that leaned forward at approximately a 20-degree angle were introduced. This led to another change in skiing style and precipitated the shortening of skis.

For years, most advancements in skiing equipment had been made by Europeans. But in 1964, the Lange Company, then of Dubuque, Iowa, came up with an idea for a unique design and construction that would eventually revolutionize the ski boot industry.

Lange realized that the problems inherent in leather ruled it out for the type of boot they envisioned. However, through the many changes that leather boots had undergone over the years, Lange had gained an understanding of what a really good ski boot shell should offer. It should provide very strong, almost rigid lateral support; permit direct control from the leg to the ski; be capable of absorbing shock and vibration; remain unaffected by temperature extremes; possess the right degree of flexibility yet retain its original shape; not absorb water; be lightweight; resist cutting and abrasion; and be colorable to complement high fashion ski wear.

In their search for a material to meet such exacting requirements, Lange learned about "Adiprene" urethane elastomer, a synthetic material which Du Pont had introduced in 1957. Adiprene was being used in a variety of demanding industrial applications but Du Pont undoubtedly never envisioned ski boots as a market for the material. Nevertheless, when approached by Lange, a joint development program to determine the feasibility of using the synthetic for boot shells was agreed upon. Thus the link between chemistry and ski boots was forged, but the pay-off was anything but immediate.

Over the next several years, countless laboratory formulations based on Adiprene were tried and re-tried; molds in which the shells were formed were designed and redesigned; literally hundreds of boot designs were tested and discarded before Lange was satisfied they had a boot which measured up to the exacting standards they had set.

In 1967, persistence was rewarded, and Lange introduced the first ski boot based on a special formulation of Adiprene which they called "Lange-flex".

To understand what a boot made of Adiprene offers the skier, it is necessary to understand something about Adiprene itself. It is a unique material in that it bridges the gap between a rigid plastic and an elastic rubber. It belongs to a class of materials called thermosets. This means that when heat and pressure are applied to it in a mold, as is done when making a ski boot, the material assumes a predetermined rigidity which it retains permanently. Once set, additional heat will not cause the material to "revert" or soften. This is just the opposite of a thermoplastic, the class of material common to plastic boots. When subjected to heat and pressure, thermoplastics soften and flow and become rigid on cooling. However, when again subjected to heat of a certain temperature, the material softens and loses rigidity.

Before Adiprene is molded, it must be combined with other ingredients including pigments for the color desired plus a substance called a curing agent. When this "compound," as it is called, is molded under heat and pressure, a chemical reaction takes place called "cross linking." This builds in a predetermined degree of permanent flexibility which is very important in a ski boot. This property permits the boot to flex or stretch when any part of the foot or leg is forced against it. "Cross linking" contributes a property called elastic memory which enables the boot to return to its original shape once the force is removed. And, it will do this repeatedly over the life of the boot allowing it to retain its original fit and feel.

Another property distinctive to Adiprene is its ability to retain its original rigidity-flexibility ratio over a wide temperature range. Even at sub-zero temperatures, where most materials become harder and stiffer, the change in Adiprene is so slight that it will not be felt. At higher temperatures, where most materials tend to soften, Adiprene remains stable—even at temperatures approaching 200 degrees Fahrenheit. Put a pair of boots on the ledge of a car behind the back seat on a sunny day and the temperature can climb to 140 degrees Fahrenheit. This exposure will cause no perceptible change in the boot made of Adiprene. Nor will prolonged storage during the summer months affect the boot's performance characteristics.

Another uncommon property of Adiprene is its ability to absorb energy. This means that vibration or shock from the action of the skis will be partially absorbed or dissipated by the boot shell. This property is, of course, of most importance to the professional, particularly when running in competition over hard-packed snow or ice.

Finally, Adiprene possesses outstanding abrasion and cut resistance. This means that boots made of it will retain their new appearance regardless of chafing from bindings. Adiprene is very difficult to cut, and even if nicked from a sharp ski edge, the cut will not grow. In short then, boots made of Adiprene will keep their new look longer.

Today, ski boots of Adiprene are available in a variety of styles for the junior, intermediate or highly skilled professional. In each case, the compound of Adiprene must be adjusted to provide just the right ratio of rigidity to flexibility for each style. To accomplish this, the boot manufacturer must possess in-depth knowledge of the chemistry of the materials he is working with. He must also know mold design and be capable of developing production processes which will assure day-to-day, uniformity of all boots produced.

Perhaps the best indication of the performance of these boots is the fact that since 1968, 34 of the 96 Olympic and World Championship medals awarded were won by skiers wearing Lange boots with shells of Adiprene.

Since Lange's pioneering development (now the Lange Co., a Garcia company), other manufacturers have recognized the advantages of Adiprene and are offering their versions of boots made of it. Currently, the Lange line is the broadest, and all their boots are made of a special formulation of Adiprene called "Lange-flex." K2 markets two styles based on Adiprene as does Raichle.

In recent years a great variety of plastic boots have appeared on the market and dealers and buyers have tended to confuse all synthetic boot shells, including those made of Adiprene, as "plastic."

To correct this misconception, Du Pont, in cooperation with the above named manufacturers, is running an extensive advertising campaign describing the properties of boots made of "Adiprene." The boots will be identified at point-of-sale to enable skiers to understand what qualities they can

Fig. 2-8: Marge's high heeled, high back Langes place her knees where they belong, over her toes!

expect when they purchase the boots.

Boots for advanced skiers should be high-backed and high-heeled, in order to keep your knees where they belong (in line with the toes of your boots), with very stiff sides and a soft tongue; they should also be *warm*. Beginners, who are probably using a much shorter ski, may move their pivot point back when turning by lowering their seat, but they too will have better control of their skis if their knees are in a plumb line with their toes. A high-backed, high-heeled boot would prevent the most common beginner error of "sitting back" too far, which, upon close analysis, is not critical *unless the knees move back*, too. Hence, it would be advisable for anyone who plans to ski for a long time to purchase the most advanced type of ski boot. It will not only help you to learn this sport faster, but the boots will probably last you longer, also. Beginners who come to ski class with antiquated laced boots that offer no ankle support are not only making the basic skill of edging more difficult, but they will also have to *press* their knees forward to the point where they would be locked if they were in a more expensive "advanced" ski boot. (Fig. 2-8) High-backed, stiff-sided ski boots also preclude the possibility of ankle injury. If you only ski one weekend out of the entire season, and your pain quotient is low, you need not make the investment—for you probably will want the closest thing to a bedroom slipper, just to get you by until you can return to your cocktail and cigarettes. The finest ski boots are made for skiing, not for walking, which can be irritating when the bar is half a mile from the bottom of your ski trail.

The pain of the boots, the frost-bitten fingers and toes, the physical effort of learning and the aggravation of traveling 6 hours to the ski area make many non-skiers think that we are masochists. Some of us are. Others will take the time to find boots that are tolerable for walking or skiing and warm enough to prevent frostbite. These *thinking* skiers will also spend off-season hours tuning their bodies to adjust to the physical effort of learning. Even the annoyance of the 6 hour drive can be made pleasant by listening to good music, reading a good book, or by writing. At this present moment, Marge and I are on Route 91 to Vermont. She is at the wheel listening to WQXR and I am in the midst of designing this chapter.

Bindings

Bindings are your next important consideration. Unfortunately, we consumers are again smitten by photographs of racers and free-style acrobats doing their thing while locked into a particular brand of binding; we immediately trade in our own hardware for the heroes' brand, confident that that brand must be the safest, for heroes can't afford injuries. That kind of logic would make sense if the heroes were independently wealthy. The truth is that for every skier who manages to earn a decent purse from winning races or hot dog contests, there are tens of thousands who are losers. Ski equipment is a heavy investment. The majority of top guns who appear in our consumer magazines are walking billboards for ski equipment manufacturers for no other reason than subsidy. If a rubber band manufacturer offered as much bread to a professional skier as a binding manufacturer, you would soon see photographs of the flippers with nothing but rubber bands around their boots and the manufacturer's picture on their bibs. Soon, thousands of skiers would be

trading in their hardware, and the "in" phrase at the local disco would be, "Man, ain't you into rubbers? Far out!" Money makes money. The bigger a corporation is, the more athletes they can put on their payroll, and the more space they can buy in the consumer magazines. Many of us are gullible; if we see anything in print, we believe it to be gospel truth. (Except for the Gospel.) *Skiing* Magazine (December, 1975) claims that the Salomon binding ". . . adorns more professional hot doggers' skis than all other bindings." In the Spring, 1976 issue of the same magazine (page 88), the editors admit: "Frankly, competitors (racers and hot-doggers) enter into contracts with suppliers for many reasons, not all related to safety." Marvelous euphemism.

Who are we to believe? If the heroes are paid to advertise equipment manufactured by wealthy corporations, and if those corporations clutter up our consumer magazines with mega-displays of their products, who can we trust? Not the ski shops; they must sell all their stock or be stuck with their speculative investment. If the month is March and all the ski shop has left in his storeroom is 50 pair of Schlock bindings, you can bet they will try to sell you a pair. One thing you can do is attend the consumer ski shows that take place every fall. I have heard a lot of derogatory comments from skiers about the ski shows being ". . . nothing but living commercials." To a great extent that is true, but there is a great difference between a "living commercial" and a magazine advertisement. At the ski show you may not only see the equipment, but in most cases you may *test* it for yourself! Empirical evidence is always more reliable than hero testimonials. At the shows you can witness live competition between all the manufacturers of ski equipment, each trying to win your vote for credibility. The large corporations dislike this kind of equalized representation, to the point where, each year, they threaten to not participate again, under the pretense of questioning the commercial value of their exposure. What they really fear is your empirical judgement. At the ski shows, it is not the testimonial of Fritz Sweinschwanze that will coerce you to buy a particular ski, boot or binding, but rather your own evaluation after comparing one brand with several others.

You can do more. You can read. Enough copy has been printed about *plate* bindings to convince any intelligent reader that they are safer than the conventional heel and toe step-in bindings. I will predict that, within the next decade, all binding manufacturers will produce a binding that follows the plate concept. You will see some of them already swinging in that direction this year. Plate bindings reduce the role of the boot in the release system. Their metal-to-metal contact is more reliable than boot-to-metal contact, as boots are susceptible to deterioration and are also not compatible with every binding design. In addition, most toe and heel step-in bindings provide no release in a backward fall. They have been instrumental in the fracture of many tibias when neophyte aerialists have flipped too early or when *gelande-sprungers* have forgotten to drop their tips before landing.

Most plate bindings also provide a pivot point in twist release closer to the tibial shaft, which enables them to react to twist loads more immediately. Some, like the Burt, also provide a fulcrum release close to the ball of the foot, which enables the mechanism to react more immediately to snapping loads fore and aft exerted upon the tibia. (Fig. 2-9) You have the advantage, in this book, of reading an honest

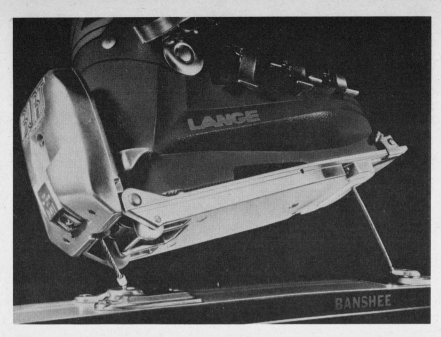

Fig. 2-9: Only the Burt bindings release at every conceivable angle and then return the ski to your foot!

opinion from a veteran professional skier who does not have to worry about losing advertisers. I highly recommend plate bindings for your ultimate protection. I prefer those models which do not necessitate the permanent addition of any hardware to your boot.

Should you insist upon using any heel and toe conventional step-in, for whatever reason, do be certain to include a good Anti-Friction Device behind the toe piece. Highly recommended over Teflon pad AFD's are the Lipe Slider and the Geze. Also be certain that the toe of your boot penetrates the cup of your toe piece as far as possible without actually touching it in the center, to prevent inadvertent release and allow for anti-shock movement.

Uli Gertsch of Switzerland introduced the first plate binding in 1967, establishing a precedent that has taken a decade to be accepted as most significant. He is still researching new modifications that will improve the Gertsch plate system. The Tyrolia PBII is quite similar to the Gertsch, but be sure to keep it clean and lubricated to avoid malfunction caused by friction. Wulf and Moog are other plate bindings worth consideration. The Lange USA Company has finally worked out the bugs in their Burt plate binding system. I blew out of their first prototype 2 years ago during my first dynamic wheelie. The post that was holding the pivoting ring housing for the front cable was attached to the base plate only by peening! After my critique, the post was redesigned with a graduating diameter that is strong enough to hold under any stress. This modification pretty near makes the Burt retractable binding perfect, although it is rather heavy. I would not have my wife in any other piece of hardware. My Burt Competition model is more appropriate for hot mogul bashing. Stronger springs return the binding to the boot faster in the event of inadvertent release. The Burt is the only binding that features an automatic return after release, obviating the use of runaway straps. They are expensive, but one pair of bindings may be used on any number of skis if the skis are mounted with inexpensive base plates. This makes them a lot cheaper for the skier who owns more than one pair of skis. The only adverse charac-

teristic of the Burt plate binding is its weight. It will not affect your stability or turns in any way, but oh, those jumps! Your skis will just not tuck as quickly, unless you have a mesomorphic biceps femoris. If you decide upon the Burts, combine them with a light pair of boots, like the new Langes or Scotts, and consider a shorter, lighter ski, but feel confident that you are in one of the safest release systems on the market (and you won't have to add any hardware to your boots).

Poles

Pole companies must be confidently secure. I tried to get a few to donate some poles to SKIER'S DIGEST for testing, in order to surreptitiously supplement my own supply and give you an honest appraisal, but we received zero cooperation. I hate to mention brand names anyway, as it creates too much animosity in this jealousy-ridden business. I am already blackballed by many instructors and ski areas because of the exposé of the blue side of the profession in my novel, *Snowballing: Diary of a Ski Instructor* (NY, Nordon Publications, 1975), and my mention of brands in this book will probably win and lose some other professional friends. Please remember that the comments and opinions in this book are based upon my own experiences and in no way reflect the conjecture of anyone else on the staff of SKIER'S DIGEST.

Your criteria for pole selection should be light weight, firm grip and ease of swing with wrist action. Lately, pole manufacturers have been following the lead of Barrecrafters in designing handles devoid of straps. This is an effort to protect you from wrenched shoulders and twisted wrists in the event of your pole catching on a slalom gate or tree trunk. These models are eye appealing in their resemblance to rapiers of the 16th and 17th centuries. I have tried them all but personally prefer the older variation with the strap. For two reasons. First, I believe that the strap gives more support for a firmer pole plant. Secondly, I have thrust the other type deep into the face of a mogul during my compression only to leave it behind as my skis continued to snake down the run. It is a bloody nuisance to climb back after it.

The choice is yours, but, again, I advise you to try before you buy. If your shoulders are not too muscular, choose the lightest model in the store. Hold the pole before you and flick it back and forth with just your wrist. Does it swing gracefully, or does it feel like a monkey wrench? What about the tip? Will it puncture ice? A skidded pole plant can throw off your timing. I especially like the dual tapered models for ease of swing. Watching the Olympics recently, I saw a bent variation used by some competitors. That's a radical variation designed especially for the downhill "tuck" position.

Pole baskets have also been subject to change. There is one model that looks very much like a plunger or plumber's helper! The ring and cross-straps model of the past is still most functional for my money, with a wider basket for deep powder. Think about these functional prerequisites before you choose the color to match your outfit.

Now that you know a little about your equipment, let us learn a little about how to use it properly.

Caring For Your Bottoms

This is not an article on deep knee bends or corsets. It is about the bottom of *your skis*. Instructors are always amazed at how some student skis can even slide, they have been so neglected. Your skis will not only function better if their bottoms are maintained in a professional manner, but your legs will also be in less jeopardy. Holes torn by stones in the base of your skis can act just like hooks, which will catch other stones, stop your ski short and send you flying, particulary if the torn sections are close to your steel edges. Deeply incised scratches can be just as functional in guiding the direction of your ski as its center groove, and those incisions are frequently not fore to aft. Damage like that should be repaired, and you need not leave the work to the ski shop. They have enough to keep them busy.

Your ski bottoms are made of a substance in the polyethylene family. After cleaning the scratch or minor hole with a knife point and some solvent, simply melt some polyethylene with a match and allow it to drip hot into the cavity. (Fig. 2-10) You can use a piece of the plastic bag that was wrapped around your skis, or you can purchase P-Tex "candles" at your local ski shop, which need only to be lit with a match and allowed to drip into the wound. Pile the patch high, well above the base, and allow it to cool. (Fig. 2-11) Then file it level with a Surform file. Finally, sand it flat with a very fine emery cloth or sand paper. P-Tex candles come in a variety of colors if the cosmetics of the repair work bother you. Large holes and missing segments are best left to the ski shop, but you can certainly take care of minor repairs. If repair work is frequent, you should consider choosing another ski area. We pay enough for lift tickets, food and booze at the ski resorts for them to spend a little on grooming their trails. Jagged rocks should be removed. Many areas have a liner of straw beneath their base. Bromley Mountain in Vermont is so well-groomed, we were able to ski there during our November certification pre-course on only 3 inches of snow! Stony areas will ruin your edges. There are only so many times that a skier can re-file a 90-degree angle on his skis' edges after beveling them on a rock pile.

Fig. 2-10: Rolled up polyethylene works just as well as P-Tex candles, which burn up fast.

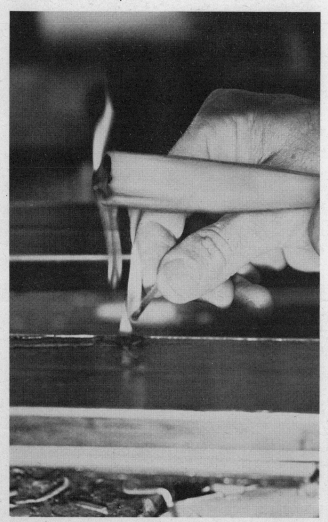

Fig. 2-11: Pile up your filling high. Then file it flat with a SURFORM file.

Your P-Tex base should also be kept perfectly flat. Check it periodically by resting a file card or flat blade on the bottom with your ski upside down on a table. (Fig. 2-12) If you can see light under the card, your base is concave. This must be rectified. A concave base means you are gliding on a "railed edge," and your turns must be extremely difficult. Only a flat filing can correct this. We will talk about that, soon. A *convex* base can also be detected by the file card analysis. If yours is convex, your skis probably wander all over the hill when you try to make them track in a straight line. The cure for this is also flat filing.

Skis that are severely railed or convex should be flat filed by a sanding machine. Most skis do not get that bad, unless they have been stored in areas of excessive heat. You can flat file your own skis on any kind of a table if you can devise a method to keep your ski from moving—usually no more than propping the tail against the wall with heavy books beneath the ski to raise it as high as the splayed tip. Your file can be (you should excuse the expression) a mill-bastard file of about 10 inches, although a heavier file may be required for really aggravated bottoms. The strokes should be long and always from tip to tail. If you don't want calluses, there is a new device on the market that will protect your hands—the "Turtle."

The name is for its shape, not its speed of efficacy. You can cut your sharpening time in half and keep some of the skin on your hands if you pick up the Webster Ski Tül (pronounced *tool*), an edge sharpener that will take the agony out of tuning your skis. (Fig. 2-13) It is guaranteed to give your skis a perfectly flat bottom with a 90-degree edge, and it is available at ski shops for under $15. Remember to keep your flat filing strokes long and from shovel to tail. (Fig. 2-14)

Filing the sides of your edges for a true 90-degree angle is very difficult without a tool like the "turtle", unless you have a ski shop bench built in your garage. As you can see in Fig. 2-15, the unique design of the Ski Tül allows you to keep

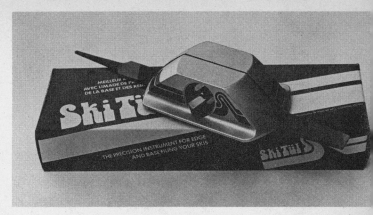

Fig. 2-13: The Webster SKI-TÜL, otherwise known as the Turtle. If your local ski shop doesn't carry it, write to: Collins Ski Products, Inc., Box 11, Bergenfield, New Jersey 07621.

Fig. 2-14: Use long strokes, from shovel to tail.

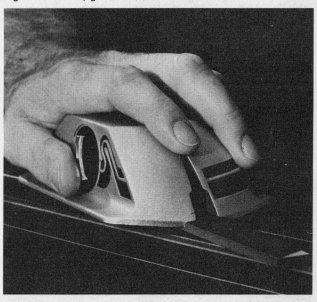

Fig. 2-12: The card test. The only air you should see is at the space of the ski's center groove.

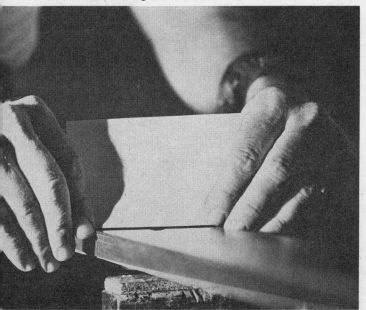

Fig. 2-15: The Turtle will keep your edges at a 90-degree angle!

your ski flat on its face when filing the sides. Strokes along the side edge should also be long and from tip to tail. Pick up a "turtle." I take mine with us whenever Marge and I travel to distant ski areas.

Some skiers dull their edges from the tips past the shovels, in order to prevent their skis from "hooking" at the end of a turn. The Austrians in our ski school did not approve of this practice, and I don't have to tell you about the precision of Austrian skiing. Some did dull their tips, but only up to the running surface. I follow this practice. You can dull or wire the edges of your ski tips by gently drawing your file down the blade a few times. After filing your skis, you should remove any inadvertent burrs that may have arisen by lightly passing some sandpaper or a stone down the entire edge length. (See photo on this chapter's title page). Your bottoms are now ready for wax.

Once your base is whole again, and flat, you should consider waxing it. Many new skiers avoid waxing because they don't *want* to travel fast. What they fail to realize is that wax will also make their turns more effortless. Under certain conditions, wax is absolutely imperative. Like on those hot spring days, when the snow cakes to the bottom of your skis, directly under your boots, and prevents you from sliding. Cross-country skiers know the value of "the right wax." Theirs is a grueling sport. While alpine skiers capitalize upon natural forces like gravity for their propulsion, *langläufers* must use their poles and their muscles. Some of them also use their heads. They wax properly. Anything you can do to reduce friction beneath your skis will pay you off in energy conservation, whether you are poling on the flat or schussing down a cat-walk.

Wax comes in color codes, with a different hue for each temperature or weather condition. Most colors are constant among the different brands, although, recently, some brands have changed the hues either to confuse the consumer and thus have him stick to one brand, theirs, or just because they are stupid. They are not stupid. Most brands are rip-offs. The prices they charge for miniscule bars of wax that are good for maybe two skis are outrageous. I suggest that you buy your wax in large size bricks, but I have never seen such a product on eastern ski shop shelves. A company called U.S. Ski Wax used to supply large bricks to our instructors' repair room at Sugarbush Valley. Their address is Leisure Research, Inc., P.O. Box 4386, Denver, Colo. 80204, and I hope they will send me a few bars for mentioning them, as I am going to recommend that you try their product as the best wax investment today.

Some skiers use a hot traveling iron to wax their skis, allowing the wax to melt on the base of the iron and drip onto the ski base. I have waxed my skis in this manner ever since my good friend, Hartwig, taught it to me when the Austrians were imported for the Sugarbush Valley Ski School. The iron is used by many skiers to melt the wax drippings into a flat coating on the ski base, which is scraped and finally buffed. Recently, however, I was cautioned by an official at the Lange plant that excessive heat in one spot on a ski base can cause the base to lift from the metal edges. He recommended the cross-country skiers' manner of *painting* on the wax, melted in a small pot. Sounds reasonable, though it does take longer. It also uses more wax. Painting the hot wax onto your ski base is especially desirable in the the spring, when hot weather demands that the bottom of

your skis *not* be entirely flat. Too flat a surface in high temperatures will cause greater friction because of the thin film of water that rides close to the surface of the snow. At such times, the wax, usually red, should be painted in steps (Fig. 2-16) from the back to the front of your skis, overlapping each brush stroke to create *steps* and thus air between them. This is followed by a light scraping and removal of the wax from the center groove and the edges.

Conversely, cold weather calls for the smoothest, flattest surface you can polish. Paint on the wax (usually green at

Fig. 2-16 (above): This method is best but it's bloody expensive, as you'll use much more wax. Save the scrappings and remelt them if they're not mixed with edge fillings.
Fig. 2-17 (below): Be sure that the tool that you use for this job is perfectly *flat*!

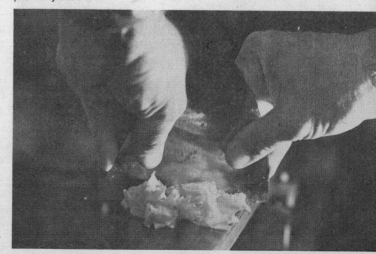

sub-zero, variations of yellow and blue between zero and freezing [Fahrenheit]. Then, scrape it flat with a carpenter's scraper, or an old electric outlet plate (be sure it is absolutely straight at the edges). (Fig. 2-17) Next, remove most of the wax from your center groove with a butter knife blade. (Fig. 2-18) Then, remove the wax from your edges by drawing a piece of plastic over them from front to rear (an old car windshield scraper will do). (Fig. 2-19) Finally, rub the bottom with a cork and buff it until you can see your face reflected. All waxes come with specifications for tempera-ture differences, etc.

Now that you have spent an hour getting your bottoms tuned, you don't want to carry your skis bottom to bottom, as your edges would dull and your wax would get rough. The answer is to separate the skis with a device like the Skeep-It, available at your local ski shop. (Fig. 2-20A and 2-20B).

You will feel a lot more confident on well-tuned skis. You wouldn't perform a tracheotomy with an old rusty butter-knife, yet just look at the equipment that some of you are using to ski!

Fig. 2-18: A butter knife works well for removing wax from the center groove.

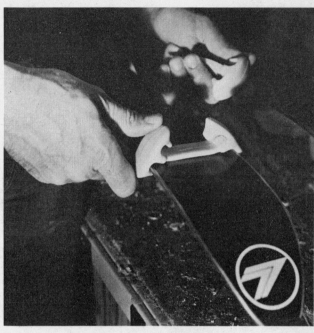

Fig. 2-20A & 20B: After spending so much time tuning your skis, you don't want to place them against each other. A wise invest-ment is the "SKEEP-IT." If your local ski shop doesn't stock them, write to: SKEEP-IT, c/o John Zelle Jr., Dept. F, 38 Harbor View Ave., Stamford, Conn. 06902.

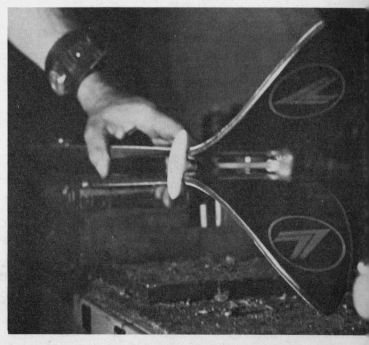

Fig. 2-19: Any kind of plastic will do. This particular scraper is made by TOKO.

Frank Covino with one of his Ski Week classes at Sugarbush Valley, Vermont.

Chapter 3
NO FRILLS
SKI INSTRUCTION

CHAPTER 3—NO FRILLS SKI INSTRUCTION
A Primer For Those Who Would Teach Themselves

FOR YEARS, the Ski School curriculum has been based upon the supposition that the learner is a kinetic idiot who skis once or twice a year for reasons other than the pure enjoyment of the sport. The effort in most schools still is to get that clown to turn as quickly as possible, so he can boast of his achievement back at the office and wait another year for his next lesson. So they teach him to spin. On the flat part of his skis. Like a propeller. He turns. He is happy. He will return. Next year. Granted, I have taught many of these day trippers, and I have taught the fat, the tall, the lean and the small, and maybe some of them were kinetic imbeciles. But a lot of them were not. A lot of them had good balance, an alert mind and were in excellent physical condition. It is to such learners that this chapter is dedicated. To the physically fit and the mentally aware, who should be taught differently than their less-capable cousins.

A ski instructor's training should include at least a basic course in psychology. Every student he teaches is as different and as individual as snowflakes. Their only common denominator is that they are in class to learn. They are uninformed. The uninformed ego is a complex phenomenon. At birth it screams for perpetual comfort, satisfaction of its basic needs, love and attention. After several years of frustration of having to *earn* these favors, it can either become incorrigibly extroverted, acceptably cooperative or passively withdrawn. The ostentatious are difficult to teach because they feel they "know it all" and are *above* needing instruction. The introverts are not easily taught because they doubt their capacity for success in any endeavor. The middle group ·usually welcomes instruction and learns with little effort because they have less "hangups" or personal inhibitions.· Although they too may be unaware if their capacities, they at least welcome stimulus that tests their potentials. This chapter is directed at all three groups; toward the introverts and extroverts who have their peculiar reasons for not taking ski lessons from qualified ski instructors, and toward those skiers of the middle group who are open to direction but who may be disappointed with the instruction they have received on the hill.

The reasons for such disappointment can be many and varied. Here are some of the comments I have heard from some disgruntled students:

"The class was too big . . ."

"The students were not all at the same level . . ."

"He (the instructor) gave all his attention to the girls . . ."

"All our instructor did was show-off . . ."

"He talked too much . . ."

"He talked too *little* . . ."

"He took us on a slope that was too difficult . . ."

"He didn't teach the same system that I learned at Paradise Peak . . ."

"I couldn't understand his accent . . ."

The list of gripes is endless, and, as difficult as it may be for a student to adjust to a typical ski class situation, it is even more of a problem for an instructor. Consider these barriers to a successful *teaching* experience:

It's the Christmas-New Year's week and the penurious corporation has sold an excess of ski lesson tickets. You have a class of 15 students! (Eight should be maximum.)

Your incompetent ski school director has neglected to separate the groups of students according to their specific level of proficiency. You have five who are ready for parallel turns, six who have never been off a beginner slope, and four who are skiing against their better judgement (to please a husband, wife or child) and are wishing they had never come.

Three students are using antiquated equipment, or skis that are too long, or mixed brand binding combinations that are unsafe. Five students haven't had their skis waxed; the snow is caking to the middle of their ski bottoms and is preventing them from moving.

Two students, whose waists are bigger than the girth of their shoulders, can't get up by themselves when they fall. While you help them rise, the class is grumbling.

Four students haven't spent a winter day outdoors in 20 years. They are red-nosed and white-faced, trembling at an ideal 28 degrees, and impatient for the class to end.

You have just glided off the chairlift unloading platform, and there stands your class, in line. Two obese specimens are eating salami sandwiches, dressed in Army fatigues with their socks outside their pants. Two recalcitrant teenagers who shared a "joint" on the chairlift ahead of you are long haired and psychedelic in their discordant colored jumpsuits replete with racing stripes. Two gray-haired women want to rape you. Two drunks are man and wife and are arguing between themselves already. Two have frost-bitten ears. Two hate your guts because of your glamorous image. Your job? Keep them all happy for two hours and *teach*.

As you can see, an instructor's list of obstacles is also endless. Add to it the facts that he probably works a 7-day week, 6 hours a day, for less than the "minimum wage," frequently in sub-zero temperatures, rain or sleet, hardly has the time between lessons to relieve his kidneys and seldom has lunch, because the only way he can earn a few extra dollars is to teach on his lunch hour, and you have a very *un*glamorous picture of the ski instructor who tries so valiantly to deliver his lesson at a level of understanding that is effective to all.

There are many pros and cons when one considers the effectiveness of a ski class lesson. The question inevitably arises: can you teach *yourself* how to ski? My opinion, based upon 15 years of teaching experience, is that the art of skiing has a *scientific* basis. Anything scientific is logical and can be taught to any reasonably intelligent mind. Few of us have the mental discipline to learn anything by reading alone, however. Vicarious learning will never replace pragmatic understanding. Thorough knowledge must be the result of exposure to salient principles that you believe will help you to achieve success, plus empirical verification of those principles by extensive practice under the critical eye of a qualified professional. That kind of cumulative awareness is possible in the sport of skiing. There are enough publications available which reveal the science of skiing, and there are a sufficient number of instructors around who are qualified to judge and accelerate your proficiency at the practice of those principles.

Errors made by many technical manuals are that they either take too much for granted from the average reader, are too verbose or pedantic for basic understanding, are chauvinistic, or simply are too drawn out and lengthy for rapid understanding. In this chapter, I will try to avoid each of those barriers to your learning experience. The system that I will present is one that I have devised which is designed to help you master the art of pure parallel skiing in the shortest amount of time possible. It is qualified by my extensive experience in teaching the Modified Austrian Technique, the American Technique and the Stein Eriksen Ski School Technique, plus by my own training as a student under the tutelage of qualified French, Austrian, American and Canadian ski instructors. It is therefore an eclectic system which should simplify your whole learning process if you have the desire to teach yourself. To avoid confusion among those of you who are being schooled on the mountain in the American Technique (probably the majority of our readers), illustrations of the sequence of the American Teaching Method disciplines currently adopted by the Professional Ski Instructors of America will appear in Chapter 6, "The P.S.I.A. Today." The Professional Ski Instructors of America has paved the way for a universal mastery of the sport by also borrowing the best theory from each of the international systems and simplifying your understanding. The basic differences between its ATM program and my pure parallel approach are as follows:

1—My Graduated Length Method, a personal adaptation of the original systems inaugurated by Clif Taylor and Karl Pfeiffer, encourages parallel movements *exclusively* while the P.S.I.A. continues the traditional approach of wedge-type exercises which I believe are invaluable to non-athletic skiers or those who are physically inadequate, but which are unnecessary, and in some cases detrimental, to the progress of the new skier who has little difficulty with other athletic or kinesthetic movements.

2—The student of the American Teaching Method and the almost identical method taught by the Canadian Ski Instructor Alliance is encouraged to employ skidding movements on the flat part of his ski in the early part of his learning process. I personally believe that the skill of positive edging should be taught to physically capable tyros on the very first day and employed as a discipline in every learning exercise.

3—Little mention is made in the ATM or C.S.I.A. program of body angulation. I believe that this classic position is so essential for controlled descents on steep or icy terrain that it should be taught early as a discipline and be consistently employed in each of the subsequent learning exercises when the skier is in a traverse attitude i.e., as the hip and knees are pressed to the uphill side of the skis for traverse leverage, the shoulders are angled to the same slant as the slope for balance. I am not alone in my defense of this form. Othmar Schneider, Olympic champion and Director of Skiing at Boyne, is vehemently opposed to the modern ski school's lack of emphasis upon this vital defense against the pull of centrifugal *and* centripetal force. Angulation is not a chauvinistic affectation. It is an imperative silhouette for optimum control and balance in most recreational skiing.

4—While other systems encourage a wide track approach for *all* beginners, (and I believe that such an approach may be necessary for the non-athletic or physically handicapped), I feel that many new skiers are as capable of learning to ski with their boots together as children are of mastering the skill of riding a bicycle without training wheels. There is no question in my mind about the "stability" of an open stance. I simply maintain that, if a student feels as stable with his feet together, he should not be discouraged from using this closed stance, as he will then add to the security of his stability the aesthetic quality of *grace*.

The current P.S.I.A. Technical Committee has adopted the mature attitude of flexibility within their teaching program. Their rejection of rigid final forms as stepping stones in the progress of every new skier is a refreshing attitude accepted by most other modern schools, bringing us closer to a universal method for teaching the art of skiing. It is hoped that my pure parallel approach, designed for the physically conditioned, alert new skier, will be accepted as part of that ubiquitous eclectic curriculum. Practice the following proposed exercises under the critical guidance of a qualified ski instructor, supplement a minimum of one week's on-the-mountain-instruction per season with at least ten private lessons from an eclectic minded ski instructor, and you will be skiing the expert slopes by next Easter!

A. PREPARATION

1. Some GLM Schools advocate 3-foot skis for the beginner. While such a ski does facilitate turning by axial motion, it also presents longitudinal leverage problems, particularly for the tall learner. I believe that the length of your first ski should relate to your height. Choose a pair of skis that are as high as your armpits (Fig. 3-2), preferably with *plate* bindings (they are safer); rent them, as you will need a longer ski in a few days (the Graduated Length Method). If you can't find a rental pair of skis with plate bindings, just make sure that the bindings which are attached to the skis that you rent are tested with a Lipe release check *while you are locked into them*.

2. Don't let any salesman con you into buying cheap beginner boots. If you are committed to learning this sport rapidly, the only boot for you is an expensive *expert* boot that fits well and will last for many years. It should have a high back to keep you from sitting back too far and raised heels to keep your knees in a plumb line with your toes, where they should be for optimum control. (Fig. 3-3) Your boots are your first and most important investment. A

Fig. 3-2 (above left): Teri shows the height of skis recommended for the beginner.
Fig. 3-3 (above center): The best boot for a beginner is one that will permit him to control his skis just as well as his instructor. A comfortable expert boot.
Fig. 3-4 (right): Teri's boots are not exactly your basic ordinary street shoes, but her poles are the correct height. Her stretch outfit is definitely *fast!*

variable would be the Free Style type boot for those of you who would eventually move into that new phase of skiing. They have a slightly lower back and flexible hinge of the upper shaft to accommodate for miscalculated landings from aerial stunts and for fast, tight mogul busting.

3. Dress adequately, and pick a sunny day for beginning. You will have enough problems without worrying about severe cold and poor visibility.

4. Select poles that tuck just beneath your armpit when you are standing on the floor in ordinary street shoes (Fig. 3-4).

5. DON'T RIDE THE LIFT. Not yet. If you can't tolerate climbing a slight grade between each exercise on the first morning, you are not physically ready for skiing.

6. The skyrocketing import census for the state of Florida indicates that most of us find the severe cold of winter a needless ordeal. Who among even skiers would not settle for a season of just *spring* skiing? As I write at this moment, the thermometer outside our Vermont home shivers at 30 *below* zero. My car has three umbilical cords running from it to the house's electrical outlet: a motor block heater, an oil dipstick heater, and a charger on the battery which was choked with ice. My right toe is burning from a touch of frostbite, and I have a dimple under my cheekbone from tissue destroyed by frostbite several years ago. Few sensible skiers ski when the thermometer dives below zero, but there will always be fanatics like Marge and myself who *have* to be out there when the slopes are white. For us, precautions *must* be taken. Here are a few tips which we have found helpful:

a. Don't overdress and stay that way when you are not outside. Even a short drive from your lodge to the ski area can make you perspire, and perspiration can freeze when you step outside that heat choked automobile. If you must drive to the area fully ski clothed, open the car windows; especially if there is a smoker in the car!

b. A dry anti-perspirant sprayed between your toes will prevent freeze-potential perspiration from accumulating there (I forgot, this morning . . .).

c. When the temp is sub-zero, a face mask is advisable if you haven't eased your face tolerance into the bite of winter winds. (They are not only made for bank robbers.)

d. Furs beat *any* kind of parka for warmth at sub-zero, hands down. Pick one from an unendangered species to appease the ecology freaks (Fig. 3-5).

e. Your head is your battery. Keep it warm and it will spark your reflexes. The Moriarty hats are adequate (for most of the season) but are not as effective in sub-zero temperatures as fur or cowboy hats (with ear flaps) which allow for air insulation. Brimmed hats also are great when it snows or rains, functioning as umbrellas. The ski school at Steamboat Springs uses cowboy hats as part of its uniform. Smart. I am surprised that more skiers don't use them.

f. A set of thermals under ballet tights is a great second skin for good insulation on the sub-zero days. The tights will help your feet to slip into your boots easier too. Fishnet shirts are recommended as the best underwear to have close to your skin; air pockets are the best insulation (Fig. 3-6).

g. A cup of hot soup in the lodge while you massage your toes will make the last runs of that sub-zero day much more enjoyable; massage hers, too . . .

h. Comfort Products, Box 9200, Aspen, Colorado 81611, has come to the aid of many skiers who have poor circulation in their extremities. Those funny looking boxes you may have seen on the back of some skiers boots are the power packs of their Footwarmer product, an electrical heating device that really works. Insoles of emboss-grained vinyl enclose a heating element that is a completely flexible etched foil circuit focused upwards toward the foot. The completely sealed power packs weigh about 15 ounces apiece and contain 4-volt systems with no shock or shorting hazard. Daily use does not affect the cycle life. They accept a full charge over a ½-hour period, with no overcharge danger. They are especially recommended for ski instructors, patrolmen and for any skier who spends more than a few hours

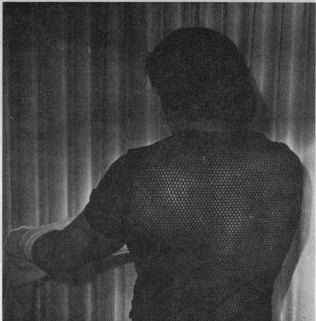

Fig. 3-5 (left): My wife says I look like *the bad guy* in an Italian western, but this is my warmest outfit on those sub-zero days. Marge sewed ear flaps onto the hat.

Fig. 3-6 (above): Best insulation you can have next to your skin is the *fish-net* type shirt.

in sub-zero or sub-tolerable temperatures. New from Comfort Products also is the world's first *electronic glove*, called the Lunar. SKIER'S DIGEST salutes this United States company for solving the most common problems of skiing comfort. We hope that their contribution will bring back many skiing deserters who fled south with frostbitten fingers and toes, and we wonder: can an electronic *hat* be far behind? (Fig. 3-7)

7. More ski accidents occur after 3 PM than at any other time of day. This is due partly to the fatigue of skiers who are in poor physical condition, partly because of icier conditions than when the sun is high, and partly because of *poor visibility*. When the sun drops, its rays no longer expose undulating terrain and cause definitive shadows. You will then experience what is called *flat light*; the terrain looks flat and deceptively easy. Yellow goggles will not only help to define the slope variations; their golden glaze will actually have a psychologically beneficial effect in warming up the bleakness of overcast or sunless conditions.

While the sun *does* shine, do your eyes a favor and protect them with darker lenses, or you will soon sport that characteristic slash of red across the whites of your eyes that is so common among foolish skiers. The higher the elevation, the darker your lenses should be.

I can speak from personal experience to skiers who wear contact lenses. It is true that they do protect your pupils and are even better than goggles when it is snowing, as they won't fog. Colored lenses offer some brightness reduction; resistance to the ultra-violet rays of the sun is provided by special lenses which have been designed with this protection in mind. Available from Sight Improvement Center, Inc., 25 West 43rd Street, New York, N.Y. is a process called Ultra-Violet Inhibitor, which guarantees elimination of ultra-violet rays from outdoor sun and even flourescent lights. The same company offers a WETreat (TM) adjustment to any contact lens, which improves optical clarity while allowing skiers to wear their lenses for a longer time; the treatment keeps lenses more moist for greater wearing comfort. My wife and I have been using UVI lenses with the WETreat adjustment with remarkable results, particularly at higher elevations.

Overexposure of your eyes to strong sunlight on the ski slopes during the day can result in poor vision after sunset, whether or not you wear glasses. Bright sunlight can destroy the normal quantity of "visual purple" in the eyes temporarily, and several hours are required to renew that supply. This accounts for reports from skiers about the "night blindness" that they experience when driving home after a ski weekend. It can be avoided simply by protecting your eyes with correctly tinted lenses or goggles when skiing in bright sunlight. Advisable colors are dark green, brown or gray tints; least acceptable for screening out harmful sun rays are yellow or blue lenses, according to the New York State Optometric Association. While yellow-lensed goggles are the ones most preferred by racers, they should really only be used on overcast days or in flat light. Most goggles are sold with interchangeable lenses for this reason. (Fig. 3-8)

B. SOME BASIC SCIENCE

1. **The Skier.** Basic science that will help your mastery of this sport should include a psychological analysis of you, the skier, which will be covered in a later chapter. At this point, let's just say that each of us has a personal motivation for taking part in skiing, and no amount of exposure to technical principles can effectively teach any individual who has a

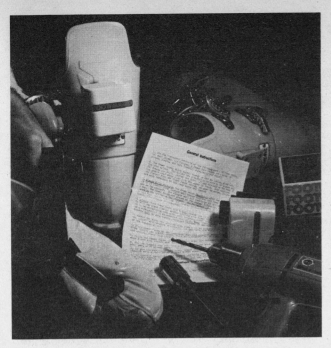

Fig. 3-7 (above): Now the *cold toed* of our species can ski! Comfort Products' *footwarmer.*

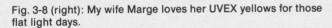

Fig. 3-8 (right): My wife Marge loves her UVEX yellows for those flat light days.

neurotic fear or apprehension of any form of kinesthetic activity. Some fear is normal and perhaps even wise, but if that emotion boils into a disproportionate form of horror, that person is asking for trouble, as skiing is an intellectual sport that demands exceptional self-discipline and control of one's mental and emotional faculties during every moment of descent.

What proved to me that *fear* is the primary deterrent to a skier's progress was the experience I had with David, a 24-year-old musician from Boston who was congenitally blind. My first thought, as I am sure you must have, is that nothing could be more fearful than not being able to see, but it was not long before I realized that David was at an *advantage*! He could not *see* the steepness of the slope; he could not *see* the ice patches; he could not *see* the uncontrolled skiers schussing before him; he could not *see* the lack of sun on that dreary overcast day. David's blindness blocked every stimulus for fear and apprehension that the rest of us experience when we begin to ski. David had only to concentrate upon the *postures* that I described. Because skiing is an intellectual sport, because turns work when physical forces are in optimum relationship for controlled changes of direction, and because David listened *precisely* to my advice for effecting those forces, he learned to ski with wide track parallel turns in *one week*! David was blind, but his kind of blindness was easier to conquer than the common blindness of *fear* that many skiers bring to ski class. That kind of darkness is the most formidable deterrent to your progress. Have faith in your instructor. If he is qualified, you need only to *listen* to his commands. He will be quick enough to spot your miscalculations and shout a correction that will prevent a fall, if you will just . . . *listen.*

2. **The Ski.** Before you take off, you should be aware of a few physical principles that will affect your movement down the slope. First, *study the shape of your ski.* Its bottom is flat. If that flatness is allowed to rest completely on the snow, gravity will pull the ski downhill, no matter which way the ski is pointed (Fig. 3-9). The tip, or forebody of the ski is curved upward. This is to prevent the ski from nose-diving into pot holes or bumps (called moguls) as it slides downhill. The curve of the tip is called tip-splay. Skis designed for short radius turns frequently are splayed upward more abruptly than skis designed for longer turns. The forebody of the ski is wider than the waist or center portion of the ski. The width of the tail or rear part of the ski is also wider than the waist, though not quite as wide as the tip. This hourglass configuration forms an arc when the skier's weight presses his skis into a *reverse camber* in a turn and allows the skier to *carve* his turns in the snow rather than skid them (Fig. 3-10). He twists his skis onto their inside *edges*. The edges are steel runners that are embedded into either side of the ski's bottom; they are meant to be kept *sharp* for maximum control. Some skis have one-piece edges, while others are "cracked" at intervals to facilitate the flexible matching of the base of the ski to the changing undulation of the terrain. One-piece edges give a greater *spring* to the ski if a skier bounces on them like on a diving board. Helping that bounce is a bow in the bottom of the ski, called a *camber*. Placed bottom to bottom with the tails and forebodies of the skis touching, a space should exist in the center, (Fig. 3-11), that's the camber. The groove running down the center of the ski bottom helps the ski to track in a straight line; this is especially important when landing from a jump off a bump or cornice. Many *ballet* skiers fill this groove with wax to facilitate 360 degree turns and other trick maneuvers.

3. **Turning With Parallel Skis.** This used to be an *advanced*

maneuver, but if the skis you are wearing are short and your legs are strong, you can point them downhill and *steer* the skis by "axial motion," twisting the feet around the axes of the lower legs early in your learning experience. Your feet and skis are twisted into the desired direction while the skis are *flat* to the snow surface. It will help to *crouch* with your feet separated the first time you try this, in order to lower your center of gravity and provide a broader base of support. If you maintain that "flat ski" attitude after the turn, gravity will continue to pull the skis downhill sideways. That's called a *skidded* turn with a *sideslip* (Fig. 3-12). To prevent such lateral slippage, you are encouraged to tilt your skis onto their uphill edges after a turn when you go across the hill. Tilted onto their uphill edges, your skis will resist the gravitational pull sideways and slide toward the cross-hill direction in which they are pointed. This is called *traversing the fall line*. (The fall line is the line that a ball would take were it allowed to roll downhill.)

For optimum control, your skis should only be *flat* to the snow surface when they are pointed directly downhill or when a deliberate sideslip is desired. Tilting the skis onto their uphill edges is called *edging*. An advanced skier, travelling at higher speeds anticipates his next traverse direction by edging while he is in *the fall line* or even before he has reached that downhill direction. He *carves* his turns on his edges. (Fig. 3-13) The simplest manner of tilting your skis onto their uphill edges is by rolling your knees uphill (Fig. 3-14). The stiff sides of your ski boots will control the tilt of your skis as you roll your knees. If you were to travel across the hill (traversing), with your knees directly over your skis, your ski bottoms would be more flush with the snow surface and a skid to the downhill side would follow. Rolling your knees *downhill* could be disastrous at slow speeds, as this will cause you to fall on the downhill side of your skis! Uphill edging while traversing can be amplified if your hips are also swung uphill, together with your knees. This position is especially advisable for women whose pelvic structure slants their femur bone inward at a greater angle (Fig. 3-15). Such an anatomical variation causes many women, and some men, to ski "knock-kneed." With the uphill knee riding directly over the uphill ski it cannot be edged properly. A swing of the hip to the uphill side of the skis will edge both skis properly when traversing. (Fig. 3-16) To balance this uphill movement of the lower body, your upper body should tilt *downhill*, at least until your shoulders are parallel with the slant of the slope (Fig. 3-17). On a gently graded beginner slope, that tilt will therefore not be very extreme (Fig. 3-18). An important principle for optimum balance when skiing is to *keep your upper body 90 degrees to the slant of the snow beneath your feet at all times*, whether traveling across the hill or straight downhill (Fig. 3-19). An exception to this rule applies to the downhill racer who sometimes assumes a low crouched posture with his torso tipped forward (the *egg position*), designed for maximum acceleration. It is curious that many beginners will crouch and sit back when they are afraid or want to slow down. (Fig. 3-20) This is precisely what a downhill racer does when he he wants to go *faster*! (Fig. 3-20A) With no friction under your ski tips, you will take off like a bullet!

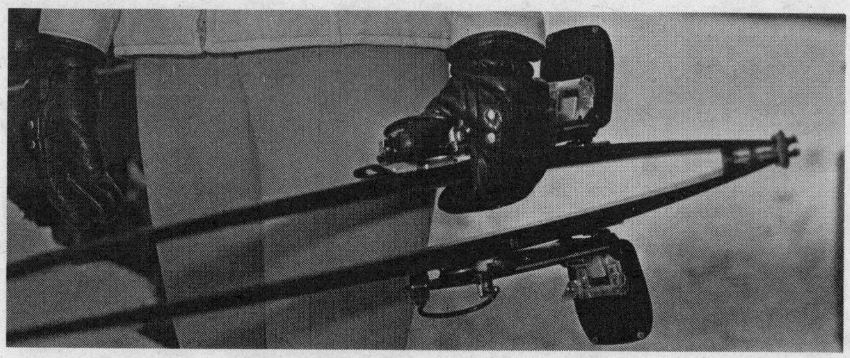

Fig. 3-9 (below): No matter which way your skis are pointed, if their bottoms are *flat to the snow surface,* they will slide straight downhill. That is what is known as *the fall line.*

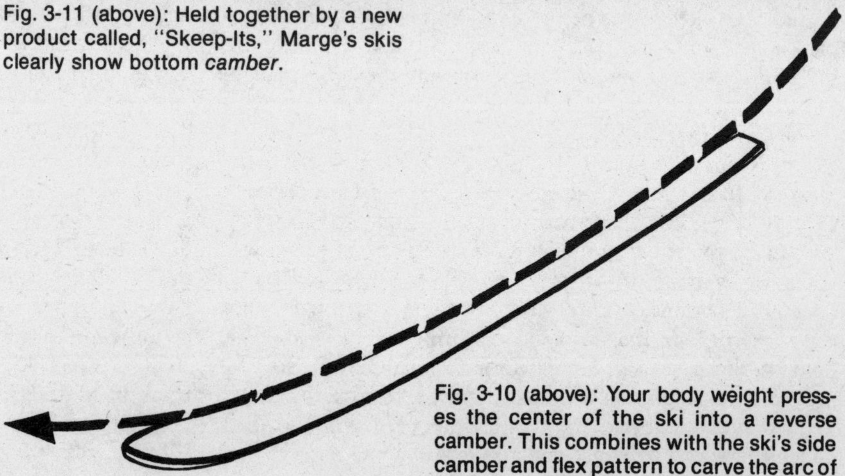

Fig. 3-11 (above): Held together by a new product called, "Skeep-Its," Marge's skis clearly show bottom *camber.*

Fig. 3-10 (above): Your body weight presses the center of the ski into a reverse camber. This combines with the ski's side camber and flex pattern to carve the arc of your turn, if you have twisted the ski onto its inside edge.

Fig. 3-12 (above): A skidded turn on the flat bottoms of your skis may easily be effected by axial motion of the feet, coupled with a down motion for weight release. Don't try it on a steep slope, though!

Fig. 3-13 (right): Carving a turn at high speed after a thrilling run down the Stauffenberg run at Taos Ski Valley, my skis ride on their inside edges. I'm in a traversing posture before my new traverse direction has even been reached.

Fig. 3-14 (below): Tilt of the knees uphill will be followed by a tilt of the skis onto their uphill edges. This will keep your skis tracking in a traverse direction. Note my hip position.

Fig. 3-15: Ginny is typical of many women and some men whose anatomical hip structure causes them to ski *knock-kneed*. Look what happens to her uphill ski!

Fig. 3-16: By reaching uphill and forward with her uphill hip, toward the twigs I've set on the ground, Ginny corrects her problem. Now look again at her skis!

Fig. 3-17: Marge finishes a high speed turn and traverses toward the camera in excellent form. Note how her upper body is 90 degrees to the slant of the slope. See how her hip compensates for her *knocked knees* in order to tilt her skis onto their uphill edges.

Fig. 3-18: My 5-year-old daughter, Cami, traversing in good form. On a more gentle slope such as this, body angulation need not be extreme. Her hip still swings into the hill, and her shoulders are still *parallel to the slant of the slope*. Notice the space under her downhill edges.

Fig. 3-19 (left): Two pros whooping it up on Mt. Norquay's North American run. Note how the torso of each skier remains in a constant 90 degree relationship with the slope.

Fig. 3-20 (above): Sit back and your skis will take off like a bullet! It's your pole baskets that belong behind your heels, not your *derriere*.

Fig. 3-20A (below): Jo-Jay Jalbert, stunting for Robert Redford in the Paramount film *Downhill Racer,* was travelling at about 60mph when the camera froze his accelerating position. Note the air under his ski tips.

Fig. 3-19A (above): Simon Hoyle photo of two skiers on Jerry's Run at Sunshine Village is another good example of the quiet upper body maintaining a 90 degree relationship with the angle of the slope, as the lower body swings like a pendulum and provides the motor force for the turning of the skis.

DR-26-27-107

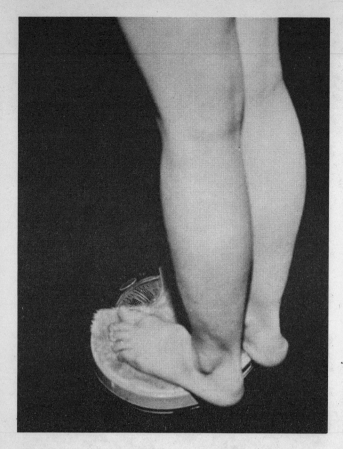

Fig. 3-21 (above): This skier weighed in at a hair over 100.
Fig. 3-21A (below): A quick drop DOWN moved the scale needle to 60, proving the most efficient manner of unweighting your skis.

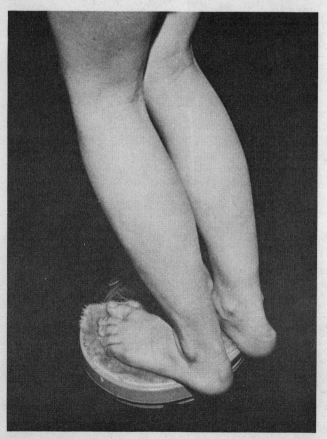

I have mentioned that short skis can be pivoted beneath the feet by axial motion if your legs are strong enough, and that you can help this dynamic movement by lowering your center of gravity—the closer your belt buckle gets to your skis, the easier it will be to twist them (as long as your knees are leading your boots!). Remember that if you ever ski out of control!

4. **Unweighting**. Long skis are difficult to turn by axial motion unless they are unweighted briefly during the initiation of the twist. This *unweighting* can be effected by a sudden *sink down* or an equally sudden spring upwards. Both methods of unweighting can be demonstrated on a bathroom scale (Figs. 3-21 & 3-21A). Most skiers have no trouble understanding how they can minimize their weight on their skis by jumping *up*, but few believe that a similar weight release will take place with a sudden drop *down*. Your scale will prove this. Long skis may also be spun like a propeller when the skier is directly over the peak of a mogul (a bump of snow) with no friction beneath his tips or tails (Fig. 3-22). During the fifties and sixties, it was the practice of advanced skiers to turn on long skis by pivoting on the forebody of their skis while the tails were lifted or unweighted (by a movement of the skier's body *upward* and *forward*). If the forebody of each ski was rolled onto its inside edge it would spoon out the turn as its greater width cut into the snow (Fig. 3-23). The resulting *short swing* was and still is an effective manner of descending steep terrain on long skis. Modern skiers, on contemporary stiff-tailed skis, can unweight and pivot on the *tails* of their skis, but their thighs must be strong enough to pull their weight forward again once their skis are pointed downhill.

C. EXERCISES ON SKIS

Following is a logical progression of exercises for those who would teach themselves with a pure parallel GLM technique.

1. *Gliding On The Flat*. Your *center of gravity* is just behind your belt buckle. When you stand in your skis on flat terrain with your feet about a hip width apart and all your joints slightly flexed, you will feel stable. Walking on skis differs from walking in shoes in the respect that you will advance most comfortably by *sliding* or gliding each ski forward rather than picking up your ski and "stepping." *Drive* each gliding step with your knee by literally trying to kneel on your ski tip. Right now, get used to leading the toe of your boot with your knee. Never allow the knees to trail behind the toes of your boots if you want to control your skis! Use your poles for balance, holding them as shown (Figs. 3-24, 3-24A), and swing your arms as you would when walking normally, i.e. your left arm swings forward as your right foot moves forward, and vice versa. Study the sequence in Fig. 3-25.

2. *Flat Terrain Step-Around*. With your poles planted on either side of your body and your skis placed together, begin to step around by moving your right ski tip 6 inches away from your left. Then, bring the left tip alongside the right, resuming a parallel relationship. Continue to step completely around. Your ski tails should be the center of your turning circle. Next, try a similar exercise, using your ski *tips* as the center of your turning circle. Replant your poles with each step and weight them forcibly. (Fig. 3-26)

3. *Sidestepping In The Traverse Posture*. The most impor-

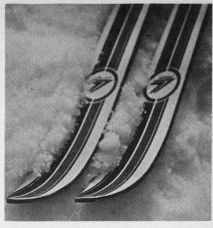

Fig. 3-23 (above): I used to advise my students to think about skiing on *the sides of their ski tips.* It is still good advice if you use a longer ski.

Fig. 3-22 (above left): Skis may easily be spun like a propeller if you shorten their *running surface,* as when you stand on the peak of a mogul.

Fig. 3-24: First, put your glove *through* the pole strap.
Fig. 3-24A: Then, grasp the strap and the pole handle.

Fig. 3-25 (below): Glide forward on the flat surface by pushing your knee forward. Don't try to *lift* your ski. Slide it, like Larry, Teri and Steve.

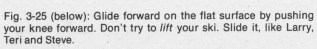

Fig. 3-26 (above): Try turning in place with your ski *tips* as the center of your circle. Keep your steps small.

Fig. 3-27 (above): When your knees are directly over your skis, your skis will be *flat to the snow surface.* They will slide downhill, pulled by the force of gravity.

Fig. 3-28 (below): Tilt your skis onto their uphill edges by rolling your knees uphill. Friction beneath your uphill edges will prevent the skis from sliding downhill.

Fig. 3-29 (above): Lift your poles as you take a step uphill, planting your ski on its uphill edge.

Fig. 3-30 (right): Plant your poles for support each time you transfer weight to your uphill ski and bring the lower ski up to meet it. Note the tilt of the shoulders; they're the same slant as the slope.

Fig. 3-31 (below): The convex part of my lower boot fits into the concave portion of my upper boot. For boots with straighter sidewalls, think about the same relationship in bare feet.

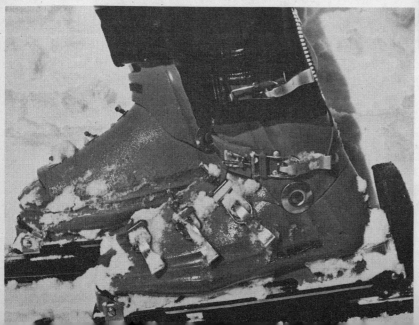

Fig. 3-32: My uphill ski has slid downhill toward my lower ski because my uphill knee is directly over the ski. This is called a sideslip (of the uphill ski).

Fig. 3-33: Starting position for your first *sideslip*. Note that my knees and hips are swung to the uphill side of the skis to keep them on their uphill edges and prevent a slide downhill.

tant position to be learned by the average recreational skier is the *traversing* posture, the stance used for crossing the slope, perpendicular to the *fall line*. The time to learn it is now, as it happens to be the very same position used for optimum balance when you climb the slope in what is called a *sidestep*.

Find a small incline that slopes upward gradually. Obviously, if you tried to climb this hill with your skis pointed straight toward it, your skis would slide backwards. Flat to the snow surface, your skis would be pulled downhill by gravity and the absence of friction between their slick bottom surface and the wet icy snow. It is advisable to climb sideways, but even in that stance, gravity will pull your skis downhill *if they are flat to the surface of the snow* (Fig. 3-27). Tilting the skis onto their uphill edges, you can provide a substantial resistance against that gravitational pull. (Fig. 3-28) Climb uphill sideways taking each step on the uphill edge of your ski. If the snow is fresh, your tracks will look like steps in the snow (Fig. 3-29). The slope I am climbing in these photos would be too steep for the average beginner, but I wanted to emphasize the parallel relationship between the shoulders and the hill. And, I just had to give you a peek at Colorado's Maroon Bell peaks from the top of Aspen Highlands. What a spot!

The simplest manner of twisting your skis onto their uphill edges is by trying to kneel on the uphill side of your skis. Any movement of the knees uphill will be followed by a tilt of the skis onto their uphill edges. Swing your hip uphill also. This is called *edging* via *transverse leverage*. Study Fig. 3-30 for the proper form when climbing or descending in a sidestep. Each time I bring my skis together (between each step), I resume a correct traversing posture with the exception of my poles which are dug in for support. Notice that my hips and knees swing *uphill* while my shoulders are maintained at the same angle as the slope on which I climb. This

is called body *angulation*. What you may not be able to detect is that my uphill ski leads my downhill ski by several inches; in fact, *everything* on my uphill side is leading—my uphill ski, uphill boot, uphill knee, uphill hip and shoulder are all leading slightly. This is an anticipatory posture that will aid your "parallel" turns later on. *Now* is the time to learn it! Each time the skis are brought together, the convex curve of the downhill boot is tucked tightly into the concave curve of the uphill boot (Fig. 3-31). The few inches lead that my uphill boot takes ahead of my downhill boot is the same lead taken by my uphill ski, knee, hip and shoulder. Finally, observe how I plant both poles with each step, for maximum support and balance. Climb up the slope several steps and then walk down, maintaining the same posture and stepping each time on your uphill edges. Perfect your sidestep-traversing posture before you even take your first run, and I guarantee you will be skiing with parallel skis in one week! But . . . be patient!

4. *Sideslip For Edge Control.* You probably noticed while stepping *down* the hill that your uphill ski occasionally skidded a bit as you stepped it next to your downhill ski. (Fig. 3-32) This will happen if the uphill ski is momentarily flat to the snow surface, which occurs when you release the hold that it has on the snow by relaxing its tilt onto its uphill edge. That kind of downhill skid is called a *sideslip*. It can also be done on both skis, simultaneously. Practicing the parallel ski sideslip early in your learning process will develop the basic skill of *edge control*, most essential to skiing proficiency.

Try this sideslip exercise, *now*, before you even take your first run downhill.

a. Stand in a sidestep-traverse posture a few yards up a graded slope (climb up with the sidestep). Your torso should be perpendicular to the slope, while your hip and knees are over the uphill side of your skis (angulation).

Fig. 3-34: A gentle roll of your knees until they are over your skis will initiate your parallel ski sideslip. Note that my hip is still uphill. Allow your skis to slip downhill to your lower planted pole.

Fig. 3-35: STOP your sideslip by snapping your knees sharply uphill. This will tilt your skis onto their uphill edges. Snow will pile beneath your skis and build a wall against the gravitational pull.

b. Plant your poles an arm's distance away on both sides of your body. Be sure to dig in the uphill edges of both skis to prevent a premature slide (Fig. 3-33). Face your lower pole. You are going to sideslip toward it.

c. *Gently* release your edges by rolling your knees directly over your skis. Keep your hips on the uphill side of your skis during this whole maneuver; torso perpendicular to the hill. When your skis are almost flat to the surface of the snow, gravity will pull them downhill and you will skid to your planted lower pole (Fig. 3-34). When you have slid to that lower pole, drive your knees uphill again to bite the snow with the uphill edges of your skis. This action will stop the skid, as the snow bunches up beneath your skis. (Fig. 3-35) You have just performed your first successful *sideslip* and the *hockey stop*. Try it several times, replanting your poles each time, until you reach the flat snow area. Then, turn around in place, sidestep up the slope facing the opposite way, and practice a series of sideslips again, with your skis facing that new direction. *Practice this exercise repeatedly*, until you feel that you can actually control your sideslip with just your knees and edges. Then, try it without planting your poles (Fig. 3-36). Learn to sideslip and stop in both directions before you take your first run downhill. This unorthodox procedure of teaching the sideslip before a straight downhill run is where my approach to ski instruction differs with most other systems. You will soon learn why.

Try to keep your body weight directly over the center of your skis during the sideslip, but keep your hips on the uphill side of your skis and your shoulders parallel to the slope. Once you feel control over this basic skill, climb higher and see if you can sideslip for progressively longer distances. Always stop your slide by driving your knees into the hill sharply, tilting your skis onto their uphill edges. As I mentioned, this will pile up the snow beneath your skis and brake your slide. Be sure to balance yourself by keeping

your shoulders slanted to the same degree as the slope throughout this exercise—you will hear me say that a lot, as I believe strongly in the educational value of repetition.

5. *Discover The Effect Of Longitudinal Leverage.* I should remind you, at this stage, that your skis should still be facing *across* the slope. You are not quite ready for your first run with your skis pointed straight downhill. So far, your sliding movements have been down the hill *sideways* via release of your skis' edges.

Because the ball of each foot (just behind the toes) is directly over the center of the running surface on both skis, a movement of your center of gravity forward or aft will be followed by greater body weight pressure on the front or rear of your skis. This is called *longitudinal leverage*, and your ability to control it is another basic skill required of the proficient skier. (Think of your "center of gravity" as a point just behind your belt buckle.)

When you were practicing your sideslip, if your body weight was not concentrated over the center of your skis, you probably experienced a moment of imbalance. If your body weight was *forward*, the tips of your skis skidded downhill faster than your tails; if your longitudinal leverage was aft, the tails of your skis led your sideslip. Both movements will be utilized later in advanced skiing maneuvers. This time, let's be deliberate in our use of the leverage principle:

a. Climb several yards up the slope again with a hard edges sidestep. Assume a good sidestep-traverse posture (angulate), tilting your knees and hip uphill and your shoulder line parallel with the slant of the slope.

b. Release your edge hold on the snow by rolling your knees over your skis and flattening their bottoms to the snow surface. Be sure to not roll those knees too far, or you will catch a downhill edge! Your hips should remain on the uphill side of your skis, at this stage.

Fig. 3-36: Sideslipping is a safe and respectable way for a novice to come down a slope that he has ventured on with poor judgement, like this steep pitch at Taos Ski Valley. Notice how my torso is 90 degrees away from the slant of the slope in this hockey stop.

Fig. 3-37 (above): Begin a sideslip by rolling your knees over your skis. Then, move your hips forward and downhill also. Extra body weight on the front of your skis will assist the gravitational pull. Your ski tips will slip downhill faster than your tails. This *forward sideslip* is the key to your first parallel turn.

Fig. 3-38 (below): The optimum posture for traversing, or crossing the hill, with your skis together. Everything that is on your uphill side should be leading. The hip is swung uphill and the shoulders are parallel to the slant of the slope.

c. As your skis begin to slip sideways down the slope, tilt your center of gravity forward by moving your hips over your boots (maintaining good knee bend, of course). Your extra weighted ski *tips* will automatically slide downhill faster than your ski tails. This is called a *forward sideslip* via hip projection (Fig. 3-37).

d. Still maintaining good knee bend but on the flat surface of your skis to continue your sideslip, tilt your center of gravity backward to weight your ski *tails*. The backward leverage pressure will drive your ski tails downhill faster than your tips. It is called a *backward sideslip*. Your hips are your most powerful motor force. Learn how to use them to your advantage.

e. Alternate forward, backward and straight sideslips until you feel control over the leverage of your skis in the sideslip maneuver. Try it from both traverse directions. Then, you will be ready to ski straight ahead.

6. *Traversing.* Your first forward movement on skis should be *across* the hill, not straight down. (Be patient!) Pick a *concave* slope so that your first traverse will end in an automatic stop. Let's review the optimum posture:

a. If you are in good shape and have good balance, by all means try to traverse with your boots together—the convex portion of your lower boot tucked into the concave part of your upper boot as when you sidestepped.

b. Bent knees and your hip should be swung uphill to tilt both skis onto their uphill edges.

c. No part of your body should trail behind your heels.

d. Shoulders should slant at the same angle as the slope.

e. Everything uphill should lead slightly—the uphill ski, boot, knee, hip and uphill shoulder are all slightly ahead (Fig. 3-38).

f. If your balance is poor or your physical condition is less than adequate, try traversing with your skis apart. Pro-

moters of the wide-track approach do not advocate a close boot relationship for the beginner, as they feel that a wide stance is more stable. With a wide stance, the need to angle the shoulders parallel to the hill can be minimized, as body weight is maintained more equally on both skis (Fig. 3-39) and your center of gravity will be above a broader base.

g. Once in a good holding traverse posture, push off with your poles, pointing your skis just slightly downhill to get some momentum. At all costs, maintain a good traverse posture and glide on the uphill edges of both skis, but keep your knees flexible enough to absorb terrain undulation.

h. Problems you may encounter while traversing:

(1). If you are falling on the uphill side of your skis when traversing with your skis close together, you forgot to slant your shoulders the same angle as the hill.

(2). A fall on the downhill side of your skis is caused by catching your downhill edges when your skis are held *too flat* to the snow surface. Traverse on your uphill edges.

(3). If your ski tips separate, your body weight is too far back. Don't *sit!*

(4). If your ski tails separate, you are probably bending forward too much from the waist and one or both skis are too flat to the snow surface. (Fig. 3-40) Minimize your forward waist bend. Rather, traverse with a sidebend, until your shoulders match the angle of the slope.

(5). If your ski tails are skidding downhill, you are sitting too far back. *Always lead your boots with your knees!*

(6). Should your ski tips cross, you probably forgot to lead your traverse with your uphill ski, boot, knee, hip and shoulder. Rather than in a purely parallel position, your skis should glide in a *parallelogram* position. When I teach kids, I tell them to point their belly-button downhill. Try it. It will keep your uphill hip forward. If your downhill hip is back, it will keep your downhill ski back. A ski tip cross almost always will follow an advance of the downhill ski when a beginner is traversing.

(7). If you ski too fast and crash into the woods, you forgot to pick a *concave* slope to slow down your traverse, or

you began with your ski tips pointed too far downhill. Try a less steep traverse.

7. *Traverse, Forward Sideslip And Stop!* Once you have perfected your traverse in both directions, link up a traverse with a forward sideslip:

a. Traverse a *convex* slope on your uphill edges. Maintain good body angulation.

b. At the crest of the convex slope, release your edges by rolling your knees over your skis. As your boots pass the peak of the bump, *project* your hips and torso down the fall line. Because of your forward momentum and longitudinal leverage, a forward sideslip should follow. Stop your forward sideslip by sharply driving your knees forward and into the hill. This will tilt your weighted ski shovels onto their uphill edges abruptly. Your unweighted ski tails will skid downhill, and a platform of snow will pile up beneath your tilted skis, eventually causing enough resistance to stop your slide. Some call this form of stopping a "hockey-stop" (Figs. 3-41A, B, C & D).

c. Try this maneuver in *both* directions.

8. *The Fan.* Once you have perfected your traverse, forward sideslip and stop exercise, try it from a steeper traverse; then steeper; then still steeper. Finally, try it from almost straight downhill (Fig. 3-42). This progressively steeper traverse forward sideslip and stop is called *The Fan* exercise. Try it in both directions. You are closer than ever to parallel skiing.

9. **The Downhill Running Posture.** It may seem strange to some readers (my P.S.I.A. colleagues notwithstanding) that I have not spoken of the downhill running position until this time. My reasoning is that a beginner should know how to *finish* his first run before he is taught how to begin it. Too many new skiers push off from the top of the slope with no conception of how to turn or stop. They comprise the greatest number of casualties on the daily accident report; they are frequently unschooled "turkeys" who give a bad name to our sport; but, sometimes, they are just unfortunate learners who have been taught inefficiently. If you have

Fig. 3-41A (below): Begin this exercise with a well edged traverse. Reach for the "X" that I've marked with your knees and your uphill hip.

Fig. 3-41B (right): Start a sideslip while you're traversing by rolling your knees over your skis. Change it to a *forward sideslip* by projecting your hips toward the direction of intended travel.

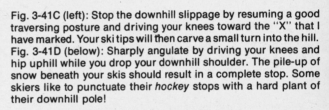

Fig. 3-41C (left): Stop the downhill slippage by resuming a good traversing posture and driving your knees toward the "X" that I have marked. Your ski tips will then carve a small turn into the hill.

Fig. 3-41D (below): Sharply angulate by driving your knees and hip uphill while you drop your downhill shoulder. The pile-up of snow beneath your skis should result in a complete stop. Some skiers like to punctuate their *hockey* stops with a hard plant of their downhill pole!

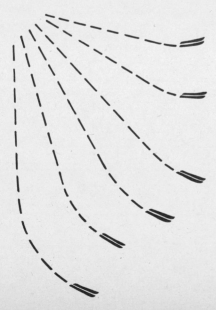

Fig. 3-42 (left): A traverse, forward sideslip and hockey stop usually results in a *turn onto the hill* with parallel skis. Start with a shallow traverse, almost 90 degrees to the fall line. Gradually increase the steepness of your traverse until you are *straight in the fall line.* This exercise is called *the Fan.*

perfected your traverse form when climbing in a sidestep or when skiing *across* the hill, and if you have had a reasonable amount of success with your sideslip and "hockey-stop," you are ready to take your first run straight down the fall line:

a. Assume the proper stance on flat ground first, to study its form.

b. The position of the skis is *parallel* to each other. If your balance is good, lock one boot inside the other, as described in your traversing posture instruction. If not, a separation of 4 to 6 inches between your skis may feel more comfortable. Allow the leading boot to be the one on the inside of your anticipated turn—i.e. skiing straight down the fall line, the right boot leads by a few inches before a right turn, the left boot leads before a left turn.

Most ski schools advocate the wide-track fall line stance for beginners, presupposing that your balance is not too keen and that you will feel more control with a broader base under your center of gravity. This is certainly true in some cases: some people can't even *walk* in a straight line *off* skis; others walk with their toes pointed outward like Charlie Chaplin's memorable silent movie character; still others carry so much fat in their middle and bottom regions that it is virtually impossible for them to *stand* with their feet together, let alone move that way on skis! For those individuals, and for anyone who is inexperienced at other forms of kinesthetic activity, I, too, recommend a wide-track stance.

On the other hand, if you have ever ridden a bicycle, enjoyed running on the beach, ridden a horse, skated, studied ballet, slalomed on a water ski, or even have learned

Fig. 3-43: Marge in a good posture for skiing straight downhill. Be sure to keep your hands *forward* and your knees in front of your boots.

how to walk steadily in a straight line, there is no reason why your first run cannot be in the classic form of a ski instructor—with the convex part of one boot tucked into the concave portion of the other. Lead with your right boot if you plan to turn to the right and with your left boot if you plan to finish your run with a left turn.

c. All body joints should be loosely flexed. If you have purchased a good boot, your knees are already locked into a position that is over the front of your toes, by the forward flexing of your ankles. If you are using Uncle Louie's hand-me-down rocker-soled boots, issued when he skied with the 10th Mountain Division, they are of no help at all, and you will have to *press your knees* forward until they hide your boots.

Drop your seat *slightly* until it is in a line above your heels, (but not behind your heels), and tip your torso forward until it is at the same slant as your lower legs. (Fig. 3-43)

Your arms should be bent slightly at the elbows, while your hands are forward and wider apart than your shoulders. Pretend that you are serving a tray of food to your downhill audience.

Your head should be flexed back to enable you to look several yards ahead. It is not good practice to look down at your skis.

d. While your pole *handles* are kept forward by your extended arms and hands, your pole *baskets* (the pointed end) should trail behind your body, about a foot above the snow.

e. If your skis are shoulder height or longer, your body weight should be concentrated at a point forward of your boots, where it will be if you ski on the balls of your feet (just behind your toes). Pretend that you have tacks under your heels. Don't step on them! If your skis are below shoulder high, and they should be if you are just beginning, distribute your body weight evenly over the entire ski.

f. Assume the correct downhill running posture on flat terrain and rock up and down, flexing your knees several times to accustom yourself to the balance. You might feel the front of your boot pressing into the front of your leg. You should *not* feel the back of your boot pressing into the back of your leg!

g. Next, climb the hill with a good sidestep reminding yourself to angulate, with your knees and hip swung uphill and your shoulders slanted, parallel to the slope, in preparation for your first downhill run.

10. **The Bullfighter Turn.** Once on top of your first practice hill—if you have climbed with a sidestep—you are faced with the problem of turning in place in order to face downhill (the fall line). The method you learned on the flat won't work on a hill, as the moment your skis would face the fall line they would shoot downhill like a rocket! Such a situation calls for the "Bullfighter."

a. Dig your uphill edges deeply into the snow to keep from sideslipping and twist your torso until it faces downhill.

b. Hold your pole handles in the palms of your hands and reach out to plant your ski poles as far away from your body as you can, directly in line with your ski boots but a shoulder width apart—(*Your* shoulders). (Fig. 3-44) Plant your poles and let them support your weight. (Fig. 3-45) There should be a straight line from your pole baskets running through your poles, your forearms and your upper arms to your shoulders. This "locked elbow" position will tax your arm

Fig. 3-44 (above left): Hold the butt of the pole handles in the palm of your hands. You're going to support yourself on them as you turn around.

Fig. 3-45 (above center): Be sure to keep your skis tilted onto their uphill edges as you plant both poles.

Fig. 3-46 (above right): Lock your arms at the elbows and keep them as straight as your poles.

Fig. 3-47 (left): You'll have no trouble stepping around if you keep your steps SMALL.

Fig. 3-48 (right): Marge takes off. She's sitting back a bit, a natural tendency with beginners of skiers who fear fall line. At this stage make a concerted effort to *kneel on your ski tips.* That will keep your body weight forward and your skis in control!

muscles less and make use of your arm bones as support (Fig. 3-46).

c. With SMALL steps, step your ski tips around until they both face downhill (the fall line) between your planted poles. (Fig. 3-47)

d. Align your boots, either locked together or in a wide-track stance, so that the right boot is slightly ahead in anticipation of a right turn.

11: **The First Run Downhill.**

a. Flex your ankles until your knees hide your boots and you feel body weight pressure under both feet as you relax your pole support. Ski right through the middle of your initial pole placement and grip the pole handles normally as you continue to slide. Assume the correct downhill running posture that you practiced on the flat. (Fig. 3-48).

b. Fix your eyes upon the spot where you wish to turn and let your skis slide. Rock up and down gently, flexing your knees. Be sure to keep them in line with the toes of your boots. Enjoy the flight. You are in control if your posture is correct

c. Rise up to an almost erect posture, hips forward, knees still leading the boots, body line 90 degrees to the slope when you are ready to turn. (Fig 3-49) Then sink (Fig. 3-50) down sharply, making an effort to *kneel* to the right of your ski

Fig. 3-49: Marge's spring upward and forward lightens her skis' weight burden in preparation for a turn.

Fig. 3-50: A drive of her knees toward the spot I've marked with an "X" tilts Marge's skis onto their inside edges. Her ski tips spoon out a neat right turn, assisted by the side camber on her skis.

Fig. 3-51: The snow will fly!

Fig. 3-52 (above): Turn completed, Marge assumes traversing posture for a new direction, with her shoulders the same slant as the slope, hip and knees pressed forward and uphill. No part of her body is behind her heels.

Fig. 3-53 (below): Marge in a left traverse. Note the similarity between this excellent traversing posture and the body position used for climbing with a sidestep.

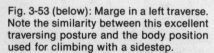

Fig. 3-54: Centrifugal force pulls outside your turn. You must lean away from it or you'll fall to the outside of your turn.

Centripetal force pulls inside the turn. With *angulation* your torso leans away from it and effects an optimum balance for skiers who ski with their skis *together*.

The *wide track* turn will allow you to fight centripetal force by weighting the ski that is *inside* the turn, as we see Marge doing here, with your outside ski functioning as an outrigger for balance. This is called *inclination*.

tips. If you edge sharply enough, the snow will fly! (Fig. 3-51) Twist your boots and knees to the right as you lead your turn with your inside hip and assume a right traverse position to cross the slope. You should have had enough practice traversing to assume this posture automatically. (Fig. 3-52) Its angulated form is designed to combat the power of centrifugal and centripetal forces which seek to destroy your turn.

Remember:

(1). Your torso remains perpendicular to the slope from start to finish. Shoulders should slant parallel to the hill when you traverse.

(2). Knees and hip are swung to the uphill side of your skis in order to edge them while traversing. The shape of the ski will then carve the finish of your turn for you.

(3). Body weight pressure remains on the forward part of longer skis, with the shovels of your skis spooning out the turn. Shorter skis may be equally weighted from tip to tail to prevent a spin-out.

(4). Everything uphill leads when traversing—the uphill ski, boot, knee, hip and shoulder. All are slightly ahead. The precise amount of lead is determined by your boots, as the lower boot locks its convex curve into the concave curve of the upper. (Fig. 3-53) If you are performing this exercise with a wide stance, lead your traverse the same way, but with your skis apart and with less angulation. (Fig. 3-54) Angulation is also less imperative in deep powder snow.

To stop sharply, drive your knees farther forward and uphill as you increase your body angulation, and you will stop with the aforementioned "hockey-stop" by abrupt *edging*, as your unweighted tails skid a few inches downhill.

Try several straight runs and turns to a stop, turning each time in a different direction. Just remember to lead with your right boot and your right hip for a right turn, and your left boot and left hip for a left turn. Body angulation while traversing is crucial if you are turning with your feet together. With a wide-track stance, it is less important, as the body weight is then distributed more evenly over *both* skis, and the broader base of support will even allow some body *inclination* during the turn.

12. **The First Fall And Resurrection.** Everybody falls. If you can accept that, you will have less hangups about falling and place less importance upon how others will react to your errors. The truth is that other skiers will be more compassionate than ridiculing, since they have all been in the same embarrassing position more than once. Falls are less traumatic today than they were 15 or 20 years ago. High modern boots with stiff shanks (if they fit properly) make an ankle injury almost impossible today, and release bindings (properly adjusted and compatible with a skier's boots) are working better than ever to separate the skis from the skier in a potentially damaging fall. Add to this the technological advances of the ski industry and the methodological improvements of the ski schools, and you will understand why accidents have decreased on a per skier comparison since the primitive years of two decades ago.

Nevertheless, you *will* fall. Sometimes, a spill is caused by *collision*—an uncontrolled skier who has never taken a lesson and does not know how to stop or turn crashes into you. Occasionally, a sudden change in terrain condition (ice,

chunky snow, a pothole or sitzmark) will cause you to relax your mental concentration upon your form. Any deviation from the form prescribed by your instructor can cause a moment of imbalance and a fall. A *sudden distraction*, like a field mouse dashing across the slope, another falling skier, or a skin tight pair of stretch pants can also bust up your concentration and cause a spill.

I should mention that, during the entire week that the blind boy, David, was under my tutelage, he did not fall a single time! He proved to me that *posture* is the essence of control. David was devoid of the distractions of sight. His posture was perfect. The positions that your instructor prescribes will prevent a fall, but the performance of those movements requires *total* concentration and rejection of any stimulus of distraction. That kind of concentration is available to all but achieved by few. Again, it's a question of *purpose*. If you want something bad enough, you set your sights on it and approach it aggressively in the straightest line possible—like the racer. Distractions are obstacles in your course. David really *wanted* to ski. I provided the prescription. He followed my directions precisely and succeeded. It might have been quite a different story if he was *not* handicapped and more susceptible to harmful distractions.

The worst distraction that an instructor must deal with is *mental preoccupation*. It causes a great percentage of falls. An instructor can spot a potential collision and shout a warning to his student; he can see terrain changes and steer his class away from them; he can stall his instruction for a moment and join the rest of the class in ogling that neat pair of stretch pants that skis by. What he has difficulty discerning is mental preoccupation, a primary deterrent to a skier's learning process: Mary is so frightened to death of moving down that 10-foot slope that she's about to wet her britches; Sam is so overwhelmed by the pretty girls all around that his head is about to unscrew, while his heart rate has jumped to 150; Alice doesn't give a rap about the posture her instructor is demonstrating as she has plans for his evening; George is only in class because his wife insisted. His mind in on the Rose Bowl game, and he'd rather be in his overstuffed chair in front of the TV with a good cigar. These students will retain little of what their instructor describes as optimum balance positions. They will fall.

Fortunately, the good Lord gave us a fine cushion to absorb the shock of inadvertent falls. The problem is that many of us don't use it. Our first movement, when a fall is imminent, is to reach out and block the impact with our hands. This can result in a fractured ulna, a dislocated thumb, a crushed bursa, or, at least, a sprained wrist. *Use that cushion.* It's located in the seat of your pants. That round thing that's got cleavage. If a fall is inevitable, stick out your seat and cushion the impact. At the same time, try to get your boots together but thrust your skis *away* from your body (Fig. 3-55). If you are on a steep slope and you begin to slide head first down the fall line, do everything you can to spin around and get your skis *below* your body and pointed across the slope. The edges of your skis are your best brake to stop that kind of a slide. Beginners need not worry, as the slope on which you practice should not be very steep. All skiers should stay away from steep terrain when wearing slick shiny clothing. That material is faster than your skis, and a fall on the steep could be disastrous! I lost a student who wore an outfit like that for a class on Stein's

Fig. 3-55: Marge takes a bummer. She'll be all right, though. She's using her cushion!

Fig. 3-56: Bring skis up close to your center of gravity, and be sure that your skis are pointed *across* slope.

Fig. 3-57: Pull with your right hand and push with your left. You're UP!

Run, at Sugarbush Valley. She made one turn, miscalculated, fell, slid and didn't stop until she'd bounced from mogul to mogul, all the way to the bottom!

Forward falls are dangerous. Avoid them. If you feel one coming on, swing your seat to the uphill side of the slope and *sit!*

Now, you have done it. You have fallen for the first time, and the other seven people in your class are impatiently waiting for you to get up. At least, that's the way it will seem to you. You will feel like the dunce, and your adrenalin will boil! In the face of that embarrassment, most men will rise up by brute force. But, some men, and most women, are not brutes. They have to use their intelligence. They must reason that it is foolish to try to rise when their skis are pointed downhill, as gravity will then simply make them slide farther. Whichever way you may have fallen, your first rising effort should be to swing your skis until they rest *across* the fall line, in a traverse direction. Some fallen positions require the skier to roll over on his back in order to swing his skis across the hill. The wise skier then *uses* gravity and the dependable assistance of leverage in the following manner:

a. Bring your boots and skis up close to your seat.

b. Dig in the uphill edges of your skis. Deeply.

c. Take your hands out of your pole straps and hold your poles together.

d. Dig in your pole tips all the way to their baskets, close to your uphill hip. Hold your poles just above the baskets (the rings) with your uphill hand—firmly. (Fig. 3-56)

e. Place your downhill hand high up on the poles on top of the handles, if you can reach that far.

f. Pull with that downhill hand, push with your uphill hand, and let gravity do the rest as you stand. (Fig. 3-57)

There are other methods, but this is by far the most successful. Unless you fall on flat ground. If you spill on the flat and you are not muscular enough to pull yourself up (as gravity will offer you no assistance), either release the binding from one of your skis and step up, or swallow your pride, blink your eyelashes and ask for some assistance. Most skiers will be happy to help you. Now, let's get back to skiing.

13. **Graduating The Length Of Your Ski.** After a day or two of practicing the exercises I have just mentioned, trade in those rented arm-pit-high skis for a pair that are shoulder-high and practice each of the 12 exercises you have just learned for a least an entire day. I know you are anxious to link your turns, but the longer you wait, and the more you practice the exercises for development of the basic skills that I have outlined—edging, sideslipping, leverage, traversing, straight running and the "hockey-stop"—the easier it will be for you to link several turns together.

On the shorter ski, you probably felt more in balance with your center of gravity directly over the middle of your skis. With a longer ski, you should move that center of gravity to a point forward of your boots. This is easy if you tip your torso slightly forward until it is at the same angle as your lower legs *and* ride on the balls of your feet, just behind your toes, feeling little contact under your heels. In either case, your knees should hide your boots, so press them forward (if the shape of your boot doesn't place them there for you) and *keep* them there! (Fig. 3-58)

14. **An Easier Way Up.** It is a bonus for learning how to turn and stop. Up until now I have had you climb the bottom of the slope with the sidestep. You probably looked with envy at the hundreds of skiers who have been riding the chairlift next to us and wondered why I have put you through this torture. Two reasons. The first is that I want to condition your reflexes to automatically assume a good angulated posture when your skis face across the hill. If you have climbed repeatedly in that traverse posture (on your uphill edges, with your knees and hip swung uphill and your shoulders slanted parallel to the angle of the slope) between each of your practice runs to a sideslip and ''hockey-stop,'' the chances are good that you will automatically fall into that position every time your skis point across the fall line. Secondly, most chairlifts require the skier to stand and ski down a gentle slope while his chair continues to move. A lift operator is usually stationed at the point of disembarkation to pull back the chair while you stand and push off. What would you expect to do at the end of that run if you could not turn? Probably what 80 percent of uninformed beginners do at the end of their first chairlift ride: stand, slide, crash and burn! Now, you can ride the lift with less apprehension, confident that you are at least capable of skiing down that narrow run when you leave your chair and making one turn or a stop. Find yourself a fox and do it! (Fig. 3-59)

15. **First Parallel Run From The Top.** You have ridden the chairlift for the first time, slid down the exit ramp and successfully turned. A short walk or sidestep has brought you to the top of the novice slope. Over a thousand feet of downhill skiing awaits you. You look down. It scares the hell out of you. You can push off forgetting all I have taught you and pray that you don't embrace a tree or another skier. You could take off your skis, ride the lift down and give up this insane sport forever. Or, you can remind yourself that it was not too long ago when another beginner stood in your same spot, thinking carefully about what his instructor had to say, pushed off and got to the bottom without falling. And . . . he was blind. . .

Let's review a few basic principles:

a. A ski will slide downhill (the fall line) if its bottom is flat against the surface of the snow, no matter *which* way the ski is pointed. Skis should be totally flat to the snow surface ONLY when skiing straight down the fall line or when deliberately sideslipping.

b. A ski that is flat to the surface of the snow can be easily turned by axial motion (like a propeller) by steering it with the feet and legs, IF THE KNEES ARE DIRECTLY ABOVE THE FRONT OF THE BOOTS! Skiing straight down the fall line, try to hide your boots with your knees.

c. Axial motion of longer skis is facilitated by an unweighting effort. This can be a sudden *down* movement flexing all body joints, a spring of the body *upward*, or a shortening of the skis' running surface, as when the skier stands on the apex of a mogul or when he pivots on his ski tips or ski tails.

d. Your skis will track *across* the hill if they are tilted onto their uphill edges, as a platform of snow will form beneath them and provide resistance to the pull of gravity downhill.

e. Edging (tilting the skis onto their uphill edges) is best accomplished by pressing your knees forward and to the

Fig. 3-58: Larry turns his short boards very well with his body weight pretty well centered. Longer skis, like mine, need more weight pressure on the forebody, achieved by tipping the torso forward slightly and skiing on the balls of the feet, just behind the toes.

Fig. 3-59: Teri and Steve going up the easy way at Aspen Highlands.

uphill side of your skis; it may be amplified by swinging your hip uphill also, but keep your balance by dropping your downhill shoulder toward your downhill heel, until your shoulders slant parallel to the angle of the slope (body angulation).

f. Parallel skiing is safer skiing although the boots do not necessarily have to be locked together. If your balance is good, your form will be more graceful in a locked boot relationship; if this is your choice, lock the convex portion of the inside of your downhill boot into the concave curve above the arch of your uphill boot. The uphill ski should always lead the downhill ski by a few inches while traversing, as should the uphill knee, hip and shoulder.

g. It is possible to ski downhill sideways by simply releasing the hold of the uphill edges when the skis are in a traverse attitude. This is called a sideslip. It is accomplished by rolling the knees over the skis to flatten their relationship to the snow. *Some* bite of the uphill edges should be maintained even when sideslipping, to prevent a catch of the downhill edges and moment of imbalance.

h. A sideslip may be terminated by a sudden tilt of the skis onto their uphill edges. Snow will then pile up under the skis and provide a formidable resistance to the pull of gravity downhill. This is frequently called a "hockey-stop." The sudden tilt of the skis is accomplished by a sharp drive of the knees uphill, coupled with body angulation to maintain equilibrium.

i. Longitudinal leverage toward the shovels of the skis will change a sideslip into a *forward* sideslip, with the shovels sliding downhill faster than the tails. Longitudinal leverage behind the heels will cause the ski tails to slide downhill faster than the shovels into a *backward* sideslip. Body weight should be centralized when sideslipping directly down the fall line, not forward nor aft.

Concentrate upon those nine principles as David did and forget about the visual stimuli of fear that confront you. If your form is accurate, you WILL succeed, as he succeeded. Your first run should be no more than a series of short downhill slides, turns to traverses and hockey-stops. Don't try to link together right and left turns. Not yet. You will be ready for that next lesson after you have completed a perfect run, practicing only the straight downhill position, the sideslip, the traverse and the hockey-stop, in *both* directions.

16. Linking Parallel Turns.

a. The Forward Sideslip. Find a steep slope and practice your sideslip. If your body weight is centralized while sideslipping you will skid *straight* down the fall line although your skis are pointed across it. You learned that a short while ago. Move your center of gravity forward and that straight sideslip will turn into a *forward* sideslip (your ski tips will skid downhill faster than your tails). This is the link between your parallel turns! Perform a series of linked straight and forward sideslips. Be sure to lead your sideslip posture with everything that is uphill—the uphill ski, boot, knee, hip and shoulder should all lead by a few inches, just as before.

b. The Change of Lead. From a holding traverse close to the fall line (Fig. 3-60), move your knees and hips over your skis and forward into a forward sideslip and *switch your leading ski, boot, knee, hip and shoulder* (Fig. 3-61). That subtle exchange, performed when the skis are flat to the snow surface and pointed close to the fall line, will facilitate the axial motion that is necessary to cross the fall line. Axial motion should begin with a downward drive of the knees into the new traverse direction. (Fig.3-62) Pressure applied to the tips or shovels of your skis, once they are tilted onto their uphill edges, will continue the arc of your turn. Once you reach the traverse line that you want, move that pressure back and ride the entire ski. Your angulated posture will automatically place more body weight on your downhill ski. Check your traverse form. Are your skis on their new uphill edges? Are your knees and hip swung uphill? Do your shoulders parallel the angle of the slope? Are the uphill ski, boot, knee, hip and shoulder all a few inches ahead? Practice the forward sideslip and change of lead in both directions. Now you can link your long parallel turns.

Fig. 3-60: Begin a steep traverse, just barely off the fall line. Note my body dynamics.

Fig. 3-61: Start a forward sideslip into the fall line by moving your hips and knees directly over your skis and *forward*. Now, change your leading ski, knee, hip and shoulder. Note the neutral position of my shoulders when I am skiing straight down the fall line.

Fig. 3-62: My knees and left hip tilt *inside* the turn away from centrifugal force. My right shoulder drops to fight the pull of centripetal force. My skis carve, and I am in perfect balance.

Fig. 3-63: Pole plant near the ski tip, when traversing at an extreme angle to fall line, must be followed by a vigorous effort to swing tails into the fall line.

Fig. 3-64: Planting the pole *in the fall line* will effect a faster turn with less effort, especially if the pole plant is followed by an anticipatory movement of the torso *downhill*.

Fig. 3-65: A pole plant in fall line allows me to *anticipate* my turn by moving my torso toward it. When the upper half of my body is blocked and can't twist any farther, the lower half will follow its lead. I can than pivot under my boots or on my ski tails! *Note change of my leading ski.*

17. **Pole Action And Anticipation.** Up until now you have read no mention of the poles other than my suggestion to keep their baskets trailing behind with their handles forward. The poles are relatively superfluous in the early stages of your learning process. Some GLM schools even take them away from beginners. I don't, because my beginners are encouraged to sidestep up the hill a lot, and pole support makes climbing easier. Poles also come in handy for rising from a fall. Now, we will see how they can help you turn.

Most parallel skiers prepare for a turn by planting their downhill pole in the snow. Many of them don't know the best spot to plant it. If the pole is planted close to the tip of the downhill ski when traversing, a strong effort must follow to swing the ski tails into the fall line (Fig. 3-63), as the pivot must take place under the shovels of the skis. This kind of vigorous turn was popular in the fifties.

The French, spearheaded by champions like Killy, Russel and Augert, taught us that a parallel turn could be made faster and with less effort if the downhill pole is planted *always in the fall line.* Thus, in a traverse that is 90 degrees to the fall line, the downhill pole is planted to the side, (Fig. 3-64), directly below the skier's body, allowing him to pivot his skis like a propeller under his boots, or if acceleration is his intent, on his ski *tails!* (Fig. 3-65)

In either case, the purpose of the pole plant is to trigger the deflection and the *projection* of the torso upward and forward *toward the fall line.* This dynamic thrust is called *anticipation.* The movement of the upper body downhill is soon followed by an uncoiling of the lower body and thus the skis. This is an automatic physical assist to the axial motion

Fig. 3-66: Preparatory phase. Torso faces intended direction of travel as pole is planted in fall line. A knee push uphill should create a "pre-turn" into the hill.

Fig. 3-67: Turn initiation takes place when torso twist is blocked and lower body uncoils to recover neutral position. Body projects 90 degrees to the slope angle, leading ski is exchanged and knees will now drive forward to place body weight on the forebody of the skis.

Fig. 3-68: Turn execution is continued by twisting knees, feet and skis via axial motion, as my hip swings into the hill and my outside shoulder drops to match the angle of the slope.

Fig. 3-69: Turn completion is simply a resumption of the new traverse position. Note how my knees and hip swing to my right, causing my skis to roll onto their inside edges.

of the skier as he pivots his feet into the new direction. It is the primary reason why I believe that even the beginner should ski across the fall line in a parallelogram, i.e. with his uphill ski, knee, hip and shoulder all leading his traverse.

Here we go:

a. Traverse in good form on a wide gentle slope.

b. Without changing your posture, advance your downhill pole basket (the ring), and freeze it, 6 inches above the snow.

c. Plant the downhill pole in the fall line with a sharp drive of your knees uphill. Such a movement will create a "pre-turn," as your shovels turn uphill and your un-weighted ski tails push downhill. This will check your speed, as in a hockey-stop, giving you a platform of snow beneath your skis from which you can spring up and into the fall line. (Fig. 3-66)

d. Spring up and move your hips *forward*, projecting your upper body and both hands downhill as you flatten your skis; this should trigger a momentary forward sideslip (Fig. 3-67), as your legs uncoil to catch up with your torso. Immediately *change your leads*, pivot your feet, and sink down driving your knees forward and into the new traverse direction. (Fig. 3-68) Check your traverse form again. Is everything uphill ahead? Are you gliding on your uphill edges? How is your body angulation? (Fig. 3-69) Try a similar turn in the other direction.

e. Practice this turn from different angles of traverse, always planting the pole that is INSIDE THE TURN downhill, then springing like a cat into the fall line as you flatten your skis and change your leads. Deflection or rebound from a platform of snow created by a "check" along with the pole plant can be explosive if the skier severely angulates and applies strong lateral downhill pressure on his skis at the moment of the pole plant. Snow will fly and the resultant uncoiling of the lower body as the torso moves downhill is frequently accompanied by a lifting of the ski tails. The pivot in this classical type of parallel turn is under the tips. The final movement of every turn should be a drive of the knees and uphill hip forward toward the new traverse as the body angulates. As you improve, the change of edges and leads will be so rapid, it will appear that your skis are never flat to the snow surface. This is the classical manner of turning with "parallel" skis.

18. **The Easiest Parallel Turn Of All.** The last exercise is the traditional method of turning with your skis together, bouncing off a platform of snow that develops under your skis after an abrupt pre-turn uphill coupled with a pole plant. Every platform is a check of your speed, as in a "hockey-stop," which among its practical benefits provides a psychological security for the timid skier who does not feel comfortable skiing at high velocities. There is another type of skier, though, and another type of parallel turn. For the racer, the speed freak, for you who are lured by the thrill of speed, there is the easiest parallel turn of all. It employs *inclination* as opposed to *angulation* but may also be combined for a very graceful, totally secure high speed turn.

a. Start in a traverse in good form, knees and hips swung uphill, shoulders parallel to the slope, body weight mostly on the lower ski if the snow is hard packed or shallow, or on both skis if the snow is powder or deep and heavy, (Fig. 3-70) then, begin a forward sideslip. (Fig. 3-70A)

Fig. 3-70 (above): From a good holding traverse, on your uphill edges. . .

Fig. 3-70A (below): . . . move your hips and knees forward and over your skis to initiate a forward sideslip. Your skis should flatten to the snow surface, and your ski tips should drift toward the fall line.

Fig. 3-71: When your ski tips have drifted 45 degrees away from your initial traverse, *incline* your body *downhill and forward*, planting your pole at about two o'clock to your direction of travel. Be sure to stay forward by standing on the balls of your feet.

b. Rise up to an almost erect posture, tilting your *entire body* about 1 o'clock to your direction of travel as you plant your pole at 2 o'clock. This upward and downhill movement will trigger a flattening of your skis to the angle of the hill and the forward leverage of your body weight will continue to push your tips downhill faster than your tails in an accelerated forward sideslip. (Fig. 3-71)

c. Assist the inception of your turn with axial motion of your skis as you change your leading ski. This should head you straight down the fall line with your body 90 degrees to the angle of the slope. (Fig. 3-72)

d. Continue turning your skis by applying pressure to their shovels with a kneeling motion, forward and in the direction of the turn's completion. This should roll the forebody of your skis onto their inside edges and spoon out the completion of your turn.

e. Now you have a choice. Follow with a traverse and good *angulation,* or tilt right into another *inclined* parallel turn. (Fig. 3-73) The choice depends upon the direction of travel you desire next. With no setting of the edges or platform position, this type of turn is designed for high velocity, minimum physical effort and maximum courage. It functions beautifully on a Giant Slalom course and on a western type slope where you have plenty of room and not too many obstacles in your path.

19. **Moguls (Those Bloody Bumps) And Avalement.** Ask the majority of new skiers what is their greatest fear. Half will say steep slopes while the other half will answer "MOGULS" as they hunch their shoulders and quiver their lower lips with apprehension. Moguls are menacing to most novices who have finally become comfortable performing their early training exercises on relatively flat beginner terrain. Some are shocked to hear that ski areas actually design their slopes to deliberately include bumps for the pleasure of advanced skiers. It is true. The better you get, the more you will seek "bump runs" for the variety of challenge that they provide.

A deep groan was heard through the entire Mad River Valley of Vermont last week when a new type of "Snow-Cat" called a Kassbohrer Pisten Bully crept down one of the steeper bump trails at Sugarbush Valley called The Mall, crushing all the moguls in its wake. For years, that trail was an arena for the best of skiing's gladiators, who could be seen in competition with each other every weekend for top gun status. It was well known that no one but the very best could negotiate that entire narrow trail of sheer-faced moguls, which divided the men from the boys, without making at least one miscalculation. A friend of mind suffered a compound fracture from a slam into one of the towers on the Mall. He died two days later. The Mall was Sugarbush's answer to Al's Run at Taos, although not as long. What makes it as interesting is that the Valley House chairlift passes directly above its entire length, and skiers have a front row seat to some of the finest skiing in the entire Northeast! The Pisten Bully turned the Mall into a ballroom carpet last week. Its weekend athletes were replaced by stem turners almost as soon as the machine chewed up its first run. Turkeys were strewn all over the trail. Sad. If this continues, Sugarbush mogul busters will have to move next door to Glen Ellen's "Scotch Mist," a very similar trail, or be content with hidden challenges like Stowe's "Goat," an hour northeast, which have no critical audiences overhead. This is one bump lover who sincerely hopes that they keep the Piston Bully off "Stein's Run." If they don't, more Sugarbush Valley skiers will follow its former Norwegian ski school director to the Rocky Mountains where the needs of athletes are as respected as the comforts and limitations of lesser skiers, who should ski on trails designed for their particular level of ineptitude. I hope they never get a Bully on "The Rumble!"

Moguls are not fallen skiers who have been snowed upon. Not usually. Curiously, it is the less proficient skier that usually is the creator of a mogul. His hesitations, doubts and fears are generated to his skis which then cut up new snow into a maze of small valleys and humps. The valleys are his erratic tracks where he has scraped off the surface snow

Fig. 3-72 (left): When your skis point straight down the fall line, *drive your knees forward* as if you were trying to kneel on your ski tips. When you can't get your knees any farther forward, push them toward the inside of the turn and tilt your ski tips onto their new uphill edges. The shovels of your skis should spoon out the right turn's completion as you ride on your inside edges.

Fig. 3-73 (right): Finish your turn by resuming your traverse posture, or incline into a left turn as I'm about to do here. The arrow points to the direction of my next inclination—forward and downhill.

This inclinated turn is designed for high speed; at a slow speed, this inclination in the downhill direction can catch your lower edges and cause a serious fall.

clear down to the icy base. The humps, bumps, or *moguls* are built up piles of that scraped off surface snow which grow taller and taller as more less proficient skiers follow the same cautious line. Adding insult to injury, the short ski aficionados have destroyed the pleasurable large round bumps that made runs down trails like the Mall so rhythmic and graceful a decade ago. Characterizing most eastern bump trails today are short choppy bumps with little space in between, sharp rises and icy faces where the short-ski skiers have checked, pivoted and skidded, scraping all the snow off the downhill side. Accepting the adage, "If you can't lick 'em, join 'em," most veteran skiers have traded in their long boards for a shorter pair of sticks. While we miss the long rhythmic turns over the bumps of the fifties, we welcome the challenge of the new terrain, which demands quicker foot work and a sound knowledge of the modern mogul mashing technique known as *avalement*.

It is a French word that we are told means "to swallow." The reference is to the "swallowing" of the bump as the skier retracts his knees and feet to pivot on the crest of the mogul. The movement requires strong *anticipation* or drive of the upper body downhill after the customary pole plant in the fall line, as the initiation of the turn finds the skier with his hips in a seated position and his ski tips in the air pointed in the traverse direction. With the upper body facing downhill, it is twisted to a maximum variance with the hips and legs. The pole provides stability and deflection as the lower body then uncoils like a twisted rubber band, spinning the skis toward the fall line, assisted by axial motion of the skier's lower legs. Projection of the upper body 90 degrees to the angle of the slope, as the legs are extended into the valley on the other side of the mogul, gets the ski tips back in contact with the snow, and a quick roll onto his uphill edges keeps the skier angulated and in total control, as his legs are extended in the valley beyond the mogul.

Study avalement from a traverse in slow motion:

a. Approach the mogul from an angle 45 degrees to the general fall line of the trail in a good traverse position, with the basket of your downhill pole swung forward for planting. (Fig. 3-74)

b. Roll your knees in a plumb line with your boot toes, as you shoot your boots forward and retract your knees to swallow the bump. (Fig. 3-75) This will lessen the weight pressing down on your ski tips and permit them to climb the bump with no shock upon contact. (Fig. 3-76)

c. When your boots reach the top of the mogul, twist your skis downhill and onto their inside edges, EXCHANGING YOUR LEADING BOOT, as you tilt your torso downhill and plant your downhill pole. (Fig. 3-77) Your turn will be carved on the inside edges of your ski *tails*.

The bite of your inside edges should not be affected by a lateral thrust, but rather by a FORWARD THRUST. Some skiers call this movement *jetting*, as the skis will accelerate. It is possible to shoot the boots and skis so far forward (flat or on their downhill edges) that only the ski tails will be in contact with the snow for that precarious moment when you must twist your knees and feet toward the fall line. This is called a "wheelie." (Fig. 3-78)

What saves you from a fall immediately after that seemingly unbalanced position is the same procedure for completing an avalement turn:

Fig. 3-74: Preparation for avalement is your basic traverse position with pole basket advanced, ready for planting. Note how my shoulder slant matches the tilt of the slope.

Fig. 3-75: The moment of avalement is when I "swallow" the bump by retracting my knees and jetting my boots forward. Note how my torso begins to move downhill, but maintains a 90 degree relationship to the slope.

Fig. 3-76: Weight release off ski tips will allow them to climb and snake *over* the mogul instead of tearing *through* it.

Fig. 3-77: An important part of the anticipatory movement is the change of the leading ski before the skis have been turned into the fall line.

Fig. 3-78 (above): It's a "wheelie" and it's a neat turn, but you need powerful thighs and tough knee ligaments to finish it! I've changed my leading ski and am about to roll my knees inside the turn.

Fig. 3-79 (right): Avalement completion. Body moves upward and forward to press ski tips back into contact with the snow. Once they point downhill, I resume my traversing posture, extending my legs in the valley below the mogul. *Note how my shoulders resume parallel relationship with the slope. This keeps the torso in a constant 90 degree angle to the hill.*

1. Your pole plant on the downhill side of the bump which gives some support.

2. Your upper body projection downhill (anticipation) *90 degrees to the slant of the slope.*

3. The extension of your legs into the valley beyond the bump as you angulate into your new traverse direction. *The torso remains perpandicular to the slope.* Observe the completion in triple exposure. (Fig. 3-79)

The final part of your avalement turn over a bump is just as important as its inception. It is a resumption of that very same posture you learned in your early lessons—the angulated traverse position. Remember, though, that mogul may have a steep downhill face. If your turn has taken you perpendicular to the fall line, drop your downhill shoulder until the angle of your shoulders *matches* the slant of that face! This action will balance the angulation of your knees and hip *uphill* and prevent you from falling on the uphill side of your skis, seduced by centripetal force.

Be sure to keep your hands always forward and your torso facing downhill when skiing a *narrow* moguled trail. This will help your anticipatory projection. Since your movement down a narrow trail will allow no traverse, you can forget about dropping your downhill shoulder. With your torso facing the fall line, you will have no downhill shoulder. I tell my students: The torso is quiet and perpendicular to the slope, whether you are skiing straight downhill or across the hill. *If you have a downhill shoulder, drop it.* Toward your heel. Advance your pole basket with just a flick of your wrist and don't hang on to your planted pole too long, or it will throw off your timing.

The very same principles may be applied when skiing over smaller bumps although the retraction of the knees and feet is naturally minimized. The idea is to keep your head at about the same level above the snow through the entire course. (Figs. 3-80A, B, C & D) Do remember to retract your knees and *jet* your boots forward when you climb the bump. Do tilt your upper body downhill immediately after that jet

Fig. 3-80B (above): She pulls up her knees and shoots her boots forward, planting her pole in the fall line. With little of her skis on the snow, her pivot will now be easy.

Fig. 3-80A (left): Marge spots a small rise with a steep drop beyond its ridge. Avalement may also be used in a situation like this.

Fig. 3-80C (above): There's a slight flaw here, but I'm going to print it anyway, because the rest of her form is neat. Can you spot it? She forgot to advance her inside ski. With the outside ski leading, a tip cross is imminent. Fortunately, Marge was quick to correct, as you can see in the next photo.

and drive your knees forward into the new traverse direction, as you advance your outside pole basket in preparation for the next bump.

20. **Wedeln.** It is an Austrian colloquialism for "tail wagging" which hasn't been too popular since the freestyle movement came on the ski scene, but wedeln is a classic form that will always be part of the proficient skier's repertoire. Explained simply, it is a linked series of short parallel turns straight down the fall line with no traverse. Edging takes place but only briefly at the termination of each axial motion of the parallel skis. The upper body is kept QUIET. All body joints are flexed as in the downhill running posture described in Exercise 9, but the bend at the waist is less appreciable. The hands are kept forward, spaced a bit wider than the shoulders, and one pole basket is always forward, poised for planting, while the other trails behind. The tails of the skis follow the advance of the pole basket as they are thrust downhill by axial motion when the skier twists his knees and feet away from the fall line. The pole is planted in the fall line as the knees drive to the uphill side of the skis. This triggers a spring upward and forward as the other pole basket is advanced and an axial motion in the opposite direction takes place. Here is wedeln, step by step:

a. Begin a run straight down a *gentle* slope. Assume a slightly taller than usual downhill running posture. Keep both hands forward, pole baskets behind. (Fig 3-81A)

b. Advance your right pole basket with a flick of your

Fig. 3-80D: A dynamite finish! Look at those inside edges bite!

Fig. 3-81A: Upright for a classic Wedeln.

Fig. 3-81B: Imagine your ski tails connected to your pole basket. As you advance the basket, bring the ski tails along with it, gently brushing the snow.

Fig. 3-81C: Remember to plant the pole by bending your knees forward and away from it.

wrist, and sink down slightly to unweight your skis, twisting your knees to your left and thrusting your ski tails downhill simultaneously, with your skis relatively flat to the snow surface, as when performing a forward sideslip. Keep your torso motionless. (Fig. 3-81B)

c. Freeze the right forward pole 6 inches above the snow. Then, plant it with a drive of your knees forward and to your left. *Plant the pole by bending your knees.* Don't plant it with an arm movement! (Fig. 3-81C)

d. As soon as the right pole touches the snow, spring up and forward to your original tall downhill running position, simultaneously advancing your left pole basket as you twist your skis back into the fall line. (Fig. 3-81D) Change your leading ski and swing the right pole basket back as you advance the left one. Only one pole basket should be forward at all times in wedeln. The poles flick like a pendulum with just wrist movement. Keep your hands forward.

e. Continue to twist your skis with your knees and feet as you sink down and ready the left pole for planting. (Fig. 3-81E) As before, plant it with a drive of your knees forward and, this time, to your right. (Fig. 3-81F) Notice the change of leading ski!

f. Continue the movements rhythmically, with no traverse interruption, straight down the fall line. Keep your upper body quiet and do all the turning with your knees and feet on relatively flat skis. The only edging that should take place is a brief setting when the pole is planted. Remember to spring upward and forward after each pole plant, simultaneously advancing the opposite pole basket. (Figs. 3-81G, 3-81H)

21. **Short Swing.** Still the safest, most controlled method of descending a steep packed slope, (Fig 3-82) is the *short swing,* another classic maneuver that will outlive all the worm turns and shoulder rolls of modern free-stylists. Essentially, it involves a pivot under the shovels of the skis and a hard setting of the edges as in the "hockey-stop." (Fig. 3-83A) The ski tails are then lifted (Fig. 3-83B), shortening the running surface of the skis to just the area under the shovels, and the skier pivots on his ski tips pulling his tails back into the fall line. (Fig. 3-83C) The skis regain snow contact when they just cross the fall line and a skid of the tails downhill follows as the skier presses his knees forward and uphill of his planted pole. (Fig. 3-83D) Another hard setting of the edges creates a platform of snow beneath the skis from which it is easy to bounce into the next turn. (Fig. 3-83E) You should feel a tension between your ski tails and your pole basket in the short swing. As the left pole basket is snapped forward by a flick of the wrist, the tails of your skis should come with it, thrust downhill on your left side, etc. (Figs. 3-83F, G & H)

This is the safest and most cautious way to ski super steep terrain, except in deep powder or on icy slopes, as every turn is a sharp check in your speed (almost a *stop*). Practice it on a moderate slope. Then gradually apply the maneuver to steeper and steeper terrain. You will appreciate the control, and, when spring arrives, and the only snow left on the trails is a catwalk 8 feet wide on the sides, *you* will be skiing!

22. **The Windshield Washer.** Do *not* use a short swing as described in deep powder, as your ski tips will dive and you will nose over! When the snow is deep your pivot must be moved back from the shovels to a point under your heels. In such a case, your spring upward from the "check" or

Fig. 3-81D: Every turn is followed by a rise UP and FORWARD to the original neutral position in the fall line.

Fig. 3-81E: The tails follow the advance of the pole basket.

Fig. 3-81F: The pole is planted with a knee bend. Note how quiet Marge's torso is. Motionless.

Fig. 3-81G: The neutral position.

Fig. 3-81H (above): Wedeln is a beautiful way to descend a gradual slope. Remember to keep your torso facing downhill throughout this maneuver.

Fig. 3-82 (right): The short swing came to my aid many times in the Bugaboos, as when I had to chop my way down this steep crevassed slope near one of the spires.

Fig. 3-83A: Each "check" or setting of your edges is like the "hockey stop" you learned as a beginner.

Fig. 3-83B: Bounce off your platform of snow and pivot on your ski tips. Note my change of leading ski and quick advance of the outside pole basket.

Fig. 3-83C: Pole ready, I will plant it with a drive of my knees forward and to my left.

"platform" position should not be forward but should be *straight up*, lifting your entire skis off the sunken base and pivoting them by axial motion (like a propeller) near or above the snow surface with just your knees and feet. The pole action, synchronized with the tails of your skis, remains the same, i.e. as one pole basket is advanced, the tails of the skis are drawn downhill with it. Another difference in this type of short swing, called by some a *"windshield washer turn"* is that the pole is planted to the side rather than close to the downhill ski tip, in an effort to keep the body weight of the ski centralized and *on both feet.* The spring upward is not an elongation of the body as when springing off a diving board. Instead, it is a retraction of the knees and feet. As with most types of skiing exercises, the knees are maintained directly above the front of the boot, although the center of gravity (a point behind your belt buckle) is moved back to centralize your body weight. You should feel like you are jumping your turns with *equal* weight on both skis, as if you were on a pogo stick!

23. **Stem Or Wedge Turns.** A more primitive method of changing direction on skis is by steering with *independent leg action.* This can take various forms, of which the *snowplow, wedge* or a variety of *stem* turns are the most basic. From a holding traverse position (hips and bent knees tilted uphill, shoulders parallel to the slope, no part of the body behind the heels), the skier spreads (stems) the tails of one or both skis. If just the uphill tail is "stemmed," this is called a *stem turn.* At least, it used to be. Every few years, new terms spring up for the same old forms. This year, we are calling the form a *wedge.* This movement points the skier's outside ski toward the fall line. By applying more body weight to the front of that stemmed outside ski and

steering it with his knee, the skier will turn, with the provision that his inside ski remains flat to the snow surface and is unweighted. (Fig. 3-84) Modern schools advise twisting *both* knees into the intended new traverse. This will automatically flatten the inside ski and twist the outside ski onto its inside edge. The American Teaching Method encourages a sequence of foot steering, leg steering and aggressive leg steering in this type of wedge shaped maneuver. (See Chapter 6, "The P.S.I.A. Today.") The snowplow, wedge or stem position is favored by non-athletic tyros who feel more secure over the broader wedged base. The maneuver is a standard discipline in the manuals of ski schools which teach the American Technique, although, at present, it is referred to as an *early basic christie,* when linked with a sideslip after the turn. It is rejected by schools employing the pure GLM technique, a system in which the new skier is encouraged to use short skis and turn *parallel* by axial motion right from the beginning of his learning experience. As the GLM learner progresses, he is encouraged to use a longer pair of skis. The pure Graduated Length Method has had phenomenal success in some areas, but it is not necessarily a faster way. I do believe that it is safer, though.

At Sugarbush Valley, several years ago, we decided to test the results of both systems. Half the beginning "skiweekers" were taught by GLM, using only *parallel* turns, and half were taken through the traditional ATM sequence of snowplow, stem turn, stem christie and parallel exercises. At the end of the week, there was no significant difference between the skiing ability of those from either group, but several twisted knees and charley horses were reported by those who were taught the awkward wedge or snowplow

Fig. 3-83D: Remember to plant your pole with your knees, not your hand!

Fig. 3-83E: As I bounce, my leading ski changes, and my left pole basket is already on its way forward.

Fig. 3-83F: Still airborne, my ski tails follow the advance of my left pole basket.

Fig. 3-83G: Regain contact with the snow when your skis are at about a 45 degree angle to the fall line of the slope. Have your downhill pole ready for planting!

Fig. 3-83H: By planting your pole with a sharp drive of your knees away from it, you'll get a good bite with your inside edges. *Note how no part of my body is behind my heels!*

posture. That ski week contingent numbered only about 150, hardly a number for conclusive evidence but high enough to cause wonder and radical conjecture.

24. **Special Techniques For Snow Variations.** Included in this segment of Exercises should be a cursory examination of techniques that are applicable to different snow conditions, as these will require constant adjustment of physical attitude:

a. *ICY CONDITIONS.* Beginners should avoid days like these. Might be a good occasion to try yourself out at cross-country or stay in bed with a good book or someone. The *langlaüf* trails are usually cut through beautiful wooded areas that have better snow conditions than the scraped off *piste* under the chairlift. Icy conditions are not for beginners.

No reason for advanced skiers to shy away from these conditions, though. It can almost be enjoyable. There are two ways for a parallel skier to ski icy or boiler plate conditions. I have read in *Ski* Magazine (January 1976, p. 25) that Dixi Nohl, of Mad River Glen Ski Area in Vermont, prefers a flat ski method, riding both skis and powering his turns by forward projection. Forward projection of the body is essential, but it can also be done on one ski, the lower ski, weighted from tip to tail and on its uphill edge, like an ice-skater, with far more control. This movement is called *Schrittbogen* (step-turn) by my Austrian friends. The theory is that all your body weight on one edge will cut a deeper incision into the ice than if your weight is dispersed over both skis. I favor this method. It also demands strong *angulation* (tilt of the lower body uphill and the torso at least 90 degrees to the angle of the slope; while the hips and legs lean away from *centrifugal force* (the force that pulls outside the turn), the torso must balance the skier by dropping downhill, away from *centripetal force* (the force pulling inside the turn). Schrittbogen is an advanced maneuver for parallel skiers—as the downhill pole is planted, lift your downhill ski tail and project your body toward the fall line in

a long arc, turning on the inside edge of your outside ski. The shape of the ski alone will carve your turn. Avoid any *lateral* slippage and make full use of your ski's *side-camber!* Resume your extreme angulation while your skis point down the fall line in anticipation of the new traverse, but keep the tail of your new uphill ski off the ground until you are ready for another turn. (Fig. 3-85) All edging on ice should be via *glissement* or forward projection. Use no side pressure, as you might use when checking or in a "hockey-stop."

b. *POWDER.* It can be up to your boots, knee high, waist high, or, if you are lucky, bottomless. Beginners should shy away from the latter three conditions. Wait until the "cats" pack it down. Here are a few tips for more advanced skiers on how to master the deep.

Boot top-high powder requires no change in your standard form; skiing just becomes more enjoyable. Deeper snow demands alert compensation, however, with disastrous results if you don't adjust. Stiff, long skis will tend to nose dive in the deep stuff, unless you plane them upward by applying more pressure to your heels. You will soon tire, though. It is a lot easier on shorter, more flexible skis, as your body weight will bend your boards into a reverse camber. The slightest roll of your knees in the direction of your intended turn will tilt that arc, and the shape of your skis will finish your turn for you. Skis must be parallel and held tightly together in deep powder, of course. Some powder freaks like to add an up and down motion to this knee action, porpoising their turns by steering with their knees when the skis are floating near the snow surface, but a constant low hip posture, called by some *submarining,* is just as effective, although you need thighs like oak trees! Because the angle of the snow beneath the skis is perpendicular to the skier's body in deep powder, he may bank his turns with *inclination* rather than angulation. It's a floating sensation.

Many skiers think that one must *sit back* in deep powder—don't. Your knees should always be leading your boots in *any* snow condition for optimum steering control. It is true

Fig. 3-84: For WEDGE or SNOWPLOW and STEM TURNS, think of your skis as arrows. One is pointed to your right; one is pointed left. The "arrow" that carries most of your body weight will move forward in the direction toward which it points. As with other types of turns, it is the outside ski that should carry more weight; a good reason for *dropping the outside shoulder,* contrary to current ATM and C.S.I.A. methodology. Angulation is so important, I believe that it should be taught in the early stage of your learning process.

Fig. 3-85: Unorthodox as it may sound, the *downhill* ski tail is lifted at the moment of the pole plant. It is kept off the snow until you have crossed the fall line. *Schrittbogen* is an effective method for skiing icy conditions.

that a lower hips position is effective and pressure on the heels as your toes curl upwards will help to plane your ski tips upward, but never allow those knees to trail behind your boot toes, or you will lose control of your ski tips and drown in the white stuff!

Try to ski close to the fall line when the going gets deep. If you should have to traverse, stay over the center of your skis and be sure to weight then *equally*. Equal weight is an absolute prerequisite to controlled skiing in deep powder. Plant your pole in the fall line and tilt your torso toward it as you roll your knees inside the turn. Once you face the fall line, try to stay in it, linking one turn after another. This rhythm can be easily triggered by advancing your outside ski pole basket to lead every turn. (Fig. 3-86) One pole basket should always be visible as the other swings back. Your arms may be more to the side than forward which will keep your weight centralized. A forward arms posture as recommended for packed snow conditions would move your weight forward, causing a nose-dive. Be sure to keep your skis tightly together. Imagine yourself skiing on a single board rather than on two. Try your best to keep your mouth shut. Most of us forget that last piece of advice and scream in orgasmic ecstasy, but an open mouth will soom be choked with powder and it could spoil a neat run.

Finally, ski the deep stuff, but don't *rape* it. If you can't handle it, don't go up there, unless it is with a qualified instructor. The tracks you leave behind will be your personal signature. If that signature is a scrawl you might get tarred and feathered by the powder freaks in your lodge. They are an extraordinary breed and their terrain should be respected. See Chapter 4 for more authoritative advice on skiing the deep stuff.

That's it. Your accelerated course for successful parallel skiing. The time it takes you to perfect each exercise, from gliding on the flat to absorbing the moguls will, of course, vary with each reader, in accordance with your ability to respond to my directions. One of my students, a

Fig. 3-86: Quick advance of the outside pole basket is a must in powder. Note how my ski tails follow that advance as I push my knees to my left.

professional hockey skater, mastered the whole course in 2 weeks. I learned to ski via the Arlberg system and didn't make my first parallel turn until 3 whole winters had passed! If you haven't got what it takes to feel comfortable with this purely parallel approach, please don't be discouraged. There is another way. A slower, more cautious way, but a method that will eventually get you to the same goal: to ski any terrain safely, efficiently and with a reasonable amount of grace. For an illustrated exposure of that system, look over the American Teaching Method in Chapter 6, "The P.S.I.A. Today."

Of course, there is a great deal more science to the total skiing experience than what I have outlined. Sophisticated extensions of the basics I have provided, like "jetting" or the various racing step-turns, plus aerial and ballet maneuvers would be your graduate education. Take your lessons from a qualified man. Unfortunately, the terms *qualified* and *certified* are not always synonymous. The qualifications of a good ski instructor can be read in the satisfactory progress of his students. Observe your instructor in action before you sign up for a lesson with him. Talk to some of his students, if you can.

If your balance is not too keen or your physical condition is a bit less than adequate, by all means learn via the traditional wedge or snowplow method. Its merits have certainly been proven. The pure parallel system I have illustrated is a radical departure from that method, but it also has proven itself in the success of my own students. It is worth a try. Any skier who learned to ski following the traditional snowplow, stem, stem christie, parallel christie, and wedeln final forms will tell you that the snowplow position is a very difficult one to lose once you are in the habit of calling upon its security. The truth is that the wedge stance should never be thought of as "a way to ski." Rather, it should be used as a teaching device early in your learning experience (if at all) and discarded as soon as possible. *There is no more dangerous way to ski than with one ski pointed directly across the other.* If you should fall with your skis in that position, your chances of incurring a fracture are far greater than if you should fall with your skis parallel and together. I especially shudder when I see children coming down a steep slope with their knees locked, their derriere back and their skis in the snowplow form. You might think it looks cute, but there is nothing cute about a fracture, and no child would stand a chance if he hit an obstacle at high speed with his skis in that awkward position. Nor would you stand much of a chance in the same predicament. This chapter was for you. Chapter 5 is for the safety of your child. The American Teaching Method is your alternative if my pure parallel system fails. Its basics are defined in Chapter 6, "The P.S.I.A. Today."

I would appreciate hearing about your experience with either or both approaches. As a teacher, my primary purpose is to help you to master this sport in the shortest amount of time possible. *No frills.* Your experiences with these exercises, successful or otherwise, would give me greater insight for developing an even more accelerated program. I would like to share those thoughts with my P.S.I.A. colleagues and instructors of other international systems, and perhaps gather substance for the third edition of SKIER'S DIGEST. Thank you.

Chapter 4
GREAT NORTH AMERICAN SKI AREAS
and how to ski them...

WITH WELL OVER 500 ski areas in the United States alone and a book limit of less than 300 pages, this chapter was the most difficult to put together. How would you select from the extensive North American listing a handful of those which may be considered *great* without driving those whom you don't include into a jealous rage? And what standard can we use to qualify *greatness*? My first thought was to consider only those areas with a vertical drop of over 2,500 feet, but that would leave out places like Sugarbush Valley, Vermont, certainly one of the top three skiing resorts in the Northeast. Such a standard would also have to include lesser areas that may reach to a higher altitude but which have long "runouts" from mid-station that make their vertical drop only exciting from the top half of the mountain. While, in most cases, the vertical drop of a mountain does add to the *greatness* of the resort, other things must be considered. The average snowfall, the variety of trails, the mountain's exposure, après ski facilities, lodging and dining accommodations, the ski school and its director, the nursery program, parking, and the comfort of its uphill lifts are just a few things to evaluate in our estimation of a ski area's greatness. In all fairness, we should also consider the many parts of the country where skiing is available. The wide back bowls of Vail might be *great* to a Denver sophomore, but a Dartmouth junior might prefer the challenge and demands of the *National* at Stowe. Another skier might feel that nothing is *great* beyond the freestyle or ballet scene or artificial snow at his local 500-foot vertical drop area, while a pilot from Air Canada will just smile confidently and drop you into Hans Gmoser's *Bugaboos*. If beauty is indeed in the eyes of the beholder, the world's greatest ski areas are equally identified by subjective experience. It is for this reason that Chapter 4 is not entitled "The Greatest Ski Areas. . ." but rather, "Great Ski Areas. . . .," as the resorts I have selected for your perusal may not be *the greatest* to *all* skiers, but have certainly earned the distinction of being *great*, at least to some.

The author and his wife in the Bugaboos, photo compliments of Hans Gmoser.

A is for ASPEN

as in Snowmass, Buttermilk, Ajax and Aspen Highlands

A is for Aspen. It is fitting that we should begin with the largest ski complex in the United States; it is comprised of four separate mountains. Dollar for dollar, Aspen could be one of your best investments if you are contemplating a ski week and are looking for vast variety of terrain, challenging runs, good ski schools, effective children's learning programs, beautiful girls, super-cool night life, easy access to town, great shops for any gift imaginable, historical charm, honestly friendly local villagers, wide, long slopes, incredible scenery, and, you name it. (I've run out of ink!) George Madsen greeted us with comp lift tickets that took some of the bite out of our condominum bill of 60 bucks a night. While that was a bit high on the hog for my taste, it was the only empty room during the popular Washington's Birthday week. One gratuity we did receive is available to you and to everyone, and it is not to be taken lightly. There is a free, let me repeat that, *free* bus which runs every 15 minutes to the four magnificent mountains, each mountain with a personality of its own. And your 6-day lift ticket is recognized at *any* of the four mountain resorts! They are **Ajax Mountain** which rises from the main town of Aspen like the back of a bucket seat and offers the most challenging runs of the group, **Buttermilk,** where we watched affable instructors coddle new skiers with a GLM system that really worked, **Aspen Highlands,** where the view of the Maroon Bells from Loges peak rises from a 3,000-foot canyon that will take your breath away, and **Snowmass,** apparently the most popular of the four because the slopes are wide and gentle enough for everyone to go home feeling like a champion. The ski school is one of the best in the nation, and the shops are called *boutiques*, catering to the needs of those who suffer from the compulsive requirements of pretentious propriety.

Generally speaking, any eastern skier who can negotiate trails marked *expert* back home will have no difficulty skiing any slope in Colorado as most of them are overrated. Add to this the fact that western slopes are wide—really wide. In some cases you have a quarter of a mile traverse ahead to give you time to think about what kind of a turn you are going to make. Seldom will you even need the short turns that are required on trails like Stowe's Goat or Glen Ellen's Scotch Mist in the East; except for an occasional surprise, like when you leap off the ledge into Lower Stein's Run at Aspen Highlands. If you like glades, none could be more beautiful than those on the Face of Bell at Ajax. If you prefer your trees closer to one another, the Back of Bell invites you to leave your face on the bark of one of its tall pines. We were lucky enough to ski both sides of Bell Mountain Ridge during a 12-inch snowfall. The weather was too uncomfortable for the turkeys and Ajax was spotted with no one but good skiers cutting up the powder from Gentleman's Ridge all the way to Ruthie's Run. Every track was a respectable one, complemented by hoots and hollers and happy faces as the powder freaks welcomed the new cover over the leanest base Colorado had ever seen during the month of February. Bell emerges from the hairy nose of Ajax like a columella, inviting only the best of skiers to accept the challenge of steep drops on either side of her ridge. Watching over her from the left side, looking up, are the protective walls of Gentleman's Ridge, another expert glade area, while on the right, more steep drops fall off the gentler Midway and

The Aspen group. Four separate mountains connected by a *free* shuttle bus and an interchangeable lift ticket! What more could you ask?

The small plane flight to Aspen from Denver is exciting. What a way to go skiing!

Sleigh rides through Aspen have become a favorite pastime of Aspen vacationists. Sleigh rides in this Victorian ski town are only a part of the skiing experience. (Photo by Bob Haden.)

Skiers of lower intermediate ability—and even confident beginners—are not relegated to the lower teaching slopes at the Snowmass Resort near Aspen. In fact, lower ability skiers can have views such as this on three of the four mountains in the skiing complex—Aspen Highlands, Buttermilk and Snowmass. Only Aspen Mountain is rated too tough for novices.

Ruthie's Run—wide intermediate terrain that allows less proficient skiers to ski Ajax from its top elevation of 11,300 feet.

Ten minutes up the road from Aspen is Buttermilk, well known as a family area and one best suited for beginners to advanced intermediates. What is not often written about Buttermilk is that it does have a 2,000-foot vertical drop with fine expert terrain in its Tiehack Area—not super challenging for eastern experts but enough of a challenge to give any expert an enjoyable day if the traffic at Aspen is heavy. Since no one ever touts Buttermilk as expert terrain, the Tiehack Area life is usually empty!

It was at Aspen Highlands that I decided to shoot many of the photographs that you saw in our "No Frills Ski Instruction" (Chapter 3). The scenery there is so spectacular. We also appreciated the challenge of Upper and Lower Stein's Runs and got caught in a blizzard on Willy's and Moment of Truth—bump runs which gave Marge and I a cheek-biting thrill we will never forget. The other expert runs at Aspen Highlands are overrated, but an intermediate skier will be in his bliss, as this area offers all the security of Snowmass without the turkeys and the crowd. I was especially impressed while watching a group of instructors at the Half-Inch lift guiding a group of beginners through their first GLM exercises. They still use Clif Taylor's 3- and 4-foot skis and progress to greater length in accordance with the beginner's progress. The ski school approach at Aspen Highlands is pure parallel, and it really works.

The *mass* in Snowmass stands for the bulk of visitors to Aspen. The lines at the lifts during Washington's Birthday week were unbelievable! We waited 40 minutes on the lower lift line and 30 minutes for each of the upper lifts, while the other three mountains had no waiting lines at all. At least the lines faced the sun. We didn't get much skiing in during our day at Snowmass, but we sure baked to a golden brown. Our cursory analysis of the skiers in line and on the slopes brought us to the conclusion that Snowmass is the Stratton of the West, at least two-thirds populated with the chic nouveau riche from Fairfield and Westchester Counties. This puts it a cut above Vermont's Mount Snow, as at least the skiing at Snowmass is more disciplined. And that is partly due to Ski School Supervisor Roberto Gasperl and his squad of crackerjack instructors, most of whom were transplanted from the Stein Eriksen Ski School at Sugarbush Valley, Vermont, about 8 years ago. I worked with those guys for 3 years, and seeing them again was like awakening from a long dream. Svein, with silver streaks in his wavy hair that make him more attractive than ever (I had to restrain my wife); my good Austrian friend, Franz, still smiling and playing the role of *Guiler Boch*; Martin, married now, but with the perpetually innocent face of a young Mickey Rooney; Walter, as intellectual as ever but so dedicated to skiing that he will teach in Portillo during the summer; Amund, a giant Norwegian who skis with the grace of a bird and melts the women with his eyes; former Easterner, Curtis, a little older, heavier and a lot wiser, with a successful construction business on the side; Jan, the friendliest Norwegian I have ever met, who reminds me of a chuck wagon cowboy; and Roberto, my old roommate, a racing champion from Cervinia, Italy. Roberto has been incredibly successful at the most underpaid profession in this country. Graduating to supervisor after Stein Eriksen's departure, he

Aspen powder is indescribable. You'll have to try it yourself.

organized one of the finest ski schools anywhere and is still skiing as fast as ever. When we saw Svein in Sam's Knob Restaurant at the top of Lift Three, I asked him if Roberto was still around. "He just left," smiled Svein, in his thundering deep bass voice. "We'll try to catch him," I answered, choking down my apple. "You'll have to ski pretty fast!" laughed Svein, confident that Roberto was probably already at the bottom. He was. We rapped a little about old times, and nostalgia filled the instructor's room as each of the boys drifted in to check out for the day.

The organization of four mountains as variable as the Aspen groups requires the mind, strength and endurance of a guy like Curt Chase, Director of Skiing, who is one of the educative giants in the ski industry. In unifying the ski schools at three of the four resorts, Curt has opted for the American Teaching Method, which is flexible enough to allow the supervisor of each ski school to incorporate some of his own variations in the complex solution of teaching you how to ski. At Aspen Highlands, the approach is via GLM or straight parallel technique with no wedge maneuvers. In his own teaching manual, Curt has been strongly influenced by the French teaching method, as documented by Joubert and Vuarnet. The combination of those French and American disciplines broadens the breadth of the Aspen Ski School curriculum. I have extracted a few of those thoughts for your perusal. While I do feel that a beginner should stick to one school—at least until he understands the basic science behind controlled descent—I have stated more than once in my feature "Ski Eclectic" which ran in *Snow Country* magazine several years ago, and in my book *Skiing Made Easy* (NY, Lancer Books, 1971) that the intermediate or advanced ski student would benefit from exposure to *many* systems. The eclectic style that will naturally develop from such exposure will bring him closer to the *total* skiing experience, or what Plato would call The Perfect Form. The chauvinistic approach of militant ski schools of the past developed hundreds of insipid automatons churning what Fred Iselin called "itchy-twitchy funny turns" run after run after run, with no variation on the theme. The most exciting facet of skiing, as compared to other sports, is that it is intellectual before it is physical. The mind is constantly at work, learning new variations and making quick decisions in the application of those learned principles. There is always another authoritative voice to whom we should listen. Here are the words of Curt Chase:

THOUGHTS ON TEACHING SKIING

by Curt Chase
Director, Aspen Ski School

There is a far more natural and effective process for learning and doing almost anything than most of us realize. Some things we learn better when we do not try too hard.

In order to learn or develop a new physical skill, we need to have an image of what it is we are trying to do, and we have to develop an awareness of what it is that we are doing. Perhaps most important, we have to make it OK with ourselves to reproduce the original image.

In getting the picture of what it is we are trying to do, it is well to remember that images are better than words, showing is better than telling and too much instruction is worse than none. In developing an awareness of what is really going on we must drop the human inclination to judge ourselves and our performance as either good or bad. In making it OK to duplicate a new image, we must abandon our allegiance to all other images.

There is a natural learning process which operates within everyone if it is allowed to. If we trust our body to learn, in a short time it will perform beyond our expectations. Fortunately, most children learn to walk before they can be told how to by their parents. If we would treat other things as we do learning to walk, we would make amazing progress.

In teaching children, following a few simple principles will insure good results. *First, instruction must be simple.* Involved explanations will only bore the child. For him learning to ski should be a form of play. Ski games that encourage movement and competition between the youngsters are excellent as teaching aids.

Children learn naturally through imitations. It is imperative that the child's instructor present the proper image through simple and correct demonstrations. *Fundamental positions and movements must appear obvious, and all unnecessary moves should be eliminated.* The basic skiing stance should stress standing solidly on the feet. Hands should be apart, forward, and better too low than too high. *If we encourage movement, the child will quickly develop his own balancing reflexes.* For the child, both edging of the skis and steering should be developed as a function of the feet. Skidding should come through the hockey stop and stem stop approach. Sideslipping should be initiated with down motion and associated with turning.

Children normally progress from gliding snowplow, through gliding snowplow turn, to a form of basic christie, and then parallel. Some small children may stay for a long time in the snowplow, while others may go almost directly to wide track parallel. The child tends to go directly to the whole turn, rather than develop one through learning its parts. We can, therefore, skip many of the exercises that may be helpful in teaching adults.

If the first duty of the child's instructor is to set a good example, his second certainly is to see that it is followed. *If youngsters are prevented from developing useless skiing habits, only effective moves are left for them to make.* Particular attention should be given to the head, hips, arms, and torso. The head should never tip to the inside of the turn, and the outside hip must not lift or rotate. The body should remain quiet and not accentuate the turning of the skis. Images should be developed by a process of awareness. "Right-wrong" and "good-bad" connotations should be avoided. Think about this. "When the child stumbles and falls, the mother doesn't condemn him for being clumsy. She doesn't even feel bad about it; she simply notices the event and perhaps gives a word or gesture of encouragement. Consequently, a child's progress is never hindered by the idea that he is uncoordinated."

Teaching children has always been considered fun and easy by the ski teaching profession. We all know that youngsters learn through imitations, and that they have few problems. We also know that as children grow to be adults, the magic learning process somehow goes away. What we don't seem to know is that the magic goes away only because we have all agreed that it is supposed to go away. *The truth about learning and developing physical skills is that adults learn best by exactly the same process that works so well for children.*

Look once again at what we have just said about teaching children. Apply the same concepts in teaching grown up people and prepare yourself to be astounded at what happens.

You say it is not that simple? True. But it is not that simple not because it is not that simple. It is not that simple because we, the teachers and the students, have interfered with the natural learning process which will operate within everyone . . . . . . if it is allowed to.

Much of what we have said will be recognized as quotes, or paraphrases from *The Inner Game of Tennis* by W. Timothy Gallwey. This book certainly should be of interest to anyone who concerns himself with teaching, with learning, or the process of acquiring new skills. Anyone who would call himself a ski instructor should become aware of what *The Inner Game* is all about.

Those who take the trouble to explore *The Inner Game*

may also recognize that its origins are in Eastern culture and philosophy. Ski teachers deal mostly with the Western mind, which has been told "how to," been "criticized" and been "corrected" since the day it first understood the spoken language. This can create some problems. But man is a problem solving machine, and this problem can be handled. Most effective ski teaching will result if we are prepared to let that happen.

Most of us have been exposed to the use of video in the teaching-learning process. Video is imagery in its purest form. The picture that we wish to emulate and our effort to duplicate that picture both flash upon the screen. Here we have the two basic requirements for learning. The image of what it is we are trying to do, and the picture of what it is that we are doing. Here we also have a solution to a problem.

When the student comes to the teacher, he wants to be talked to. He expects it. He may even demand it. He wants to be told "how to." One answer is: "Talk to him." The real answer is: "Talk to him like the video." The most effective teacher will use words to create an image of what we are trying to do, and an awareness of what is going on. He will use words in such a way that they do not appear to judge results as "good" or "bad," but to create an atmosphere in which the student does not interfere with his own natural learning process.

In teaching and in learning there is an age-old game that is played between the teacher and the student. The ski teacher's game involves developing fundamental skiing skills. The student's game may be to go up the mountain and slide down, having fun . . . . . . as soon as possible. A happy conclusion occurs when both teacher and student can feel that they have won their game.

* * *

Thanks Curt. Skier's Digest appreciates your lucid description of the Inner Skier philosophy to which I referred in my editorial on the "Three Storey Mountain" in Chapter 6, and we believe strongly in the awareness of the concept by the truly *qualified* ski instructor. It is this type of qualification that we would like to see incorporated in the training of a *certified* ski teacher. It has been my recent experience to note that the terms *qualified* and *certified* are not always synonymous.

Some P.S.I.A. examiners have allowed the personal free-skiing style and racing proficiency of the P.S.I.A. candidate to affect his grade more than his knowledge of basic skiing skills, his perception in detecting student faults and his ability to empathize with particular student obstacles, be they mental or physical. Obviously, I consider myself a victim of such prejudice. Without stepping on any particular examiner's feet, I am going to pose a few questions and answer them with direct quotes from your recent *Guide for Teaching Skiing,* for the benefit of our readers, but especially for the benefit of some of the E.P.S.I.A. hierarchy, who may, in the future, place a little more emphasis upon the intellectual awareness of their candidates. Their written examination is a farce.

1. In my recent Certification course, I was criticized for angulating as I traversed the slope, no more extreme than tilting my torso perpendicular to the hill. My posture was ridiculed as posed and unnatural. To test that judgement, I walked across a steep slope without skis; my "natural" posture was decidedly angulated. In fact, I felt most in

The author moves farther down Loges Peak at Aspen Highlands. Those are the Maroon Bell peaks in the background. The scenery from the Highlands is really spectacular.

balance when my shoulders were parallel to the slant of the hill, and I walked on the uphill "edges" of my boots.

Curt Chase (page 1): *"We define natural positions and natural movements on skis as those which keep the body in balance, and which at the same time allow it to efficiently perform its skiing functions. . .* When the skier is in a traverse, or in the process of turning, the necessity to adjust balance as we edge the skis makes angulation a part of natural position."

2. Stu Campbell, author of the highly respected *Ski With The Big Boys* (NY, Simon and Shuster, 1976) claims that modern turns rely so much upon the tenacity of centrifugal force, *inclination* is replacing *angulation* as the advanced skier stands *against* his outside ski rather than *on* it.

Curt Chase (page 3): "The thousands of photographs of champions published each year show the racer in an angulated position most of the time. The fact that this angulation is more moderate than that of the average skier is understandable: the principal characteristic of the champion is his moderation. [Ed.: because of his high velocity.] The average skier, whose angulation is less effective, must angulate more in order to obtain similar results."

Curt Chase (page 23): "As we traverse, we begin to learn about angulation which enables us to control our lateral balance as we edge our skis. *Actually, angulation is the result of proper balance and edge control.* The action of our lower body relates to edging, and that of our upper body to balance. . . In turns we must increase our edge-set angle to resist the centrifugal force. [Ed.: and the *centripetal* counterforce generated by the turn.] The hip moves to the inside of the turn to increase edging as the upper body moves to the outside to maintain balance. *When our skis are skidding,* or *sideslipping, angulation* is the key to stability and control."

3. Another movement which the E.P.S.I.A. stresses is the position of the shoulders square to the direction of travel when traversing with little or no lead of the uphill ski. I find that this position places too much weight on the uphill ski and is extremely difficult to maintain on steep icy terrain. A constant criticism of my own free skiing form was incorrectly referred to by some of my peers as a "counter" movement, when in fact the *slight* retraction of the downhill shoulder is an *anticipatory* gesture that will be followed by an automatic uncoiling of the lower body and hence the skis once the twist of the torso is blocked by the next pole plant deflection. I should emphasize that my lead of the uphill shoulder is no more than my lead of the uphill hip, knee and ski, and that precise distance is regulated by fitting the convex portion of my lower boot into the concave portion of my upper boot. I am the first to admit that the old Austrian reverse shoulder position aligning the shoulders with the traversing skis is too extreme and unnatural. My readers and I would like to hear your description of a proper (and by *proper*, I mean most functional) traversing position.

Curt Chase (page 23): *"Traverse.* Crossing the slope, the skis are on their uphill edges. More weight is on the downhill ski. The uphill ski, hip and shoulder are slightly advanced and the upper body is angled over the weighted ski."

Thanks again, Curt. I could go on and reproduce your description of the Jet Turn and Carved Jet Turn to corroborate my opinion that a *qualified* instructor should be aware that there are times when the *tails* of the skis are in fact weighted for an instant before projection, edge change, anticipation and use of the skis' side camber for carved turn execution, but that would only confuse my colleagues who took delight in pointing to the fact that I "sit back" occasionally. Please take my advice and publish your *Guide for Teaching Skiing* for distribution beyond the three mountains of the Aspen Ski School, as I believe it should be in every serious ski instructor's library.

B is for BOYNE

Othmar Schneider, Ski School Director

B is for Boyne Country, an umbrella name for four popular Midwest ski resorts located in the northwestern corner of Michigan's Lower Peninsula within 30 miles of Boyne Falls.

Boyne Mountain, oldest of the four and nearest to Boyne Falls, opened in 1948. It was one of the first ski areas in the Midwest. Boyne Highlands, in Harbor Springs, Michigan, was acquired in 1963, and Walloon Hills and Thunder Mountain, two nearby day ski areas, were added to the Boyne Country enterprises just in the last few years.

With some of the highest verticals in the Midwest—625 feet and 600 feet at the Highlands and the Mountain respectively—Boyne Country offers ample challenge and variety for even the most advanced adult skiers, but Boyne owner Everett Kircher says, "We're programmed for beginners and children."

Boyne's specialties, Family Ski Week packages and a unique Boyne Country Children's Ski Program, are especially popular, attracting skiing families from all over the Midwest and as far away as Kentucky, Pennsylvania and Mississippi.

For a set package price per person, families on Boyne's Family Ski Week enjoy daily ski instruction by a predominantly Austrian ski staff in the famed Austrian ski style for which Boyne is known, lodging, all meals, unlimited use of the lifts and heated outdoor swimming pool, and participation in planned aprés ski entertainment.

All family members 6 years old and older can register, but parents may wish to enroll 6- to 12-year-olds in the Children's Program.

Youngsters enrolled in the all-day Children's Program are under the supervision of certified Austrian or American instructors. Boyne finds its young Austrian National Ski Team girls especially good with children. Children ski from 10 AM until Noon, break for lunch with their instructor and, following a 1-hour free period, enjoy two more hours of ski instruction.

Meeting again at 6 PM, they dine with their instructor, who then supervises them in a variety of evening recreational activities including swimming, ice skating, movies, sleigh rides and marshmallow roasts.

While youngsters participate in the children's aprés ski activities, adults enjoy cocktail and hors d'oeuvres parties, fondue get togethers, tea dancing, pizza parties and moonlight sleigh rides with bonfireside refreshment stops. In addition to heated outdoor pools, Boyne Mountain has an outdoor skating rink and Boyne Highlands features saunas for added aprés ski relaxation.

As an added bonus, Boyne's Ski Weekers are always pleased to discover that after several days of instruction in the graceful Austrian ski style, everyone in the family not only skis in control, but looks great doing it.

The new, shorter, more easily maneuvered skis have been incorporated into Boyne's teaching program for several years, but the classic Austrian style is stressed, and a good basic technique free of bad habits has not been sacrificed to currently popular ski fads such as wide track or gorilla position.

Pre-skiing tots aren't left out at family-oriented Boyne. Austrian ski governesses care for youngsters 3- to 6-years of age in Boyne's Alpine Nurseries located at the Mountain, the Highlands and Walloon Hills. While parents ski, children play in a colorfully decorated environment equipped with a wide selection of toys, books and games. Outdoor snow and ski play and hot chocolate breaks help pass the time happily. Governesses will also supervise lunch if desired. Babysitters for children under 3, or for night hours, are also available at $1.50 an hour.

In Boyne Country there are 1,400 accommodations at the slopes in Alpine-motif lodges and mountain villas. There are an additional 8,000 accommodations in the immediate area.

A just-completed 44,000-square-foot Ski and Convention Centre at Boyne Mountain enables Boyne Country resorts to serve a total of 10,000 skiers a day. The Ski Centre houses

Nothing better between Boston and Denver, Boyne Highlands' fans say of this Michigan ski resort. Lodge facilities look like a toy castle at the foot of the slopes.

Snowy evening hay rides are a favorite apres ski activity for children at Michigan's Boyne Country resorts where youngsters can enroll in an all-day Children's Program that combines ski instruction with other supervised recreation, meals, snacks and planned evening entertainment.

the ski rental and repair department, a large skier's cafeteria and registration facilities for lift tickets, lessons and accommodations.

Such improvements and expansion were instrumental in Boyne's recently receiving one of 21 four-star ratings awarded by the Mobil Oil Travel Guide, indicating an outstanding resort worth a special trip.

Boyne Airport, the resort's private aviation facility, makes Boyne Country especially convenient for fly-in guests. Facilities include a 4,200-foot-long lighted, paved airstrip, complete hangar and instrument facilities and an attractive air terminal, all located just 300 yards from the main lodge.

Full American rates for Boyne's Family Ski Weeks vary depending on accommodations. At Boyne Mountain families staying in either the Boynehof or Boyne lodges pay $180 per person for the Ski Week based on double room lodging and $190 per person when staying in a family room based on double occupancy. The third and fourth person in a family room pay $160 each. Children 6 to 14 staying as the third and fourth occupants of a room pay $92.50 each. Non-skiing children under 6 pay $55 each when staying in the same room with their parents.

Full American family weekend rates are $70 per person in a double room, $75 per person for the first and second person in a family room and $65 per person for the third and fourth person in a family room. On weekends children 6 to 14 pay $39.50 and children under 6 pay $22 when staying in the same room with their parents.

One- two- and three-bedroom mountain villas are also available for a day, week, month or season.

Enrollment for the Children's Program is $4 per day per child for a Ski Week house guest and $6 per day for weekend house guest.

Boyne also offers room-only rates for skiers preferring to make up their own package, and children can be enrolled in the Children's Program on a daily basis.

Rates quoted for Boyne Mountain are comparable at Boyne Highlands.

Lift tickets, good at all four Boyne Country ski areas, are $10 for adults and $7 for children under 12.

For information and reservations call (616) 549-2441 or write Boyne Mountain Lodge, Inc., Boyne Mountain, Mich. 49713. For bookings at the Highlands, phone (616) 526-2172 or write Boyne Highlands, Harbor Springs, Mich. 49740.

LEARNING THE BOYNE WAY

by Teddee Grace

The Boyne Way, a ski teaching method developed 16 years ago by Othmar Schneider for Michigan's Boyne Mountain and Boyne Highlands ski resorts, has aged gracefully. Modified only slightly since 1960, the Boyne Way continues to produce skiers with excellent basic technique who not only are able to ski in control on all types of terrain, but look great doing it.

A modified Austrian technique, the Boyne Way is a direct result of Schneider's long-term residency at Boyne. The Austrian Olympic gold medalist who helped develop the Modern Austrian Ski Technique that revolutionized skiing back in the fifties, Schneider brought that graceful skiing style to the U.S., first to Stowe, Vt., then to Boyne.

As Boyne's director of skiing, Schneider runs one of the most highly disciplined ski schools in the U.S. Half of Boyne's instructors are Austrians who sometimes wait as long as 3 years to come to the U.S. and work at Boyne. All of Schneider's instructors must have at least 5 years of teaching experience and be fully certified, a process that takes 3 years in their native Austria. Instructors attend weekly teaching clinics at Boyne and are required to race in giant slalom competition weekly. They keep strict schedules, sometimes teaching as many as 7 hours a day. One of Othmar's assistants, Sigi Grottendorfer, left to direct the Ski School at Sugarbush Valley. It was there that instructor Frank Covino was influenced in his teaching methodology, and Othmar is pleased that Frank is trying valiantly to preserve this classical, basically Austrian, tradition.

This same discipline is obvious in the exacting teaching methods on which Schneider insists. Except for a concession to shorter skis in 1970 that cut teaching time in half, according to Schneider, there are few short cuts at Boyne. Pupils are still required to learn all the basics before progressing to parallel skiing even though many students, in true Yankee fashion, look for a quicker, easier way.

"American people have not enough patience," says Schneider. "A lot of students, especially weekend skiers, look for short cuts. They would like to learn to ski in one day and skip a lot of these maneuvers. But you can't do that with skiing. You've got to learn all these steps, one after the other."

Good basic technique is stressed. "Good basic technique means knowing the snowplow, the snowplow turn, how to traverse in a nice proper position and have the so-called angulation," Schneider says. "We insist our pupils know these things before they go on, and I think that is our main difference in teaching. We follow our system. None of my instructors is allowed to teach any other way." While Frank

Covino's exclusion of the snowplow in his radical departure from the traditional approach illustrated in this book may take the average student longer to make his first turn, at least his turning form will be classical, on his edges, with sufficient angulation and proper leverage. This proper traverse form is the most essential posture in recreational skiing. The snowplow turn is simply a slower way of learning it.

Such uniformity and imperviousness to the passing fads governs even the teaching terminology at Boyne. "Two or three years ago everybody started saying 'wedge'," says Schneider. "A complete new word. Why wedge? For 50 years we were talking snowplow. Why go away from snowplow to wedge?" At Boyne they didn't. Snowplow it was and snowplow it stayed. And today, of course, most areas are returning to the old familiar term.

Boyne encourages skiers to get the basics they consider so important by offering rock bottom prices on 5- and 7-day family ski weeks that each season lure about 4,000 ski weekers to Boyne to learn the Boyne Way.

Schneider says he insists on good basic training, not only because it makes skiing safer and therefore more fun right from the beginning, but because it makes better skiers.

WEIGHTED SKI

Left—Boyne believes in teaching the basics, including the snowplow turn. Here Othmar Schneider, director of skiing, demonstrates the Boyne snowplow turn—body erect, arms out for balance, weight on the downhill ski. The dotted line clearly shows the relationship of the snowplow form to a more advanced parallel technique, with the shoulders the same slant as the slope.

Right—In a typical five-day Boyne Ski Week, pupils master the traverse and basic turn the second day. The turn is accomplished standing rather straight in the traverse position, then opening up both skis into a sliding snowplow. Skis are closed by dropping *down* as opposed to up unweighting.

Left—Even in the early stages of learning, the Boyne way, a modified Austrian style, stresses angulation . . . leaning the upper body down hill to shift, and keeping the weight on the downhill ski. Upright posture and extended arms are Boyne trademarks. Everything uphill leads the traverse: the uphill ski, knee, hip and shoulder all lead, with the torso 90 degrees to the slant of the hill. Compare this to author Frank Covino's traversing position in Chapter 3.

Right—Close parallel skiing is the goal for every pupil at Boyne. Beginners using short skis are allowed to keep skis 5 to 8 inches apart, but as soon as they start going over the fall line parallel, they are then encouraged to close the skis. By maintaining his quiet torso 90 degrees to the hill and always facing the fall line, Othmar's upper body is always coiled in anticipation of the next turn. The dynamics of the turn are from the hips down.

Boyne specializes in children and families. More than 400 children enroll in Boyne's mid-week Children's Ski Program, part of the Family Ski Week packages for which the Boyne resorts are famous.

Snowplow turns and basic turns, he points out, are essential to teaching pupils to use their edges and carve their turns. The flat ski used in GLM allows the skier to slide too much for good control on steeper terrain.

"Perhaps we aren't moving as fast at the start as some other schools by sticking to the snowplow and snowplow turn," he says, "but when we come to the advanced skiing, to the safe skiing and to the mogul skiing then I'm quite sure we'll show the pupils who had basic training."

Today, after 16 years at Boyne, Schneider can pick out the skiers who started at Boyne. "They look great. Perfect form. In control. Left and right turns just alike. Good position on the skis, and they can go on all kinds of mountains and have no problems skiing the terrain."

Schneider says that Boyne's terrain, excellent for the Midwest, but modest compared to the Rockies and the East, has been a help, not a hindrance, in developing competent skiers chiefly because Boyne's teaching reputation, not its terrain, has had to be one of its main attractions. "Where there are big mountains, the ski instructor may find himself serving primarily as a guide," Schneider says. "In the Midwest, we must go into the ski lessons. We must teach, we must keep pushing or we lose a lot of customers."

Boyne's modified Austrian method stresses skiing efficiently, using less energy, less effort. "When we say modified Austrian we mean right away that you don't move your upper body as a turning force," says Schneider. "The skiing is done from the hips down with your legs."

In a typical 5-day Boyne ski week, skiers master the snowplow and snowplow turn the first day, traversing and the basic turn the second day. Boyne's basic turn is accomplished standing rather straight in traverse position, then opening up both skis into kind of a sliding snowplow and by dropping down, closing the skis. "The Americans like to close the skis by coming up," says Schneider pointing out the difference in the two turns. On the third day skiers learn beginning parallel turns that take them directly into parallel skiing on the fourth day. "By Friday our ski week students have very good basic technique with no bad habits," says Schneider.

With shorter skis Boyne does not expect beginners to ski parallel at first, but unlike many areas using GLM, Boyne encourages skiers to bring their skis together when they progress to the parallel stage.

"Many ski schools say as long as you are paralleling you are OK," says Schneider. "The French, for example, say you don't have to have your skis together to be a good skier. They are right. But you look so much better if you do. As soon as you put your skis apart, you don't look graceful. I must agree with Frank Covino that gracefulness is as important as efficiency, and they often are one and the same."

But this is difficult for the beginner, especially with short skis, because he needs stability, so Boyne relaxes the system. "We say skis apart 5 inches to 8 inches," says Schneider, "and don't try to be perfect right away. Later after 5, 6 or 10 days of skiing, we tell you to bring the skis back together. Once a skier starts going over the fall line parallel, then we ask him to close the skis, to be graceful, to have a nice position."

This, of course, necessitates a longer ski. Whereas GLM students start on 3-footers and often never ski on anything longer than a 5-foot ski, at Boyne students never use the very shortest skis and are encouraged to move on to longer lengths.

"The 3-foot skis turn very easily by axial motion, of course," says Schneider, "but they don't track well because their edges are not used properly." Boyne ski weekers start on 4-footers, move to 5-footers on the third day and are skiing on 170cm skis by Friday. After a few more weeks of skiing, intermediates are encouraged to move up to 180cm or longer and make use of their skis' side camber.

"It depends on how fast you progress and how fast you ski," says Schneider. "At higher speeds the longer ski is much more stable, and when it comes to hard pack skiing, the longer skis hold better, you have more edge and can make precise turns with good control and little skidding."

In addition to maintaining a graceful upright position (with knees slightly bent forward, the body only slightly bent from the waist and the arms out for balance) and using the legs for turning, *the Boyne Way stresses angulation*—leaning the upper body downhill to shift and keeping the weight on the downhill ski and bending the knees and hip into the hill for proper edge control.

Although Boyne no longer stresses the extreme reverse shoulder position, a hallmark of the original Modern Austrian Ski Technique, beginners who steer their turns are told to keep their shoulders quiet and have them facing down the hill.

"When we started the *gegenschulter* 23 years ago, we had to have an extreme position because everybody had the habit of rotating," says Schneider. "Today we don't need to do that."

Boyne promises to have the average beginner skiing parallel by the end of a Ski Week. "The average Ski Weeker should be able to ski parallel with short skis under average conditions on an intermediate slope by the time he leaves," says Schneider. "We can almost guarantee that, and we couldn't 15 years ago with the long boards."

The difference among ski teaching techniques are minor today, Schneider says, and he predicts a time when all ski areas will use the same method.

"The Official American Teaching Method today and Boyne's modified Austrian technique, for example, are very similar, except for our greater emphasis upon angulation," he says. "I think Boyne, Sun Valley and Park City could exchange instructors and pupils with no trouble, and I think one day we will have a universal teaching method for all the ski schools in the U.S." The parallelogram principles and angulation in the traverse that Frank Covino emphasizes in this book are totally in tune with Othmar's teaching methodology. He is opposed to the E.P.S.I.A. square stance and inclination after the turn, especially on steep icy terrain, as it invariably places the student on his uphill ski and causes imbalance due to the pull of *centripetal force*.

How to Ski Boyne Highlands

Boyne Highlands fans may well be right when they say this Michigan resort has the best beginner's terrain in the Midwest—nothing comparable between Boston and Denver. Grooming is meticulous in a continuous effort to live up to the slogan, "There's never any ice at Boyne Highlands."

Kathy's Run is perhaps the favorite beginner run. Named for owner Everett Kircher's daughter, it is the result of extensive earth moving efforts that combined two narrower runs. The result is a wide—¼-mile—open, ½-mile long run that's constantly groomed for a surface that is absolutely free of bumps and ice. Kathy starts out gentle then runs into a steeper section that's just right for practicing snowplow turns. The bottom is flat and is especially nice for teaching purposes.

Amy's Run is probably one of the most scenic runs at the Highlands. It's kept closed during the week and opened on weekends for deep powder skiing.

Heather is the longest ski run in the Midwest at ¾-mile. There are no trees, and the terrain is excellent for skiers through the intermediates. MacGully is steeper than Heather and excellent for more adventuresome intermediates, according to Peter Obermouser, Highlands' ski school director.

Tournament is closed during the week, its beautiful expert terrain saved for weekend hot doggers and advanced skiers. Olympic and Challenge are great for racing and racing instruction. Olympic is left ungroomed for mogul build up. Rob Roy, a not quite so steep expert run, is used for weekly NASTAR races.

How to Ski Boyne Mountain

When beginners leave Boyne Mountain's bunny slope after mastering the snowplow turn, they can take the Victor, Hemlock or McLough chairlifts to the top of Boyne Mountain and Cold Springs Trail.

Cold Springs, a very easy back trail, leads down to the south side of the resort complex via Top Notch. Top Notch is a run that's easy to ski, beautiful, peaceful and wide

Boyne Mountain with its Alpine-motif lodges and village complex is one of the oldest ski resorts in the Midwest. Terrain offers ample challenge for advanced skiers, but the resort caters to families, beginners and children.

enough for beginners to make turns comfortably, according to Boyne Mountain's director of skiing Robert Kirschlager. Top Notch offers beginners a variety of terrain good for practicing all the basic maneuvers stressed at Boyne, including traversing, side slipping and the basic turn.

Ramshead, the longest trail at Boyne Mountain, almost wide enough to qualify as a bowl, offers a variety of terrain also, slightly steeper at the top, very gentle at the bottom. Ideal for the advanced beginner and intermediate skier.

Deer Run, very easy, gentle and wider than Cold Springs, is also good for intermediates.

The most famous run at Boyne Mountain is Victor, popular because of its halfway house where skiers party and enjoy cookouts with a scenic view of the resort and surrounding countryside below.

The Meadow, which ranges from intermediate to advanced intermediate, and North Boyne, not usually as heavily skied as Victor, are good alternatives for the intermediate.

Hemlock is the steepest of Boyne's long slopes. FIS approved for slalom competition, it is regularly selected as the site for Pro and Can-Am races.

McLouth is Boyne's permanent racing hill. It features permanent starting and finishing houses and can accommodate two races simultaneously. It's best for intermediate and expert skiers.

Mogul hunters should seek out Nosedive, a very steep trail tucked in between North Boyne and Deer Run that is left ungroomed for challenging skiing.

C is for COLORADO and its Summit Skiing

Copper
Breckenridge
and Keystone

C is for Colorado's Summit Skiing.

What if someone told you that you could ski three major Colorado resorts on the same lift ticket? Would you believe him?

Maybe not, but it is true and it is happening right now in Summit County, Colorado, at the top of the nation, where a variety of skiing awaits the visitor.

In Summit County, three completely different ski resorts decided to formulate a program which would allow the visitor to experience the advantages of all three resorts during one vacation and on the same lift ticket.

The program, the latest innovation in the ever-changing sport of skiing, is called "Ski the Summit." The three resorts are Keystone, Copper Mountain and Breckenridge, all located within 15 miles of each other and within easy driving distance from Denver's Stapleton International Airport.

Actually, Ski the Summit is three resorts rolled into one. Altogether, the three combine 25 lifts, 123 miles of ski trails and an uphill capacity of 25,200 skiers per hour. The highest vertical drop is 2,450 feet. More than 50 restaurants and bars also are located at the resorts and in nearby towns.

Ski the Summit is sold in two separate packages which include either 7 nights' lodging and 6 days' skiing at any of the three resorts, or 5 nights' lodging and 4 days' skiing. The packages may be purchased through travel agents in major cities in the United States or through airline tour desk personnel. A person purchasing a Ski the Summit package also may qualify for reduced tour-basing air fares.

Visitors may arrive in Summit County any day of the week and stay in lodges and condominiums which are located at the resorts themselves or in lodges situated throughout the county. Package rates differ at each resort depending on the cost of accomodations. However, most lodge prices range from $63 to $120 per person for the 5-night rate and from $86 to $163 for the 7-night rate. These prices also include lift tickets.

Per person prices at condominiums based on double occupancy range from $73 to $98 for 5 nights and from $99 to $138 for 7 nights. The economy-wise skier can spend as little as $99 for 7 nights' lodging and 6 days' skiing by sharing a condominium with a minimum of three other persons.

Here is how Ski the Summit works. A skier, for example, may stay in the Keystone Lodge with its three restaurants, cocktail lounge, heated, outdoor swimming pool and therapy pools for 7 nights for $162 a person based on double occupancy and ski for 6 days at either Keystone, where the Lodge is located, Copper Mountain or Breckenridge. A free bus service makes frequent trips between the three resorts.

Although the Summit County resorts all have skiing in common, they differ markedly in both character and atmosphere. Keystone is a contemporary, all-seasons, final destination resort situated in the shadow of the Continental Divide only 72 miles west of Denver. Copper Mountain has a youthful exuberance, a larger base area and a steeper mountain.

Breckenridge grew out of an old mining town by the same name and retains much of the original, rustic charm. Altogether, they offer an abundance of powder glades, steep mogul pitches and wide, manicured boulevards.

Keystone offers a variety of recreational and intellectual activities ranging from skiing and tennis to lectures sponsored by the Keystone Center for Continuing Education.

Skiing, however, is the main winter sport, and Keystone Mountain, which has 35 miles of trails served by seven lifts, offers something for everyone. A fun mountain for all abilities, 65 percent of the runs are for intermediate skiers, 20 percent are for beginners and 15 percent are for advanced skiers. Two day lodges, one at the base of the mountain, the other at the 11,640-foot summit, serve everything from hamburgers to crepes.

Shuttle buses connect the mountain to the village where there is ice skating on Keystone Lake and cross-country lessons and equipment available through a new ski touring center.

The village centers around a variety of restaurants, shops and nightspots. The Lodge itself houses three distinctively different restaurants, in addition to the cocktail lounge. One

Keystone (left), Breckenridge (middle), and Copper Mountain (right), all located within 15 miles of each other in Summit County, offer the skier more slopes, more lifts, more restaurants, more bars, more shops, more variety. Through the Ski the Summit program, skiers can ski all three resorts on the same lift ticket.

A backdrop of stately evergreens loaded with snow overlooks this skier who ventured out early one bright, sunny winter's day at Keystone to *schuss* some fresh powder. Keystone has plenty of that light, Colorado powder and a variety of good slopes on which to ski it.

of the restaurants, the Garden Room, specializes in Continental cuisine.

A Keystone winter bonus is the prestigious John Gardiner's Tennis Club which has 12 all-weather, outdoor and two indoor courts, a pro shop, where tennis equipment can be rented, and a mezzanine lounge.

From Keystone it is 15 miles to Copper Mountain located on the east side of Vail Pass. Copper Mountain, named after a mine farther up, also has a base area with shops, restaurants, tennis courts, nightspots and a fine mountain which has 37 trails ranging from beginning to advanced, six double chairlifts, one of them covered, and a Poma.

Copper Mountain's skiing is different from that of both Keystone and Breckenridge because it has more advanced terrain and an entire area devoted almost exclusively to moguls. Copper also has some fine powder skiing, a midway house called Solitude Station, and a base lodge with a rental shop, a cafeteria and a large seating area which overlooks the slopes. Most of the buildings at Copper Mountain, including the base lodge, are copper-colored.

In keeping with the current avid interest in freestyle skiing, Copper has established a freestyle school which offers extensive training for all ages in jumping, mogul-running, and ballet.

From Copper Mountain, it is another 15 miles to the old town of Breckenridge, named by the townspeople the "Kingdom of Breckenridge." One of the oldest ski resorts in Colorado, Breckenridge now is owned and operated by the Aspen Skiing Corp.

Breckenridge has two ski mountains, Peak 8 and Peak 9, both with separate base areas, but connected by trails and lifts. Peak 8, which was the first to be developed, has 34 runs served by six lifts and two day lodges. Peak 9, which was constructed more recently, has 18 runs and four double

Breckenridge Ski Area, not super steep, is an intermediate's Paradise.

chairs. Both Peak 8 and Peak 9 are part of Summit County's Ten Mile Range.

At the base of Peak 9 is the Four Seasons Village which features an enclosed shopping area with more restaurants and bars. Skiing at Breckenridge is primarily for beginners and intermediates although there are a few advanced and expert runs.

The town, however, is unique. An old 1890s mining village, Breckenridge has many single-fronted buildings facing the street and shops tucked into unlikely spaces in these buildings. The town also has a selection of restaurants and nightspots ranging from pizza joints to first-class gourmet delights. Bars vary from the Gold Pan, where fussball is the highlight of the evening, to the crowded Miner's Camp, which features dinner and top-rate entertainment.

From Breckenridge, then, it is only 15 miles back to Keystone and another day of fun and relaxation on the slopes or the courts or in a Jacuzzi whirlpool.

Ski the Summit is a far cry from the days when a person was willing to ride in the back of a pickup truck with his old Head Standards just to get to the local ski area. But then, skiing has come a long way in a few years. All the way to Ski the Summit.

SKI LESSONS AND G.L.M.

by Hans Garger, Director
Breckenridge Ski School

Before discussing GLM (Graduated Length Method), it is most important to mention something about ski lessons in general. While GLM has made learning to ski a much more enjoyable and easier experience, one should never attempt to learn to ski without competent instruction regardless of whether such an attempt is made on a shorter GLM ski or the standard length ski. In either case, bad habits develop easily and quickly but are frustratingly hard to get rid of later on. It's the later on that depends a great deal on the fundamental skills taught correctly in the beginning stages of the sport. Ski instructors know this. They know skiing, and the mountain, and will, first of all, always find the best terrain and snow condition for your ability to ski and learn on. Careful terrain selection means that you will have more fun. Why? You will enjoy learning while you progress more rapidly. Instructors are meticulously trained in the latest teaching methods—methods that from the very beginning relate body movements directly toward advanced maneuvers. Thus, unnecessary and exaggerated body movements which result in complete distortion and extreme muscular forces are avoided, and the ultimate goal of the learner—to become a good and avid skier—can be achieved.

For the beginner skier, the GLM is beyond any doubt the quickest and easiest method of learning yet devised. It is simply exhilarating. And that is no exaggeration! Shorter skis to learn on are easier to handle, and they turn with less effort, making the very first day a day of fun and progress rather than a psychological frustration and physical destruction. GLM has been effectively applied for several years and has greatly contributed in making fine skiers out of people who otherwise would have either given up on the sport or never would have given it a try in the first place. With such almost phenomenal results, it seems that no more needs to be said! Well, that is true as far as GLM in its true and realistic concept is concerned. Unfortunately, however, we still encounter discrepancies when it comes to the actual length of GLM skis for the beginning skier. One can easily be misled into starting out with much too short a ski. When the

The Breckenridge Ski School is all smiles.

Genia Fuller looks determined as she spins a beautiful reuel, competing at Keystone's Challenge of the Sexes.

The inimitable Wayne Wong appears ready to do in the bull as he flies down the mogul course at Keystone, Colorado, beating his counterpart, Genia Fuller, by less than one point!

ski becomes so short that it ceases to perform its basic function as a stable base for a skier to stand in balance on, it seems obvious that we have encountered an extreme in the opposite direction. Certainly, there is some fun in sliding around on real short skis, but the body movements and skills used with these skis have little or no relation to the sport of skiing as we understand and teach it today. Most instructors will, therefore, recommend a learning length of chest to shoulder height. This is not only an excellent length to start out with, it also avoids the how-many-centimeter-longer or shorter-question that many people get a little confused about at this stage. Since people vary in height, let the learning ski be equal to the need of the learner. Although graduation to longer skis comes rather rapidly, let's not be overly hasty about it. How much time (days, weeks) out of one ski season you have to spend on the slopes and your own progression are the major factors that will determine the graduating procedure. Your instructor will guide you. He (or she) will let you know when you are ready for longer skis. On the other hand, there is nothing that says you MUST go to a longer ski. In the long run it will be you yourself who will have a "say so" on what length of ski you feel best on. As your skills develop toward and into the more advanced skiing maneuvers, the chest to shoulder length ski most likely will no longer be the right "tool" to do the job. When you are ready for higher speeds, steeper terrain and deep powder snow, the time has come then to use a longer than shoulder height ski—a ski that will provide the essential stability and performance in conformity with speed, terrain and let's not forget, your more developed and refined physical skills.

You, then, have "Graduated!" Another "Freshman" will take over your learning length ski and eagerly look forward to and ski toward the same objective—Graduation Day.

After all, if one's goal is to acquire a chauffeur's steering skill it seems a waste of time to keep on practicing on a motorcycle. By the same token, there is no point either in fighting today's modern creation of "artwork" that faintly resembles the good old moguls on the slopes with too long a pair of skis. Unless you are racing for a train, hit every mogul at a slower speed instead of going too fast and hitting every third on-hard!

Consequently, a good ski length for average or better recreational skiers would be (now that we know what we are talking about) anywhere from 170 to 200 cm, give or take a few centimeters according to what feels best. The racer or otherwise aggressive type skier will have different ideas and will determine his ski length according to the purpose the skis are used for.

While GLM was basically designed for the beginner skier, it is equally effective for skiers of any level who wish to overcome, if necessary, problems with a more advanced maneuver or maneuvers. So, never be "ashamed" to use a little shorter ski than normal to help you get the feeling of that particular maneuver you are experiencing difficulties with. You will be surprised how much easier it will be for you to get the feel of it. On top of that you might even be mistaken for a "hot-dogger!"

At any rate, whether you come for a day of a season of skiing, let your instructor be your guide and host. Lessons will give you a great return for your dollar. Lessons solve some of energy problems too. Especially with GLM. When we recall the days of John L. "Snowshoe" Thompson who chopped down an oak tree and fashioned himself a pair of 10-foot long skis back in 1856, GLM has come a long way indeed.

D is for DENVER

as near
**Winter Park,
Colorado**

D IS FOR DENVER

D is for Denver, and the closest major ski area to that capital city is Winter Park and its neighbor Mary Jane. We have a good article on freestyle skiing from Bruce Bowlin at Winter Park, but first, let me tell you about *him*.

Bruce Bowlin started skiing 12 years ago at Winter Park. He attended the University of Colorado and received a degree in aerospace engineering in 1972.

The lack of jobs in the aerospace industry was a lucky break for skiers, since Bruce turned to ski teaching on a full-time basis. He currently teaches freestyle skiing with Bill Eisenhart's Winter Park Freestyle/Racing Society. Bruce was chosen as one of the ten members of the United States demonstration team sent to the 10th Interski held in Strbske-Pleso, Czechoslovakia in January of 1975.

Bruce gave the U.S. demonstration of freestyle skiing, and tells here how it fits into the overall teaching philosophy of the ATM; and talks about the Winter Park freestyle program.

FREESTYLE AND THE ATM

by Bruce Bowlin

The 10th Interski held in Strbske-Pleso, Czechoslovakia in January of 1975 brought 20 skiing nations together to communicate their ideas on skiing techniques and teaching methods.

I was chosen as one of the ten members of the demonstration team representing the United States. The team was selected at tryouts in Aspen, Colorado, by the Professional Ski Instructors of America (P.S.I.A.). Instructors from all divisions participated in the tryouts.

Each team puts on a demonstration at the Interski, showing their methods of teaching. Papers are also presented on many subjects, such as safety and the unification of world skiing instruction.

The demonstration presented by the United States team had a different orientation from those in the past, and therefore it was fairly controversial. We are trying to orient our teaching to the development of skills, such as balance, edging, weight transfer, unweighting, terrain absorption, pole plants and steering or twisting, rather than a perfecting of maneuvers as the end result.

Our philosophy is to adapt the teaching to the skier, rather than the other way around. These skills were developed through various teaching maneuvers. For example, we demonstrated a straight run, and then various advanced skills were added, such as a straight run backwards, or a straight run through the moguls to show terrain absorption.

We used freestyle in our demonstration as an integral part

Winter Park, Colorado.

of teaching new skills. Freestyle teaches such advanced skills as independent leg action, edge control, and using both edges of the ski. The major benefit of freestyle is in the confidence it gives a skier.

I was chosen to give the freestyle demonstration for the team, and it consisted of a variation on a single routine that I put together.

Several other nations also included freestyle in their demonstrations. Wayne Wong from Canada did a whole progression of stunts, and Futzi Garhammer from Germany also did a presentation.

I teach freestyle skiing with Bill Eisenhart's Winter Park Freestyle/Racing Society, and our program works on the same philosophy of teaching skills. We take a skier who can do parallel christies, and do more advanced skills, or "tricks," to try and turn that person into a very good skier by increasing his skill level.

With the proper instruction and equipment, freestyle can be safe and easy to do. It does require a fair amount of physical conditioning, but last year we had no major injuries to any of our students. The average age of the participants at our program in Winter Park runs from 14-29, but we are beginning to see some older skiers try it, too.

Winter Park Freestyle/Racing Society

The Freestyle/Racing Society was started during the 1974-75 season, and is directed by Bill Eisenhart. We hold several 5-day freestyle camps during the season, or you can choose any 5 days and take lessons in a specific area, such as freestyle, racing, ballet, or aerials.

Bruce Bowlin, member of the United States Demonstration Team and coach at the Winter Park Freestyle/Racing Society. (Photo by Steve Stone)

Mary Jane at Winter Park.

Bill Eisenhart, director of the Winter Park Freestyle/Racing Society, demonstrates his form on the NASTAR course. (Photo by Steve Stone)

Lance Wood demonstrates a helicopter on the freestyle jump above Snoasis at Winter Park. (Photo by Greg Albracht)

The lessons begin in the morning with lectures and films. These lectures include biomechanics and technique analysis, equipment tuning, waxing, racing and course setting, buying equipment, conditioning and health, binding analysis, and the psychology of competition.

The lessons then move outside for on-the-hill practice and are broken down into four different ability levels. Videotapes are used to critique the student's skiing, and there are special guest coaches at some sessions.

The program stresses the safety and fun of learning freestyle techniques. With the proper conditioning and coaching, almost any parallel skier can be doing basic maneuvers.

In our 5-day clinics, we emphasize good technical skiing on the first day of the class. Carved turns are stressed, and we also run some gates. Here, any problems that the skier has will be magnified, and corrections can be made in pole plants, body posture, and arm and hand position.

Four Phases of Freestyle

Teaching of the stunt and ballet skiing is divided into four phases. In Phase 1, the skills of balance and edge control are increased. The maneuvers taught are: skiing backwards, skiing on one ski, and skiing on the uphill ski. The basic 360 spin is then taught, which allows for development of refined edge control of the flat ski.

In Phase 2, timing and edge control are emphasized in such maneuvers as the Charleston, cross-overs, one foot spins, and the Butterfly.

Phase 3 is the learning of new tricks, and putting them together in a smooth routine. The tricks taught are the reuel 360, reverse cross-over, Shea-Guy, 360 tiproll, and shoulder roll. The emphasis is on perfecting these tricks and making the routine look professional.

In Phase 4, the student works on timing, rhythm and difficult stunts. All classes are divided into three different levels of ability, so the student can progress at his own level.

The students are also introduced to aerials early in the program. Students are shown the proper way to go off prepared jumps. Concentration in the inrun is important, with steady and equal weight on the skis, and even balance. The student is taught to spring up, look out, and thrust the chest out. Basic aerial maneuvers such as the spread eagle and the tip drop can be attempted when the student feels confident in the air.

The mini-tramp is also useful in developing the basic skills used in aerial acrobatics, without the weight of skis. Safety is provided by controlled spotting of trained coaches.

Mogul technique is also taught. Eisenhart's school stresses a balance position on the skis, with all joints flexed. Terrain absorption is also important, and again, carved turns are the secret of good mogul technique.

MARY JANE AT WINTER PARK

Winter Park's new Mary Jane development is tops for teaching mogul technique. Of the 18 new runs, over 65 percent are rated "most difficult," and 28 percent "more difficult." This new addition to Winter Park, which included 350 acres of new terrain, makes the area a haven for the

Jeff Jakelich, coach at the Winter Park Freestyle/Racing Society, performs a reuel, one of the the tricks learned in Phase 2 of the freestyle program. (Photo by Greg Albracht)

super hot skiers, along with its vast terrain geared to the beginner and intermediate.

The new area includes 18 new trails, with names taken from the colorful railroad history of the area. Winter Park is located at the west portal of the famous Moffat Tunnel, the 6-mile railroad tunnel underneath nearby Rollins Pass. The tunnel was the first east-west railroad link between Denver and the mountains west. Denver skiers would ride the train to the west portal, and get off here to ski the old logging roads in the area, and use the abandoned construction shacks for warming houses.

The Mary Jane development marks a turning point for Winter Park. It is now no longer the small day area it once was. With a capacity of 5,000 beds in the valley, it is looking toward the status of a major destination resort.

Besides the 18 new trails, the Mary Jane area has a new base center housing the cafeteria, ski school, ski patrol, ski shop and rentals, and first aid room.

It is possible to ski between the Winter Park and Mary Jane areas, and one lift ticket is valid at both. A shuttle service is also available between the two base areas for those who do not ski.

The original Mary Jane trail was cut in the early 1930's by members of the Colorado Arlberg Club, a club of prominent Denver businessmen and outdoorsmen. There were several ski races held on the trail in the early days, and the racers had to hike up the trail in order to reach the race start.

The total amount of skiable acres at Winter Park is now 770, and there are 51 different trails to choose from. These range from the gentle and wide Allan Phipps trail to the steep and challenging Needle's Eye at Mary Jane. Winter Park is now the second largest ski area in the state, and will soon be taking its place among the best known areas in the west.

Ski School

The ski school at Winter Park is under the direction of George Engel, who has been the director since 1948. George heads a staff of over 120 instructors, who teach both the Cliff Taylor direct parallel method, and the American Teaching Method's Graduated Length Methods (GLM).

The ski school has kept abreast of the new changes and trends, and besides the Freestyle/Racing Society which holds classes here, there is an extensive handicapped skier program.

Program director for the handicapped. Hal O'Leary teaches classes for the blind, amputees, and mentally handicapped skiers. O'Leary works closely with the Children's Hospital in Denver, and the method of teaching amputee skiers which was developed here is now used nation-wide.

There is also an extensive nordic program at Winter Park for junior jumpers and cross-country racers. The Pop Sorenson jumping complex is located at the base of the area, and includes five jumping hills ranging in size from the 3-meter hill for the youngest skiers, to the 50-meter hill for the Class A jumpers. There is free coaching for the nordic program, and jumping and cross-country meets are held throughout the season.

The nursery at the area accepts children from 6 months to 8 years old and is open daily from 8:30 AM to 4 PM.

The children's ski school is available for ages 5-12. A special Day Care program offers lessons, lunch, and supervision from 9 AM to 4 PM daily.

E is for EMO

Stratton Mountain, Vermont

E is for Emo, as in Henrich, at Stratton Mountain, Vermont, where *form* is not dead. Here is a report by Bob Schaefer:

In 1961, Austrian ski racer and ski instructor Emo Henrich accepted the position of ski school director at Stratton Mountain, Vermont, before the mountain opened, even before there were any lifts on the mountain.

Today, Stratton is one of the East's finest ski resorts where families from New York's Westchester County and Connecticut's Fairfield County mingle with singles from Manhattan on immaculately groomed slopes. So many Stratton skiers and families have come to call Stratton their skiing home base, or have become second-home owners in the mountain community, that the Stratton Ski School is now teaching many second-generation Stratton skiers. The success of the Stratton story, in fact, closely parallels that of Emo Henrich and the Stratton Ski School. The reputation for excellence and doing things the right way that Stratton has acquired over the years certainly doesn't exclude Emo's ski school.

Emo Henrich is a big man who is full of intensity and love of life. His *joie de vivre* extends naturally into his philosophy of skiing. "Skiing is happiness," says Emo, and one has only to watch him ski to feel that happiness radiate from him. Emo skis in a classic style that exemplifies the graceful poetry that skiing at its best can be. And he is very adept at passing on the technical intricacies of the sport to others, for Emo loves to teach almost as much as he loves to ski.

Emo skis with a controlled exuberance, and it is his goal to pass that on to his students. The two terms, control and exuberance, may seem contradictory, but Emo stresses that a skier must develop good technical skills before he can really begin to express himself on skis. And with control and confidence, the skier is free to express the joy of moving on skis.

The main forces in skiing, gravity and centrifugal force, are always the same; ski design and boot design may change somewhat, but the essential things that the skier's body must do to make the skis turn remain virtually unchanged. But Emo has made a recent discovery which may well reshape the emphasis of ski instruction.

In 1975, Emo was watching movies made in the '30s of expert skiers skiing powder. Noticing that these early skiers were technically as proficient as skiers today, and yet knowing that there were significant differences in equipment, he sought to find the common denominator that linked the good skiers of the past to those of today.

"Suddenly it came to me," says Emo. "It seemed so obvious, that I couldn't believe that no one had noticed before—the key was *rhythm!*"

Rhythm in skiing is so important, explains Emo, that skiers on the hill can be classified more accurately by that criterion than by the kinds of turns they make; skiers with rhythm are good skiers, while those without rhythm are mediocre skiers at best.

After some experimentation with teaching skiing using rhythm as a cornerstone, Emo was very pleased with the results. He found that the concept of rhythmic skiing can be introduced very successfully at the snowplow or wedge turn stage of learning, or at any point thereafter.

"To become a rhythmical skier," says Emo, "learn to use the rebound of a turn as the source of energy for the next turn. Turns are almost automatically linked together if the skier does a motion before the turn is over, in the rebound stage of the turn, which leads into the unweighting for the next turn." This basic idea, he points out, can be done as early as the carved snowplow stage of skiing and at all levels above that.

"Rhythm is *needed* in more advanced stages of skiing,"

Like a melting ice cream cone, this popular eastern ski area provides a variety of terrain for every level of proficiency, as its trails drop from the peak 1,900 vertical feet.

Classic angulation marks the elegant style of Stratton Mt. Ski School Director, Emo Henrich. He and Frank Covino have more than skiing methodology in common; Emo is also a very fine landscape painter. (Photos by Hubert Schriebl)

Don Lamson goes upside down in a full layout backflip as a World Trophy Freestyle competitor at Stratton Mountain. (Photo by Wendy Walker)

Emo says, and cites effective mogul skiing as an example. A skier who has no rhythm in his skiing gets into real difficulty in the moguls; he can't decide where to make his turns and so keeps going straight continually looking for a "good" place to make a turn. But the rhythmical skier can bounce through the mogul field with the same rhythm of the good skiers whose turns built up the rhythm of the moguls in the first place.

"Every skier has some hang-ups as he learns to ski," says Emo, "but they are more easily overcome if a skier has rhythm than if he doesn't."

Does Emo's new "discovery" portend a change in the way he will ski or the way that his ski school "graduates" will be skiing? Not really. Emo still envisions the ideal final form for the recreational skier much the same as he has in the past, and one can still recognize the stylish skiing of his students on Stratton's slopes, as well as at Vail, Snowbird, and at Europe's finest ski resorts.

"The beauty of elegant skiing is the highest goal the recreational skier can strive to reach," says Emo, in complete agreement with SKIER'S DIGEST author, Frank Covino. He also feels that skiing with the feet together and legs closed, not in the more recent "wide track" style, is the ultimate standard by which recreational skiing is judged. Stressing that skiing technique is always affected in the short run by fads resulting from the publicity of a popular skier's technique, Emo points out that Jean-Claude Killy is a prime example of this effect. Immediately following his unprecedented racing success, recreational skiers began "sitting back" on their skis, not understanding that they were emulating a move of acceleration that the French team racers were photographed doing, but which was only a momentary changing of weight during a turn, not, as most skiers thought, a position held throughout a turn.

Now he sees the "wide track" stance, also popularized by Killy, beginning to give way again to the skis-together stance that he has always skied, promoted, and taught. "It's more comfortable, especially in deep snow, and it helps prevent

tip crossing, too. "Besides," he reminds, "skiing with the skis together *looks* better."

Emo has, in his many years of skiing and teaching skiing, done a lot of observing of skiers and their habits and realizes that most skiers like to "show off" their abilities. He observes that the trails under chairlifts are always the ones with the greatest number of skiers; he can only conclude that this is because skiers like to be seen skiing. His convictions about skiing elegantly are also reinforced by the fact that skiers usually ski in groups, or at least in pairs, and often ski a distance one at a time so that the others in the group can observe one another while they ski. Even when a skier is skiing alone, he notes, if the sun is at his back, the skier will often watch his own shadow to see how he looks.

How does Emo regard freestyle skiing? Is it a logical extension of his perception of skiing as a spectator sport? Is it a passing fad, or is freestyle here to stay? Emo views freestyle primarily in relation to its impact on the sport of skiing—the big picture.

"We always admired Stein Eriksen and his aerial acrobatics," Emo says. "And in 1960, when I was assistant ski school director in Portillo, Chile, I was impressed by the elegant Royal Christies that ski school director Othmar Schneider would do. Then, when Hermann Goellner came out with his incredible flips in the film *Ski the Outer Limits,* it was unbelievable. Back then we thought that that was just for a few of the most talented athletes.

"But then, freestyle skiing came to the public, and it was the dynamic thing that skiing had been waiting a long time for," he says. "The general public, even the skiing public has traditionally had little interest in racing. Racing, even with the recent development of the dual slalom format, is too technical and filled with fine points for the average non-skier to appreciate. But freestyle brought excitement into skiing."

In the winter of 1975-76, Stratton made a real commitment to "go for it" in freestyle skiing. Feb. 6-8, Stratton hosted its first World Trophy Freestyle competition, in conjunction with the first annual Winter Festival. Men's overall winne

Skiing on Stratton's scenic North American trail.

of the event was veteran freestyler Scott Brooksbank, and none other than Genia Fuller, already twice women's world freestyle champion, and representing Stratton on the World Trophy tour, took the women's combined title.

Perhaps even more important in Stratton's freestyle commitment was the development of a full-scale freestyle teaching movement. Mike Shea, former Eastern National Stunt and Ballet Champion, joined the Stratton staff to coach while not on the World Trophy tour, and to bring his Mike Shea Summer Freestyle Camp to the Stratton Freestyle Training Center. Mike's summer camp is based on a somewhat revolutionary concept in freestyle training. Mike perfected his stunts using poly-surfaced ramps and jumps to do aerial maneuvers on skis while landing in water, and as a result, introduced the training-into-water idea when he started his summer camp in 1974. Two advantages to this approach to training are obvious: safety is foremost, as a bad landing in water doesn't even hurt, and the season for training virtually becomes twice as long.

What's involved in becoming a freestyle skier? Mike Shea explains that first, one must arrive at the decision that he wants to do something different with skiing than "just go down the hill turning right and left."

Mike emphasizes that the new image that freestyle skiing is achieving is oriented strongly toward safety and responsibility, unlike the earlier "hotdogging" phase of the sport that smacked of recklessness and danger.

"After one has become motivated to try freestyle skiing," says Mike, "the next step is to find out what the alternatives in freestyle are." By watching freestyle skiing, especially a competition, or even watching freestyle on film or television, the potential skier can get some idea of what's involved in the three basic categories—ballet, moguls, and aerials.

"To become an active participant in freestyle, the *best* way, and the *safest* way, is to get into a formal freestyle training program," Mike emphasizes. Training programs offer the best instructors available, usually top professional freestyle competitors, and the necessary equipment to learn safely.

MEET STRATTON MOUNTAIN

How does one ski the mountain at Stratton? The mountain itself is a big one, with 1,900 feet of vertical that runs from the 3,875-foot summit—southern Vermont's highest peak. Seven chairlifts and one T-bar speed skiers uphill to ski the terrain of their choice. Each area of the mountain has its own personality; the Sun Bowl, Snow Bowl, and the Upper and Lower North Face—they're each a little different.

There are 47 alpine trails of every description, from gentle narrow trails like the Wanderer or Old Log Road that meander through the forest, to wide open slopes like Big Ben, to the steep expert winding trails with varying pitches like the popular Spruce, or to the wide, straight mogully runs like Liftline, where exhibition skiing is usually on display for chairlift riders.

Experienced Stratton skiers often start their day with first runs in the Sun Bowl, an east-facing bowl with its own chairlift that catches the first warmth of the morning sun. Trails there are comfortably wide, with pitches that are just right for skiers of any ability to warm up on. As the sun moves across the sky, skiers move to the North Face, with the experts heading for the upper mountain, and the beginning and intermediate skiers gravitating toward the more gentle lower mountain runs where the snow is perhaps the best-groomed anywhere.

Stratton has always been famous for managing the skiing surfaces, both with snowmaking and with snow grooming by a team of eight snowcats that work the snow at night while the skiers sleep. But with the advent of the million-dollar summit snowmaking system, even the more challenging trails like the FIS approved Rimeline provide man-made snow to increase base depths and touch up the skiing surfaces.

An added dividend of the snowmaking system comes into play in the spring, perhaps the most enjoyable time of all for skiing. Coupled with Stratton's snow-saving northern exposure, the added snow depths derived from the winter's snowmaking insure good spring skiing long after many other

Above—Beginning skiers get the feel of their skis moving on the snow with the Stratton Ski School's Dopplemayr Carousel, the first of its kind in the United States.

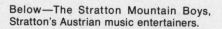
Below—The Stratton Mountain Boys, Stratton's Austrian music entertainers.

mountains are bare. Those skiers who know the delights of skiing in the rapid-tanning spring sun wearing sweaters, not parkas, ski the snow into magnificent corn snow moguls, breaking only for a leisurely lunch in the sun.

Learning is Easier

But what if you're new to the sport of skiing, but want to learn to ski? How do you ski Stratton, or any mountain, for that matter if you don't even know the basics. Here's where Emo Henrich and his staff of 75 professional ski instructors come into the picture. Emo has taught thousands of beginners to ski—and to ski well. And learning how is getting easier all the time.

One thing that is simplifying the first stages of learning to ski at Stratton is the rotating, four-armed Dopplemayr Carousel, which made its U.S. debut at Stratton early in the 1976 winter season. Imported from Austria, the Carousel helps beginners get the feel of their skis moving on snow. Located on flat terrain, not the usual hill on which most beginners customarily clamber up for their first lessons, the Carousel pulls them around in slow circles. Under the watchful eye of a ski school instructor who is always at the controls, to control the speed and to stop it abruptly if necessary, the students receive suggestions and pointers

about body position, balance, and how to start learning to control the skis. And there's none of the beginners' apprehension about getting "out of control" on the hill before they know how to turn and stop.

Most beginners at Stratton now start their skiing careers in the GLM (Graduated Length Method) program, where they start on short skis that are very easy to learn to turn and maneuver, and then gradually progress up in ski length as they learn until they are skiing comfortably on skis the right length for them. And, of course, there are special ticket and lesson packages to make the whole thing really easy —and the Ski Week package is the most popular way to learn to ski (or to learn to ski better).

Ski weekers have the opportunity to learn in a week-long series of lessons with other skiers of their own ability level, and the same instructor is on hand all week to really get acquainted with each skier in his group and really personalize the learning.

Almost as popular as the skiing among Stratton skiweekers is the apres-skiing. Here again, Emo Henrich really comes into his own. "The day is not over when the skiers come in off the slopes," says Emo. "Skiers like to be entertained, too. So, I hire certified ski instructors who are entertainers too."

These Austrian entertainers, the Stratton Mountain Boys, were organized by Emo in 1961 and since have become widely known for their Tyrolean Evening entertainment program offered to Stratton skiers twice weekly in the evenings throughout the ski season. They also provide entertainment every afternoon in the base lodge.

The group, composed of eight Austrian musicians, professional ski instructors all, have become more than just local entertainers. Each fall they tour the East playing to enthusiastic crowds of thousands at Oktoberfests, ski shows, and ski club gatherings. They have been guests on national and regional television programs.

Playing at the Rochester, New York, Oktoberfest, one of the largest in the country, they were received so enthusiastically that the enormous crowd there expressed their unwillingness to let the boys stop playing.

The Stratton Mountain Boys are also now recording artists, having recently recorded an album of their most popular Austrian folksongs, waltzes, yodels, and instrumental numbers.

Emo, an entertainer himself, is a part of the group that includes Otto Egger, who plays accordian and is the group's M.C. Otto is a veteran instructor and a supervisor of the Stratton Ski School.

The bandleader is Stefan Schernthaner, former Eastern National Freestyle Champion who is the head freestyle coach of the Stratton Ski School. Stefan plays trumpet, and his extensive experience with the instrument includes a stint as an Austrian Army trumpeter. Hans Kremser, guitarist and yodeler, is assistant director of the Stratton Ski School, and summers find him back in Austria serving as a tour guide in the Alps.

Racing coach and high ranking NASTAR pacesetter Gerhardt Gregor plays bass guitar, but also occasionally joins Stefan for a haunting duet on their unique 10-foot-long Alphorns. Fredi Strobl plays clarinet, saxophone, guitar, and sings and yodels, but his most unusual instrument is the "singing saw," an ordinary saw which he plays melodically with a violin bow.

Rounding out the group are schuplatten dancers Kasi Lindlbauer, also a freestyle coach, and instructor Hans Brantner. Emo dances, sings sometimes, plays guitar, offers explanations of songs and dances, and generally provides the spontaneous spark of enthusiasm that characterizes their performances.

There's plenty more to do, too. Many alpine skiers try ski-touring at the complete Stratton Ski Touring Center, where they find well-maintained marked trails, instruction, and complete equipment rentals. Wednesday nights, ski-tourers gather for a unique after-dark tour lighted either by the moon or, if the night is not clear, each skier wears a miner's headlamp to light his way. And, of course, there's a party afterwards when everybody relaxes over wine and cheese, and joins in the music to the accompaniment of a couple of the ski instructors' instruments.

Evenings offer plenty of activity, too. The area abounds in superb gourmet restaurants the likes of which are not usually found outside of Manhattan. And nowhere else is the charm of the New England countryside better exemplified than where quaint villages contrast with rugged wilderness in the heart of Vermont's Green Mountains, where there's all the skiing you want, and more.

Beneath a backdrop of cascading Alpine trails, cross-country skiers stretch toward the woods at Stratton's new Ski Touring Center.

F is for FUN

Which brings us all, eventually, to Purgatory

F is for fun which brings us to Purgatory where skiing is at its best in southwest Colorado. Purgatory Ski Resort is in the best of two lands—the sun warmed southwest and the snow-blanketed Colorado mountains. The average annual snowfall is 300 inches (over 450 inches fell last season), yet the sun persists in warming the slopes. You'll enjoy skiing here so much, you'll think you're committing a sin; maybe that's why they named this area *Purgatory!*

The spectacular peaks of the San Juan National Forest surround Purgatory with breathtaking scenery and you'll find genuine mountain friendliness.

There's room to move at Purgatory. Nearly 40 trails and slopes are spread over 400 acres of beautifully groomed terrain. Experts are challenged with runs like Hades, Pandemonium and an exciting new trail called "Styx." Intermediate skiers have more than 50 percent of the mountain to enjoy on an endless variety of long, ego-boosting trails. Beginners will find learning easy on miles of gentle terrain. All this is served by three double chairlifts, a poma and a beginner's rope tow.

Six condominium complexes with fireplaces and kitchens and a deluxe 50-room lodge with two lounges and a restaurant are all within walking distance of the lifts. The newly expanded Powderhouse at 10,300 feet allows skiers to spend the whole day on the mountain. The 50-instructor ski school, the sports shop, rental shop, Day Lodge, Purgy's Pub, Asgard restaurant and bar, nursery and drug and package liquor store provide service and convenience for skiers.

The new resort, just 10 miles from Purgatory, is Tamarron. A classic hotel-condominium resort, Tamarron offers indoor tennis, swimming, an exercise room, masseur, massuese, saunas and steam rooms, a whirlpool, game rooms and more. There's nightly entertainment in three unique cocktail lounges, along with gourmet dining in the Le Canyon and casual dining in the San Juan Club.

Nearly 30 hotels and motels in Durango, 25 miles south, offer package plans for every pocketbook. There's always room for skiers in Durango. The old west town comes alive at night with dining, dancing and drinking at the many fine restaurants and night spots.

Purgatory is just 235 miles from Albuquerque, 430 miles from Phoenix, 360 miles from Denver and 157 miles from Grand Junction. There are no mountain passes from the south and west; stunning scenery from the north and east.

Frontier Airlines serves Durango from Denver, Albuquerque and Phoenix daily. Continental Trailways serves Durango from all major cities.

PURGATORY OFFERS PERSONALIZED, PROFESSIONAL TECHNIQUE

Ski instruction has come a long way in recent years with modern systems such as the Graduated Length Method and the American Technique Method. Teaching a person to ski, however, cannot be completely standardized, according to

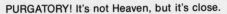

PURGATORY! It's not Heaven, but it's close.

Deep indigo skies, the Southwest's brilliant sun and deep powder are the perfect combination at Purgatory.

strenuous. Fritz suggests that skiers be aware of altitude changes when they come skiing and that they be in shape to compensate for the thinner air found at high altitudes.

The Purgatory Ski School offers a program for almost anyone—beginners to advanced with the Graduated Length Method and American Technique. Ladies Day and Children's Ski School are also available.

Class lessons are suggested for mid-week days because they are generally uncrowded, especially in the afternoons. On weekends, when class lessons are larger, private lessons are the best buy.

Parents who enroll their children in the special kids' ski school will be able to ski worry-free all day from 10 AM to 4 PM while the child has fun. Lunch is included in the full day child's lesson.

A common question by parents is, "Can you teach my 3-year-old to ski?"

Until a child is 6 years of age, his attention span is short and he would rather play than learn to ski. It is suggested that kids under 6 be placed in Purgatory's Nursery. There, he can play in the snow and learn to like it rather than be forced to ski. Children should never be forced to ski.

In addition to ski instruction, a lesson is an experience in which you meet people and share the experience of skiing.

PURGATORY AND CRESTED BUTTE OFFER JOINT SKI PACKAGE

Purgatory and Crested Butte Ski Resorts offer a special, week-long, joint ski package. The package includes 3 days of skiing at each area and 7 nights of lodging.

Frontier Airlines will fly skiers on this package to Durango (gateway to Purgatory) from Denver. After 3 days at Purgatory, ski-weekers drive a skierized rental car to Gunnison for completion of the package at Crested Butte and then return to Denver on Frontier

Lodging for the package includes 3 nights at the new $30 million Tamarron Resort, 8 miles south of Purgatory, and 4 nights at the luxurious Village Center Condominiums at Crested Butte.

The package, which ranges from $186 for double occupancy to $126.50 for quad occupancy, is designed for skiers who want a different and varied Colorado skiing experience.

Crested Butte's big, friendly mountain has 31 trails which are served by five double chairlifts, one cabin chair and a "T" bar. The old mining town and the many services of the new resort provide a delightful contrast.

The Village Center Condominiums are right at the base of the mountain at Crested Butte and are within walking distance of the lifts, shops, restaurants and night spots. All units have full kitchens and guests may take advantage of the health spa.

Both resorts are located less than 45 minutes from the Durango and Gunnison airports. Ground transportation to the resorts from the airports is available at nominal cost and transportation is provided free of charge between Tamarron and Purgatory.

Skiers should contact their local travel agent ot Tamarron P.O. Box 3131, Durango, Colorado 81301—(303) 247-8801, for reservations.

Purgatory's Ski School Director, Fritz Tatzer.

"Skiers are individuals with different physical and learning abilities," Tatzer explained. "A professional instructor is trained to recognize such factors as balance, coordination, physical condition and then teach accordingly, using a variety of techniques."

Emphasis is placed not only on learning to ski but also on learning how to choose the right equipment for the individual and tips on conditioning.

"I'm frequently asked, 'What is the best size ski to learn on?" Tatzer said. "Again, it depends on the individual. A man who is 6 feet 3 inches should use longer skis to learn on than a lady who is 5 feet 2 inches. A common error made with the GLM technique is to suggest that everyone use 150cm skis for their first lessons."

"All skiers should be in good shape," says Tatzer. He suggests a varied menu of exercises and recreational activities. Running, jumprope, tennis and weight lifting are a few exercises he suggests. Exercising must be fun and not overly

G is for GLEN ELLEN, VERMONT

in the author's back yard...

G IS FOR GLEN ELLEN

G is for the great skiing on the summit of Glen Ellen in the Green Mountains of Vermont. Glen Ellen is my back yard. I built a chalet south of its novice area, choosing the location because the land at neighboring Sugarbush is so ridiculously overpriced. Three major ski resorts follow each other across the same spine of this section of the Green Mountains, beginning with Sugarbush at Lincoln Peak, then, Glen Ellen, 500 feet taller, and ending with the lowest elevation of the three, Mad River Glen. The Long Trail, known further south as the Appalachian Trail, cuts a neat swath over that ridge permitting us to walk over the three peaks during the back-packing season. Because of its higher elevation, Glen Ellen provides summit skiing long after Sugarbush and Mad River Glen have turned to mud. Many skiers continue to hike to the top after the lifts have shut down for the season. Marge and I usually take our "last run" on Glen Ellen's FIS slope well into the month of May. It is about a 2½-hour climb to the peak, but, once you get there, you can enjoy several runs on the FIS, as it is only about a 45-minute climb from the point where it flattens out.

Expert skiers at Glen Ellen will like the FIS, which is a lot like Stein's Run at Sugarbush, replete with giant moguls but it hasn't been cut on a bias. And it is wide. Exceptionally wide, for an eastern trail. On the left, looking up is the challenging Scotch Mist, directly under the chairlift. One straight narrow ribbon of bone jarring moguls that never allow you to enjoy a rhythmic run because they follow no logical pattern. Too many turkeys, skiing a trail on which they don't belong, have cut traverse ridges and have scraped off most of the snow from the downhill face of the bumps with their wedge defenses. If you can jump into the Mist after a heavy snowfall, you will have a fantastic run. Oh, yes, I forgot to mention: the trail is split up the middle with a steel girded lift tower every 50 feet. Better sharpen your edges.

The view from the summit of Glen Ellen is most magnificent on a clear day. Lake Champlain hems her northwest side, which accounts for all the powder that is dumped onto this sleeper of a mountain every time a cumulus thunderhead rolls in from the west. Glen Ellen really is a "sleeper." It has been overshadowed for too many years by its neighboring resorts. Many skiers don't even realize that its summit is a lot higher and the powder stays a lot longer.

One of the reasons that Glen Ellen is snubbed by better skiers has to do with the design of its trails. For the most part it is novice-intermediate oriented, and that kind of a ski area will never draw advanced skiers, despite the challenge of its Scotch Mist, FIS and mogul studded High Road. Glen Ellen has a vertical drop that tops Sugarbush. Many skiers don't realize that it is as steep as Taos! Harvey Clifford should take a good look at how Ernie Blake has designed his trails if he is interested in creating as magnificent a ski area as Blake's Shangri-la. The fact of the matter is that, with the majority of skiers, the weekend ski trip might well be called an ego trip, for reasons mentioned elsewhere in this book. For John to tell the boys back at the office that he skied Glen Ellen this past weekend would be like telling them that he took a pony ride. He would much rather say that he has been to some area like Paradise Peak, where the trails are steep and the broads are wall to wall. The truth is that John probably spent half the day in the bar and went to bed with a Penthouse propped below his navel. But the bar and the magazine stand were at Paradise Peak!

When Glen Ellen was in financial trouble, I spoke with Damon Gadd, principal stockholder of the Sugarbush Corporation. "Why don't you buy it, Damon? With a tram strung from peak to peak, you could create the biggest single ski complex in the East, and offer a reciprocal pass, like at Aspen." Damon just smiled and said, "Maybe, Frank, if I was younger. . . ." He has about had it with the ski business and plans to phase out and spend more time with his family. Too bad. For you and me. And, for Glen Ellen, because only big money can pull it out of the red. Money that will cut chutes from the peak that will rival Stowe's Starr, Goat or National; money that will take that terrible waste of a building, once destined to provide hotel-type lodging a

Glen Ellen is one of the highest ski area peaks in Vermont, with a vertical drop of over 2,600 feet. Here, the author shoots a wheelie into the heavily moguled FIS run after a fresh powder drop.

stone's throw from Glen Ellen base lodge, and complete it; money that will develop slopeside condominium lodging and create a shopping mall close to the base lodge. I don't know if the new owner, Harvey Clifford, has that kind of bread. My guess is that his recent purchase of the mammoth mountain cleaned his pockets. That means opening the potential to heavy investors. Investors are usually not too quick to buy a piece of any business that has just gone bankrupt, but if enough speculators can be herded by a smart marketing man, Glen Ellen has the potential of becoming a giant of the industry. If that ever happens, they might even get around to paving the ungravelled mud roads through their village, where some 19 homeowners including Marge and I get bogged down every mud season.

Another mistake has been the marketing office's traditional touting of the mountain as "a family area." No area can survive if it appeals only to a group that must necessarily watch its budget. The spenders are the singles and the couples, and they will spend big if you wave the right carrot in their faces. Every successful ski area has made its mark by the power of *the promise:* the promise of wide exciting terrain; the promise of a dynamic effective ski school; the promise of convenience, comfort and luxury service; the promise of friendliness and (admit it) sexual fulfillment or, at least, arousal; and, especially important, the promise of safety.

One service that Glen Ellen does provide is unique but should be required at every ski resort. They have doctors *in residence,* who will not only X-ray your injury moments after you have been victimized (the Glen Ellen ski patrol is among the top squads in the country), but they will also cast injured limbs right on the spot! One of the doctors has an assistant who is so incredibly beautiful you will forget completely about your injury. Until you find out that she is his wife. Don't let her take your pulse; it is guaranteed to be higher than normal.

Inside that twin trailer that is set up next to the base lodge is the brilliant Carl Ettlinger, the world's foremost authority and analyst of bindings and lower extremity equipment related injuries. He is conducting a survey at Glen Ellen that has been forceful enough to influence the various designs of our release mechanisms, as his knowledge is highly respected in the manufacturer's end of our business. I know of at least one well-known binding manufacturer that has had to recall their recent switch to a *plate binding* design because Carl pointed out a few bugs. SKIER'S DIGEST holds a great deal of respect for Carl Ettlinger. He has dedicated himself to this important project largely at his own expense, and he really does his homework. His presence at Glen Ellen is not only an asset for the area; it is a gratuity for us all.

Glen Ellen has had a variety of ski schools, most notable of which was that of Neil Robinson, who had the charisma of Stein Eriksen and the dynamic drive of a top sergeant. You would believe that his aggressive style of skiing was ultra-masculine, until you got to see his beautiful blonde wife "Zip" follow him down some of the more challenging runs. Her movements seemed the same, but she made it, somehow, sexy. They were a great team, an asset to the mountain and the sport. Neil's precise, militant ski school was highly respected throughout the industry, and the huge mountain began its career on a good strong note. But the resort on its south flank, with the handsome blonde Nor-

Frank Covino blasts through a cornice on the FIS.

wegian ski school director, had too great a reputation with which to compete. It is still not unusual for the lift lines at Sugarbush to be a quarter of a mile long, while empty chairs rise to the summit of Glen Ellen, just 5 minutes away. When Zip and Neil split to enter another business near Pico Peak, Glen Ellen started sliding downhill. It hit rock bottom a few years ago, was sold, went bankrupt and was sold again. They had a great mountain to offer, but no one was coming. Except a few "families"—who brought their lunches in brown paper bags; who borrowed their antique ski equipment; who dressed in Army fatigues and rolled their hockey socks outside their rocker bottomed ski boots. Together, they came, like poverty stricken immigrants, to the "family area." They didn't spend much. And Glen Ellen nose-dived.

There is new hope. Harvey Clifford is an enterprising man whose business head is as sharp as his proficient skiing history. His prior position at Stratton was a great influence in the successful development of that increasingly affluent area. Before that, he helped Mount Snow rise to the level of profitable enterprise.

Clifford was a 1948 Olympic contender and coach of the Canadian team. His new ski school director is Rich Messer, whose personality is as dynamic as his skiing. P.S.I.A. oriented, Rich will stick to the American Teaching Method at Glen Ellen, offering a special *intensive* ski week that includes morning and afternoon lessons plus vital clinics on equipment and technique. Messer's appointment is a step in the right direction for Glen Ellen, destined to become one of the Northeast's finest ski areas.

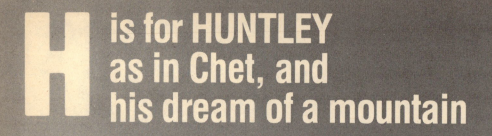

H is for HUNTLEY as in Chet, and his dream of a mountain

Big Sky, Montana

H is for Huntley as in Chet, and his dream of a mountain.

It's a pity that the late newscaster is not around to see what a fine job Don Kast is doing with the Big Sky Ski School. The accompanying photo of Don doesn't tell you much about the mountain, but Don's perfect *angulation* tells you much about the man. Here is the substance of an interview with this expert skiing stylist.

BIG SKY: OBTAINING YOUR WINGS IN PARALLEL

"Skiing was intended to be easy, and the easier it is, the more fun it will be." Such is the initial lesson conveyed by Big Sky Ski School Director, Don Kast. When you come to Ski The Sky, Kast will be the first to note when "you work much too hard on your turns," as this is your greatest obstacle in learning to parallel. For a skier to go through his turns at Big Sky, Montana, is the thrill of being on top of the world, with 11,166-foot Lone Mountain in the background, and out in front, the marvelous vista of the valley floor and the Spanish Peaks Primitive Area. From the first run down alone, which Big Sky locals term the "solo flight," it's a simple step to "obtaining your wings in parallel."

Don Kast pursues his two favorite interests in Big Sky's mountains and meadows. During the winter it's smooth skiing and the study of this achievement, and during the summer it's trout fishing on the near by Gallatin River. Both interests reflect patience as the key element to success.

Kast's perspective of skiing emphasizes motion and ease: "Most skiers get too anxious during the turn and won't wait for the ski to come around. As a result, they make sudden, jerky motions which upset their rhythm and make turning harder than it should be," he explains. "In the turn, the skier should exert gentle, yet firm pressure on the turning ski and have patience for it to turn around."

Kast rejects the method of constant edging as one which requires too much exertion.

"We went too far into the edging thing in the past. Now the thrust in instruction is getting these same people to ride a flatter ski."

He sees smoother skiing derived from a combination of skidding and edging.

"We think about carving only in the final stage of the turn and then only the amount of edge needed to turn smoothly and firmly."

Turning an edged ski demands twice the effort and therefore detracts from the enjoyment of smooth skiing.

"That's why the last couple of runs of the day usually are your best—you're generally tired and can't use the edges that much. You release the edges and ski better.

"You should feel your skis and the snow with the whole bottom of the foot rather than just the edge," Kast con-

tinues. "You can ski much better when you feel where the pressure is on your entire foot."

Kast sees the largest drawback to effective ski instruction in the past has been a dogmatic approach, largely "the result of nationalism." The simpler the communication to the student the better, because the initial motion in skiing takes place in the mind, he says.

"Our main problem now is in terminology—using words and analogies which elicit certain thought patterns in the student. If the instructor is reaching the mind, then the body can function.

"The sport never really changes," Kast notes. "It has always been the relationship between the skier, the skis and the snow. Instruction simply is getting the best elements of this relationship across to the skier. The common denominator is getting the feel of the skis and the snow which involves using the terrain and the ski to the best advantage. By using the terrain properly in turns, the skier can ski with much less effort and muscle and skiing becomes less tiring."

He thinks that few skiers get the most from their equipment.

"Utilizing the ski is the key to good skiing. Ski companies have spent an awful lot of money on engineering for us to do otherwise."

Kast describes the elements of a good, effortless turn with his palms extended flat to indicate a pair of skis.

"In initiating the turn, eliminate the traverse by putting early pressure on the uphill, or outside ski. This prevents the tendency to stem. Flatten the skis, begin the edge change, and then put pressure forward on the skis to complete the turn.

"Flatten the ski in the early part of the turn and put leg drive into the latter stages," he concludes simply. [Ed: Notice also, how Kast's torso maintains a 90 degree relationship with the angle of the slope.]

The terrain at Big Sky provides both the parallel and the "solo" skier with a perfect opportunity to put Kast's words into motion. Andesite Mountain features steeper pitches and plenty of powder for the advanced and upper intermediate skier. This mountain is served by a double chair and offers plenty of moguls for practicing those turns. The gondola sends the intermediate and beginner skier up 1,500 feet of vertical for a more gentle workout on Lone Mountain's packed slopes. For the powder hound seeking to carve his name in untracked terrain, the triple chair climbs 800 vertical feet into the Lone Peak bowl area.

But all ski areas today offer the skier lifts, lodging and nightlife. If Don Kast makes obtaining your wings in parallel sound smooth and easy enough, it's time to set your bindings for the Big Sky, and in Kast's own perspective come ski "another average day at Paradise."

is for IDAHO

SUN VALLEY

I is for Idaho, and of course that means SUN VALLEY. Sun Valley has all the basic raw ingredients that automatically rank it with the world's best resorts: sun and snow and spectacular mountains. These indigenous attributes alone would seem to guarantee its premier reputation. But it's the thoughtful extras adorning the simple life that make Sun Valley and its resultant lifestyle, truly unique.

A Sun Valley guest is pampered and coddled even before he arrives. Gateway airports are smilingly staffed with members of the Ambassador team. These amiable charmers know everything about Sun Valley from the quickest (and cheapest) way to get there to the best time of day to ski Baldy's famous bowls.

Good looking, yes. Good skiers, yes. But this elite fleet is chosen for their loving knowledge of Sun Valley. Not only do Ambassadors meet, greet and help with Sun Valley arrivals at airports, heavy check-ins at Sun Valley hotels, but they are strategically stationed on the mountain to acquaint, assist and guide Sun Valley skiers. In constant radio contact with the Mountain Manager, they have instant reports on changing conditions—like a closed run opening. They can do anything for you from cheerfully adjusting a safety binding to finding the best way out of the maze of runs that grid Baldy.

An eleven-man, one-woman crew mans the 22-machine grooming fleet. This armada is the world's most awesome array of Pisten-Bullies, Thiokols, Snow-Cats, etc., and their bump-busting accessories: mogul cutters, harrows, compacters, rollers and powder makers, to name a few of the attack implements that coax, cajole, flatten and mash, to make new snow out of old, to reclaim a wrecked run or discipline a new fall of snow. On duty 24 hours a day, a small crew handles emergency repairs during daylight skiing hours; a big crew works shifts from 4:00 PM to Midnight, and Midnight to 8:00 AM on major maintenance, like re-working an entire 2-mile run.

All runs, even "Exhibition's" 800 quite vertical feet can be groomed; however, "Exhibition's" belovedly furrowed brow is usually left intentionally intact to please the hot dogging fast crowd and the true expert.

A Courtesy Patrolman may kindly advise a too-speedy skier terrorizing an intermediate run, to head for "Exhibition." This 15-man Courtesy Patrol is the muscle behind the Ambassadors' smiles, policing the mountain and stopping anyone skiing too fast, out of control, or dangerously.

Still another group, a 20-man Trail Crew, hand grooms—they're the good old fashioned shovel brigade. They also troubleshoot any emergencies. If a Sun Valley skier is really in trouble, there's always a reliable ski patrolman within visual or radio contact.

Ski racing is more popular than ever and Sun Valley pleases more ski racers than most resorts. Besides weekly ski school races on Dollar/Elkhorn and Baldy, Wednesday NASTAR races on Baldy, and Friday NASTARs on Elkhorn, a dozen experienced race experts mastermind an average of three special races per week; everything from the Kennedy clan's slalom to a serious downhill for fast moving airlines employees.

This year snowmaking climbs to a new high, less than a thousand vertical feet of Baldy's auspicious 9,150-foot summit. Winter now begins at Thanksgiving. The snow-making system now augments natural snowfall to cover one of Baldy's favorite runs, "Flying Squirrel." The snowmaker covers about 60 acres or 2,300 vertical feet. It even turns out more consistent white stuff than Mother Nature. This man-made snow is more dense and more durable, hence only about a third as much is needed.

One of Sun Valley's newest triple seated chairlifts, the former "Plaza Lift," a high-speed link between Warm Springs and College Runs, has been re-named "Flying Squirrel Lift" in honor of its most popular destination. Its upper terminal gives choices of Lower College, Graduate, Roundhouse Lane and its numerous offshoots, but "Squirrel" with its inviting intermediate terrain, woos more

SOLITUDE awaits the skier who gets up early for the first run. At Sun Valley, that usually means putting the first tracks in a new powder blanket, or figure-eighting the tracks of the Ski Patrolman who got there first.

skiers in its direction. The fastest way to enjoy it is via "Flying Squirrel Lift" just below the Warm Springs II Lift.

In the Valley, Sun Valley and Elkhorn Villages are a delight to explore. The Sun Valley Boardwalk Shopping Mall is a shop-lined lane linking Sun Valley hotels. At Elkhorn, Sun Valley's sister village, shops and restaurants encircle its ice rink. Some stores open at Thanksgiving, all open in mid-December, their shops blossoming with the newest, latest and most unusual. Sun Valley's Konditorei serves up frothy Capuccino, live zither music and authentic Austrian pastries. A popcorn wagon shuttles the village exuding irresistible aromas and another wagon plies the Mall enticing appetites with sizzling crepes.

Food for thought may be a Literature or Creative Writing class; or one of the intensive Ceramics, Dance or Photography Workshops at Sun Valley's 4-year-old Center for the Arts and Humanities. The school is tucked into a bend of Trail Creek on a 7-acre site and attracts well-known painters, artists and teachers, some of whom don't even ski, but wish to teach at Sun Valley for the temporary escape it provides from the metropolitan merry-go-round. Most courses can be taken for college credit and the fulltime student enjoys an attractive daily discount on his lift ticket.

More extras that make Sun Valley guests feel loved: no lift lines, foam insulated and padded chairlift seats to keep you warm, optional lift robes and capes to keep you even warmer, helicopter skiing to whisk you to your own private mountain, interchangeable tickets between alpine and nordic ski schools for a change of pace, free buses with capacious ski racks, the original glass-enclosed warm water swim pools, a masseur and masseuse on call, three ice rinks—one indoor regulation size for serious skaters, another at Elkhorn complete with skating elk mascot for the not-so-serious, and, a nice place to ride out a snowstorm, a lighted and heated indoor horseback riding arena.

Christmas brings on a jovial Santa holding forth in the Mall, and the 36-year old beloved Christmas Eve tradition, the Torchlight Parade. Some 200 Sun Valley ski instructors with lighted torches slowly descend nearby Dollar Mountain. The glowing parade is followed by Santa's arrival at the Inn, and Christmas caroling warms the night. A gentle snow, another Sun Valley tradition, is apt to fall.

At night while sleigh bells toll departing Trail Creek diners, evergreen trees give out their soft glow of lights and old fashioned gas lighted lanterns illuminate pathways throughout the village. Sun Valley employees remember last year's guests, smile spontaneously and welcome visitors to their very own special home, Sun Valley, the resort with something extra.

LIMELIGHT—NEW EXHIBITION RUN

By RAINER KOLB as told to SUZI GILLIS

It's 4,000 feet long, 300 feet wide and drops 1,800 self-conscious feet. An expert can make it look like poetry, and an intermediate shouldn't even try. It is a deceptively simple, straight-forward looking run, merely following the line of chairlift towers up most of Baldy's Warm Springs II lift. However, it flexes its considerable muscle in a sea of bumps,

Diversification of skiing Sun Valley is illustrated by "Chief" Jack Rabbit Johannsen shown here at the age of 100 touring one of Sun Valley's three cross-country touring courses free to all Nordic skiers. This oldest skier in the world is one of many senior citizens who find resort ideal for touring.

walled by trees and interrupted by towers. It is the Pied Piper, little David to many a Goliath, and sings a song, both swan and siren. It is Limelight—a Sun Valley status symbol. But many a skier can't take its glare.

It can be a tough run but not so tough as some skiers seem to make it. It becomes unmanageable only to skiers who can't handle its publicity. Limelight unfurls under a long, lonesome span of the lift and the chair has a thousand eyes—560 pairs of eyes to be exact, all waiting for the show to go on. By the time a skier can handle this kind of pressure, we say he can handle any run, anywhere.

Limelight began right under everyone's nose. In 1965 it was only a series of linked clearings under the new lift luring an intrepid few. In 1967 it was widened to better than bobsled width and immediately attracted skiers like lemmings to the sea. Its reputation rose in 1968 when Jean-Claude Killy called it his "favorite chute." By 1970 the run was widened to its average width now of 300 feet and with instant fame, it became the prestige run—Baldy's new "Exhibition." Many a Sun Valley skier's goal is negotiating its 1,800 vertical feet.

When you reach the top of Baldy aboard Warm Springs II lift, Limelight races over the bank your chair just ascended. It hurtles its way off Baldy like an express train taking the shortest line between two points. And that's fall line skiing. Its upper *steilhang* charges downhill with an average pitch of 57 degrees. If a skier is not quite up to the rigors of its upper reaches, a sneaky cattrack via soothing

Left—The incredible LIMELIGHT. (Photo by Bank Wright.) Above—Ski racing takes a new turn toward the beginner in the Sun Valley Ski School. Now beginners as well as intermediates and advanced skiers are finding their way around slalom poles after four days in the school. Youngsters at four and oldsters over 70, race on courses either on Dollar or Baldy mountains depending upon ability. Winning racers receive awards during a festive party which concludes each ski school week.

College Run, circumvents it. College may be a tranquilizing approach but the skier is soon catapulted into the spotlight, having bypassed only about one-tenth of Limelight's exposure.

From the crossroad of the cattrack, an abyss of bumps now ripples away with a pitch of 40 degrees and a width of 350 needed feet. A 100-year-old forest guards its sides. Warm Springs lift is heavy with upcoming skiers, and it is so quiet you can hear a snowflake drop. Now you can feel some of Limelight's stare.

An expert can dance down the Limelight. And when he does a cheer may rise from the onlooking lift. However, an even bigger hurrah can follow a skier's disappearance in a puff of snow. Everybody enjoys Limelight in one way or another.

Limelight is more than just a show-off spot for cheap thrills however. It is genuinely lovable in lots of ways. It now rolls off kindly sustaining its 40 degree slope, and only the surprise of an intersecting cattrack upsets this consistency.

There's always a nice offbeat rhythm to Limelight. If you can forget you're on display and get in the groove, you'll enjoy it. The run is built right for good skiing. Because it tempts only the best skiers, who seem to favor a longer ski, 190-205 cm, the bumps are rounder, more friendly. And though the run is seldom groomed, it doesn't develop the electric moguls of Baldy's eastern facing counterpart, Exhibition.

This north facing slope is seldom touched by the sun and the snow that swaths Limelight maintains its plush long after the skies blaze blue again. In late winter afternoons the sun will smile briefly, gilding skiers with light, and backlight the showers of powder in their wake. When a foot or more new snow powders this run, skiers slow to a ballet, spinning off in bigger, wider swoops. Deep snow relaxes some of Limelight's urgency and muffles its demands. Fresh snow attracts skiers to Limelight like fingerprints to fresh paint.

Baldy's north face is dense with trees and Limelight was carved from the thick of this forest. This forest lines the length of the run and makes it a favored trip when the lights are out during a snowstorm. Tall pines and fir (some were seedlings when America was born), shelter the run from any wind and aid in defining contours in flat light. And if you plan on meeting a friend, Limelight is one of the few places you can't be missed on a big mountain like Baldy.

After the illumination of center stage, Limelight finally sweeps aside into Middle Warm Springs run. Here at last the skier escapes the chairlift gallery and dissolves into grateful anonymity, glad to share gentle Warm Springs with experts, intermediates and even a novice or two. The skier can continue to enjoy this run to the lower Warm Springs flats or slice across it via a strategic cattrack to the delicious isolation of lower Greyhawk, bottom half of Sun Valley's World Cup run.

Whether you want to waltz or boogie, Limelight demands a skier exercise knife-edge control, execute deadly fall line turns, and perhaps most of all—maintain a lot of cool.

J is for JACKSON HOLE, Wyoming

Ski School Director Pepi Stiegler

IN THE SHADOW OF THE TETONS

by Harry Baxter

Sooner or later, every skier has to try Jackson Hole. For the past 10 years, the best skiers in America have been skiing this monster of the Tetons. Jackson Hole is best known for its deep dry powder, breathtaking bowls, challenging chutes and wide slopes. Deep powder is the stuff skiers spend summers dreaming about and go searching for in winter. It is no myth that Jackson Hole has some of the finest powder found anywhere in the world. The moisture-laden weather fronts that sweep across the dry, temperate plains have nothing to stop them until they run into the Rockies. The sudden climb to over 14,000 feet cools the moisture to the point where it's ready to turn to snow. Since the Rockies are in the temperate zone, the critical temperature is most likely reached at night, which explains the cycles of overnight snowfalls and sunny days. One of the most welcomed qualities of Jackson Hole powder is the absence of wind both during the storm and in the days that follow.

Your first run down Jackson Hole after a good snow fall may not seem much different than at any other great Rocky Mountain Resort, but what makes Jackson Hole *so* different is the fact that you can cut new tracks all day. At the others, you're lucky if by the second run you're not following someone else's path.

Jackson Hole's annual snowfall is nearly 500 inches, and when the snowfall becomes too deep or too tough to handle, slope maintenance crews groom it into a smooth packed condition that miraculously remains more powder than packed.

Jackson Hole is not a preserve for the expert skier. There is much to offer the beginner and intermediate as well. If you're a beginning powder buff, there is none better. This massive mountain can offer an unlimited variety of skiing, and every skier can find the terrain that best matches his or her ability.

The area itself is composed of two mountains. Rendezvous, which stands 10,450 feet above sea level with the greatest vertical of any ski mountain in the country with 4,139 vertical feet and Apres Vous, which has a top elevation of 8,450 feet with a greater vertical than most of America's major resorts. The two mountains are connected by the newly-opened Casper Bowl with its own triple chairlift and ten new runs and trails for the intermediate skier. Casper Bowl did more than just add additional uphill facilities and ski terrain, it connected Giant Rendezvous Mountain and Apres Vous Mountain with a network of cross trails.

Jackson Hole skiers are served by an aerial tram that takes 63 passengers over 2.4 miles to the top of Rendezvous Mountain in just 12 minutes and five chairlifts that allow you to ski across 3,200 acres.

Jackson Hole is located in the northwestern corner of

J IS FOR JACKSON HOLE

Wyoming and extends into the interior of Grand Teton National Park and is at the Gateway to Yellowstone National Park. The overwhelming beauty of the towering granite peaks, the famous Snake River cutting through the valley floor, and the many lakes, both large and small, are what make Jackson Hole perhaps the most desirable and definitely the most beautiful resort in the country.

At the base of Rendezvous and Apres Vous Mountain lies Teton Village, an all-inclusive resort village featuring numerous lodges, condominiums, restaurants, cocktail lounges, and shops. Teton Village is a complete winter and summer resort with all its facilities within walking distance to the ski lifts on both mountains. During the summer months, it's the home of the Grand Teton Music Festival with its distinguished performers, base for scenic and wild water float trips on the Snake River, pack trips, rock climbing and aerial tram rides to the summit of Rendezvous Mountain, an outdoorsman's paradise, and a complete convention center. During the winter months the village condominiums, lodges and hotels are filled with skiers. For those seeking something out of the ordinary, they may choose from the snowcat tours into Yellowstone Park's untracked winter wonderland, horse-drawn sled trips to the wintering home of the world's largest elk herd (8,000-10,000), swimming in the mineral hot springs, or ski touring

It takes a fair amount of courage to ski Jackson's *Rendezvous*.

on the frozen lakes and forest lands in the mountain valley.

The Jackson Hole Airport is served by Frontier Airlines from Denver, Salt Lake City, and Billings. Skiers and summer visitors also fly into Idaho Falls and bus or drive the 1½ hours to Teton Village. Large groups often utilize the Idaho Fall's Gateway serviced by the much larger Western Airlines and Hughes Airwest equipment and connect with the Star Valley Jackson Stage Bus Company. The round trip fare from the Idaho Falls International Airport to Teton Village and return is only $10 per person for seven or more people. Rental cars are also available at all the Gateways and are used by both skiers and summer tourists. Frontier's schedule into Jackson Hole features a *free* half-day of skiing and is designed to arrive in Jackson at about noon, giving the skiers half a day to ski on the day of arrival.

Jackson Hole has initiated a long list of Customer Service programs for the skiers. A special welcome party to greet all the new skiers on Sunday evening is held weekly. Jackson Hole's Ski Hosts are on the mountain daily to ski with and assist guests in choosing the ski terrains that best match their ability. They also provide special activities both on and off the mountain for the guests. Ice skating and broomball is offered as well as ski touring. Gordon Lipe and his staff of experts will check your ski bindings free. When the lights go on in the evening, it can be gourmet dining or entertainment in Teton Village or a short drive into the old Cowboy Town of Jackson for a night at the Cowboy Bar. The town of Jackson is truly a western town with saloons, boardwalks, and rodeos as well as fine restaurants, shops, art galleries, and you will be pleased by how friendly and courteously you will be treated.

In 1965, Pepi Stiegler, an accomplished World Class racer and Olympic Gold Medalist became the director of the Jackson Hole Ski School. Pepi was born in 1937 in Lienz, Austria and began skiing at the early age of 6. At the age of 14, he was already competing in alpine ski races with success. Selected to the Austrian National Team in 1957, he went on to win the Blauherd Downhill in Zermatt in 1957, the Coup Emel Allais in Megeve in 1958, the Lauberhorn Combined in 1960. At the Squaw Valley Olympics, Pepi won a silver medal in the Giant Slalom, and in 1961 he won four of Europe's most important slaloms including the Austrian Championships. Pepi continued his winning way, finally winning a gold medal in the 1964 Olympics.

After the Olympics, Pepi accepted the position with the Austrian Ski Federation as men's Alpine Coach for one year. The following season Pepi became the Ski School Director at Jackson Hole in Wyoming, and that's where he has spent the past 10 years. From his knowledge and background of racing and teaching, Pepi has chosen each of his instructors personally, and he oversees each class.

During this 10-year period Pepi has established Jackson Hole as a training center for young racers. Racing camps are conducted during the early winter and spring for both adults and juniors. Racing clinics are held throughout the winter season.

It was only natural that Pepi would develop a NASTAR program at Jackson Hole with twice-weekly races.

This past December at the Rocky Mountain Regional Pacesetting trials at Vail, Colorado, Pepi Stiegler at 38 years old became the Nation's Number One Pacesetter by earning a zero handicap for the seventh year in a row. To establish himself as the Nation's Fastest NASTAR Pacesetter, he had to beat out such greats as Hank Kashiwa, World Professional Ski Racing Champion of 1974/75 skiing for Steamboat, Colorado; the late Spider Sabich, former World Professional Ski Racing Champion; and many other top-ranking professionals topping out a field of 75 racers.

Zero is the best possible score and sets the standard against which all NASTAR participants will be compared when they race in this recreational program.

Under a joint program with Pepsi Cola and the Jackson Hole Ski Corporation, Pepi has produced an exciting new film entitled *Stiegler: The Style of a Champion*. This is a 14-minute film featuring the life and racing style of Olympic Gold Medalist Pepi Stiegler. It covers the fundamentals of modern day racing and is an essential tool for racers inter-

Knee deep powder is a common commodity at Jackson Hole. Find out for yourself with a visit!

SKIER'S DIGEST gives Pepi Stiegler our vote for the sport's *greatest* racer. He has shown the ideal combination of speed, endurance, and graceful style in every one of his contests. Pepi also has another characteristic that is very rare in sports' champions. He is friendly and humble.

ested in the finer points of the carved turn and the skating turn. The movie also deals with the pure joy of skiing and the beauty of Jackson Hole. A booklet by the same name and designed to give the movie greater depth has also been produced. It contains a sequence of drawings and graphs that make the movie a very valuable instructional tool.

The film is currently available, along with the booklet, by contacting the Jackson Hole Ski Corporation, or, the booklet may be purchased separately for $2.50 per copy. Whether it's racing, a lesson in deep powder skiing or GLM, the Jackson Hole Ski School has to be one of the best.

Pepi has donated one small part of the booklet which accompanies his film, *Stiegler: The Style of a Champion* to SKIER'S DIGEST for your perusal. Here is what Pepi had to say about the most important maneuver in giant slalom racing.

THE SKATING TURN

by Pepi Stiegler

If asked what were the most important thing in giant slalom racing, I would have to say the "skating step" that results in the "skating turn." It has been established that the most significant factor in acceleration is the pull of gravity. However, if you wish to beat the others, you will have to work harder and put your muscles to work. Acceleration by muscle force plays a significant part in succeeding in a race. It is a prerequisite that the racer be master over a perfect technique in order to use acceleration maneuvers. Strong accelerating maneuvers can cause disturbances to balance and the carving action of the skis. Then nothing is gained. Low friction sliding on the snow must never be sacrificed for futile acceleration attempts. Economy of motion, balance and good carving remain extremely desirable goals. The skating step leading to the accelerated skating turn is by far the most important part of giant slalom racing. It incorpo-

rates both gravity acceleration through extending the fall line phase and acceleration through muscle force—like a speed skater on ice.

The prerequisite is to carve a round and smooth arc. Only through extensive practice can the skier develop the exact timing necessary for an effective skating step. It must be done at the proper moment in the turn, toward the end of the turn, otherwise it will be without much effect. The "how to" for the skating step is as follows:

1—Ski with all the weight on the outside ski. (Inside ski glides over the snow just for maintaining balance.)

2—Outside knee and ankle must be flexed before extension occurs.

3—Ski must be well-edged (done by pointing knee inward in the sense of the turn) so that a firm platform exists when pushing off. Caution needs to be taken when snow is softly packed as platform may break away.

4—Movement of body while skating is forward and lateral. Body is being thrust forward; arms are assisting this movement. Weight is transferred from downhill ski to uphill ski. At this moment all the body weight must be committed to the new ski. Uphill ski is being turned by rolling the knee into the new turn's direction. Inside ski is brought by closely over the snow.

5—The initiation of the new turn is assisted by an anticipatory movement of the upper body. The shoulders turn toward the new direction prematurely, drawing the skis into the new turn once the weight is shifted to the new outside ski.

Recommendation

In order to become a master in the skating turn technique you must develop your skiing toward independent leg work by constantly changing weight from one ski to the other while initiating a turn. For practice it is good to ski on one ski, including skiing on the uphill edge of the uphill ski. You need to become secure and comfortable in carving on one ski.

K is for KILLINGTON, VERMONT

K is for Killington, Vermont, traditionally the first eastern ski resort to open in the fall and the last to close in the spring. From November to May, 6 months of the year, skiers find at Killington better skiing conditions on more diverse terrain than at any other eastern resort. Killington's long ski season enables the skier to test his "ski legs" early in the year in order to whet his skiing appetite for superior conditions in mid-winter and to enjoy the blue skies and warm days of spring skiing long past the time when skis are normally put away.

In fact, over the past 10 years Killington has averaged 180 days of continuous skiing annually. This means that a skier can plan weekends and ski holidays at Killington with the assurance that if there is skiing to be found anywhere in the East it will be at Killington. And to skiers who normally have only a limited number of weekends and vacation days to allot to skiing, Killington's dependability is a measure of security.

Once at the resort the skier will find among Killington's 50 trails and slopes terrain exactly suited to his skiing ability, be he novice, intermediate or expert, and so much mountain that in a given day the best of skiers can ski to his heart's content and never ski the same trail twice.

For the skier looking for a best-of-a-lifetime experience or for the person who knows he wants to become a skier, Killington is the ski resort with something for everyone and a lot more than many will ever be able to use.

Snow—Natural and Man-made

The mountains—Skye Peak, Killington Peak, Snowdon Mountain and Rams Head Mountain—are a formidable team of four peaks which form the complex called Killington in Vermont's Green Mountain chain. The highest of the peaks, 4,241-foot Killington Peak, towers above the range and is the hub around which many of the resort's attractions focus.

The four-mountain complex is located in such a way that it creates a mini-climate of its own. Nature is lavish here with snowfalls. At almost no other spot on the eastern seaboard is there so much snow between the end of October and the middle of May, averaging 300 inches annually.

At Killington, however, to ski or not to ski is a decision which is not left to the discretion of Mother Nature. The resort's asset of a naturally heavy snow yield is supported by the most extensive snowmaking system in the Northeast which literally guarantees skiing without a flake of natural snow.

Snowmaking, the supreme example of how man adapts the environment to his own needs, in this case recreational, is typical of Killington's ingenuity, resourcefulness and commitment to skiing. The snowmaking system coupled with the annual snowfall adds up to so many skiing days that the heartiest and most dedicated skier would be hard-pressed to pursue the sport for the length of time Killington is open every year.

Why should a resort like Killington, which is more fortunate than almost all other areas in the extraordinary amount of natural snow that falls every year, go to the trouble of pioneering in the development of snowmaking systems?

The answer is that where skiing is concerned, there is never too much of a good thing. Snowmaking means not only that the resort is able to offer the longest ski season, but that the best skiing conditions anywhere in the East will usually be found on Killington's snowmaking trails. A phenomenon of Killington is that regardless of how much natural snow Mother Nature sends this way, snowmaking machines are in constant use around the clock. Even during snowstorms visitors are amazed to see man-made snow mantling the trails.

Snowmaking assists the resort's operation in three major areas. First, it enables Killington to open early and continue operating longer so that more skiers can enjoy the sport for a greater period of time. Second, the base on snowmaking

A four-mountain complex, Killington receives more than its share of snow every year. The highest mountain, Killington Peak at the left with an elevation of 4,241 feet, towers above Snowdon Mountain in the middle and Rams Head Mountain to the right. The fourth, Skye Peak, nestles below Killington Peak on the far left. At the base of the mountains Snowshed Novice Slope offers beginning skiers one of the best teaching-learning slopes in the country. (Photo by Bob Perry)

Snowmaking at Killington covers 12 miles of novice, intermediate and expert trails of four mountain areas serviced by 8 chairlifts. These trails are all interconnected and can be skied without a flake of natural snow.

trails is more substantial so that in the event of a warming trend those trails with man-made snow have a better chance of withstanding inclement conditions and remain skiable. Third, snowmaking is an integral part of trail grooming operations. Snow cover on trails and slopes must continually be replenished to maintain trails in the best possible condition at all times.

Yesterday fewer skiers, using wooden or early-model plastic skis, needed only natural snow to have a good season because they skied more slowly and with little fancy footwork.

Today ever-increasing numbers of skiers are on the slopes. The equipment they use and the speed at which they travel take a toll on the trails. Skiers chew away at snow cover because their performance is harder, tougher and more daring. Unlike yesterday's skiers, they won't take bad weather conditions sitting down. They search for the mountains that have been covered by snowmaking, and that is where they go for action.

But having snow, man-made or natural, on the ground is

This four passenger gondola tramway at Killington is the world's longest ski lift, running 3½ miles one way on its trip to the summit of Killington Peak.

only half the battle. The trick is to maintain it in good condition. With snow-cats, rollers, powder-makers and mogul-cutters, Killington's Skiing Service Department grooms the most popular slopes and trails 24 hours a day and less frequently used trails on a regular basis to insure that Killington's conditions are always the best to be found in the East.

The Inter-skiable Mountains

On Killington's four separate mountains are six skiing areas which are all interconnected. This means that a skier can begin skiing anywhere at Killington and still ski everywhere. Killington Peak, Skye Peak, Rams Head Mountain and Snowdon Mountain all have lifts and trails of their own which have been designed to dovetail together. From the skier's point of view, Killington's four mountains are inter-skiable and offer "something for everyone"—trails on any mountain to match any skiing ability.

The skier who spends a few minutes examining a trail map of the area will have no trouble setting the course he wants. Experts will find challenges to test their skills, and intermediates will have ample opportunity to practice newly acquired competence.

Most expert trails flow from Skye and Killington peaks to the Killington Base Lodge. The most popular is Cascade, a 1¼-mile trail. Catwalk, another expert trail, starts at the summit of Killington Peak, plunges down a steep, narrow chute, and curves as it drops to cross Goat Path and links up with Big Dipper and Downdraft. Both of these are expert trails which experience has shown are the places to find great powder—loose or packed. Downdraft and Big Dipper then run down the headwall that makes up the face of the Killington basin.

The trails on Snowdon Mountain are advanced intermediate and intermediate including upper Bunny Buster and the popular Chute. A delightful intermediate course is the Four-Mile Trail which runs along the ridge between Killington and Skye peaks and then drops down the southern face of Skye in a series of steps, twists and turns. After crossing Great Eastern Trail (novice), the Four-Mile Trail has some wide slopes with excellent pitches for intermediates to ski. It flattens for a while, barrels through two ski tunnels, and joins Great Eastern at the ski bridge that spans Roaring Brook Road. From there on it weaves in and out of Great Eastern until the two trails join on the final approach to the gondola base.

The desire to ski Great Eastern, a gentle 5-mile descent and the longest ski trail in the East, is a good excuse to take the Killington Gondola tramway to the top of Killington Peak where the trail begins and continues along the ridge of Skye Peak. The Killington Gondola, the world's longest ski lift, offers 3½ miles of snug transportation and spectacular views on the ascent to the summit.

The Killington Peak Restaurant at the top of Killington Peak is a delightful place to stop for lunch or a cup of hot chocolate, long enough, at least, to take in the nearly 360 degree view of five states and Canada afforded from the summit. Its reputation as one of the most dramatic panoramas in New England is well deserved.

Over on Rams Head Mountain long intermediate runs are the specialty on such trails as Timberline and Header. Interesting perspectives of the rest of the mountain complex can be viewed from the summit of Rams Head Mountain. This area, incidentally, is the only section of Killington which does not receive snowmaking coverage. The other three mountains, Snowdown Mountain, Killington Peak and Skye Peak because of snowmaking, comprise an inter-ski-able network among themselves even without a flake of natural snow.

Not to be overlooked for beginning skiers is Snowshed Novice Slope which sits literally in the lap of the four mountains and is generally acknowledged to be one of the best teaching-learning slopes in the country. Snowshed has a smooth, even pitch all the way and is serviced by three double chairs and snowmaking which insures that at all times novices have the best conditions for learning and practicing newly acquired skills. In fact, Snowshed Novice Slope is so versatile and friendly that skiers of all abilities often take warm-up runs on Snowshed before moving to more challenging parts of the mountain.

After ranging briefly on a trail map across the 37 miles of trails, 15 of which are covered by snowmaking, the skier is aware that at Killington "you can get there from here,"— that from any point on the mountain the skier can get to any other point through the interconnected network of 50 trails and 11 lifts—without removing his skis!

"Something for Everyone" Programs

The skier who comes to Killington will ski more and ski better thanks to the fact that skiing conditions and programs at Killington are constantly upgraded and innovated to assist the skier in his desire to perfect technique and have a good time. In fact, Killington's reputation in the ski industry as the ski resort "first with the most" is unsurpassed.

Practice makes perfect. To this end the Killington Ski School offers more than 10 specialized kinds of classes designed to meet specific requirements of skiers with particular abilities, experience and equipment. Such specialization with "something for everyone" allows Killington to place a skier in a class that operates precisely at his level.

The skier who skied last year but who has not skied since does not have to start all over again at Lesson One. There will be a special Advanced Accelerated class for him. The skier who learned with standard length skis years ago but who still cannot get his skis together before he is in the fall line will be enrolled in an Accelerated class that meets his specific needs.

What about the skier who is on that hard-to-cross plateau between intermediate and expert? Who whizzes down the intermediate Chute but who can only look wistfully at expert Skye Lark?

Killington has lessons for such skiers emphasizing confidence and control. The theory applied is that the skier can learn to ski well on any trail if he can ski well on one trail. In addition to expert instruction from the Killington Ski School, one of the largest in the country with nearly 100 instructors who are selected for their ability to teach, Killington offers assistance through videotape clinicing and facilities for ski tuning, two innovations which were pioneered at this resort.

Videotaping is a new approach to assist in better skiing used in many of Killington's Ski School programs. Students in any class may receive optional videotape analysis as part of their instruction, and in some programs such as the

Skiers at Killington who are enrolled in any of the resort's ski lesson programs may opt for the video tape clinic during the session.

Mountain Ski Week the application of video instruction is an integral feature of classes.

Skiers are recorded on videotape while actually maneuvering a run. The instructor takes the tape and moves down the mountain with his class to the Skiing Diagnostic Center located near the Killington Base lodge at the foot of Highline Racing Trail. Students file through the Center, on skis, and receive personal critiquing by their instructor as each demonstration comes on the screen. The instructor can freeze a shot or slow up a sequence to point out strengths and weaknesses. For the skier, one picture of himself in motion is worth a thousand words from the instructor.

Another innovative concept involves ski tuning. Many skiers ski better than they realize, but their skis conceal the truth. Surfaces on skis may have deteriorated so they fail to respond as they did when they were new. Killington's positive-performance ski tuning includes wet-belt sanding to make the bottoms flat and smooth, filling in holes and scratches, sharpening edges and final waxing. This service is included in the fee of some package plans but may be purchased by any skier. A feature of Killington's Accelerated Ski Method is a weekly ski tuning clinic where skiers may watch experts demonstrate the process of proper ski maintenance.

The accelerated ski method emphasizes the use of 3 foot skis in the first few lessons. As skiers become more proficient, they graduate through two more sizes until they are on skis which suit their height, weight and skiing ability. Here three Killington Ski School instructors demonstrate the three lengths of skis used in the Accelerated Ski Method.

Several Killington programs, including the highly successful Mountain Ski Week for intermediates and the Weekend Ski Clinic for expert skiers, depend on videotape feedback and ski tuning to assist the teaching-learning process. The Mountain Ski Week offers a rare learning experience to a skier who skis reasonably well but who wants to ski better, who likes the idea of a lesson but does not want to miss a minute on the trails, and, most important, who would be happy to ski with a small group of like-minded persons whose abilities match his own.

Mountain Ski Week classes meet for 3 hours of skiing Monday through Friday on upper mountain trails with intensive instruction based on the instructor's on-the-spot diagnosis of skiing faults and strengths. For many skiers the constant observation by a professional skier is enough to create the edge of self-discipline that prevents him from slipping back into bad habits.

The special Weekend Ski Clinic, supporting Killington's "something for everyone" emphasis, is open only to advanced skiers who can handle Killington's most challenging expert terrain. Skiers follow top instructors of Killington's Ski School on four non-stop runs down expert trails with videotape instruction during the second and fourth runs. The 2-hour lesson focuses for the first time on the super skier who in the past has been paid scant attention, if any, at resorts across the country.

And for beginners Killington pioneered the popular Graduated Length Method (GLM) of instruction and has refined it to today's Accelerated Ski Method. The technique emphasizes the use of short skis with gradual advancement to longer skis until eventually the skier is on equipment suited to his height, weight and ability. The Killington learn-to-ski promise states that small classes, special teachers, short skis and a perfect novice slope (Snowshed) will turn Monday's beginner into Friday's skier through the Accelerated Ski Method.

Killington's Accelerated Ski Method is a total skier concept. It is, in fact, virtually impossible for a student to sign up for a class, attend, leave and come again the next day without receiving extracurricular attention from the Ski School and various programs. And it is in this extra attention given to preparing the student psychologically through pre-school clinics and films, attention to his equipment which is all standardized and safety inspected through the rental shop, and attention to his social needs through fondue parties and other gatherings that makes the Accelerated program such a unique package.

Only at Killington can a skier order a complete learn-to-ski package—lifts, lesson and equipment—and attend a ski tuning clinic where emphasis is put on proper care and maintenance of equipment. The Killington skier receives the extra attention from instructors which virtually guarantees that he will learn to ski. Does he perhaps need wedges or cants for his boots? The instructor is trained to spot problems and will advise students accordingly. Is one student too advanced for a particular class or is another having extreme difficulty learning to ski? Students are moved to other instructors and other classes until they are in a situation where they feel "at home" and can make the most rapid progress.

In addition to "something for everyone" in the way of mountains, snow and ski lessons, the resort offers a staggering number of package plans in various combinations for any number of days up to 7. For instance, the Killington Lodging Bureau can help a family plan lodging, meals, lifts, lessons and equipment rental all at one time. Lodging may be in one of the resort's own condominium units with meals served at the Angus Tavern Restaurant, or reservations can be placed at one of the Killington community's 86 lodges and inns which offer variety from sophisticated contemporary facilities with pools and saunas to cozy "typical Vermont" rooms and country inns.

The choices for dining and entertainment around Killington are so numerous that the skier trying to cover all the mountain in one day or trying to ski all the days Killington is open would find the same challenge trying to hit all the restaurants and night spots in the area. This is not an entirely impossible assignment but certainly a long season's work—at least 6 months worth.

Killington Ski Resort is happy to extend the challenge to any skier to try all the trails and ski all the days and enjoy all the festivities that the mountain offers. The reward? One of the finest skiing opportunities with "something for everyone" any skier will ever find.

IMPROVING SKI SCHOOL SUCCESS THROUGH PSYCHOLOGICAL PREPARATION OF THE BEGINNING SKIER

Prepared in consultation with Leo Denis, Vice President, Skiing, Killington Ski Resort by Sara Widness

A person's ability to recognize and acknowledge the fact that he may be apprehensive or even downright afraid when confronting a new experience may make the difference between success and failure in pursuing that endeavor. When a person approaches skiing for the first time in his life he is, probably, experiencing a degree of anxiety which, unless circumvented or channeled, can and probably will interfere with learning to ski.

After years of testing and research in the Killington Ski School, the staff has concluded that probably all skiers or would-be-skiers, if they are honest with themselves, fear some aspect of skiing, be it getting on and off the chairlifts, falling, or even cold weather. Rather than shunting this seemingly negative set into the background and ignoring it, the Killington Ski School, working with a carefully designed program called the Accelerated Ski Method, forces the skier to acknowledge and define his fear, to understand that his apprehensions may be shared by fellow students, to learn to deal with and to overcome the variables and attitudes which may be fear-provoking.

Recognition of fear subsequently imposes a structure on ski lessons, an immediately reassuring framework that a group of strangers have in common at their first meeting. This consciousness also becomes a peg on which to hang a number of ski-related hats which might otherwise be overlooked and indeed cause danger and mishap if they were ignored.

This is not to say, however, that F-E-A-R is spelled out in bold letters and paraded in front of the skiers' noses. Instead it is treated lightly, comically and methodically in a manner designed to strengthen the skier's confidence in his ability to conquer the strange new world of skiing.

The Accelerated Ski Method which began at Killington as GLM (Graduated Length Method) has been expanded and refined to influence practically every aspect of a beginning skier's first experience on skis, from helping him to recognize fears in the first place, to finally overcoming them during that second or third run down Snowshed Novice slope when he has, at least, become a skier.

Beginning with the premise that skiing is fun and all steps leading to that maiden voyage down Snowshed should also be enjoyable, the Accelerated Ski Method's primary concern is to insure that the novice skier in the strange new world has to deal with as few variables as possible which might be fear-inducing or in the least confusing. The Accelerated method confronts directly three basic fears and constructs a skier support system around those fears.

Fear of the unknown, fear of failure and fear of injury have been defined through various testing devices which have

Beginners learn to ski under ideal conditions. Snowshed Novice Slope is gentle, broad and always carefully groomed to provide the best conditions for learning to ski. The Accelerated Ski Method emphasizes the use of short skis and gradual advancement to equipment which suits the ability of the skier.

from time to time been administered to Killington's skiers on a volunteer basis.

Imagine for a minute what some of the unknown elements of skiing might be. How do I know where to get equipment? How do I know what kind of equipment to rent? How do I put on my skis? How do I find my lesson meeting place? How do I get on the chairlift? What's at the top when I get up there? How can I ever begin to get back down that hill? How do I meet my friends or family for lunch? How do I get tickets?

Fears related to failure might be—What if I goof up trying to get on the chairlift and everyone laughs at me? What if I fall down and make a fool of myself? What if I'm so afraid I won't be able to ski down that hill and get left behind? What if I never learn how to turn like that guy over there? What if I have trouble getting my bindings on and have to ask for help while everyone else seems to be doing OK?

And, of course, the fear of injury is self-explanatory.

How does the Accelerated Ski Method help to overcome these dilemmas to insure that Killington has practically 100 percent positive success in teaching people to ski? By removing the necessity on the part of the student of having to make choices and decisions related to skiing and by making the Ski Week emotionally and physically supportive of the skier's initial desire to learn to ski. The Killington Ski School "graduates" thousands of new skiers every year.

A ski weeker arrives at the Ski Vacation Center on Sunday evening. He is skillfully guided through registration during which time he is questioned as to previous skiing experience, advised on class time, given tickets, assigned to a class and fitted with equipment, all in a painless, step-by-step procedure.

The following morning he attends a pre-lesson film clinic where short movies outline in detail exactly what the skier may expect the first time up the chairlift, the first time he stands on skis. The new skier sees people falling, laughing and picking themselves up out of the snow. He sees instructors talking and joking with their classes. He learns how to carry skis and how to adjust the bindings. He sees new skiers who are awkward and clumsy just the way he knows he will feel. And he sees skiers at the end of the week who look as if they've been skiing for years, but who have just begun a few days ago.

In addition to the film clinic, Killington's Ski Vacation Coordinator or instructors from the ski school talk about "special help" teachers if someone is having difficult time grasping the fundamentals of skiing. They find out where to go if they have questions during the week, who to ask for if they lose a ticket. And finally they are shown where to go for their first lesson. By the time the clinic is over, new skiers have actually experienced in mini-version a complete ski week, exactly what they'll be doing as soon as their first lesson begins.

Out on the hill students are asked to "ski off." This implies a short demonstration of their skiing proficiency so that students can be grouped homogeneously. Already the skier can begin to feel confident because he is no different from the rest of the group. Many fellow students look just as clumsy as he feels he looks.

From this point on the technology developed around the Accelerated Ski Method and the sensitivity, dedication and teaching skills of individual instructors take over. The short,

3-foot skis are all equipped with the safest binding-release systems on the market and prior to being rented have been carefully inspected by the Rental Shop. Because the equipment is uniform for all students, teachers do not have to worry about the performance of this, that or another kind of ski or binding. Students do not use poles in the early stages of instruction so hands are free for maintaining better balance.

Snowshed Novice Slope, a ¾-mile long hill graded to a gentle descent, receives more attention from snowmaking and trail grooming crews than any other part of the 50-trail complex at Killington. Here all beginning students test their wings under as near-perfect conditions as possible. The reputation of Snowshed as one of the finest teaching-learning hills in the country is undisputed, and beginning skiers are aware that utmost care has gone into preparing the hill to make learning to ski as effortless as possible.

The Killington Ski School is staffed with men and women who bring to their teaching assignments a desire to assist others to levels where they, too, can enjoy skiing. The fact that a person skis well does not immediately presume that he will be a teacher. Killington instructors are selected for their sensitivity, good humor, tact, and above all ability to teach; qualities which time and again are praised in letters from persons who have learned to ski at Killington. A primary concern of the teacher, working with a maximum class size of eight students, is that each person individually receives as much of his attention as possible.

If a person accelerates beyond his class or on the other hand is having more difficulty than other students, he will be moved to another class which better suits his ability level. For extreme cases "special help" instructors are ready to take the problem student under wing for extra instruction. Instructors are also alert to physical problems which may hamper progress. They will advise if skis should be canted or tuned to assist performance.

And after class, every day through the week, a full social program provides opportunity for classmates to mingle, commiserate and discuss their victories, and have fun. The Monday afternoon fondue party mixes future friends with mulled wine and cheese fondue. That evening ski tuning and equipment clinics introduce skiers to selection and maintenance of equipment. On Tuesday and Wednesday evenings ski films and feature-length movies provide diversion. And, finally, on Thursday students have a chance to demonstrate their new-found skills during the afternoon Ski Week Race. That evening at the Ski Week Party awards are presented to winners of the race. Live music and a festive atmosphere climax the Learn-to-Ski Week.

By this time most skiers have graduated from 3- to 4- to 5-foot skis and are probably ready for skis which suit their own height, weight and ability. Their instructor has taken them to the tops of other mountains and they've skied down novice and maybe even intermediate trails. They know Snowshed Base Lodge like the back of their hand, can point out the Rental Shop, Ski School Desk and Ski Vacation Center to new arrivals. They can probably discuss the relative merits of Yodeler and Idler trails and have their own preference. Through Killington's Accelerated Ski Method they wonder, if they even remember to ask, why they were ever afraid; because now, at the end of 5 days, they themselves are skiers.

L is for light, as in powder, as at SNOWBIRD, UTAH

L IS FOR LIGHT

L is for LIGHT, as in POWDER, and it's like flour in the Wasatch Range, Utah, where the Little Cottonwood Canyon looks up at one helluvva mountain called Snowbird. The two peaks that rise up like a woman resting on her back flank have some of the greatest powder skiing in the United States. Peruvian Gulch and Gad Valley, the two bowls that drop from Hidden Peak, provide that bottomless stuff for which you have been searching. Better bring a snorkel. And some courage. That first drop off the ridge will seem like a floating fall into space. Keep turning. And keep your tips up. Near avalanche grades off the lip will give you a thrill you will never forget, until they get more negotiable at timberline.

You would think that an area like Snowbird would be content with merely having some of the greatest ski conditions in the country. Not resting on those laurels, the corporation has installed one of the most luxurious, fastest and roomiest aerial trams in the entire world. The view alone, while riding up, is worth a visit to Snowbird. And don't turn your heels if you are an intermediate skier. There are several gentle routes down from the peak's tram station. While you are traversing to them though, at least take a peek over the ridge to prepare yourself for what you may be skiing someday in the future!

Snowbird is Corky Fowler territory. I personally think that Fowler is one of the greatest, most versatile skiers in the world. His book, *Ski Techniques,* a Petersen publication, should be in your library. Corky covers the gamut, from the basics via GLM to acrobatics and somersaults. He is a fine technician, and he has really got it all together.

Snowbird's tram is if the most modern uphill facility of any ski resort in the United States.

As if a celebrity like Corky is not enough, Snowbird also is Junior Bounos country. For at least two decades he has developed a reputation as powder snake. The PR office at Snowbird must have been lean on photos or we would show you Junior, usually buried up to his chin in the white stuff, churning his way down a headwall. I was able to get a short article from him through, which you should read before you buy that ticket to salt Lake City, no more than a pipe smoke away from this fantastic ski resort.

TEACHING POWDER SNOW

by Junior Bounos

Few areas in the U.S. are teaching or even promoting powder or off-trail skiing. Snowbird is one area that can promote powder skiing. We have the natural ski terrain for this type of skiing and our teachers have the background to ski and teach at all levels. Much of Snowbird's beauty can only be experienced by off-trail skiing.

"Powder snow"—two words which cause completely different reactions from skiers! For those who like powder and can ski it, "Powder snow" means their greatest thrills for the entire season, the feeling of floating without contact with a hard, noisy surface under your skis, the freedom of dashing down the mountain in any direction, seeking out all the hidden nooks, hollows and steep pitches that few would venture onto with hard pack conditions. For the powder skier the one day or one run makes the whole ski season worthwhile. For the non-powder skier the words, "powder snow" remind him of a long run with many bathtubs marking his changes of direction, goggles filled with snow, cold hands and skis that are difficult to put back on. It reminds him of the struggle to get untangled and back on his feet after a fall, of the tired and exasperated feeling from struggling. We have two different skiers, worlds apart.

In our modern skis of today, because of increased performance from engineering and design, we find three factors that aid us in powder snow skiing. These three factors are softer, more flexible skis, short, and with less bottom camber. If you can have a choice of skis for powder, those are the three factors to watch for.

If you can combine those three factors with the mounting of the bindings back behind chord length center 1 to 1½ inches, you are ready to tackle any powder. With any of today's equipment you can ski most of the powder offered at Snowbird. There are exceptions—heavy wet snow, wind-blown or crusted snow, which are difficult to ski. Then the best powder snow ski is a real advantage. Also a real powder snow nut will seek out the hidden places in which good powder might linger for a day or two longer after the storms have passed. After that, the same skier might spend a day or two skiing the chopped up snow or crud before he gives in to skiing packed snow. The average skier will ski only the cream of the powder the first few untracked runs before it is cut by skiers or changed by wind or sun.

The greatest boon in clothing for powder snow is the advent of warm-up pants. We can again be in style with baggy pants. Some of the very best powder snow skiing will be during the storms or soon after. This means skiing in snow and wind, or before the ice has melted off the chairlift seats. Warm-up pants increase a skier's comfort in the elements many times. Even in warmer weather, a wet seat is uncomfortable. A warm hat and parka should be worn to keep body heat from escaping around the neck and the small of the back. You shouldn't be overdressed. This causes perspiration and eventually makes you cold. Seeing during storms is one of the biggest problems. Avoid open slopes during storms or in flat light; choose narrower tree-lined runs or runs through trees. The trees mark the slope so you can see the contour. This is important for your balance. Goggles in powder are as important as the skis. It's not fun to ski blind down any run. Keeping goggles clear has developed into an art with the powder skiers. The problem multiplies greatly if you are one who falls once in a while. Very few skiers go through the day without tipping over once or twice.

A word of caution about the dangers involved in powder. Most skiers feel the dangers are breaking a bone in a fall or running into a tree. Both dangers are minimized in powder compared to packed snow skiing! In powder the skis are apt to pull free from the snow in a fall. Should you fall in powder there is little danger of sliding into a tree because the stops are more abrupt. Caution should be used in skiing in areas where you don't know what lies under the snow. This is especially true of the early snowfalls or in an area with a winter of very little snow. A fall in the fluffy snow can be serious if there is a hidden rock or cutoff tree stump under it. If you do not know the area, ask a teacher or ski patrolman about the safe areas. If you cannot find out, it is best to ski on or near the edges of the main runs.

At any ability level it is best to start out powder skiing with less depth of snow. This means you are really skiing the base under the powder and not floating. In small amounts of powder confidence is the major factor, not the type of skis or even your ability. Hundreds of skiers see a little new snow and become tense and fearful. This causes a complete loss of the basic body positions. The snow would have very little effect on the maneuverability of the skis; but with the loss of confidence and body position the skier would not be able to ski well under any snow conditions. Most of our powder snow teaching is trying to get our students to ski with as good a *basic technique* as they already use in packed snow conditions. Once a little confidence is established, we can begin our progress in improving our powder snow skiing.

For the lower level ability skier, powder snow can be taken right in stride with normal learning or practice. At this level there is very little conscious fear of powder, and confidence is quickly established. The snowplow-stem turn student generally skis on gentle terrain, well groomed and mogul free. The powder snow holds down the speed of a skier, and the snowplower soon finds he can ski under control with less width in the plow and much fewer turns. He soon finds gripping hard with the skis' edges is no longer required, and he now can ski in a much more relaxed position and find skiing much less tiring than compared to

Corky Fowler jumps for joy in his natural habitat called Snowbird.

the harder snow conditions. These advantages far outweigh the difficulties of getting up after a fall or the chance of running into the very deep bottomless powder that presents greater problems.

The body balance from side to side is the most critical, with forward and back position just maintaining a comfortable balance over the feet. At the snowplow stemming level every effort should be made to maintain *equal* weight between the skis at all times. At this level most students instinctively want to be even with weight on both skis. The major change comes when he has learned the traditional stemming of the uphill ski without weight and wants to carry the weight heavily on the downhill ski. If the skier is at this stem turn stage, it is a great advantage for him to keep his skis in a small snowplow position most of the time. This allows keeping the weight more evenly distributed and still maintaining control of direction and speed. This seems to be working backward in technique a little, but it keeps the skier from going too early into the traversing and sideslip stage.

The intermediate skier is the one who probably goes through the most problems with powder skiing. But a little guidance in the right direction and a few pointers will greatly reduce his problems. Our intermediate skier has ability to slide the skis during part or all of the turn. He is proud to be able to sideslip the skis and change quickly from side to side. He also has the courage to ski on the steeper terrain and depends on his sideslip or traverse to keep him under control. He has pretty well engrained a habit of a good weight change to help him achieve his control and can now almost count on his natural reactions to keep his weight on the downhill ski to guide him back uphill after a long runaway turn.

As this skier goes into powder snow, the snow takes away some value of his two strongest points for controlling himself, weight change and sideslip. If this skier could do two things which both require overcoming pride, his powder-snow-day would be improved by 200 percent. The first one is to stay away from the steeper terrain that forces him into traversing. The second is to drop back a little in his technique, like the example of a stem turner who has to drop back to snowplowing and depend more on a stem to produce a greater part of the beginning of the turn. If the hill is a little steeper, this skier should allow the stem to turn him at least to the fall line. This would compare very much to our beginning stem christie.

The skier will soon gain needed confidence to work on a few tips to improve his powder skiing. The easiest is to begin to balance weight on both skis while traversing. This leads us into the next step, which is to learn to sideslip in powder. This takes a little practice because the edge control in powder is more delicate than in packed snow skiing. Edging is a much lesser degree in angle. The whole bottom of the ski has contact with the snow, not just the steel edges. With the full ski holding, it becomes necessary for skiing the skis flat so they will cut sideways through the snow.

We begin with a practice of a turn similar to the christie uphill, but for powder we emphasize the sideslip and try not to make the skis carve in the traditional manner with weight on the downhill ski. Practice should be directed toward leaning away from the hill and keeping the knees well over the skis, but still using both skis equally with weight and turning force applied. This practice is very good in learning the necessary edge control to ski powder.

During this practice time we try to develop in the skier his balance on the skis and his control of turning from the fall line to a stop. You may have to combine extra work on turning power and unweighting.

Following the training of the christie uphill, we are ready to cross the fall line. At this stage two points of emphasis are:

1—The stem phase is held until the body is facing the fall line, and this delay allows the outside ski to cross the fall line and point toward the new traverse.

2—The upper body is over both skis, and the unweighting comes equally from both legs or skis. Following the unweighting the skis are closed, and the weight returns on both skis evenly. The body continues in a down motion to a low body position as the turning power is applied to keep the skis in the christie stage.

This critical end phase is also where the previous training in edge control will help us with the correct edging to make the skis sideslip for the christie. Throughout the whole turn every effort is made to keep the weight distribution *even* on both skis. This includes the unweighting coming up from both skis. If all weight goes to one ski, that immediately sinks deeper in the snow and the other rises to the surface, causing a loss of balance.

Practice is the word for progress in improving ability in skiing. Practice time in powder is limited because the availability of powder is much shorter than packed snow. In most ski areas packing is a big part of keeping good snow conditions for the majority of the skiers. At Snowbird we do have a lot of area untouched by packers, and you should be aware of both the steep and gentle terrain areas left for practice.

For most small, light powder storms, there is very little change of technique needed. What is needed is confidence to maintain a good body position and just plain good skiing technique. From here on our improvements start developing by keeping weight more evenly distributed on both skis to keep snow from pulling the skis apart, holding a little lower body position to improve stability, using slow motion movements with the body for unweighting and turning power to give the skis more time to turn rather than using quick forceful movements, and trying to keep a rhythm going in linking one turn into another.

Now I will go into the exercises for the more serious powder skier who wants to try the deep snow. We have a few terms which have been used for some years in powder: *flotation, submarine, lateral unweighting, down-up-down, tip pressure, boot pressure, controlling the turn with the tails of the skis.*

If you are suddenly faced with 1 to 2 feet of powder, your best approach is to practice on gentle terrain going in a straight line to develop your balance on both skis evenly weighted. This gives you a chance to feel the reaction on the skis if you shift weight too much, lean too far forward or back and to feel unweighting with little down-up-down movements. Once a feeling for the snow is developed, practice should begin on an uphill christie and a stop christie. Confidence is soon established when one finds he can turn uphill or stop. In deep powder snow the skier needs to be moving with enough speed to feel that the skis are not mushing in the snow but *floating* as a boat would do as it picks up speed. The turning into the hill can be produced by a slow motion bounce which produces a porpoising action of the skis. In porpoising the skis come up near the surface and then go deeper into the snow. The correct timing is starting the turn while the skis are near the surface and applying pressure to the back of the skis to push them sideways and deeper into the snow. The working with the *tails* of the skis keeps the tips floating near or on the surface. This practice should be done while traversing on steeper terrain. For building confidence, crossing the fall line should be started on terrain the skier would feel safe in schussing. While practicing turns into the hill or stop christies, the weight should be maintained on both skis. The greatest number of falls occur in powder because of stopping with too much weight on the lower ski, causing the ski to sink in and the skier to fall downhill. Because of this reason, one should choose stopping places carefully. Stopping on a steep hill increases the chance of tipping over downhill. You should plan out the powder snow run with a goal in mind of skiing to a particular stopping area, much like a slalom racer planning to ski through the finish gate.

Lateral unweighting is used to decrease the pressure from the skis for a slight moment while the change of direction takes place. This is when the skier's body is angulated, providing stability for a turn in either direction and also avoiding the totally upright position with the body which is a very unstable position for powder. Ankle bend is maintained continuously by pushing the knees forward. This is known as boot pressure and is used in powder to maintain stability and control. [Ed: Many thanks, Junior!]

M is for MONTANA

where you'll find the BIG MOUNTAIN, WHITEFISH

M IS FOR MONTANA

M is for Montana, where you will find The Big Mountain . . . The Big Mountain is a harmonious blend of snow, nature, and congenial people, located in the Flathead National Forest, Whitefish, Montana.

It is an easy kind of place to visit, ski, and make a lot of friends. Fact is, that on The Big Mountain you are not just a guest but a good friend as well. That's the easy going way they approach the ski resort operation.

While they may seem easy going, they are making every effort toward your skiing enjoyment, with a new triple-chairlift, new slopes, new slope grooming equipment, and a conservative, yet sensible expansion of base area facilities. The daily operation too is always carried out with the skier in mind—fabulous food from their own restaurants, a newly expanded ski shop and school facilities; in fact, everyone on the staff is on The Mountain with but one thought—you.

As to size, The Big Mountain is a more comfortable version of the complete resort. Overnight accomodations for 400 skiers right at the base of the lifts in a Chalet, Lodge, and Alpinglow Inn, not to mention many winter homes right on the mountainside, await your occupancy. Then of course, there's all the rest; a bar and a Bierstube, a cafeteria, heated pool, sauna baths, day care center for the kids; it's all there for your relaxation and enjoyment.

Headed by nationally known racing coach and Ski School Director Martin Hale, The Big Mountain Ski School and its staff of specially trained, certified instructors will guide you to skiing excellence with either the modified American or GLM instruction techniques. You will find their teaching is friendly and casual and you will be pleased with your progress by their friendly persuasion. Ski school classes form the daytime social hub of The Big Mountain's dedication to skiing fun.

YOU DON'T HAVE TO BE A SKIER . . . TO BE A SKIER

by Martin Hale, Ski School Director At Big Mountain, Montana as told to Norm Kurtz

Each year, The Big Mountain, along with the 800 some odd ski resorts and areas throughout North America, spends thousands of dollars on advertising pieces, brochures, radio and television and other media commercials, telling skiers how great skiing is at their "Mossy Mogul Ski Resort."

Fact is, they are talking to each other about how great skiing is at their area, not what skiing is like to literally millions who for some reason or another never gave it a try. Whether by reason of fear, cost, or circumstance, these would-be skiers never go skiing or even try it because, while all of us skiers are talking to each other, they hardly know where to start or what to expect.

I thought I'd like to say a little about how it is, or how it goes, for someone just starting into skiing with us in the ski school from Day One; how much fun it is, and how easy it is to get started and become really quite proficient in 6 days or less, as a recreational skier.

After having preferably made some arrangement with the ski shop and ski school by phone, mail or whatever, you have just entered the ski school building. In finding your way to the ski school desk, which is just inside the door, your ears are assailed with all kinds or enthusiastic generic terms which, except for the friendly treatment, kind'a makes you feel you just got lost in the Greek Embassy.

So, with more than just a little trepidation, you walk up to the ski school desk for your appointment with some excitement, and with one hand protecting your pocketbook. It's

Big Mountain's new triple chairlift cuts down the lift lines. (Photos Big Mountain Photograph)

A lone skier looks out over western Montana's Flathead Valley from the Big Mountain's "Big Drift" area.

with that in mind that you vaguely remember tip number one—prepare yourself with comfortable dress and gloves and/or mittens (you don't need the latest fashions), and, if you don't already own your equipment, don't buy any equipment yet for a couple of reasons. First, you may find after giving skiing your very best shot several times, that you just plain don't like it (there are a few folks like that, but not many). Second, before you make a big investment in equipment, rent it once or twice. The money you spend in rental will probably save you in the long run by assuring that you are skiing on equipment that suits your needs. Then when you've made up your mind, received the best start you can get, along with the best professional advice available, you can buy wisely and economically. So start off by renting. If you already do have your own equipment, make sure you get it checked out for function, proper fit, and comfort. This includes boots, skis, bindings, and even poles. Starting with the wrong gear can develop in some an immediate hatred, if not an outright fear, of the sport. You'll want to have someone check and tell you a little about wax anyway.

Now that we have you properly equipped, you're ready to go outside to the ski school meeting place and get acquainted with your classmates and your instructor. You'll find from the start that even though your learn-to-ski-adventure is called "school," the emphasis is on "FUN," and the entire experience will blend a lot of laughter and smiles with the learning process. Your instructor will know your name, just as you will soon know the names of your classmates on the mountainside.

Your first learning adventure will soon dispel the apprehension you had, as the instructor has no intention of taking you to the very top of the nearest mountain and saying, "Follow me."

Instead, your instructor will first teach you to walk on your way to your very own practice area. Now—silly though it sounds since you already know how to walk—having 2½ to 3½ feet sticking out from under both ends of your boots and being firmly affixed to them has considerable effect on what your feet want to do, as opposed to what you want them to do. As a result, your first experience with walking will be good for a few smiles as you firmly retrain your feet somewhat away from their previous independent movements. Then, having a few walking steps passing easily under your skis, you'll find that turning around is no trick at all after a few moments of doubt. All the time you are doing these few basic things, the whole teaching experience will be gently and almost unconsciously poking and connecting painless new thoughts into your mind with each step, instilling in you the confidence to manipulate your skis, feet, legs, arms and body in the various and sundry directions you wish them to go.

Even before you go to any kind of lift, those few walking steps and static turns will see you ever so gradually learning to climb and maneuver. Suddenly you're atop a very small and gentle incline, where for the first time, you point your skis downhill, if only for a few feet, to find what gravity can do for you. You won't be going very fast at all, and the first couple of times, you won't even have to attempt a turn; just letting your skis run straight ahead to a gentle stop. All the while, you're having a good time and those words, actions, and urgings you've been receiving are starting to make a little sense after all.

The Big Mountain's Alpinglow Inn.

This, you realize, is all taking place over a very brief span of time. And most of all, you're having fun at trying.

Next, it's back up the very small incline a few more times to slip from the straight running you've accomplished into the "V" or wedge position, making some very slight directional changes. Surprise again, you can do it. While learning this position, you're introduced almost casually to the "wide track" position, where skis are positioned in a super stable mode under your body, almost hip wide. In this position, you do some traversing across the slope and are pleased at how stable you're beginning to feel on skis.

Now it's over to the lift. Next trauma, you feel? Nope. It's

Part of "The Big Face" off chairlift one at Big Mountain.

The scenery beyond the Big Mountain Base Lodge is a curious combination of rolling hills of pine, flat valleys and towering snowcapped peaks.

easy too, for there's a new triple-chairlift replacing the old poma lift. Getting up the hill merely means standing in the right place and sitting down at the proper moment, as the big new chairlift gently scoops you up and takes you up the hill.

Getting on the chair and riding it is easy. And after that, as you look around, you get a chance to reflect on it all until . . . "holy mackerel, it's not just me alone, there's two other people on this chair with me! Great guns, when I get to the top, how do we all get off? And all at once!"

Then you remember what the operator and your instructor said about merely standing up as you pass the sign on top and sliding down the gentle incline away from the chair. And you figure too, that if 1,200 people per hour are supposed to be able to do it on this lift, you can too. There is still a little nagging doubt this first time, however, that this particular chairlift may have an hourly capacity of 1,199 skiers and one beginning idiot.

But as the top terminal of the lift approaches, you see the sign, "Stand up, glide off, and Nice Day" . . . a little shaky, but you made it!

On top! By golly, you're doing what you came to do and alternately either enjoying it or getting away with it, some of this and some of that.

"That to you, Walter Mitty! I'm a little overage, overweight, undertrained, and either better than I thought I was, or these ski instructors are geniuses. But I'm doing it! I'm skiing!"

Back into class, for while reflecting on past and future glories, your instructor has been gathering the class and waiting for you. He has a slope that you can handle, one that gently descends more than half a mile back to the base of the hill, and you think, "My gawd, half a mile! Better call a cab or call someone."

Once again, the instructor amplifies the logic of the situation, stating simply enough that the slope is still gentle and you're just going to eliminate the climbing between those practice passes.

So, it's some more wide tracking, and once again, you feel more and more stable, and at the same time, more confident as you make long gentle traverses and learn something called a "hockey stop."

Wide track traverse to the left, then a hockey stop up into the hill to stop, then the same to the right. A "hockey stop," by the way, is a skidding turn in either direction where the skis are both steered in the same direction and in such a fashion as to produce a simple and easily accomplished turn into the hill. Today's ski equipment being both more responsive, and at the same time forgiving, make these maneuvers easy to come by with instruction.

By now, your instructor has gently urged you into a slightly longer running period between each maneuver and you, still in the comfortable wide track stance, are ready to link up those easy steering turns from left to right and back, thus getting into those long continuous runs that total the skier's experience.

The first few efforts at linking your turns down the hill are a little trying on your confidence, but once accomplished, you wonder what you were worried about. A few more runs increase your confidence and with continued practice and instruction, you find your runs in class are getting longer and longer between stops.

Before the week is out, and depending on what you want to do with skiing, and where you want to go, you'll have the ability not only to ride to the very summit of The Big Mountain, but to enjoy the run back down.

(A note from Martin Hale—In this brief article, I've tried to point up how easy it is to get into skiing and enjoy it. We've stayed away as far as possible from all the technical points. We've tried not to engage in explaining the teaching techniques and equipment needs for GLM, or Modified American, or whatever.

We've not gotten into physical requirements or age limitations, as we feel for instance that you should be somewhere between the ages of 5 and 85 and healthy enough to walk around outside. The only other real requirements, beyond those of your own thoughts, is a need for enthusiasm and an enjoyment of the out-of-doors in winter and a desire to participate in the world's greatest winter sport—skiing! NICE DAY!)

N is for the Northwest Territory
TIMBERLINE, OREGON

The Timberline Lodge has the most beautiful backyard in the country. Its rustic structure was largely hand hewn by western craftsmen and artisans in the early 1930's. It is not unusual for the snow depth to rise to roof level during high season.

N is for Northwest Territory . . . Timberline Lodge at Government Camp, Timberline, Oregon, has to represent our Northwest as a strong contender for some of the country's *greatest* skiing. Unfortunately, we can't tell you too much about it, as their PR office was a bit remiss in sending us only the photos that you see and no text. Marge and I found it impossible to visit *every* resort, so we had to count on the PR offices for explicit information, in those areas that were not in our itinerary. Timberline does have a great reputation propagated by afficionados who have skied there, so I've done some minor research and have come up with these facts which you might find attractive.

Directly from the lodge, three double-chairlifts and a poma provide access to the 9,300-foot elevation, from which you can dive into miles of exciting runs including a popular one called the Magic Mile. If you want to go higher, two 20-passenger snow-cats are available to transport you to the barren snowfields that lead to the peak.

The ski school is run by Bud Nash who probably follows the ATM manual.

For the hours after skiing, a heated year-round pool invites your pink bod, which you can then fatten in the Cascade Dining Room as you feast your fawn by firelight. For booze you can tip at the Blue Ox Rathskeller which swings informally, or find yourself a fox and whisper sweet nothings in the more intimate setting of the Ram's Head Cocktail Lounge. Guests are treated to free movies, occasional Bingo and dancing every evening.

You can reach Timberline off U.S. Route 26. Take 80N east from Portland; turn right at Arata Road, then exit to U.S. 26, which goes east to the Lodge. There is a regular Continental Trailways bus service from Portland to Government Camp which is dependable.

I'd like to tell you more, but we'll have to wait until Marge and I get enough bread together for a trip to the great Northwest. I sure like the looks of the Timberline peak.

O is for Oregon and the Bob Beattie Ski Camp

Mt. BACHELOR, BEND, OREGON

O IS FOR OREGON

O is for Oregon and the Bob Beattie Ski Camp in Bend.

Racing camps have become very popular in the higher elevations. SKIER'S DIGEST believes that the Bob Beattie Ski Camp provides one of the finest quality programs in the country. I've asked Director Bill Marolt to tell a little about it.

BOB BEATTIE SKI CAMP

BILL MAROLT, DIRECTOR, BBSC

A day at the Bob Beattie Ski Camp in Bend, Oregon begins at 6:30 AM with one of the coaches waking everyone up. The campers are all required to go outside and do some light calisthenics before returning to the dorm. Once back in the dorm, each boy and girl is required to dress in appropriate ski clothing for the day's activities and then make his bed and straighten out the area adjacent to his bunk.

Breakfast is served at 7:15 AM and the campers then proceed to their dorm to put on boots, sun lotion, and make last-minute adjustments of equipment. By 8:00 AM the skiing day begins, and each racer is put into the ability group that reflects his skiing capabilities. These groups vary from beginner to expert, and as the campers progress they can move up to a higher ability level. The groups are determined by results from a handicap race that is held on the first afternoon of each session. A later handicap race will determine who has reduced their handicap by the largest margin and has earned the "most improved award."

While skiing in the ability groups until 10 AM the coaches will work generally on skiing courses and making error corrections as each participant runs through the gates. This is repeated every day at the same time and only during the day when everyone is fresh and strong.

At 10 AM the campers all descend on the lodge for a glass of juice and a 30-minute rest. We want the concentration to stay at a high level and feel that frequent rest is as important as the training itself.

After the break, the group all gets on the chairlift and skis to the racing area for some dual slalom team races. Here again, we make teams up from the handicap races and match people of equal ability to race each other head-to-head. These are all electrically timed, and the results are accurate and carefully calculated and watched. We keep team scores as well as handicap scores for awards that will be made at our banquet which will be held the last evening of each session.

The team racing concludes the morning activities and a lunch break will not conclude until 2 PM when everyone goes out to run drills. The drills are set all the way from the top of the chairlift to the bottom. A coach stands at the bottom and the racer goes down a course working on one special drill. An example might be 1) Planting the Pole, 2) Stepping or 3) Running hairpins. We will have 4 or 5 different drills and each camper moves through the courses practicing certain things as he works his way through the drills. This is a most effective way to teach because it is concise, easy to understand, and the kids all enjoy the freedom of the individual courses and coaching.

After the coaching ends, everyone reports to the top of the mountain for the final slip of the day. This is done so that the courses for the next morning are all ready and we slip everything out at night so when the snow freezes it will be smooth the following day.

The evening activities will be as constructive as the daily activities with lectures by the staff concerning techniques, ski preparation, waxing, training, and just good rap sessions. Our visual aids include video and movies which are always a great help to any teaching situation. By 9:30 PM everyone is ready to hit the sack, and lights are turned off after everyone inspects the official scoreboard to see how they skied for the day. The coaching staff lives with the campers in the dorms, and supervision is 24 hours a day. The coaches are all professionals, and they work at their job year round. Working with kids is their vocation and we stress total involvement from our staff.

If there are any minor injuries or sicknesses, we have a registered nurse on duty all the time, and she will make sure that everyone has their medical problems taken care of. The hospital is a short distance away if anything serious does happen.

The *physical* facilities—chairlifts (no portable lifts here); snow—the most dependable in North America; lodge—at the base of the mountain. *The Staff* of professional coaches and teachers and all necessary kitchen, medical and mountain help. The extras—1) *Salting machines* put the snow in excellent condition so that it is and stays hard, 2) *More Gates* because of the nearness of everything and the snow quality, 3) *More Races*. We believe in racing to learn how to master the skills and pressures of the competitive skiing situation.

Each of these concerted efforts makes this camp the ideal summer training situation. We guarantee no one will be disappointed.

* * *

Thank you, Bill. Here is a fact sheet on the Bob Beattie Ski Camp:

Location:
Mt. Bachelor
Bend, Oregon
Lift Facilities:
7000 ft. Double Chairlift
1800 ft. Vertical Rise
1300 Skiers Per Hour
Slopes:
The natural terrain of Mt. Bachelor makes it an ideal summer ski area for both the beginner and expert. The slopes vary from very gentle to the demanding race course terrain and will let any skier thoroughly enjoy the week.
Snow Conditions:
Are the most consistent in North America. Our staff has been working at Mt. Bachelor for the past 10 years and has always found great snow. In normal years we will be able to ski to and from the lodge from our ski activities.

P is for POWDER

Mt. REBA at BEAR VALLEY, CALIFORNIA

P IS FOR POWDER

P is for POWDER . . . Mt. Reba at Bear Valley, California.

Jon Reveal is a familiar name to many skiers. He started skiing in 1947 and racing in 1951. In 1958, Jon was the youngest member of the Far West Ski Association's Junior National Ski Team. He remained a member until 1962 when he turned 18! In 1963 he was admitted to the roster of the Utah State University Team. Two years later he became coach to the Dodge Ridge Ski Team and received full certification from the Far West Ski Instructors Association. In 1967, Jon was chosen as one of the top ten ski instructors in the United States after his ski school unanimously passed the certification exam. The peripatetic Reveal went to the National School for Ski Instructors in Chamonix, France, in 1968, and later taught skiing in Courchevel. FWSIA welcomed Jon back to the States in 1970 after a summer of race coaching at Mt. Ruapahue, New Zealand, by awarding him the title of Ski Instructor of the Year in Vail, Colorado. He placed second in downhill and giant slalom in the Veteran's national at Bear Valley, California in 1971.

Many of us remember Jon Reveal as the winner of the "Super Hot Dog Contest" sponsored by Beconta in 1972. We followed him to Steamboat Springs to compete in the national event and watched him place sixth. We also watched Peter Hershorn break his back. So did Jon. He has never competed in this type of event since.

In 1973 Jon placed fourth in "overall" on the Sierra Tahoe Pro Circuit. He won the first race and placed consistently in the top eight. He has worked with Doug Pfieffer testing skis for *Skiing* Magazine and has starred in many Warren Miller films. Jon was the Assistant Ski School Director at both Dodge Ridge and Mt. Reba at Bear Valley ski areas. We have a great deal of respect for the man and have asked him to enrich this book with a few thoughts on skiing the powder at Mt. Reba. Here, then, is Jon Reveal.

Powder Principles

by Jon Reveal

Powder skiing, if one were to speak to Warren Miller, the famous ski photographer, is enjoyed because the initial feeling that all humans have is that of floating in the aminonic fluid of the mother's womb prior to birth. This is a secure feeling, and most humans try to return to this feeling as much as possible. It is for this reason that most humans enjoy a warm bath, swimming and the floating sensation of powder skiing.

Powder skiing to a skier that drives 200 miles, or flies for 16 hours or spends $1,500 a week on a helicopter, is the ultimate in skiing. A powder skier of this caliber will tell everyone that he knows himself better after a week in the powder. He is at peace with himself and the world around him. Any number of "strange" statements might be uttered by a powder skier.

Whooping through the fluff on Mt. Reba at Bear Valley. (Photo by Puccinelli)

However, there are still those who only have one feeling for powder snow—FEAR. For those in this class, I am writing this article. I would like nothing more than for everyone to be able to experience something of what Warren Miller is talking about. To become so involved in powder skiing that a $1,500 vacation would be a necessary experience. Ready? Let's start with equipment.

Equipment is such that one does not need to buy specialized ski equipment to ski powder snow. One's normal skis, boots and poles will work fine. When skis were long and made of hickory and ash, it was necessary to buy a specialized ski for powder. Now that skis are shorter and made of synthetic materials like foam, fiberglass and plastic, it is very easy to ski in powder snow with the same pair of skis that are used on packed slopes.

There is one piece of equipment that every powder skier needs that the packed slope skier might not find necessary. This is a good pair of non-fogging goggles. These goggles are known by the powder skiers as "Smith's" or "Scott's." The necessary element is that they be soft and seal well on the face and have a sealed double lens. Even though this does not seem to be very important, in fact it is. Before their creation one would ski as far as possible until the goggles filled with snow or fogged up, then stop and clean the goggles. Now this is no longer necessary. These new goggles have opened up areas that were previously unskiable to powder skiers, i.e. wooded areas and cliffs with rock outcroppings (I remember as a young skier an old expert powder skier telling me, "When your goggles fog always remember to miss the dark objects. They are probably rocks or trees.") One can now see where he is going.

The most important element in learning to ski powder snow, of course, is powder snow. But there is a way to get ready for the powder snow through a series of exercises on packed slopes so that one can be ready for the powder snow when it arrives.

Exercise 1

Find a gentle slope, one that could be schussed if it were necessary. The objective of this exercise is to go straight down the hill and make small turns in the fall line. From the top of the slope start in the fall line and let the skis run until enough speed is attained to turn the skis. Try to make a series of small turns from the fall line. Do not traverse across the hill between the turns. The feeling that one should have is that of acceleration. The skis should continue to accelerate down the hill. If by chance they decelerate, try to make a less pronounced turn.

Find a little steeper slope. Work on the turn. Try for a short radius turn and eliminate all long radius turns. If your best effort only produces long radius turns, do two things: 1) edge the skis more by pushing the knees toward the inside of the turn and, 2) weight the outside ski more by angulating the upper part of the body over the down hill ski. As these two movements are performed you will notice that the turn comes quicker, so be ready to quicken the rhythm of the other parts of the turn such as the pole plant, weight change and edge change. This is the type of exercise that is good for all skiers, and it can be practiced for weeks before it is done well. It is especially good for those years when there is not much snow and the only slopes open are gentle.

Exercise 2

Another exercise that can be practiced and felt on packed slopes is the sitting-back position that is necessary in powder skiing. Be careful not to be confused by the expression

Early morning ski patrolman takes advantage of the fresh powder at Bear Valley.

"sitting back." The expression is a good one, but you should not think about leaning back. Sitting back is a position you obtain by actually bending the knee more than usual. This will lower the seat, and you will feel pressure being applied to the heel of the foot. The ankles must remain bent forward and the back rounded in a normal skiing position. This position is very stable since it lowers the center of gravity. A fault that some skiers get into is "leaning back." By this I mean straightening the upper body and knee joint and tilting the upper body backwards. In this case you can feel pressure from the top of the boots against the back of the leg where the boot and the leg meet. There will not be pressure down on the heel of the foot. A visual impression is that of a person leaning against a wall. This is not a very stable position and should be recognized as such. Work with this position standing still. Feel for the proper pressure on the heel of the foot.

Find a gentle slope that is well packed. Make the same type of turns as were described in Exercise 1, but this time add in the powder skiing position. You will feel the tails of the skis slip easier (due to the increased weight) so it is important not to over turn the skis and traverse them between the turns. This exercise should be worked on until the proper position is obtained. The most obvious way of knowing this is the feeling in the lower leg and foot. If there is pressure on the lower leg, bend the ankle until the pressure is felt on the heel of the foot.

Exercise 3

Another exercise that can be practiced on the packed slopes and used in powder snow is the unweighting motion. In the new teaching methods of today where short skis are incorporated in the learning process, unweighting becomes less important than it was in the past. Ten years ago when everybody was skiing on 210cm skis nothing was thought about a beginner starting his skiing experience on 210cm skis. One can imagine how important it was to unweight the skis, even at times to hop the entire ski off the snow to make the turns. This is no longer true. With today's skis and the new teaching methods, one can start on 140cm or shorter skis and work his way up to a "normal" length ski. One can spend the entire time never learning how to unweight the skis while turning until the advanced intermediate level of skiing proficiency is reached. Even then the stress on unweighting will not be harped on like it was 10 years ago. So, for those who have not been taught to unweight and know very little about it, this exercise is very important.

Unweighting is the reduction of pressure that is applied to the snow thru the ski by the skier's weight. There are several ways to go about reducing the pressure, but the two most important are "up" unweighting and "down" unweighting. "Up" unweighting is accomplished when the skier assumes a lower than normal body position and then rapidly straightens the body. This straightening of the body projects the body mass upwards and reduces the pressure of the skis on the snow, or "unweights" them.

The second major type of unweighting is done from the normal skiing position. The knees and ankles are bent rapidly, and the body drops toward the snow. This rapid dropping lowers the pressure of the skis on the snow and is therefore an unweighting motion. You can experiment with this by standing on a bathroom scale and trying the motions

and watching the scales drop and rise through the un-weighting motion, as Frank Covino has described in Chapter 3 of this book.

There are, of course, advantages and disadvantages to the two different types of unweighting. The "up" unweighting is advantageous because the length of time the skis are unweighted is very long. The beginning powder skier can use this time to make all the necessary movements in order to make the turn. However, to make an "up" unweighted type turn the skier must first prepare by assuming a lower position. This takes time. Then, once extended, the beginning powder skier finds himself in a very unstable position at a time when many other movements must be made in order for the skis to turn. But, for the beginner in the powder, the advantages of the "up" unweighting overshadow the disadvantages.

"Down" unweighting has the advantage of lowering the center of gravity and making the body more stable. It is a movement that can be done without any preparation. But, the duration of the unweighting is very short-lived and consequently the other movements necessary to make the skis turn must be well-timed and coordinated. For this reason most students learn with an "up" unweighting and perfect their powder skiing with a "down" unweighted type turn.

Now, back to the exercise that can be used on packed slopes prior to entering the powder. On a gentle slope start straight down the fall line and try to make the same type of short radius turns that were described in Exercise 1. After obtaining a rhythm, wait until the end of one turn and sink down farther than normal (by bending the knees and ankles). With the planting of the downhill pole spring up to the normal skiing position (knees and ankles slightly bent). Be careful not to straighten out the lower extremities entirely. This position is very unstable so do not add more instability to it. Try to feel just a lightening of the skis and not a total separation of the skis from the snow. It will take a little time to learn how much motion one needs to lighten the skis, but with some practice and patience it can be done.

Once the skis are light on the snow, it is time to make several rapid and coordinated movements. The changing of the edges can be done easily for the skis are light. This is done by bringing the knees under the body and pushing them toward the center of the upcoming turn. The feet can be twisted at the same time and just as easily because of the unweighted nature of the skis. This will all happen when the skis are unweighted. Once they are weighted again continue the push of the knees toward the inside of the turn and the steering (twisting) of the feet in the desired direction. Get ready for the next turn by sinking down and preparing the lower pole to be planted.

Exercise 4

The final exercise that you can work on is very important, and it is not used very much at all outside the realm of powder skiing. This is the equalization of weight on the two skis. On packed slopes every skier has heard "weight the down hill ski." This is fine for the packed slopes. In powder, the weight must be kept close to equal, for if it is not, the ski with the most weight will sink further into the powder and slow down. One can imagine the consequences when one ski moves at 5mph and the other moves at 10mph. Something

Bear is really *powderful*.

has to give somewhere!!!

Go back to the gentle slope and make the same type of short radius turns that were covered in Exercise 1. This time try to feel the weight remain fairly equally distributed on the two skis except when the skis are finishing the turn. The rest of the time feel for the equal weight on the two skis. A good way to do this is by weighting totally the outside ski and then the inside ski. This will set up the two extreme cases that one could possibly feel. Now, try for something in between. This will take a little practice and a lot of feeling, but learn it well. It will save a lot of time getting up in the powder snow later on after a fall.

There are no more exercises to be learned. The only thing left to do is to wait for the powder snow. No matter where one skis the powder will come some day. I ski in Bear Valley, California, because it is well known for its powder and steep slopes. When looking for a good powder skiing area, it is best to look at the area statistics a bit differently than the normal skier who goes on a ski vacation. It is best to find an out-of-the-way ski area where not everybody goes, because once the powder falls, it will all be gone in 30 minutes if too many people get in and chew it up. It is best to find an area with several thousand vertical feet and the longest run of about 2 miles. This will mean that the slopes are steep enough for good powder skiing. Finally look for the percentage of sunny days at the area. If it advertises 60 percent sunny days, this means to the powder skier that 40 percent of the time there will be powder snow skiing.

With all the exercises well learned, go to a slope with untracked powder that is considered to be intermediate. This will be steep enough for a starter. Point the skis straight across the hill so that it is not necessary to turn to stop but so that the skis will stop by themselves when they run out of momentum. Push off and assume the sitting back position of Exercise 2. *Remember to feel the weight on the heel of the foot and not at the point where the top of the boot and the leg meet*. The tips of the skis should start to float up onto the surface of the snow. When they emerge do not sit back any further. This is the proper skiing position for powder snow. Now it is time to make a half-turn in the powder.

In a traverse assume a normal skiing position for powder snow and glide along in a well-balanced position. In order to make half a turn it is only necessary to sink down (just like the movement that was used to prepare for the unweighting) and at the same time twist the feet up the hill while pushing the knees toward the inside of the turn. Remember what was learned in Exercise 4 and keep the weight equal on the two skis. Continue turning until the skis stop. This can be thought of as the end of a turn.

Do this exercise from steeper and steeper traverses until the skis are heading straight down the hill. As the skis become more and more parallel to the fall line, the speed will pick up and longer and longer radius turns will result. In order that all the parts of the turn are incorporated, at the end of each half-turn when the skis stop, plant the downhill pole. At this point, when the spole is planted and the skis have stopped, the *upper part of the body should be facing down the hill*. This position, called "anticipation," is very important to the advanced skier and the powder skier. Anticipation assures that the lower part of the body (legs and hips) is doing the turning of the skis, and the next turn will be easy to begin. Now it is time to make an entire downhill turn in the powder.

Start from a steep traverse, sink down and turn the skis up the hill while preparing the downhill pole for planting. Prior to stopping completely, plant the downhill pole and up-unweight forcefully to lighten the skis. When the skis are unweighted, turn them under the body down the hill. As the weight returns to the skis, keep the weight back on the heel of the foot and relatively equal between the two feet. Finish the turn out of the fall line by sinking down and twisting the feet (steering) in the direction of the turn while pushing the knees toward the inside of the turn. If by chance, equilibrium is still well maintained throughout the entire turn, make another turn and continue for as many linked turns as possible.

A few words about falling in powder snow. It is enjoyable. It is like falling into a million pounds of feathers. The problem arises in getting up after the fall. Many times when it has been snowing for several days in a row and 4 or 5 feet of new powder has accumulated, the ski poles become worthless. Every time they are used to get up they sink into the powder snow up to the handles. In this case get the skis below the body and do a normal sit-up.

If a ski has come off in the fall, pack a place out so that the ski can be put back on again without getting snow between the boot and the binding. It is usually best to check the bindings again at the bottom of the lift, where it is well packed, to verify that they are still functioning properly.

Skiing the powder is great fun and anybody can do it if they try. To ride back up a lift and see a set of tracks that have a very personal closeness is a thrill that all skiers should experience. The immersion of the body into the powder snow and the closeness that one feels to nature is not easily described. The powder is there waiting for everyone to revel in the joy that it holds. But be careful, it is habit forming.

* * *

Thank you, Jon. SKIER'S DIGEST encourages every reader to visit Mt. Reba at Bear valley to test your advice and join the rest of us powder hounds.

Q is for QUALITY

WATERVILLE VALLEY, NEW HAMPSHIRE

Q is for quality, and I can think of no eastern area that can top the one found at Waterville Valley in New Hampshire. Tom Corcoran can do a better job of telling you about it than I can. He is president and founder of the Waterville Company, Inc. which owns and operates the two major ski areas in Waterville Valley and is the master developer of the mountain village that lies between the two ski areas. Tom was formerly a member of the 1956 and 1960 Olympic Ski Teams placing fourth in the 1960 Olympic Giant Slalom in Squaw Valley, the highest placing to date for an American in this event. Tom was educated at Dartmouth College and has a master's degree in business administration from the Harvard Business School. Before coming to Waterville Valley in 1966, he was Assistant to the President of the Aspen Skiing Corporation in Aspen, Colorado. He as also been a Director of Vail Associates, President of the Eastern Ski Areas Association, and a Director of the National Ski Areas Association. He is a member of the U.S. Olympic Skiing Committee and a Trustee of the United States Ski Educational Foundation, which manages the U.S. Ski Team. Most ski professionals hold Tom Corcoran in the highest regard.

WATERVILLE VALLEY, NEW HAMPSHIRE

by Tom Corcoran

Waterville Valley is located in the heart of the White Mountain National Forest and is New Hampshire's largest and most popular ski resort. It consists of two ski areas facing each other and a ski village lying in the valley between. There are only 500 acres of private land on the valley floor where the ski village is located; virtually all of the ski facilities are located on the adjacent slopes of the White Mountain National Forest. There is only one road into Waterville Valley, Route 49, which originates at the Waterville Valley exit off I-93 and follows the Mad River 11 miles into Waterville Valley, most of which goes through the White Mountain National Forest.

If you can visualize the geographic relationships that I have briefly described above, the uniqueness of Waterville is probably apparent. It is a totally protected community that is truly a destination resort, one of the few in New England. Fortunately the valley was one of the last places to be developed as a major resort that had the potential to become one. The result was that we were able to benefit from the experience of other resorts that had been built since World War II in the French Alps, the Rockies, and in other parts of New England.

We decided from the start in planning the resort that we wanted to build a resort second to none in New England— that it should be totally self-contained; that there should not be a need for a car once a visitor had arrived; that there should be a wide variety of things to do and places to stay for all pocketbooks; and that the resort had to be year-round in nature. The skiing and ski facilities had to be first-rate in every regard, balanced as well as possible to serve equally the needs of experts, intermediates, and beginning skiers. The ski facilities had to be family-oriented with attention given to the separate needs of adults and children. It was also a major premise that the entire resort should achieve and maintain a reputation for friendliness and courtesy second to none.

How well did we succeed? The results really speak for themselves. By the end of our second year of operation, the winter of 1967-68, we had become the largest and most popular ski resort in New Hampshire, a position we have held every year since. The planning of our ski facilities, the design of our lifts and ski trails, the architecture of our base buildings, even the design of our parking lots—all have received national attention. If imitation is the greatest form of flattery, we have reason to be flattered because our facilities have been extensively copied by other resorts. Perhaps best of all is the reputation that we have maintained for attracting and holding employees who really do care

The Mt. Tecumseh Ski Area in Waterville Valley offers a vertical drop of over 2,000 feet, with five chairlifts, a J-bar, and a T-bar serving 32 slopes and trails for plenty of variety for plenty of variety for beginning, intermediate and advanced skiers.

A group of freestyle skiing fans follow the "Pied Piper" of skiing down Valley Run at Waterville Valley, Wayne Wong. Wayne, a guest coach in the Waterville Valley Freestyle Program, was the 1972 Freestyle Skier-of-the-Year.

about the needs of the skiers who come here.

As of this writing we have eight lifts on our two different mountains, Mt. Tecumseh and Snow's Mountain, six chairlifts, a T-bar, and a J-bar. We have a major snowmaking capability that covers the slopes of four lifts on Mt. Tecumseh. The slopes on which we can make snow range in difficulty from complete beginner to expert, so that we are protected against the elements for every ability level of skier.

Snow conditions in Waterville Valley are extraordinarily reliable. The CCC (Civilian Conservation Corps) first cut a walk-up ski trail on Mt. Tecumseh in 1937, and there have been skiers here ever since. I skied in a race on the walk-up trails in the late '40s, and I recall that even then Waterville Valley had a reputation as a snow pocket. There used to be a saying: "If you can't find snow anywhere else, you can find it in Waterville Valley—but you've got to climb for it." Times have changed and the old CCC trail has been swallowed by the Mt. Tecumseh Ski Area, but we still have a trail called Old Tecumseh which, in a widened state, follows the alignment of the old CCC trail.

The reasons for Waterville Valley's snow protection are geographic. The base of skiing is at 1,800 feet, which is high for the East, and if you look at a contour map you will see that surrounding Waterville Valley there is a ring of 4,000-foot peaks of the White Mountain National Forest which draws snow storms into it and protects the Valley and our ski slopes from high winds. As a result of the Valley's snow reliability, we are able to guarantee an opening of our ski facilities no later than Thanksgiving, and we typically operate until the latter part of April with good ski conditions. More often than not we close not because we have run out of snow, but because we have run out of skiers, who no longer believe there can be snow in the mountains because they haven't seen snow in the cities for a month or so, and who are now caught up with mowing lawns, putting boats in the water, or playing tennis.

In any event, we typically operate about 150 days out of the year, which is as long or longer as most of the Western resorts. Last year, which was an average year for snowfall for us, we operated 156 days, as long to the day as Vail, a week longer than Aspen, and substantially longer than Sun Valley.

How do you ski Waterville Valley? A vacationing skier will probably spend most of his or her time at the Mt. Tecumseh Ski Area, which is the larger of our two ski areas in Waterville Valley, offering a vertical drop of over 2,000 feet, with seven lifts serving 32 trails, all wide and in the fall line, cut like western ski runs. As you walk up to the base buildings you will be entering a courtyard formed by the base buildings, a concept that we borrowed from the village at Mont-Tremblant up in the Laurentians built in the late '30s. Our courtyard is really the hub of the ski area. Ski School classes are organized in it, skiers on their way to lifts walk through it, and skiers coming off the mountain for lunch or hot chocolate ski down into it.

Above the square are five lower lifts that go off in different directions like fingers in a hand: a J-bar for complete beginners; a short, slow double chairlift for novices; a longer chair for lower intermediates; a still longer chair for upper intermediates; and a T-bar serving our slalom hill for experts and racers.

This kind of lift configuration would seem obvious, but it is surprising to me how few ski areas have tried to arrange their base lifts this way. The principal advantage is that everyone in a family or group of skiers can ski slopes of their own ability level but easily get together for lunch in the Base Lodge. Parents can easily check on the progress of their kids (or vice versa!).

Higher up on the mountain there are two other lifts that serve special purposes. The Sunnyside Chair serves four truly expert runs so that experts do not have to ski down through easier slopes near the base until lunch or the end of the day. We have another chair called High Country, which begins at the top of our upper intermediate lift and goes still higher and is really a small self-contained ski area for intermediate skiers. It starts from the point adjacent to the warming hut that is at the top of the Sunnyside lift.

With this kind of lift configuration the skiing possibilities are virtually endless depending on each skier's ability level. Many of our skiers are intermediate or advanced skiers, and when surveyed, they cite the variety of our trail system as one of the reasons why they like Waterville Valley. If they are real gluttons for skiing variety, there is an option available to vacationing skiers that allows them to ski, for a very small surcharge, five other nearby ski areas in addition

Personalized instruction characterizes Waterville Valley's approach to the beginner skier. This approach is continued as the new skier progresses into our more advanced mountain classes.

to Waterville Valley: Cannon Mountain, Loon Mountain, Mittersill, Bretton Woods, and Tenney Mountain—all of which are within a reasonably short driving distance from Waterville Valley.

SKI INSTRUCTION IN THE VALLEY

By Paul Pfosi, Director, Waterville Valley Ski School

(Editor's Note:

Paul Pfosi has been Director of the well-known Waterville Valley Ski School since the ski resort opened in 1966. He is a former member of the Swiss National Ski Team, a registered Swiss mountain guide, and is certified by Professional Ski Instructors of America (P.S.I.A.). Before coming to Waterville Valley he directed the ski school at the Valbella ski resort in Switzerland. He is also the owner and manager of Pfosi's Lodge in Waterville Valley, one of the five attractive inns in the ski village.)

The Waterville Valley Ski School has been organized and designed to best serve the needs of three different kinds of skiers: a) complete beginners b) novice, intermediate, or advanced skiers with their own equipment who want to further improve and c) children of all ability levels.

Each one of these categories of skiers requires different teaching approaches and methods, and in the 10 years or so since the founding of the ski resort at Waterville Valley, there have been giant improvements made in the way ski instruction is given, whether to beginners, children, or other skiers. At Waterville Valley we pioneered a number of these teaching innovations that have subsequently become accepted practice at all ski areas.

We feel that our ski school is large enough (50 instructors at peak times) to offer specialized instruction, but small enough so that personal attention and consideration can be given. Class sizes are generally smaller than at most ski resorts, and we expect our instructors to be particularly friendly and to make ski instruction a warm, fun, and safe experience for those who come here to learn.

Because of my Swiss background I am able to locate a number of highly qualified Swiss instructors whom I bring

over each year, and the Swiss contingent always adds an international flavor to the Ski School that we find popular and beneficial. The majority of the Ski School instructors are Americans, recruited and trained here at Waterville Valley. A substantial percentage are Certified Instructors who have taught in the Waterville Valley Ski School for a number of years.

Let me try to briefly describe our varied approaches to meeting the needs of the following kinds of skiers:

Complete Beginners

We were one of the first two ski areas in the ski world to subscribe to the Graduated Length Method (GLM) approach of teaching skiing to complete beginners. It's been a vital part of our ski curriculum ever since we opened our doors 10 years ago. In recent years it's been picked up by virtually every ski area, and it's now universally described as the best way to teach beginners.

It wasn't always so enthusiastically accepted in ski teaching circles, and frankly we feel that some of the ski schools espousing the GLM today still don't understand it or believe in it, but are touting GLM only because it's popular. Not so at Waterville Valley. We are real believers because we have seen, for many years now, how quickly and safely it can make skiers out of non-skiers. Like other ski schools that understand the system, we have continually refined and improved the approach to its present state of the art.

As an example, a group of travel agents from the deep South visited us after taking a similar trip to a *very* prominent Colorado resort (which shall remain nameless!). The travel agents tried GLM instruction in both resorts. The result— unanimous in our favor! Why? A very simple reason. We start beginners on 3-foot skis, not 5-foot skis, and there's a world of difference. Our students "graduate," on the personal advice of their instructor, to 4-foot skis typically by the second or third day, and to 5-foot skis by the third or fourth day. In a 5-day midweek ski vacation (our most popular vacation plan), about half of our beginners will be skiing comfortably on 5-foot skis by the end of the fifth day, and the other half will be skiing on somewhat longer skis. To start complete beginners on 5-foot skis the first day means that they must be taught to ski in the conventional way, starting with the snowplow, etc., which does not recognize or take full advantage of what really short skis can offer the complete beginner.

Obviously, there has to be a close rapport between the individual ski school instructor and the area ski rental shop, which provides all equipment necessary: skis, boots, and poles. As mentioned above, the average beginner will "trade in" his skis for longer ones three times during his stay! At Waterville Valley both the ski school and the ski rental shop are divisions of the ski area company, so that cooperation is not a problem. Incidentally, the ski rental shop offers the absolutely finest rental equipment available: Special GLM K2 skis; comfortable new Nordica buckle boots; Scott poles; and Spademan bindings, considered by many experts as the safest binding.

Our slopes and lifts are another advantage we offer complete beginners. Our easiest slope is served by a slow, easy Pasture J-bar lift, designed especially for beginners, and they ride it the first day on skis. The hill itself is as smooth as a ballroom, and covered with man-made snow, assuring the adequacy of snow, but more importantly, assuring that the snow surface is just right for rapid learning, not too hard and not too soft. After a day or so on the Pasture J-bar slope, the beginner progresses to the Lower Meadows Chairlift, also specially designed for new skiers. This lift serves three longer slopes, each covered again by man-made snow, and graded to reflect different levels of difficulty. By the fourth or fifth day, the new skier moves to the Valley Run Chairlift, 4,000 feet long of novice/lower intermediate terrain, also covered by man-made snow. The beginner is now a skier, with a good foundation for further improvement which practice will bring!

Novice, Intermediate, or Advanced Skiers with Their Own Equipment Who Want to Improve Further

For existing skiers with their own equipment we offer the conventional American Technique system of instruction. Emphasis is placed on allowing each student to develop his or her own natural style, with a comfortable, unforced stance on the skis. We see skiing as a dynamic sport in which the body position should never be static or rigid, but is continually adapting to changes in terrain, fall line, snow conditions, speed, etc. Skiing should be fun, and what a skier looks like is really secondary to his or her ability to effectively control the skis on any slope or in any snow conditions.

Our instructors are excellent skiers who themselves ski in a natural way. We offer instruction in either class or private lessons. We also offer a unique mountain class for up to seven skiers of roughly equal ability. This is really a semi-private lesson with typical line-cutting privileges and led by one of our top instructors who serves more as a guide than as an instructor, although he is expected to provide whatever level of instruction is requested.

Children of All Ability Levels

The Ski School offers a greater variety of children's instructional programs than any other ski resort that we know of! Even before kids get on skis, there are two separate nursery programs, one for kids in diapers and one for kids out of diapers. Then there is a program we call Nursery on Skis, which is a beginning skiing program combining some skiing instruction with conventional nursery. This program has specially trained instructors who use a variety of games and techniques designed to get kids on skis in a way that is fun for them. Beyond Nursery on Skis we have an entire section of the Ski School called the Kids' Ski School, with its own director and staff, which again uses special teaching methods for children. For those kids who are advanced skiers, there is a freestyle program headed by Floyd Wilkie, with George Askevold as head coach, and Wayne Wong as a guest coach. All three skiers are very well-known professional freestyle skiers with international reputations. Incidentally, the Waterville Valley Junior Freestyle Program is the largest in the country with over 100 kids enrolled on a regular basis. Some of the most important amateur and professional freestyle competitions are annually held in Waterville Valley. The current format for professional and amateur freestyle competition originated in Waterville Valley, and the first professional freestyle competition was held here in 1971.

On the racing side, advanced juniors can have instruction on weekends and holidays from the coaching staff of the Waterville Valley BBTS Ski Club, which conducts the junior program here in Waterville Valley. This program has produced several members currently on the U.S. Ski Team! The junior racing program has its own slalom hill (covered with man-made snow) with its own lift and built-in timing equipment. This racing hill was used for the finals of the World Cup Series in 1969, nationally televised with the finest skiers from all over the world competing!

Cross-country skiing, ski touring, takes a number of forms in Waterville Valley. Gentle, quiet tours through the White Mountain National Forest or races such as the Waterville Valley Derby.

R is for Réal, Monsieur Charette

Director of the Snow Eagle Ski School
Gray Rocks, Quebec, Canada

R IS FOR RÉAL

R is for Réal, Monsieur Charette. Go skiing in eastern Canada with Réal Charette and the Snow Eagle Ski School, Gray Rocks, Quebec, Canada and improve your style!

Eastern Canada does not have the majestic, rugged, above timberline terrain of the Canadian Rockies. It does have Continental charm. It also boasts of providing one of the finest ski schools in all of North America. High up in the Laurentian Mountains near St. Jovite and Mt. Tremblant, is Gray Rocks Inn, home of the famous Snow Eagle Ski School. It was here in 1930 that the first organized ski instruction was given in Canada without charge by an amateur; then in 1932 the ski school had its first professional, Bill Pauly, a ski instructor from Germany. Bill's ski technique consisted of a very low crouch, which was known here as the "Berlin Squat." The skis were kept quite wide apart and edged inwards as in the modern snowplow. Apparently it was the latest style in Europe and Bill introduced it at Gray Rocks.

In 1934, Dr. Wagner, just arriving from Austria, took over as the new director of the ski school. He too introduced the latest developments in European skiing. He used the stem turn and also skied a lot more erect than Bill Pauly. Dr. Wagner left in 1936 immediately after the *anchluss* of Austria by Germany to join the German Air Force. Mr. George Von Lillianfeld, former assistant instructor to Dr. Wagner at Gray Rocks Inn, then took over as head pro in the fall of 1937.

The management of Gray Rocks Inn was instrumental in bringing to Canada the next directors of the ski school, Hans Falkner and his cousin Herman Gadner, from the Austrian Tyrol. It was that year that the ski school took its present name, Snow Eagle Ski School. This was the name under which Hans and Herman had been operating a very successful ski school in their native village of Obergurgl high up in the Austrian Alps. They were now transplanting their Snow Eagle Ski School to Gray Rocks in the Laurentian Mountains of Canada. The following year, in 1938, Hans Falkner left Gray Rocks and moved just a few miles away to Mont-Tremblant where Joe (Fortune) Ryan was busy building his multi-million dollar resort. Herman Gadner, Han's cousin and assistant, then took over as the next ski school director. Herman remained here for 7 years until his tragic death in the spring of 1945 in the Canadian Rockies; he was killed in an avalanche while conducting one of his annual spring tours around Banff, Alberta. Later his body was brought back and buried in the Mont-Tremblant Catholic cemetery.

While with the Snow Eagle Ski School, Herman taught and coached many skiers of international fame such as the Wurtel twins, members of our Canadian Olympic Ski Teams in 1947 and 1952, and Jack "Porky" Griffin, member of the men's Olympic Ski Team in 1952. Herman Gadner was also Lucile Wheeler's first ski coach and instructor. He gave her her first ski lesson and also guided her in her first ski competition, a downhill race at Mont-Tremblant where she placed seventh in a field of 21 *Senior* ladies. This was on her tenth birthday. Lucile Wheeler, now Mrs. Kay Vaughan, in 1958 won two Gold Medals for Canada in world competition in Europe and also won top honors in other races such as the U.S. Nationals, Canadian Championships, Quebec Kandahar and the Harriman Cup.

The next director of the Snow Eagle Ski School was one of Hannes Schneider's great disciples, Luggi Foeger. Luggi was a great ski school organizer and was at Gray Rocks for 3 years. He is often credited for having solidly put skiing on its feet in the Laurentian Mountains.

Today, the ski school is directed by Réal Charette, a native French Canadian from the Laurentians who learned under the direction of both Herman Gadner and Luggi Foeger. Réal has been the director of the Ski School since 1948 when Luggi returned to Yosemite National Park in California. I first met him on the Fall International Ski Show Circuit about 10 years ago, when he directed four of his excellent instructors in an instructional performance on the rolling carpet "Ski-Deck." Réal has a magnetic personality, is a dynamic speaker and most authoritative Ski School Director. He is directly responsible for thousands of skiers' annual return to eastern Canada's Gray Rocks and Mont-Tremblant ski areas. Réal was quite active in ski competition at an early age, but today has settled down to the operation of the Snow Eagle Ski School and the continuation of its high standards. From three instructors in 1945 the school now employs 40 full-time instructors and since 1972, has given over 100,000 ski lessons each season. There is no doubt that today, the Snow Eagle Ski School is the largest ski institution of its kind in Canada. Réal is also a past examiner and president of the Canadian Ski Instructors' Alliance. This national organization in Canada teaches the latest ski techniques to would-be ski instructors. Every year, just prior to the Winter Season, the C.S.I.A. gives a course of instruction on the teaching of skiing and certifies those that pass the exams.

This method taught today by the Snow Eagle Ski School is that of the Canadian Ski Instructors' Alliance. Through membership in the International Ski Congress, which holds sessions every 3 years, the C.S.I.A. is in close touch with the latest developments in skiing techniques and teaching methods throughout the world. The instructors of the Snow Eagle Ski School are all members of the C.S.I.A. and comprise an elite group of expert skiers. The instruction is based on their daily observation and evaluation of the elements that make up "fun" and modern skiing. Since 1973 the Snow Eagle Ski School has adopted the "Short Ski Progression" method (similar to G.L.M. in the U.S.A.). This method appears to be the logical outcome for the search of a rapid, effective and safe way of learning the modern ski technique!

I have searched the Canadian Ski School Manual for differences between their current technique and the American Teaching Method, but have found no significant conflicts of opinion or methodology. Although they still refer to the "wedge" position as a "snowplow" and the "early basic christie" as a "glide christie," all progressions and forms are identical to those described in the ATM manual, even to the

Practicing what he preaches, Gray Rocks' Ski School Director, Réal Charette, is still a master of precise form. He knows his craft.

lack of including a tight feet-together final parallel form as a level of aspiration, except in the paragraph which describes deep snow skiing. This omission of prejudice, to many instructors of both countries, was a *faux pas* on the part of both technical committees, as there are few proficient instructors anywhere, except perhaps in France, who do not ski with their feet together when free-skiing for exhibition.

All the illustrations for advanced techniques in the C.S.I.A. manual illustrate the parallel skier with his feet a hip-width apart. The ATM manual at least recognizes the existence of a feet-together form which still represents the mark of an expert to most recreational skiers. There is no question in anyone's mind that the open stance is more stable for a beginning skier, but neither is there a question that advanced recreational skiers have the desire and capability of skiing, quite stable, with their feet together. For too many years, ski educators have patterned their final forms after ski racers. At the speeds which a downhill racer must travel, the open stance is tantamount to his stability. The slalom racer is also constantly separating his skis to step into a faster line. What must be considered is that these options are simply means to a common end—beating the clock. This is hardly the object of the average recreational skier. His motivation is more aesthetic. He not only wants safety and efficiency in his turns, but he also wants to look graceful. An ice skate with two blades instead of one would surely be more "stable," but one wonders if the turns they would carve might be as graceful as those performed on a single blade. The analogy can be extended to include a comparison between a tricycle and a bicycle, or between a sailboat and a catamaran, or between a glider and a two-engined airplane. The theory of "independent leg action" notwithstanding, a recreational skier should have the option of choosing to ski with his skis together. To leave out such a final form from any instructional manual is to publish an incomplete manuscript. I fear that modern ski technicians, in an effort to appear progressive, have eliminated from their current meth-

odology significant contributions of ski theory from technicians of the sixties which are applicable to the contemporary recreational skier's needs. *Technical committees must reccognize the difference between skiing to race and skiing to look graceful.* It is my considered opinion that the majority of recreational skiers fall in the latter category. They are the masses; they support our profession; their aesthetic needs should be satisfied.

Beyond that omission, it would appear that, at least with our Canadian neighbors, we are finally arriving at a ubiquitous ski technique that has no chauvinistic connection. We are embracing an eclectic system of skiing style which has been influenced by each of the great skiing countries of the world. We are accepting the fact that there is no "vun vay to ski," and we are respecting all systems as meaningful contributors to a scientific awareness of the problems involved in controlled descent. We should salute the Canadian Ski Instructors' Alliance and Directors like Réal Charette for bringing about this peaceful coexistence and hope that they have established a precedent for the rest of the skiing world.

Here is what Réal had to say about modern skiing, eastern Canada style, in an interview with SKIER'S DIGEST:

SD: Is there a difference between what the ATM calls a wedge *and what the C.S.I.A. refers to as a* snowplow?
Réal: None whatsoever, except that, at Gray Rocks, we emphasize edging with a more narrow "snowplow" in an effort to teach proper weight transfer and *correct* turning principles. Spinning on a flat ski has little to do with advanced skiing, and parallel inside edge skiing is our primary goal.

SD: How early in your teaching program do you teach edging *principles?*
Réal: During the very first hour! The body position and

transverse leverage of the outside ski is no different in the snowplow turn than in the parallel turn. We teach edging of the outside ski early, so as not to create the bad habit of spinning on a ski that is flat to the snow.

SD: Does your ski school advocate a Graduated Length Method of learning?
Réal: Yes. In Canada, we refer to it as a Short Ski Progression, but we *do not* advocate the use of a "shortee" ski (under 135cm). While our beginners may start with a ski that has no side camber, we try to get them on a correctly shaped ski quickly to fully benefit from their edging efforts.

SD: What do you recognize as the most significant difference between the modern ski teaching methodology and that practiced by ski schools of the past?
Réal: After 28 years of ski teaching, I have seen many systems come and go. Today the primary concern of the ski teacher should be to get his student into parallel skiing with good style as quickly as possible. We are no longer adamant about the perfection of early exercise like the snowplow, stem, or various stem-christie turns. The quicker we can get the student with his feet together and on his edges, the better.

SD: Does your ski school discourage a skier who wants to learn to ski with his (or her) feet together?
Réal: Absolutely not! While a wider stance may be beneficial for the majority of new skiers who feel more balanced in that position, there are always the natural athletes who are perfectly balanced with their feet together. If we see that happen naturally, we certainly do *not* discourage it, as this ultimate form is eventually the goal of everyone! My instructors are encouraged to *always* ski with their feet together, no matter what phase of the learning process they are teaching, as I believe they should be symbols of the final perfect form toward which their students aspire!

SD: Gray Rocks is well known as one of the finest ski areas for learning how to ski. It does not, however, have a "Ryan's Run." Does an advanced ski-week enrollee at Gray Rocks get a chance to ski Mont-Tremblant? How close are you to that mountain?
Réal: We don't have the long runs of Tremblant, but we do have one of the finest teaching areas in America. I have personally designed many trails with a particular teaching need in mind. Of our 22 trails, 5 or 6 are quite steep, and we have enough moguls for anyone. We use Mt. Tremblant for mileage. Advanced students ski there twice a week, intermediates, once. It is only 10 minutes away.

SD: Do you feel that eastern ski resorts breed a more proficient skier than the resorts of the western part of our continent? Why?
Réal: There is no doubt. The eastern American skier is the best in the world. He (or she) is the most stylish, because he is always performing before a crowd. He takes more lessons and is more serious about self-improvement. With narrow steep mogulled trails, he must be more courageous, have more stamina and quicker reflexes than his western cousin, who can descend his spacious environment with few turns in a more relaxed manner. The western skier who banks his turns and does not edge appreciably in his deep powder would have great difficulty descending a typical eastern trail, where edging and angulation are imperative.

Thank you Réal. Over a million ski lessons have been administered through the Snow Eagle Ski School at Gray Rocks since Réal took over as Director. His is an authoritative voice based upon that extensive experience. He still skis every day and exercises friendly but firm control over the teaching methods of his instructors. A ski week at Gray Rocks will reward you with a unique Continental experience that is as colorful and romantic in fringe benefits as it is instructive.

Follow the leader! After a teaching session, a class from Gray Rocks' famous Snow Eagle Ski School wend their way down the mountain. The school teaches the Canadian version of GLM called "The Short Ski Progression Method."

S is for SUGARLOAF, MAINE

S IS FOR SUGARLOAF, MAINE

S is for Sugarloaf, Maine, the giant of the East.

When Sugarloaf is discussed by the general skiing public, two comments almost always surface—either, "isn't that in Vermont," or "Sugarloaf—that's some big mountain!" For the uneducated skier Sugarloaf is very often confused with Sugarbush, in Vermont, which, by the way, is also a fine mountain. To skiers who know the sport and have traveled, Sugarloaf is known as having the best big mountain skiing the East has to offer. And, with a 2,600-foot continuous vertical drop, above timberline lift-serviced snowfields, five chairlifts, five T-bars, a 8,500-foot four-passenger Gondola, and 39 miles of trails and slopes, Sugarloaf *is* big.

Located in the western mountains of Maine, surrounded by a group of 4,000-foot peaks, Sugarloaf is one mountain, with all the trails falling down the pitches simultaneously, and in plain view of the skier approaching from the north and south. The season at Sugarloaf runs from mid-November to early May and has an average yearly snowfall of 180 inches (15 feet!). Because of its more northerly and easterly exposure Sugarloaf usually gets snow when every area in the East gets rain, and once the snow is on the trails, it lasts longer.

The area has always been famous as a skiers' mountain, with its super steep front-face trails and backside snowfields giving even the most accomplished skier a run for the money. Site of the 1971 World Cup Downhill, Sugarloaf has also become a center for freestyle, with many of its skiers big winners of the pro and amateur circuits. But the mountain is not all 'blood 'n guts'—the lower section of the mountain is groomed daily and is a paradise for the novice and intermediate skier who wants nice, easy-to-turn-on terrain. The ski school was one of the first to use GLM, Graduated Length Method, and still specializes in teaching those new to skiing the fundamentals of enjoying the sport. Sugarloaf has snowmaking, too, top-to-bottom, for the world's longest system, and has a fleet of snow-cats (including three brand-new

Thiokols) that are intelligently and expertly driven, to groom trails and pack powder—always with the skier in mind.

At the base of the mountain and in the surrounding valley, Sugarloaf has achieved a unique blend of cosmopolitan sophistication with down-country folksyness. One hundred condominium units line the trails, and the adjacent village center includes a grocery store, gift shop, laundromat, restaurant and pub, and ski shop. The mountain-owned Sugarloaf Inn, at the base of the slopes with its own lift, is a full-service lodge for those who want the convenience of parking their cars and being right at the slopes for the duration. In the valley, the architecture is unique, ranging from the tyrolian Capricorn, to the swinging Red Stallion, a restored horse barn. The lodges all fit together, amid the rugged wilderness, to provide warm comfortable accommodations with excellent food and good service. There are over 20 lodges in the valley and a bed capacity of 2,000. Whether for singles, families, or large groups, these lodges are bent on making the skier's stay at Sugarloaf a good one.

But Sugarloaf is more than just a big mountain with lots of snow, lifts and lodges—it has retained the intimacy and straight forwardness of skiing as it was 10 or 15 years ago. The lift lines are short, the staff goes out of its way to help the skier, and candid, unpretentious honesty is the rule. Amos Winter, the founder of Sugarloaf, (back in 1949 when the hearty climbed Sugarloaf to ski) is still out there working, selling lift tickets. Sugarloaf has worked hard to retain the fun and enjoyment of being outdoors on the snow—lollipop races and Easter parades for the kids, canoe races on snow, wild New Years Eve ski jumps, the Spring Festival of Madness, the World Heavy Weight Ski Race, (illustrated with the photo of John Trudden on our title page), and Old Timers' Day are just some of the events that make Sugarloaf special.

Sugarloaf has come a long way since the days when the big

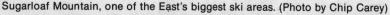

Sugarloaf Mountain, one of the East's biggest ski areas. (Photo by Chip Carey)

Left—The 9,000-foot gondola provides 2,600 vertical feet of skiing at snowcapped Sugarloaf, the "western" mountain that is "down east." Right—United Skiers of Virginia skier at the Sugar-loaf T-shirt contest. Center—The ski dorm at Sugarloaf is popular with large ski clubs.

excitement in the winter used to be "going down to Kingfield to see who rented the room in the Herbert." A big mountain, covered with lifts, with condominiums on the trails and a valley full of lodges, Sugarloaf/USA is big time, but not so much that it has forgotten the true goals of a ski vacation—enjoying good friends, the fresh air of the Maine woods, and the exhilaration of a fast run down the side of a mountain.

I have asked Tom Hildreth, Director of Skiing Sales at Sugarloaf to tell you a little about ski clubs. They still offer one of the least expensive alternatives to going broke from the expense of our sport.

SKI CLUBS—HOW TO ORGANIZE AND RUN SUCCESSFUL SKI TRIPS

by Tom Hildreth, Director of Skiing Sales Sugarloaf/USA

The last five years have seen an amazing growth of amateur ski clubs throughout the country. Whether these clubs be youth, college, adult or business groups, the motivating factor of a ski club is to provide a great ski vacation for the members, drawing on a ski area's facilities and services at a price not available to the individual skier. Skiers are coming to the realization that organizing as a club can increase buying and bargaining power at a ski area, reduce transportation costs, and provide a nucleus for social activity throughout the year. The latter is especially true for younger couples and singles working in a metropolitan area.

The following article will go through the basics of how to organize a ski club, how to set up and sell a ski trip to the club members, and finally, how to cover all the details that make a trip a success, as well as a bargain. The content for these topics will be drawn from the experience of the group sales staff at Sugarloaf/USA in Kingfield, Maine, using for a case a large club trip by the United Skiers of Virginia.

How to Organize a Ski Club

Organizing a club requires diligent work by a small group of sincere skiers who want to spread the enjoyment of skiing to a larger, unorganized mass of skiers. The major cause of a ski club's demise is almost always the lack of leadership and direction at the top. Clubs are fairly easy to organize. The hard part is stimulation and motivation by the leaders.

Schools, colleges, businesses, or apartment complexes are the major social structures to work with in developing a club. The best time to start is the early fall. Start out by posting notices of an organizational meeting in highly visible areas, and send out mailings to people who have shown interest in forming a club. At the meeting outline reasons for organizing the club, especially stressing the discounts available to the members. A wine and cheese party after the meeting with ski movies, adds a nice touch. Dues should be required, about $5 per individual, to cover printing costs, rental of meeting rooms, etc. Pins, ID cards, etc. are good to have for the members, giving them the true "club spirit." Once the club reaches a membership level of 50-75, immediately set up two or three ski trips. This is when relations with ski areas, bus companies, airlines, and sometimes tour operators and travel agents become important.

How to Set Up and Sell a Trip to a Club

Most ski clubs, at a general meeting, appoint one individual as a trip chairman, and at the same time, vote on what areas to visit in the coming season. The trip chairman then contacts the ski areas for detailed information and prices on lodging and lifts.

It is mandatory to know the dates of the proposed trip, an accurate estimate of the numbers on the trip, and most important, the type of lodging desired. Lodging arrangements usually consume most of the trip chairman's time in planning. An evaluation of the make-up of the club dictates the type of lodging desired. A youth or school group generally is happy with dorm or hostel type accommodations, with bunk beds and cafeteria style dining. The Sugarloafer's Ski Dorm at Sugarloaf is this type of a facility, with a capacity of over 200, broken down into 6 bunkrooms, male and female, with a common area for recreation. The Ski Dorm also boasts a urethene foam dome dining area. The usual dorm rates are $9 to $11 per night with two meals. For

They call them *rat packs* down east. Sugarloaf mogul busters "git it on."

adult groups and more affluent school and college clubs, there are many options open—4 to 6 to a bedroom with a common bath and no menu choice, 4 to a bedroom with a private bath and a limited meal selection, double occupancy, first class room with private bath and full menu, and finally, condominium and efficiency apartments. The latter accommodations are becoming increasingly popular with groups because of economy (condominiums rent out by the unit cost, break down to $9 to $12 per person per day) and location. At Sugarloaf the condominiums are on the ski trails. On-the-mountain lodging is very desirable for groups, especially those coming by bus. Once the group arrives, the bus is parked for the duration, saving mileage costs, and the club members are free from rendezvous times for going to and from the lodge to the slopes.

Once the trip leader has decided the type of lodging, basing the decision on economy, privacy, and comfort, a letter or phone call should be made to the ski area with detailed proposals and questions. At Sugarloaf many times one phone call can confirm a booking for a large group weekend or week long trip, with an exact per person figure, including taxes and gratuities. With condominium lodging the process is generally more involved, requiring a more accurate head count to determine how many units will be needed to accommodate the group, with every bed filled to keep the per-person costs as low as possible. Prices for both skiing and lodging for groups are generally 10 to 15 percent off the individual rates, and in low season (January and early February) they sometimes are further reduced. Lodging rates are usually more negotiable than skiing group rates. Over the holiday periods little discount is available; supply and demand sets the price. A written confirmation of the rates should always be required by the club to avoid confusion.

Once the ski area prices are confirmed, the next project is to line up transportation. For a long journey with a big group (40+) a bus is best; bus capacities are usually 39, 41, 45 or 49 passengers and rates are based on mileage. Sometimes a price reduction can be arranged if the club commits to one bus company for a series of weekend of week long trips. A long term deposit will be required, and can be drawn from the club's treasury.

If the trip is to a distant ski area, requiring an airline,

check for airlines with group rates, and with tour brokers for charters. Most charters have to be confirmed 60 days before departure time.

When all this material is assembled, print up a club newsletter promoting the trip and listing all the positive assets of the area. Price out the trip in one lump sum, including tips and taxes. Mark up the whole package 2 or 3 percent to buy wine and cheese for the bus ride and to cover any emergencies while at the ski area. Have a sign-up sheet available through the mail, as well as at a general meeting, where slides (the best) or a movie of the ski area can be shown to stimulate interest. A deposit of 35-50 percent is the safest amount, definitely locking the members into the trip, as well as paying for the lodge deposit and the bus company, which requires full payment before departure. Have the closing for deposits well before departure time, at least 1½ months.

The question often arises about travel agents and tour brokers. As a rule of thumb—except when dealing with airlines—always work directly with the ski area and lodge. Because most group rates are already significantly reduced, ski areas dislike having to give an additional 10 percent to a travel agent. Sometimes the group rate is marked up to absorb this. With tour brokers, the price may be slightly less, but experience at Sugarloaf has shown that communications sometimes break down with the addition of a third party, and the club doesn't get the service available when working indirectly with the ski area. Any major ski area, like Sugarloaf, encourages clubs to approach the resort directly. Most times a lower price and better service is the result.

The lodge should have a floor plan—obtain it and assign the skiers to rooms or units. Check with the mountain on complimentary ticketing policy. At Sugarloaf it is one complimentary ticket for every paid 15. This is one of the few rewards for the trip leader and family.

Once the pricing and lodging arrangements have been made, the details that make the club trip successful have to be worked out.

The Details That Make the Difference

A sound ground work for the trip has been laid. Reservations with the lodge or condominiums have been made and confirmed with a deposit, the bus is lined up, with a

The drop from the Sugarloaf snowfields is respectably steep.

departure time set, and the money is in from the club members going on the trip. Through all these negotiations, the trip leader should be constantly aware of all the details that make the trip run smoothly. A quick look at a Sugarloaf trip will bring the details and extras that make the difference out.

The United Skiers of Virginia is a consortium of seven different colleges in Virginia. The group started and grew through the same process as described earlier—introductory meetings, mailings, film festivals, etc. The trip to Sugarloaf was discussed the previous June, and most of the arrangements were settled by September. By the time of the trip, the United Skiers on the 14-hour bus journey to Sugarloaf had grown to 480 in ten buses; the original projection was 250 to 300. Housing was solely in condominiums. Meals, except for one party, were up to the skiers. Of the skiers 185 were new to skiing, starting out in GLM, with 23 instructors keeping the classes to a maximum of eight.

The trip leader spent long hours correlating skiers' names, condos they should stay in, lessons (if desired) and level of skiing, and whether rentals were needed. This detailed list, which is a must for all clubs, big or small, enabled the Sugarloaf staff to make up package tickets in advance, with the skier's name on it, and place the tickets in each condominium unit, saving lengthy processing and ticketing time. The list also enabled the rental shop to check inventory and make sure there was enough equipment to handle the 300 or so renting equipment.

On any destination club trip, where the group will be skiing two or more days, always mail one list to the group sales manager with a breakdown on skier's names, level of ability, lessons and rentals, and home phone number or guardian to contact (for the first-aid crew). Mail a housing breakdown to the lodge or condominium complex. If the trip leader doesn't have this information prepared 5 days before arrival at the ski area, then chaos will result. The skiers have had a long bus or plane ride; nothing irks them more than to wait in line to be processed for ticketing, or not knowing what room or condominium they are supposed to be in.

On day group trips, the trip leader should give the group sales manager a call a few days before arrival, telling him the name of the club, the trip leader's name, and the exact number on the trip. The price and complimentary policy can be settled over the phone. When the club arrives the trip leader only handles ticketing, paying the group sales manager for the bulk tickets. If arriving by bus, the trip leader should always have the skiers stay on the bus until the tickets are picked up and then ticket the skiers as they exit the bus.

If the club is driving up in cars, the trip leaders should arrange for a rendezvous point for ticketing. The most important thing a trip leader should keep in mind is constant communication with the ski area and lodge. If there is some problem in making the deposit deadline, call the lodge immediately to reassure them. Never leave a lodge hanging when the owner has reserved every bed in the building, and then call the day the deposit is due and say sorry, can't make the trip. It is never too soon to start planning a club trip, usually the late summer or early fall is sufficient. For the big trips, especially to western areas, the season before is mandatory.

If possible, the trip leader should visit the ski area in the off season or well before arrival, to get a feel for the resort and work out any problems that might be foreseen. This all stems back to the basic premise of good ski clubs and club trips—to keep a club strong requires stimulation by good ski trips, which in turn come from an effective trip leader, who works closely with the resort and transportation companies making sure all the details are worked out for a successful, smooth-running, and event-filled ski club trip.

The final facet of a club ski trip are the extras, that with planning, a resort can arrange for a club. For the USVA, some of the highlights were a Down East Lobster bake, a three-legged slalom, wine and cheese parties on the slopes, a Tuborg T-shirt contest, a NASTAR with 300 contestants, a beer blast that consumed 18 kegs of beer in 4 hours, and finally, a fantastic time skiing and lessons that the students will never forget.

Any ski club, big or small, with proper communications with the resort and long range planning, can arrange for these extras, all at package group rates. Don't settle for just lift tickets and a place to sleep; the trip leader should strive for the extras that make the trip unique. At Sugarloaf, the staff has learned that packaging a full schedule of activities for the group keeps the skiers happy and makes the chance for a return trip that much greater.

T is for TAOS
and Taos is not for turkeys...

Author Frank Covino races an avalanche down wilderness slope of Taos Ski Valley.

T IS FOR TAOS

T is for Taos, and Taos is not for turkeys. I have spoken, elsewhere in this book, of the varied motivations that bring people to skiing. For those who wish to satisfy no more than the need for freedom of controlled flight at high altitude in the close embrace of the brilliant sun, deep in dry powder with a seemingly endless variety of terrain and incredibly steep chutes, Taos is waiting. Taos Ski Valley is the dream of Ernie Blake which has reached fruition. It is a Shangri-la for real skiers who want to escape the plastic replicas that appeal to those who are into skiing for other reasons. The night life is quiet and soothing, complementing the peacefulness of the entire resort complex. Marge and I have never been hosted as royally as we have this week by the affable Swiss owner and Ski School Director, Ernie Blake, who personally escorted us over his entire mass skiing complex, turning his skis like a man half his age. The walkie-talkie tucked into his yellow parka keeps the elf-like 62-year-old Director aware of all that is occurring on his mountain, from ski accidents, which curiously are few, to new VIP arrivals.

To appreciate the art form, you should know a little about its sculptor. Who is this Swiss dynamo with the redoubtable name of Ernie Blake? Georgia Hotton, Assistant Manager to Taos Ski Valley told Skier's Digest this adventurous story:

"For awhile he conducted ski tours for Saks Fifth Avenue. Every weekend he loaded his tour group onto one of the green-beige Pullman Sleepers and headed off for the Adirondack ski slopes with other weekend escapees from metropolitan New York.

"It was a rush to get to the train and a rush to get to the ticket window. Then a standing in line to buy tickets, then a rush to the rope tows and another standing in line. If anything, the weekend excursions were more hectic for Ernie Blake than life in the city itself. After all, it was his responsibility to see to it that everyone else had *fun*.

"As a young skier in Switzerland and northern Italy, Ernie had known the challenges and the solitude of vast above-timberline mountain terrain. As one of the real pioneers in skiing, he often climbed and skied far beyond the few lifts then in existence.

"One of his earliest ski touring experiences taught him a lesson the hard way: Don't go ski touring or mountain climbing alone. One morning before the low clouds had burned off, Ernie was skimming over the snow when he sailed out over an unseen 60-foot cliff. The exhilaration of the floating over light powder snow was heightened as he literally floated through the clouds. The landing broke his thigh, and he had several hours to reflect on the awesome beauty and solitude of the surrounding majestic peaks before an Italian customs patrol found him late in the afternoon. Honorable men, these border patrolmen—instead of just taking Ernie's expensive camera, they agreed to exchange assistance in getting to the nearest hospital for the camera. Ernie was in no position to bargain.

Right—Taos is bordered by some of the steepest ski slopes in North America. Jan Walden, visiting Finnish ski expert, is shown at the base of Stauffenberg, an avalanche-prone 37 degree slope in Taos' West Basin. The area gets so much snow it becomes a problem.
Below—By day or by night, it's an impressive mountain. This nighttime photograph of Taos Ski Valley clearly shows the lodges and condominiums which are located right on the slopes. Skiers glide right to their rooms. That long gash is Al's Run.

"During World War II, Ernie served with Patton's Third Army in Europe. He became an intelligence officer on loan to the British, who christened him with the code name, Ernie Blake. Then back to New York City for 3 years of working in the export-import business. On a short vacation, he visited the Rockies and it was not long thereafter that he and his wife Rhoda decided to escape from the New York City scene.

"But they were no ordinary dropouts off to find a mountain top from which to meditate on the follies of ordinary mortals. Skiing still held a fascination.

"The Rocky Mountains rose out of their backyard in Sante Fe and though the mountains might be blood red in the afternoon sunset, they were brilliant snowcapped white against intensely blue skies most of the year. The lure of these mountain snows led Ernie to accept the managership of Santa Fe Ski Basin where he operated a lift made out of a converted 1882 ore conveyor. The ore buckets were replaced with surplus B-24 bomber seats, and this unique lift provided Ernie with many 'experiences' he did not want to advertise.

"He did, however, want to advertise the skiing, and so he went off into the vast hinterlands of Texas to introduce a new sport to a different breed of skiers. The results were impressive, for today not only is New Mexico skiing largely supported by Texans but so is much of Colorado's skiing. Prior to Ernie's forays, skiing was a sport known to Texans only from television or the movies.

"Not content to manage someone else's ski area, Ernie decided to carve out his own ski domain. He searched for a mountain with good snow and a lodge. He found these in a tight little valley shown on the maps of 1890 as Twining,

New Mexico, just 2 miles up the canyon from another famous mining town—Amizette. There was an unfinished four-room summer lodge located at the base of a spruce and aspen covered mountain that rose straight up above the lodge itself. When Ernie discovered his Shangri-la in May 1954 there were 100 inches of snow on the ground, and it was inaccessible except on snowshoes or skis.

"When the people of Taos, 19 miles down the canyon from Twining, heard about the crazy Swiss who planned to build a ski area at Twining, they just laughed and said there would be no way to keep the road open in winter. Ernie wasn't laughing. He and 18 Indians were hauling the first ski lift into place. There were no roads on the mountain. All lift parts had to be hauled by manpower. The burro that was supposed to assist was too smart; he refused to go up the mountain.

"Indian power combined with Ernie's determination put that lift in place. By the time it was completed there was enough snow to start skiing. The only run was the Showdown section of Snakedance, a near-vertical slope above the Hondo Lodge. One of the first guests asked for her money back after an hysterical sidestepping down the mountain. (Ernie thought she should pay double for his gallantry in sidestepping down with her through tempting powder.) About 2 o'clock every Sunday afternoon the lift cable would derail, and the help of the guests would quickly be enlisted to lift it back on the sheaves. Those early skiers were almost as crazy as Ernie; in those days the bar was not open on Sunday.

"Perserverance, insanity or an instinctive sense of great skiing? It is hard to determine which of these ingredients or combination of ingredients really drove Ernie Blake. His has

Below—Katchina Basin. The steep pitches in the photograph are skied by experts, but of more universal appeal are the easy-skiing bowls lower on the mountain. This Rock Mountain skier's haven holds dry powder snow in such great depth that skiing is still enjoyed into June and early July.
Left—Ernie Blake leading Frank Covino below the Katchina ridge.

not been the 9 AM to 5 PM office executive life—far from it. It might be characterized as the 5 AM to 9 PM life of the early western settler.

"Dropout, pioneer, or smart businessman—whatever you call the man, Ernie Blake has created one of the most exciting and charismatic areas to be found anywhere. As a concession to the novice he has slowly added a variety of beginner and intermediate slopes that provide easy ego-building skiing for the not so expert.

"With a twinkle in his eye, Ernie insists he is the original dropout, for as director of his own ski school he wears a bright gold ski instructor's jacket instead of a grey flannel suit. Suntanned and happy, Ernie still zooms down his sun-bathed powder slopes while his former business friends continue to fight the hectic battle of survival in the East."

Thank you, Georgia. Here is what Ernie had to say about taming the powder at Taos:

"Taming the Taos powder is largely a matter of courage, and the rewards are in the realm of pure ecstasy as it is actually delightfully easy to ski Taos powder.

"In the first place, Taos powder is found in super abundance on the steep runs, and at Taos there are 26 of these. They range from the popular runs on the lower front side of the mountain (off lift #5) like Showdown, Snakedance, Edelweiss, Inferno, Al's Run, Spencer Bowl and Psycho-Path to the plunging slashes of Zagava, Castor, Pollux, Reforma, Blitz, Oster, Fabian and Stauffenberg (from lift #2). The steep powder runs also include the wide bowls of Lorelei and Longhorn, the exciting couloirs named Juarez, Hidalgo, Treskow, and the wide (traverse for a half-mile if you like) face of Kachina. Then too there are the glades of Papa Bear, Mama Bear and the special solitude and marvelous pitches of El Funko.

"The very steepness of these powder runs makes the floating, gliding, soaring through extremely easy. All the skier need do is point his skis downhill, then let the tips float up and out as he swings close to the fall line, moving his skis (both together, both equally weighted and unweighted) with a light up-unweighting permitting a smooth displacement of the ski first to one side of the fall line, then to the other.

"It's an incredible sensation as the light dry powders provide minimal resistance to the turning skis—an incredible sensation as the powder flies even over the skier's shoulders as he glides down, down, down through the fluffy white stuff.

"Don't follow too closely or you may be blinded by the flying powder, jet-streaming from the skier in front of you.

"Do practice figure-eights with the tracks developing in front of you for the sheer fun of looking back at quintessential patterns.

"Or better yet, get out early and lead the way, etching your own distinctive mark on the vast white blanket dropping away below.

"These famous powder runs at Taos represent approximately 50 percent of the skiable terrain, and they are too steep to be packed by machines. After they are sufficiently sliced up by intrepid powder seekers, the ski patrol may come along to ski pack the entire course into a soft packed powder condition that is also great skiing. But once this has happened, the powder no longer flies, and the skier wisely reverts to those turns involving weight transfer from ski to ski.

The icy crust at the peak turns into corn as Marge carves a neat inclined turn at Taos Ski Valley.

"On a steep run, the skier has lots of advantages. Once the turn is initiated correctly, gravity and speed bring the skis on through the turn. It is virtually impossible to catch edges in light powder and/or on steep slopes. Should a skier fall on a steep slope, he may momentarily be flying free; the landing is likely to be a gliding not the sudden stopping of a high-speed edge-catching fall on a flatter slope.

"Skiing the powder at Taos is easy not only because of the steepness of the powder slopes, but also because of the quality of the snow. Rocky Mountain powder has been called "champagne," for it is a light sparkling sort of stuff.

"It is necessary to weight and unweight both skis equally; otherwise a skier will find one leg fully extended and the knee of the other leg hitting his chin, for great powder is a bottomless, unresistant substance.

"It is necessary to find that fine point of balance that keeps you over the skis, but with tips floating rather than diving.

"It is necessary to keep a cool head if you fall because it can be a suffocating feeling until you roll over and get your head up and out. It is a bit like the long dive of an underwater swimmer. Eventually you must and will come up.

"And that is the story of deep powder skiing at Taos. For the beginner and intermediate there is the ballroom experience of packed powder. Now, let's sneak across the boundary, so I can show you how I discovered and planned this fantastic ski terrain. For their own safety, however, crossing the boundary ribbon is *verbotten* and will be punished by surrender of the offender's lift ticket. We want visiting skiers to enjoy their week at Taos and are proud of our low casualty and missing person rate."

There is one sign on a tower in Katchina Basin that I can't forget. It is posted at a point where the chairlift suddenly glides from a 60-foot elevation to a 3-foot elevation, then to a steep cliff once again. The sign says, **"NO UNLOADING HERE. SURVIORS WILL BE PROSECUTED!"** Whoever painted the warning misspelled the word *survivors* but the tragi-comic intent of the caution is fully understood, and I doubt that many skiers have been recalcitrant. Much of Ernie's empire is military oriented, because of his past experience, but we found him to be the least pretentious, least officiating and most affable of all ski school directors that hosted our journey across the continent. Whatever militancy does come through in Ernie's control of his ski area is always softened by a note of humor. Like when he mentioned that the crossing of boundary lines by skiers is *verbotten,* he added: "Sometimes the powder hounds can't resist. They sneak under the boundary ribbon and occasionally are never heard from again." The avalanche proclivity in the high peaks of Taos Ski Valley is a very real danger. "But that is all right," smiled Ernie. "This is a Catholic state, and there must be some kind of control over the population explosion . . ."

"The expert powder hounds will look for a flatter run when the overnight snowfall has only equalled 1 or 2 inches. The cushion of a few inches of powder makes for fine floating on an intermediate run, whereas skis may scrape through to hard snow when there are only 2 inches of new snow on a steep run.

"However, at Taos when it snows the gods usually laugh generously and up to 36 inches may fall in a single night.

"Get up and out early, for there are lots of powder lovers at Taos."

And that is exactly what Marge and I did, as Ernie had a special powder run planned for us outside the boundary line in the wilderness area, where every thousand feet was

Three feet of snow still forms a wall beside this stream that I found in the Taos Valley, and the date is April 9!

punctuated with the scar of an avalanche, either of natural origin or detonated by the 105mm cannons of Taos. We took Bruce, one of the top Ski Patrol officers with us as a guide and to have an extra radio along for rescue.

Ernie interrupted our run through the wilderness area to reserve a dinner for us via walkie-talkie at the St. Bernard, a delightful French restaurant in a Swiss type chalet. The St. Bernard is owned by Jean Mayer, who also is Blake's top ski instructor. Mayer's brother Dadou owns the neighboring Edelweiss Lodge, and both men are geniuses in hotel management. Personally serving each table, with seating arranged family style for those who need social assistance, Jean takes great pride in the production of every meal, and they are indeed banquets. You will know you have been fed when you leave the St. Bernard. Jean is an artist.

On the mountain, Mayer usually leads the super-expert class. Every smart skier who comes to Taos includes ski lessons in his week. It is one of the few ski areas where even a professional may need guidance in descending some of the steeper avalanche prone runs. Areas most susceptible to slides are fired upon or detonated with hand-placed explosives in the wee hours of the morning long before the lifts start running, though, so you may feel reasonably secure. Jean Mayer is the inaugurator of the "Step-Into-Parallel" technique which boasts the accomplishment of successful wide track parallel turns by beginners on their second or third day.

Jean's principal effort is to keep the student's body in continuous motion, with the skier on packed slopes utilizing *independent* leg action, as opposed to simultaneous steering. He likes to relate movements on skis to natural walking movements. Opposed to static body positions, Jean admits to the necessity of hip-into-the-hill angulation only when the terrain is steep or icy, but recognizes the benefits of such a movement for women or men whose thigh bones are extremely angled. "There is no one way to ski," says Jean. "At Taos, we expect the instructor to adjust his teaching approach to the specific needs of each student. Of most importance is the development of basic skills like edge control and weight transfer. We also like the student to understand how the shape of his ski will help him to turn. Finally, we stress forward ankle flex more than some schools. Beginners are discouraged against the use of too short a ski and propeller-like skidded turns."

Yes, beginners do come to Taos, despite the fact that 27 of its 52 runs are expert slopes (and not overrated as in some other western resorts). Twelve trails are marked *Easiest,* and a whole new bowl that holds plenty of snow well into June has been recently opened up for the prime purpose of serving novice-to-intermediate skiers. Embracing these ballroom slopes are expert drops that will keep your knees well oiled. My favorites are the Katchina runs off the peak, which require a bit of hiking to reach, but the unbroken powder below makes the climb worthwhile.

Marge and I also cast our vote for Al's Run as the most pleasurable steep bump run we have skied. It is the first trail you see when you enter Taos Ski Valley, and many new visitors are intimidated by its steepness, narrow width and incredible length. You can get a nice rhythm over the moguls on Al's. They are not too close and ice-faced like the bumps in the East. We saw very few short skis at Taos. Ernie likes to promote the "compact ski" for mastering his mountain.

That's somewhere in between the shorts and the 210's of yesteryear.

"Please tell them that we are not just an expert mountain," asked Ernie, and to prove it, he took a run with Marge on the flats just below the Katchina peak, hand-in-hand!

I would like to have held somebody's hand during my first descent down the Blitz, a 34-degree pitch that is but one of the chutes which drop off the ridge serviced by chairlift #2 into the West Basin. Were it not for the moguls, that run would surely feel like a drop into space. I could hardly feel the snow beneath my feet, and each turn touched off its own minor avalanche to accompany my descent. These chutes are about two ski lengths wide, so forget about traversing. Marge tried to get a shot of me exploding through a bump but had trouble standing on the slope without sliding! The purple parkaed Ski Patrol at Taos boasts some of the most proficient skiers in the country, and they are always on hand to guide you across the ridge if you would like to take the plunge down Blitz, Oster, Fabian or Stauffenberg. But, bring your own parachute!

Some of the patrol at Taos are also masters of the practical joke. On our last day, I was compelled to jump off the cornice on High Line Ridge into a neat steep headwall that hadn't been tracked. "We will guide you to the Ridge," smiled the Patrolman, "but then, you are on your own." We didn't detect his sardonic smile. Marge set her camera, as I dangled my ski tips over the cornice and felt the warm but formidable southwest wind nudging me. The pitch was about 30 degrees, and I began to think about how far I would slide in the satin-like parka I had been foolish enough to wear if I miscalculated. Fifty feet below the cornice was a sheer rock cliff, but I figured that I could crank out at least four turns for the camera before reaching that point. As I added up the odds for survival against that beautiful carpet of virgin snow, I could feel the eyes of the Patrol, waiting for that turkey to make a move. I leaped. Not into the fall line as I should have, but into a chicken traverse. That was my first mistake. The snow was deep, old and obviously hadn't been skied for a long time. It was like wet cement. As Marge clicked away, I tried desperately to jump my turns around. Already heavy, with their Burt bindings, my Langes felt like a set of Olympic barbells. Every windshield wiper turn began with "Oof!" and ended with "Aargh!" as the cliff got closer. Marge

clicked away but my form was considerably less than classical. I decided to sidestep back and try again. Three feet from the cornice, I had difficulty stepping. The angle of the slope beneath the cornice was vertical. I had to chop a step into the face as Marge held the camera in her hand and her heart in her mouth. The harder I tried, the more I could hear the watching Patrol, "Look, that Nerd is going to try it again! Har! Har! Har!" The finks could have told me it was cement. "Screw it," I thought, "I'm committed, now," and off I went again. "Ooof! Dirty rats . . . Aargh! *Turn* you mutha!" I fought valiantly but the mountain won. I didn't ski it. I raped it. The clean white blanket was now scarred with choppy jump turns and chicken traverses, and I felt ashamed, as I continued screaming down the headwall. With Marge close behind, camera strapped to her chest, we traversed past the cliff to a more gradual decline. I continued my "Aargh!" turns, while Marge sideslipped. Close to the bottom, I turned to check out her progress. That was my second mistake. The headwall ended abruptly with a 10-foot cliff that met with the flat Honeysuckle trail on its way to Katchina. I took air and landed with a thud!

The sudden landing on the flat must have aggravated my old skydiving injury. It is a nerve in the sacroiliac area, but I won't bore you with the anatomical details. Suffice it to say that our week in Taos ended with this loud cacophonous note, and right now I am wondering if the pain will subside before Marge and I reach the Bugaboos.

Taos has a reputation for being exclusive because it offers everything a real skier would want and is not too easy to reach. Up until a few years ago, the 19-mile road to Taos Ski Valley from the town of Taos was dirt. It has since been paved, making the area more accessible, but you are still required to make the drive whether it be by rental car or via Louis Lucero's taxi service. Zia Airlines will fly you to Taos Municipal Airport from Albuquerque if they are hungry enough. We tried to book a flight with them and were informed that they were not working weekends during the spring! That meant renting a car when TWA dropped us into Albuquerque, and I really wasn't looking forward to the 3-hour drive. Boy, was I mistaken. It was one of the most beautiful drives Marge and I have taken, particularly the last half through the Rio Grande Gorge. With all the dry brown desert around us, though, I began to wonder if we had taken a wrong turn. Then, like a smoky mirage rising above the shimmering heat waves of the golden sand, there they were—The Sangre de Cristo Mountains, a miraculous happening with Wheeler peak watching over Ernie's Paradise, Taos Ski Valley. Avis really went out of their way to help us. Since the drop off point was in the town of Taos, the manager of the local company drove us to the Kandahar condo himself and offered his services should we need anything from town. His name is John, and I suspect that he is especially gratuitous since he has recently set up shop in competition with "you know who" and is determined to provide better and more reliable service. We must fly out of Albuquerque Saturday morning at 10:30 A.M., and John will have our Avis car at our door at 6:00 A.M.!

Service is one of the plus factors of this fantastic area. We have not felt the least bit uncomfortable, on or off the slopes. A surplus of lift systems and relatively few visitors means no lift lines, and I think that is incredible, when you realize that Taos probably provides the finest skiing for the seasoned veteran in the entire country! That's a pretty strong statement in a chapter that advertises the facilities of so many great ski areas, and I am sure it will cost me some friends. Consider it a personal evaluation, all things considered. Taos is Jackson Hole, without the occasionally fierce weather. It is Aspen without the turkeys. It is 300 days of sunshine at the high, dry altitude of almost 12,000 feet. Taos is light powder, cooled and dried as it moves eastward across the desert after dropping wet and heavy in California. One disbeliever filled a bathtub with Taos powder snow and watched it evaporate into a single pint of water! The resort is exceptionally warm, in temperature and comradery. On the same latitude as the Southern Isles of Greece, it is equally noted for its brilliant sun and indigo sky. Taos is also noted for smiling faces like that of an adorable cherub named Sally who serves drinks at the Chalet Suisse where Marge and I ate most of our meals. You will want to pinch her cheek. But, stop there. She has a man in Taos.

On the mountain, there is a curious respect exchanged between most of the skiers, who know that only the best can challenge the plummeting chutes of the West Basin or the thrilling powder runs off the ridge of Katchina. The radio-equipped Ski Patrol is made up largely of modern day mountain men, replete with beard, who could probably survive living alone in the wilderness below Wheeler peak for years. And, they can ski! The instructors are capable, affable and necessarily chauvinistic in their methodology, in deference to the iron hand of Ernie Blake and his first lieutenant, Jean Mayer. Their system is basically ATM, with modifications by Mayer that accelerate the student into parallel turns more rapidly. I heard one instructor wisecrack to his partner as they skied off the Katchina lift, "Hey, there's Stein Eriksen, still skiing *reverse shoulder*. Har! Har! Har!" referring, of course, to my preferred skiing style down the steep Katchina runs. Then, he skied down the gentle Patton trail with his skis apart and in the currently popular square stance. Body angulation is not always essential at Taos because the snow is usually ideal, but neither is a wide track stance essential when you are on a ballroom carpet. Different strokes for different folks, mon ami. It is curious that fall line skiing is all alike whether you are Austrian indoctrinated, Swiss, French or American. Some changes in ski form, on the other hand, are significantly different, like the way we ski moguls. Ernie stays high in the bumps, while I prefer the modern avalement. Both methods work. The more traditional form requires less physical effort.

Ernie doesn't like to talk about ski technique. He has lived through too many changes in skiing style and is tired of the chauvinistic battles for technique supremacy. He would much rather lead you through some of the exciting trails of his mountain and stop, if he likes you, for an occasional swig of a martini which he has hidden in Spanish *porrons* at strategically marked areas in the forest.

Physical effort doesn't seem to tire Ernie Blake. He has incredible stamina and did not even object to a little climbing, for the sake of the camera. "Most Americans are too lazy to climb," smiled our Swiss guide. "We must close our lifts Easter Sunday because people stop skiing then. But the snow stays on top of our mountain well into June, and some skiers enjoy the hike to summer skiing." He is not putting us on when he says the snow stays late at Taos. Marge and I talked to surveyors Gerry Pesman and Mark Dunbar, who were taking measurements for still another chairlift that will parallel #2. They had just dug a hole in the snow to reach the dirt. *Eleven feet!* And this was on April 7th!

How do you ski Taos? For the most part, you don't. You *fly* down the Taos slopes, and you had better keep your tips on the ground! It is fall line skiing. On your edges. It is bump swallowing with your knees in your chest. And, there is always more wilderness for the powder hounds, always more virgin snow, waiting for your personal track. Please don't rape it.

While you are gorging yourself with all that hedonistic ecstacy, your mate can feel safe in the Taos Ski School, even if she is a beginner. She will be riding the lift to the top with you in a few days as there are a few ribbon trails that wind around this super steep mountain to cater to the novice. There is also an excellent nursery and children's ski program at Taos. The Kinder Kafig is especially designed for your child's vacation. It offers ski instruction, games, arts and crafts, and, most important, other children his age. Children between 3 and 8 are accepted.

The most recent acquisition, and a real asset to the ski area, is the inimitable Ruedi Wyrsch, famed free-stylist acrobat and clown on skis. He will work with the ski school, adding some extra fun to the children's ski program and some knowledgeable guidance for freestyle, ballet and acrobatic routines. I traveled with Ruedi on the Harry Leonard Ski Show circuit and can attest that this man is not only an incredible athlete but also a dynamic performer. He has the strength of five men and a kinetic sense so acute that he can ski *on stilts*! I am sorry that we missed Ruedi during our stay at Taos. He was busy renovating his recently purchased El Patio restaurant in town. Guess he plans to stay a while.

That is the way it is with many who discover Ernie Blake's empire. They decide to stay. I say that as a warning, for, if you come to Taos Ski Valley, and experience for yourself what I have been unable to totally describe, you may never return home. For a real skier, Taos may very well be the end of the line. I would like to take my last run there. I hope that comedy of errors on High Line Ridge wasn't it.

TAOS
is waiting for you

U is for UNPRETENTIOUS
as at MAD RIVER GLEN, VERMONT

U IS FOR UNPRETENTIOUS

U is for unpretentious and that is what you will find if you take your skiing abilities to Mad River Glen on Route 17, just outside Waitsfield, Vermont. It is a skier's ski area. Mad River Glen is the third, smallest and most northern peak in its segment of the Green Mountains. Its neighbors are Glen Ellen and Sugarbush, all within 15 minutes of each other. Curiously, Mad River provides the toughest skiing of the three. Steep, narrow moguled trails are common at Mad River. So are overalls, knickers, long hair, beards, and tough women. Some skiers call it a miniature Taos. There are no turkeys at Mad River. If you dig tough challenging skiing but still have enough energy for some apres ski action, the Sugarbush Valley resort and its dens of iniquity are only a stone's throw south of Mad River. In between is a neat rock joint called Gallaghers, which is much like the Blue Tooth at Sugarbush but bigger, so the sounds don't blast you as hard. Gallaghers also draws a slightly older ski bum contingent and very proficient skiers, mostly from Mad River Glen. You know you have been *accepted* in the Valley when they hang your old license plate on their bar room wall. Above the Confederate flag. Marge and I like to eat at Gallaghers because of its warm atmosphere and non-pretentious customers. The bar room is barn style, with a quiet fireplace and checkered tablecloths. The light is warm. So are the people.

The trails at Mad River Glen are notoriously steep, bumpy and narrow. Veterans like to ski off the marked trails into the woods, where there is enough space for a natural slalom. These areas are especially fun after a heavy snowfall which is usually light powder excreted from the constipated thunderheads of Lake Champlain. Because the skiing is so challenging at Mad River, its aficionados take great pride in "their" mountain. Many of them wouldn't be caught dead at neighboring Glen Ellen, though a few will visit Sugarbush once or twice. The curious thing is that some of these self-labeled hot shots could not make a decent run down Glen Ellen's steep and narrow Scotch Mist, but they would prefer to be identified with a "skier's area" rather than a "family area" (Harvey Clifford, take note). One generous gratuity offered by the Mad River Corporation (and perhaps another reason why this is the favored area among the ski bums of the Valley) is a $70 weekday season pass for locals! Anyone can afford that even from unemployment checks. It is a decidedly generous offering when compared to what the close neighboring ski areas of Mad River have to offer, and it could be the reason why overalls and knickers are more popular at the "skier's area" rather than the mink and vicuna that are resplendent at Sugarbush.

Despite its reputation for expert trails, Mad River has a completely separate area for beginners and novice skiers. They call it Birdland, and it is a great place to pick up some foxy looking birds if you are still in the market. Dixi Nohl, director of skiing at Mad River likes to call his mountain "a particular place for the *particular* skier!" Mad River Glen, founded in 1947, has been called the "most challenging" and also the "most lovable" ski area in the East. Well designed, with all major lifts meeting at the same base area, it provides the best possible skiing for all types of skiers.

The *single chair* takes you to a spectacular view on top of General Starks Mt. and to some of the most exciting expert trails in New England. Marge and I like to climb Stark in the summer and walk across the Long Trail South past Glen Ellen and Sugarbush. It is great for a day's backpacking.

The *double chair* brings you to well groomed intermediate trails winding their way back to the Basebox.

The *birdland chair,* built halfway up the mountain to insure good snow conditions at all times, gives the novice skier the thrill and adventure of being "right up there" on gentle open slopes. Parking, unfortunately is limited.

The *practice slope chair,* wide and gentle on the top and broad and steep at the bottom, serves as a great training area for racers and skiers to improve their style and technique.

The *Basebox* and *Gen. Starks Pub* provide you with all the refreshments you need while you take a break and watch your children or friends skiing the slopes outside.

The *Birdcage* restaurant located next to the loading station of the Birdland lift, specializes in "natural foods," a refreshing innovation that we have found at no other ski area. It is justified by the startlingly healthy countenancy of most Mad River skiers.

"Oldtimers" and young skiers alike have found that good skiing, a great variety of trails and the very friendly atmosphere of Mad River Glen all make it a very "particular" place for the very "particular" skier. They may not be the tallest mountains, but many easterners believe they offer the *most*.

Here are a few words of advice from Dixi Nohl on how to descend the cliffs of Mad River Glen without looking like a hack.

RHYTHM ON SKI SLOPES

by Dixi Nohl

In most sports, from boxing to iceskating, rhythm plays an important part in the sports person's efforts to perform well. So is it the case in both racing and recreational skiing.

A racer needs to make only a small mistake and he loses his rhythm, his timing and his speed. In slalom and in giant slalom ski racing, rhythm is enforced by the gates which have to be skied. In recreational skiing it is the terrain which dictates the rhythm. Many skiers are not aware of this, and thus find themselves struggling from the top of the slope to the bottom whenever they ski. Instead of following the natural line of the hill and skiing down with rhythmic turns, many skiers criss-cross (traverse) and are at a constant battle with the mountain. In most sports it is important that the body motions are fluid and relaxed, and so it is in skiing. When traversing a slope and turning only occasionally, the only time when the body moves is just at the moment of the turn. In between these turns the skier remains tight and rigid. This is very unnatural and very tiring. So, try to ski rhythmically, descending a slope linking turn after turn. You

The intricate trail system at Mad River Glen. You need fast knees to ski the Green Mountains of Vermont.

will find yourself getting a lot less tired, you will enjoy each run and your skiing will improve rapidly.

How do you achieve such rhythm? If you are a beginner, and still in the snowplow stage, from now on make the attempt to link these turns rhythmically—don't worry about body-positions etc. Just keep turning those skis from right to left!

If you are already a more advanced skier, practice for some time on easier slopes, just linking turn after turn. Again, disregard your form for the time being, ignore the fact that our skis might be apart—just turn. It won't take very long for you to feel how simply and relaxing those skis are turning.

Another important thought should also be given to ski equipment. A skier may be trying very hard to link turns rhythmically, but without success because the skis are just too long to allow any fluid motions for him. The right length of skis, based on body-weight and ability, is very crucial to achieve rhythm in skiing. [Editor's Note: Let the length of your skis match your ability, your most comfortable velocity and the type of trail on which you ski most.] The long ski gives the ride of a Cadillac, but you wouldn't choose a Cadillac to drive through the gates of a tight slalom course. Most eastern trails are narrow, steep, hard packed and heavily moguled. Use a functional ski that will feel like merely an extension of your foot and keep its edges sharp.

The idea of skiing to music would certainly be another useful aid to achieve rhythm. To pretend you are skiing to the music of a waltz on an easy slope, or to some rhythmic beat when going through moguls, could very well do the trick.

Once the feeling of rhythmic turns has been achieved on easy slopes, an attempt can be made to apply this to the rest of the mountain. On steep terrain with large moguls, it is now the question of applying one's own rhythm to the rhythm demanded by the slope. All this takes practice, but once you have it, you will find that your skiing will have improved tenfold, as well as your enjoyment of the sport. . . . Then, we would like you to test it at Mad River!

Thanks, Dixi. We'll see you this season!

V is for VAIL...

V must be for Vail, which claims to be the largest single ski complex in America. Following are answers to the questions most frequently asked by visitors to President Ford's favorite ski resort. Vail has 14 major lifts with an uphill capacity of 18,550 skiers per hour.

ACCOMMODATIONS, INFORMATION & BOOKINGS

The Vail Resort Association (Box 1368, Vail, Co. 81657, Ph. (303) 476-5677) handles bookings for the lodging community. A brochure listing all of Vail's lodging facilities and their package rates (4- and 7-night packages include lodging and lift tickets) can be obtained by contacting this organization.

TRANSPORTATION TO VAIL

Air: Major airlines serve Vail's three gateway cities of Denver (100 miles), Grand Junction (150 miles) and Colorado Springs (150 miles). Rocky Mountain Airways has daily flights from Denver to Eagle (30 miles west of Vail). Tie-down, aviation and jet fuel and other private aircraft services are at Eagle.

Bus: Continental Trailways provides daily bus service from Denver and Grand Junction, as well as direct buses from Denver's Stapleton Airport. Charter bus services are available.

Auto: Vail is located west of Denver on Interstate 70. Rent-a-car facilities at all gateway airports; Avis at Eagle Airport. Avis and Hertz drop stations in Vail. Limousine service from both Denver and Eagle. Vail Cab Co. to Denver, Eagle, neighboring resorts.

LIFT TICKETS

These can be included as part of a total Vail package which can be purchased from a travel agent or airline tour desk and which includes transportation to and from Vail, plus lodging. Individual daily all-lift tickets—Adults $11; children under 12 and adults over 65 $5.50—can be purchased at the main ticket offices at the Vail Village Gondola Terminal, at the Vail/LionsHead Gondola Terminal as well as at the Golden Peak Ticket Office.

GETTING AROUND THE MOUNTAIN

A supply of printed maps can be found at lift ticket sales windows and at the base of each lift. In addition to showing the location of lifts, trails and their degree of difficulty, the map includes information on how to get from one area of the mountain to another. The four mountain restaurants are indicated on the map, so one can plan where to meet family or friends for lunch or a picnic.

The Vail Hostesses, Ski Patrol, Ski School and Lift Operators will be happy to assist anyone who is unfamiliar with the mountain.

BUSIEST LIFTS

The Vail Village Gondola (#1), and chairlifts 1,2,3,4 and 7 are busiest in the morning and after lunch. Best bets: Chairs 10,11 and 14. Ski the busy lifts during the Noon hour, stopping early for brunch, or later for lunch.

HAVE YOU TRIED LIONSHEAD OR THE NORTHEAST BOWL?

LionsHead, the "newer" end of Vail is normally not as crowded as the rest of Vail Mountain. Served by the LionsHead 6-passenger car gondola and two high-speed double chairlifts, LionsHead has one new trail—"The Glade."

In addition, beginning skiers will delight in the new "Beginners' Bowl" located on top of LionsHead at Eagle's

The largest single mountain ski complex in North America, Vail Mountain contains over 10 square miles of skiing terrain served by two gondolas, 1 triple chairlift, 13 double chairlifts and 3 surface lifts. Right at the base of the mountain, Vail Village has 47 hotel and condominium lodging facilities, 61 bars and restaurants, numerous shops and services and free bus transportation.

Nest. Served by a double chairlift, the area will be perfect for early season ski school lessons.

The Northeast Bowl section of Vail Mountain continues to grow, with the addition of Vail's first triple chairlift and three more trails: "Sourdough," "Whiskey Jack" and "Roger's Run." The Bowl is most easily reached by taking the Golden Peak chairlift from the Village.

Both Vail/LionsHead and Golden Peak feature complete lift ticket sales, ski school, food and beverage, equipment rental and child care facilities just as "downtown" Vail Village does.

TRANSPORTATION WITHIN VAIL

A fleet of free "ski buses" circulates every ten minutes from 7:00 AM to 1:00 AM daily between Golden Peak at the east end of the Village and the parking lots west of Lions-Head, with stops at key points in Vail. Hourly buses serve Bighorn (east of Vail) and Sandstone, leaving from Vail's transportation center.

The shuttle bus service eliminates the need for a car in Vail. In fact, the two core areas at LionsHead and in Vail Village are restricted to pedestrian traffic.

Vail Cab Company is available on call for in-Vail or Vail to airport transportation.

VAIL SKI SCHOOL

The country's most successful ski school features the Graduated Length Method of teaching for beginners. There are two meeting places in the Village: Golden Peak and Vail/LionsHead, with meeting areas also located on the Mountain at Eagle's Nest and Mid-Vail. Rental equipment including GLM, nordic and alpine skis is available at both Village locations.

WHAT SHALL WE DO WITH THE KIDS?

The Ski School sponsors two programs, each designed for a family's needs.

"Small World" is a nursery for youngsters 2 to 9 years. Snow play (at a nominal additional charge) ski lessons are featured. "Small World" is located in the Vail Valley Medical Center (the bus stops there) and is open from 8 AM to 5 PM daily.

"The Bratskeller," for children ages 5 to 9, includes lunch and ski lessons according to the individual ability. "Bratskeller" classes meet at both LionsHead and Golden Peak and will occupy your children from 9 AM to 5 PM daily. A daily rate of $12 includes lunch.

SPECIAL CLASSES

One of the most popular Vail Ski School programs, this is for advanced skiers. Sign-up is at any one of the Ski School offices. Skiers meet their guide-instructor at Mid-Vail at 11 AM—after they have had a chance to "warm up" on their own. Seven to eight persons in the group will spend the day doing a lot of skiing and, depending on the group's desires, socializing. The group breaks for lunch, photos or a "breather" whenever they wish. Skiing in a Special Class means skiing at one's own speed, cutting lift lines, learning the mountain, mobility—no standing around working on exercises. It is really like having a mountain host. Cost: same as a lesson—$12/day.

The Bwana chairlift and the six-passenger gondola rise from the center of Vail/LionsHead at the foot of Vail Mountain. Now 5 years old, LionsHead has "come of age" with its own complete village complex of 12 bars and restaurants, 17 shops and 15 lodge and condominum facilities located on a central pedestrian mall. The free Vail shuttlebus runs from the western end of LionsHead to the eastern end of Vail Village.

SKI TOURING

Ski touring is an aspect of skiing that is growing in popularity every year. Director of the touring school Steve Rieschl—whose book, *Ski Touring For the Fun Of It,* is in its second printing—heads up a staff of knowledgeable instructor/guides. Take a touring lesson in the morning; go on an afternoon ski tour. It is a wonderful way to "get away from it all" and to enjoy the spectacular scenery surrounding Vail. Touring equipment is available for rent at the touring meeting place at Golden Peak and also from many Vail ski shops. For a new experience, take an overnight tour—they are available through the Vail Ski School. A special segment on ski touring at Vail will follow this briefing.

SKI PATROL

The professional Vail Ski Patrol has 33 full-time and 15 part-time staffers who are thoroughly trained in first aid and mountain rescue, as well as avalanche control and advanced para-medic techniques. One hundred-thirty trailside on-mountain phones, supplemented by 49 portable radios and 17 mobile radio units make assistance readily available to an injured skier. Skiers who need a BandAid, minor repairs or information can stop at the three manned Patrol stations located at the top of Lift #4, at Eagle's Nest and at the top of the Golden Peak chairlift.

ON-MOUNTAIN RESTAURANTS

There are four restaurants on Vail Mountain—at the Golden Peak, Mid-Vail, Eagle's Nest and the LionsHead Gondola terminals. Traditionally, Mid-Vail is the most populated—so try others for a more relaxed lunch. The "Cook

Steve Rieschl, personable director of the Vail Touring School. (All photos by Peter Runyon)

SKI TOURING—FOR THE FUN OF IT!—IN VAIL, COLORADO

Steve Rieschl, director of the Vail Ski Touring School, is dismayed by ski touring's image as a strenuous sport. In appealing to the non-skier or the person just interested in exploring the winter environment, Rieschl emphasized the experience of ski touring for the sheer pleasure of it is available to anyone with the ability to walk around the block. He and his staff of 14 instructors offer a step-by-step learning progression to touring, starting with selecting the proper equipment, getting the "feel" of it, doing simple exercises on flat ground and then beginning to glide almost effortlessly on the "skinny skis." From a first-day stroll across the Vail golf course students graduate rapidly to an all-day tour on the network of 20 Vail area touring trails. Advanced touring skiers are exposed to downhill touring techniques, including the beautiful "Telemark Turn" for deep powder snow. In addition, students are taught the proper clothing and waxing procedures for the changing terrain, temperatures, and snow conditions encountered on a back country tour.

Popular Vail Area Tours

The first day program usually includes a half-day of instruction followed by a half-day tour. The Ski Touring School has developed some tours into the backcountry in conjunction with Vail Guides, Inc., an organization which offers snowcat trips, ski bobbing and jeep tours in and around the Vail area. Oriented to tourers who want to see a lot of spectacular Rocky Mountain scenery, but who really don't want to climb uphill much, the tours start with a snowcat ride into the isolated Piney Lake area, 13 miles from Vail. After a short ski tour amid craggy mountain peaks, everyone meets at the old Homestead Cabin for a hot lunch or a steak dinner on the lake's shore before making the scenic snowcat trip back to Vail. Groups also like the Meadow Mountain tour where, 3 miles west of Vail, snowcats take them up 1,500 vertical feet. After a picnic lunch among the pines, the group meanders down the wide open slopes on the mountainside.

An easy 3-mile (one-way) tour for friends with a Sunday afternoon picnic in mind is Beaver Creek, about 8 miles west of Vail. The proposed site of a new ski resort to be built by the same people who built Vail Mountain, the track winds through mountain meadows and wooded areas to an old ranch site perfect for picnics and sunbathing. Park your car approximately 1 mile west of the Avon general store (U.S. Route 6) and please, leave your dog at home as Beaver Creek is near an elk winter feeding range.

A favorite tour of many Vailites is the Shrine Pass trip from the summit of Vail Pass to the town of Red Cliff 11 miles away. The first 3 miles are uphill; the 8-mile downhill run is often followed by a dinner and a pitcher of margueritas at Reno's restaurant in Red Cliff. For those who are in shape to ski 11 miles, the tour is well worth it in terms of scenery and backcountry experience. Remember the arrangements must be made in advance for return transportation from Red Cliff to Vail.

For those in excellent shape, "The Commando Run" may be just the thing. It is a one-day trip, about 13 miles long, that starts at the summit of Vail Pass and ends at the east end of Vail Village. The route from Vail Pass includes the 3-mile

Shack" downstairs at Mid-Vail and the balcony level "Rouges Gallery" at Golden Peak feature hearty foods, limited menus and table service, as do the popular "Bier& Wein Stube" at Eagle's Nest and "Frasier's" at Vail's Lions-Head.

VAIL HOSTESSES

A girl in a green and yellow uniform with a Vail hostess patch on the front is on the mountain or in the lift line to serve the customer. She will help attach lift tickets, assist in lift line control and have the answers for, "How do I get to . . . Where do I get help . . . Where are the shortest lift lines and best snow today?"

IF YOU DON'T FEEL LIKE SKIING

Vail Village and Vail/LionsHead offer an overwhelming variety of shops and boutiques which feature imports from all over the world plus American handicrafts and fashions. Over 60 bars and restaurants feature international cuisines and unique atmospheres. When dining, try to arrive before seven or after eight in the evening if seeking a leisurely dinner. Many establishments take reservations—advisable at peak periods. Almost all offer entertainment from dance bands to belly dancers.

Other activities include: ice skating (day and night) at the Golden Peak rink; sleigh rides; swimming in heated pools; relaxing in a sauna. The Crossroads Cinema offers the latest films with an occasional classic mixed in. Or, for a change, a quiet evening by the fire with a hot buttered rum may suit one better.

A QUESTION WE HAVEN'T ANSWERED HERE?

Ask a friendly native. Or, visit or call the Vail Resort Association which is located in the Vail Transportation Center—303/467-5677.

Ski tourers glide across Piney Lake near Vail with the magnificent Gore Range in the background.

climb to Shrine Pass, a 1,000 vertical foot climb to the head of Lime Creek and another climb of 900 vertical feet from Two Elks Pass to Siberia Peak. The amount of snow to break through and the number of people breaking trail will determine how long the trip takes. It is advised only for advanced touring skiers in good shape who are prepared, carrying the normal safety gear. In past years, this tour has been a clinic run for all the instructors in the Vail Touring School.

Special Touring Programs in the Vail School

Rieschl and his staff have noticed a marked increase in the number of persons who come to Vail requesting downhill skiing lessons on touring skis. As a result, the Touring School has developed a program to fulfill this need. Students learn unweighting, edge control and sideslipping techniques, along with stem christie and parallel christie turns. Skiing deep powder on "skinny skis" is the ultimate experience, but the school teaches techniques for skiing ice and hard pack snow as well.

Rieschl, in conjunction with Horst Abraham (technical director for the Vail Ski School and for P.S.I.A.) are experimenting with a new ski teaching method whereby

beginning skiers who wish to learn alpine skiing spend their first 2 days on touring skis before transferring to traditional alpine skis. Their learning progression, balance and reaction surpass those of students on conventional alpine equipment—a development which astonished the two teaching pros. The group program, composed of students enrolled in a ski week at a special package price, will be continued for at least one more ski season before Rieschl and Abraham compile and publish the results of the teaching experiment.

For the touring enthusiast interested in a truly unique experience, the Touring School offers overnight tours, complete with sunsets and cookouts, by reservation only.

For Further Information

. . . contact the Ski School at Vail, telephone 303/476-3116, or write Steve Rieschl, Box 819, Vail, Colorado 81657. Persons wishing to "bone up" in advance, can obtain a copy of Steve Rieschl's *Ski Touring For The Fun Of It,* © 1974, Little Brown & Co. The book is available in both hardback and paperback editions.

WHY VAIL IS DIFFERENT

by Horst Abraham, Technical Director, Vail Ski School

I'm often asked what makes skiing at Vail different from other ski areas. I believe that superb snowfall followed by unsurpassed slope grooming techniques account for Vail's quality skiing experience. Good snow conditions enhance every skier's performance and enjoyment regardless of ability level. On Vail Mountain there are two very challenging runs I'd like to take you on, as a sample of what I believe is the finest snow/mountain combination available in North America.

Prima/Pronto—

After arriving at the top of Vail Mountain, the skier meanders towards Riva Ridge past Zot, Expresso and Swingsville. Instead of making the left turn down Riva Ridge, the skier remains on the ridge to start down Prima. It's critical at this point—where the moguls begin but where it's not too steep yet—to get a feel for the rhythm of the bumps. Feel the weight mid-foot, let your legs do the

When you get tired of playing Yo-Yo, try a little *langläufing* on "skinny skis." You will discover a lot more of the country, the way the first pioneers must have seen it.

"Prima" looking south from chair #6. Pronto drops over the other side of the ridge about one-third the way down Prima.

turning, and keep your hands and poles well forward and to the side, ready for immediate use. Stay in the troughs to turn around every mogul that you come upon. After about 50 yards, the slope's pitch will increase and the moguls will get larger—don't stop if you've got a good rhythm going. As mogul sizes increase, your limberness and absorbtion capability must increase, but otherwise, all else remains essentially the same. About halfway down Prima Face, the slope's pitch again increases—don't panic! You *must* begin each turn yielding to the push of the mogul towards you by allowing the knees to come to your chest. Now plant the pole towards the desired turn center and guide the skis into the next trough by extending the legs as you turn them. By ensuring that the downhill ski starts carving down the trough immediately (by consciously shifting the weight after the absorbtion), the skier will maintain his speed the length of the trough and be ready for the impact of the next mogul. Remember to keep the shoulders faced downhill and the poles out front and to the side. Plant the pole, feel its kickback, use it to stabilize you, but bring the hand holding the pole along with you. Thus you avoid the common mistake of turning "around" a *planted* pole and letting the shoulder drop back, which results in the loss of balance and/or the inability to initiate another turn swiftly.

Stop at the bottom of Prima Face—you deserve a rest! Take a look back up. It's hard to believe that you just skied one of the most challenging runs in the world. But the experience isn't over yet—now you've got to make it down Pronto to the bottom of Chair 11.

By now your nerves should have settled so leave your vantage point at the bottom of Prima Face and ski to the right towards the trees at the edge of the slope. A sign will lead you to the top of Pronto and what appears to be a snowcat road. Don't be misled! When you see a group of skiers standing motionless looking straight down, you've reached Pronto. Although Pronto has an average slope of 65 percent (slightly less than Prima), there is no way to gradually work yourself up to the steepness—it's tough from the very onset. To make the 100-yard slope seem steeper, the outrun not only flattens out but actually rises up to meet the base of Chair 11.

The moguls on Pronto are characteristically tighter though not as large as those found on Prima. Therefore, the skier must charge the slope by keeping his weight well centered and be ready for each individual mogul by never letting the poles and hands drop back. Quickness is more important on this slope than style so keep your skis slightly apart for more stability, quicker edge change, and a more powerful leg rotation. Remember that the key to speed control is "snow contact," so absorb and twistingly extend to equalize pressure on the skis while you turn them. On steep slopes like Pronto, I quite often extend more pronouncedly than usual to ski "snow contact" in the second half of the turn. To do so, think of forcing your toes downhill after the compression and letting your weight move from your heels to your toes on the flexed ski. If you've done it properly, by the time your weight moves to your toes you should be on the top of the next mogul, fully compressed, the pole planted, anticipated and ready to release the skis into the next turn.

When everyone in the Chair 11 lift line acknowledges your arrival with smiles and a little hero worship in their eyes, you will know that you've done a good job.

Bustin' Powder! Rocky Mountain powder snow—the stuff skiers' dreams are made of—is some of the driest and lightest snow in the world. "Powderhounds" come to Vail to ski the famous Back Bowls. The less venturesome find that Vail's fleet of snowcats pack the powder to silken smoothness on the front side of the mountain.

By the way, the Vail Ski School offers the prestigious Prima Pin to skiers that successfully ski Prima Face non-stop under control. When you're ready, let me know!

Back Bowls—

Vail's Back Bowls offer a unique experience to those that are seeking the ultimate thrill—powder skiing. Until you see it for yourself, it's difficult to imagine the expanse of snow that awaits the powder skier in the Bowls.

There are three major routes used to gain entry to Vail's Back Bowls. Guests residing in the LionsHead village should take Gondola 2 to Eagles Nest, ride Chair 7 to the top of Game Creek Bowl and drop into Sun Down Bowl. Confident powder skiers should try Morningside Ridge for really deep snow and the less-confident should traverse west to Ricky's Ridge. Vail Village skiers should take Gondola 1 and Chair 4 to the top of Vail Mountain which provides easy access to either Sun Up or Sun Down Bowl. Golden Peak guests should utilize Chair 6 to Chair 10, ski to triple-Chair 14, and enter Sun Up Bowl to ski the sparsely-set trees on the eastern side.

Because there are very few trees in the bowls, there are no real trails—just designated "areas." One of my favorites is Milt's Face, named after Milt Wiley, Vail's first ski patrol leader.

Milt's Face—

To reach Milt's Face from the top of Chair 4 follow the signs to Sun Up Bowl and continue around the western lip of the bowl along High Noon Ridge until it begins to drop sharply. This is a good point to pause a moment and look into the Sun Up valley and marvel at the spectacular surrounding scenery. Because Milt's Face is on the leeward side of High Noon Ridge, the snow here is quite often deeper than other areas of either bowl. Make sure that your jacket and powder pants are zipped completely for protection against the deep snow. I recommend goggles be worn and be wiped free of fog prior to heading down the face.

There are various methods for skiing powder, but I prefer to turn my legs under a quiet torso while flexing and extending them. I push the skis out and to the side then retract them underneath the body and swiftly push them out to the other side.

To begin, head the skis straight down the face weighting them equally. Let the ski tips ride on the top of the snow, but don't sit back! Turn your feet as your legs extend. Feel the skis turn out of the fall line and push toward you. Plant your pole downhill and bring your knees to your chest as you gently steer the skis towards the next turn. As you turn towards the fall line, swiftly extend your legs as you continue turning the skis and feel yourself glide toward the next pressure buildup, another flexion, pole plant, and a new turn initiation.

Sound simple? Well, it takes a great deal of practice. A couple of reminders—always start in the fall line, don't sit back, and keep up the rhythm. You don't necessarily have to be an expert hard-packed skier to learn powder skiing. But you do need to practice a lot in order to turn confidently in the bottomless fluff in Vail's Back Bowls. I heartily recommend a powder lesson from the Vail Ski School as a step towards enjoying this fantastic experience.

See you on the slopes—*Horst*.

W is for WILD

WESTERN CANADA
Let's go on Skifari with Air Canada

W IS FOR WESTERN CANADA

W is for wild western Canadian skiing, *real* skiing at its hospitable best. Any recreational skier who has put away some bread for a week or two of sunny powder skiing, dreamt of the promise for almost a year, tuned up body and equipment, and stoked the mind with volumes of skiing magazines and books like SKIER'S DIGEST, has *got* to feel a little pain when arrival is met with dark, rain-filled clouds, icy slopes, and surplus crowds, while departure is accompanied by rock scarred skis, lift line-aggravated nerves, indigestion and no sun tan. Yet year after year after year, this kind of loser returns to his chosen *mecca* for more of the same punishment. We are such creatures of habit. Not all of us, but many of you who are reading this right now. Have you been groveling in the one-ski-area-rut? Are you one of of the many who says, "Well, they had a bad season, but we will try them again next year?" or, "Sure they are crowded. They are crowded 'cause they're the *best*. We're at the best resort, so we have to put up with the lift lines." And the ice. And the inflationary lift ticket prices. And the dark gray skies. And the filthy rest rooms. And the overpriced food. And with a host of other inconveniences for the simple reason that you won't risk *change*. It is high time that you opened your tunnel visioned eyes and demanded a little more for your investment.

If skiing represents anything at all, it stands for *freedom*. Freedom of flight. Freedom of self-dependence. Most of all, it offers freedom of *choice* whether it be between ski trails, ski lifts, or ski technique. The biggest choice available to you is the selection of a particular ski area. One that best suits your own needs. With so many hats in the ring, haven't you been cheating yourself by settling for the barest of necessities when you could be enjoying gratuitous service beyond your basic needs? There are ski areas who realize that their existence is dependent upon your frequent patronage. There are resorts which take pride in their appearance. There are resorts which understand the ill effects of overkill and keep their lift ticket prices and food bills moderate. There are ski areas which disperse their crowds by installing an adequate number of lifts. There are some that even offer reciprocal tickets which will allow you to ski more than one mountain in the same week, using the same lift ticket! Curiously, in our travels over North America, we have found that the most generous ski resorts are also the ones that consistently provide the best skiing, whether it be due to persistent trail grooming, prolific snow guns or the Grace of God providing consistent, adequate powder and exciting terrain; resorts like Taos, New Mexico, where Ernie Blake starts construction of another chairlift the moment that one of his lifts develops a 15-minute wait. Some of these utopian destinations also are blessed with an abundant amount of radiant sunshine which will paint your face a healthy color rather than send you back to the office with the same jaundiced pallor you have had all year from living like a mole. There are many such ski areas in our country, but there is a mountain range across our northwestern border where the plus factors I have mentioned are at *every* resort. In short, it's an area where you are *guaranteed* a pleasurable

return for your investment. You owe it to yourself to book a flight with Air Canada and visit the ski areas of the Canadian Rockies, at least once. My guess is that it will be an experience memorable enough to lure you back many times again.

Frank Covino carves a perfect track into one of the many spacious snow fields at Sunshine Village, Banff, Alberta, Canada.

I never really knew what *steep* was . . .

The Banff Springs Hotel. Chateau luxury at its finest for those who want more than the average ski lodge.

Marge and I were required to return to New York before embarking for the Canadian Rockies, which would not have been so bad except that my hip pain was so excrutiating that I could not possibly bend. The embarrassment of having Marge carry our luggage while I did nothing but sweat, hurt more than the sciatica. We arrived at LaGuardia about 7:30 PM and were due to fly to Calgary at 10:30 the following Sunday morning. Have you ever tried to get a doctor in New York City on a Saturday night? Forget it. We turned to the Yellow Pages under *Chiropractors* and picked the first Italian name listed. Sure enough, after digging back far enough, we came up with a distant relative. "Well, if it's in *the family*," smiled Dr. Conti, "rush him right over."

Before you put down all chiropractors as quacks, let me tell you that I have already been helped by three very good ones, after subjecting myself to orthopedic diagnosis and long expensive hospital therapy. "Doc," I pleaded, "that's my story. The Bugaboos and Canadian Rockies have been

my dream for 20 years. Can you get me there?" "What you want is a miracle man," Conti said sternly. "C'mon, Doc. You're an Italian . . ." I winced. X-Rays showed no fracture, but did indicate one sacrum higher than the other and a good deal of nerve damage. He stretched me out on some weird black table that looked like a Henry Moore statue, brought one of my thighs up into a figure four position, asked me to inhale, exhale and, with that, pressed all 200 pounds of his body weight directly onto my hip. There was a snap! Another X-Ray showed normal alignment. Following some ultra-sound application and wet heat, I walked out of there standing taller, a lot happier, $75 poorer, but with new hope that Marge and I could close out the latter portion of this chapter with a few shots of more magnificent ski scenery on the other side of the northwestern border.

The enflamed area spread across my hip Sunday morning, but somehow Marge and I managed to board our Air Canada Skifari flight for Calgary on time. There are many ski-week packages offered to the public for skiing Western Canada. We chose the attractive plan called "Skifari," offered by Air Canada, as it offered the most options. Their basic package included 6 nights of hotel accommodations (we stayed at the luxurious Banff Springs, a baronial castle that is appointed with period furniture that would make an antique buff's mouth water), transfers from Calgary airport and return (we chose a Tilden rental car, compact, but big enough to carry our ski bag with three pair of 190s *inside*,) plus 5 days' lift tickets which are interchangeable at all three major areas (penurious U.S. Ski Resorts, please take note).

The drive from Calgary airport to Banff is one you will never forget. Leaving Calgary you won't be too impressed by the cement and plaster boxy bungalow type homes stacked back to back. My first thought was "Italian Ghetto" as it reminded me of my own diggings when I was a child with Grocerias and Pizzarias scattered through every block. Then we saw some taco signs. Then, taco plus pizza signs, but it wasn't until we spotted a Chinese food and steak house that we decided to call Calgary our United Nations town. It sure is flat. And brown. Driving west, it was about an hour before we noticed the brown hills begin to roll with higher undulation. Neat horse and Hereford ranches bordered the

Big horn sheep, grazing beside the Trans-Canada Highway west of Banff, pose for Marge's camera. Our Skifari with Air Canada is an experience we'll never forget.

highway, but the Rockies still seemed quite distant due to a lingering ground fog that kept teasing us. It was outside of Calgary that I noticed the first brown golf course I had ever seen, and it was loaded with compulsive duffers. They were not the only Calgarians who were rushing the season. Marge stopped for a Dairy Queen to quell some of the 80-degree Fahrenheit heat and the place was loaded with young sweethearts in silky summer clothes. Short shorts. White and tight. Neat. They looked at our ski-loaded car like we were two freaks from another planet. When Marge stepped out in her long-haired Italian goatskin after-ski boots, they were sure that we were strange.

But the hills began to roll higher, and the tall stately pines began to equal the number of birches. Gradually the ground fog lifted and the snow blanketed peaks of the Canadian Continental Divide began to emerge. Magnificent. I remember saying to Marge, "*Never* have the Rockies looked rockier." We have mountains in the East where the vertical drops are just as steep. Our home is on Glen Ellen with a vertical drop of over 2,600 feet, but the peaks of the Green Mountains are not nearly as rocky and the valleys are thousands of feet lower. They are tree laden to the top and curvilinear because of their lower elevation. First to impress our view was a steep cliffed limestone mountain on our right side. The sun had already melted most of the new snow off its southern face. To our left were spectacular peaks that still managed to retain snow in between their timber crags and crevasses. Straight ahead was the snow capped Canadian Continental Divide, the rockiest of Rockies, a giant spine of undulating razorbacks not yet spoiled by smog and other forms of pollution. Now, on the right, a small frontier type town of log cabins and stone fireplaces where I almost wished I might like to live, until I saw the scars of trailer camps on its outskirts. Why they don't surround those camps with trees, I will never understand. They are uglier than tennis courts in mountain country. There are all kinds of pollution. What's this? A toll booth! Are we gonna have to pay to get into Banff? "Ayup," smiled the collector, with a Vermont drawl. "Two bucks f'four days, ten bucks fer the season." "Air Canada never mentioned *that*," quipped

Marge, but I looked up, down and around as far as my eyes could see and said, "Marge, the Lord is here. He's just passing the collection box." Our mouths froze open in awe as we continued our drive through the Banff National Park and were presented with one picture postcard view after another.

Located in the heart of the Canadian Rockies, Banff and Lake Louise offer the most spectacular scenery available for the skier. Banff and Lake Louise towns are both located in Banff National Park and each is unique in its own way. The only "industry" allowed in the National Parks is tourism and serving visitors. Thus Banff and Lake Louise are geared to meet all the tourists' needs.

Banff is famed for its natural hot springs which flow freely year 'round. Located on Sulphur Mountain in Banff is the Upper Hot Springs Pool. Each day the pool is drained and refilled from these waters—average temperature is 100 degrees Fahrenheit. Visitors can also explore the natural cave where the original explorers first located the hot springs here, which is the site of the first national park in Canada. Connected with the Upper Hot Springs Pool are steam baths and a complete massage service—a great end to a hard day's skiing.

Wildlife is prevalent in and around the three ski areas as well as along the highways of the National Park. Although winter visitors would be surprised to see a bear (they sleep while you ski), you can expect to see numerous Rocky Mountain big horn sheep, elk, deer and coyotes all year round. Marge clicked a photo of some big horn grazing right by the side of the road.

The early beginnings of Banff stretch far back into the pages of time, most of it shrouded in Indian lore and legend. Only the footsteps of the white man have been traced with some degree of accuracy.

David Thompson, one of the earliest explorers of the Rocky Mountains, arrived in 1800 at the Gap—about 19 miles east of Banff. In 1807 he returned, crossing the mountains by the Howse Pass and Saskatchewan River.

The August of 1841 saw the arrival of Banff's first tourist. He was Sir George Simpson, governor of the Hudson's Bay Company's fur empire, and this was part of his trip around the world. He was accompanied by the stoney Indian guide Peechee, and was led past Minnewanka, place of the Evil Spirits (Devil's Lake) and camped at the foot of Cascade Mountain, continuing west to Healy Creek and over Simpson's Pass.

Simpson was followed to the area in about 1859 by Sir James Hector who was accompanying Captain Palliser's expedition, one of the main objectives of which was to search out passes through the Rocky Mountains. It was Sir James who renamed the mountain, referred to by the Indians as "The mountain-where-the-water-falls," Cascade Mountain, and also left the name of "Rundle" on a massive peak shaped like the fin of a shark in memory of Rev. Robert T. Rundle, the brave Methodist who was the first missionary to visit the Banff Area.

The town of Banff had its first beginnings with the coming of the Canadian Pacific Railroad surveyors around 1881. The surveyors, who were sent to find a route through the mountains for the CPR, were headed by Major A. B. Rogers, for whom Rogers' Pass is named. Rogers was ably assisted by Tom Wilson, the famous outfitter who supplied the survey crews. Wilson is renowned for his discoveries of Lake Louise and Emerald Lake in 1882.

During the building of the railroad, Banff was known as Siding 29 and located on the present-day site of the animal paddocks at the base of Cascade Mountain. Around the same time development was taking place at the site of the Sulphur Mountain Hot Springs. These springs were known to early visitors to the area but it was not until the early 1880's when McCardell and McCabe erected a so-called 'hotel' there and attempted to operate the springs as a commercial venture that a small settlement began to appear. Soon this settlement became the most popular of the two as people, believing in the miraculous curative properties of the hot springs, flocked to the new site. The new townsite became known as Banff, named after Banffshire in Scotland, although I doubt very seriously that the rolling hills of Scotland can compare to the jagged peaks of the majestic range surrounding Banff, and they are nowhere near as foggy. Banffshire was the birthplace of a one-time governor of the Hudson's Bay Co., Donald Smith, later Lord Strathcona.

Following an Order-in-Council, November 25,1885, Banff Hot Springs reservation was created. An area of 10 square miles was reserved around the Sulphur Springs as a national holding. In 1887, under George A. Stewart, the first Superintendent of the Park, the area was extended to 260 square miles and the name changed to Rocky Mountains Park.

Banff National Park now extends over an area of 2,000 square miles and has an estimated permanent population of 4,000. It is administered by the Federal Department of Indian Affairs and Northern Development, National Historic Parks Branch.

Skiing has been enjoyed in Banff and the vicinity since 1900, and the first ski club was organized in 1928, with Mount Norquay as a base of operations. In 1930, ski lodges were built by private enterprise in Skoki Valley and Deception Pass (Halfway Hut). Park authorities built a jump on Mount Norquay in 1936. The nucleus of Sunshine Village was built in 1936, and a private developer in Skoki Valley built Mount Temple Lodge in 1939. A chairlift was constructed on Mount Norquay in 1948 by private enterprise, and additional tow installations were introduced to this development in 1951, 1961, and 1964, including a double chairlift in 1962.

A gondola lift was constructed on the lower slopes of Mount Whitehorn near Lower Lake Louise in 1959, and supplementary lifts were added in 1960 and 1963. The Whitehorn ski complex was improved by the erection of chairlifts in 1966 and 1967. A day lodge was erected at the base of Mount Whitehorn in 1973.

Sunshine Lodge made a series of improvements commencing with additional lift facilities in 1956. Following the sale of this development in 1960 a new group enlarged the accommodations and erected additional lifts. This was followed by the building of three chalets in 1963, a T-bar lift in 1964, a double chairlift and additional accommodations in 1965, a new lodge in 1967, and a second double chairlift in 1968.

Marge and I related the three-mountain complex to a generous spread like Aspen, although the buildings of Banff are not as rustic. They are sturdy, though, with many a foundation constructed with six-by-twelve hand-hewn bricks

from Mt. Rundle.

Clothing is no problem when you visit Banff as the average winter temperatures range from 10 to 30 degrees above during the day and usually drop to 15 to 20 degrees during the night. The humidity is generally 35 to 50 per cent which is comparatively dry and makes it very easy to dress for the colder days.

A warm nylon ski jacket, light sweater and turtleneck T-shirt, together with stretch pants, would provide you with a versatile outfit. On warm days the jacket could be removed and the sweater worn with or without a light shell jacket. For the few cold days in mid-winter, it would be wise to bring along some heavier articles such as warming pants and down-filled jacket or extra sweater.

After-ski activities are many and varied, but the scene is usually a casual, relaxed atmosphere. The ladies may dress to suit their own preference: pants suits, long skirts, short skirts, no skirts—all are acceptable, within reason. The men can, for the most part, feel at home in a sweater and slacks, but a jacket and tie is quite proper for the better dining rooms and some of the other activities such as the Winter Theatre. The torn and patched jeans groups should eat at Loucas's Pizza and Spaghetti House where they will feel more comfortable. The numbers on the juke are cool and bluesy, and the college age girls you will find there are wholesome and loose.

It would be wise to have a bathing suit along to take advantage of the hot springs mineral pool or the heated swimming pools provided by some of the hotels. Note: Bathing suits can be rented at the sulphur pool if you prefer not to bring your own.

The cold, if you can call it that after a year or two in the

Inversion and one step closer to Heaven at Sunshine Village. Simon Hoyle's camera captures a unique weather phenomenon known as *inversion* where clear warm air hangs aloft while clouds and cold air sit in the valley. Temperatures vary as much as 60 degrees from the valley to the peaks. That's Mt. Assiniboine imitating the Matterhorn in the distance.

northeast, is DRY. Easterners used to wet, penetrating, sub-zero temps won't even need a hat on the clear days. I saw one chick in shorts, but that's insane, as the snow can be like sandpaper when you are sliding on your thigh.

Right now, I am flat on my back in the Banff Mineral Springs Hospital under the care of Dr. Turner while Marge is out checking the skiing at Sunshine. The plane ride to Calgary must have re-aggravated my sciatica, so I have no choice but to cop out and rely upon my wife's skiing experiences here plus a few authoritative interviews in order to describe for you the total ski scene in this beautiful area. It bugs me to not be on skis. The only consolation is that I can view the majestic Mt. Norquay from my bed. We are still scheduled for some helicopter skiing with Hans Gmoser beginning Sunday, but that will depend largely upon how fast these old bones heal.

While I am stretched out, this will give me a good opportunity to tell you a little about the Banff Springs Hotel and its skiing activities.

Already well-known as the hub of activity for winter sports enthusiasts of all sorts, Canadian Pacific Hotels' Banff Springs Hotel offered a new and exciting total ski program this past winter season. A consolidation of forces with the Ski School of the Canadian Rockies and the former Banff Springs Ski School created a unique ski program designed to fit the needs of skiers of all abilities and interests.

The Ski School of the Canadian Rockies developed the program to match the levels and capabilities of all skiers. An unusual feature of this new program, however, is a special inducement to the above-intermediate ability skiers to continue their skiing education. The program includes the full services of a traditional Alpine ski school plus a number of ski-weeks designed to take the intermediate skier to the expert level.

A staff of seven highly qualified ski instructors, headed by Peter Honrung,—former assistant director of the old Banff Springs Hotel Ski School for 4 years, is stationed at the hotel. Regular class lessons, private lessons and ski-weeks for beginners up to intermediate skiers are offered at Banff. Special children's programs are also available. For the experienced intermediate skier, advanced parallel ski-weeks, freestyle ski-weeks, recreational racing weeks and introductory weeks to helicopter skiing are all available.

Cross-country skiers will have an equally comprehensive lesson program available to them. A staff of cross-country instructors and ski guides, headed by Walter Batzhuber, who was with Canadian Mountain Holidays for the past 3 years, will offer both class and individual lessons. In addition to actual cross-country ski skills, participants in this portion of the Banff Springs Ski School will receive special training in compass and map reading and winter survival. Yet another attraction to the avid cross-country enthusiast will be half-day, full-day and overnight ski tours to some of the most scenic areas in Banff National Park. Special one-week tours are offered in March and April for the really adventurous. I can think of no finer territory for the *langläufer* than the terrain above and beyond Sunshine Village.

Skiers who don't wish to take part in the extensive ski school facilities offered will find exciting and challenging skiing to match all abilities at the three nearby ski areas. A

Jerry's Run at Sunshine is for those skiers who like to put down the resort as an intermediate area!

wide variety of advanced-intermediate and expert slopes are served by nearby Mount Norquay's two double chairlifts, two T-bars, one handle tow and a rope tow. The "North American" is the longest run with a vertical drop of 2,450 feet, and it's all expert terrain.

About 14 miles from the Banff Springs, via the Trans-Canada Highway, is Sunshine Village Ski Area. Nestled in a high Alpine valley, the well-groomed slopes receive an average of 400 inches of snow per year. Marge is skiing there right now to check out the terrain for you. At this time, Sunshine holds the greatest amount of snow on its trails of all the three neighboring areas. It is April 13th. Sunshine just happens to be directly under the heaviest "snow belt," and they ski there usually well into the month of May.

More than 6,500 skiers an hour may be whisked to the tops of the Sunshine slopes by a triple chairlift. Three double chairlifts, a T-bar and a rope tow also provide rapid up-hill transportation.

Greatest vertical drop encountered at Sunshine is only 1,820 feet, from the top of the Brewster Chairlift to the base of the valley near the main lodge, but the scenery around that vertical drop is quite Alpine and above timberline. Here's an account of Marge's day there.

Sunshine Village

She met Public Relations director, attractive Audrey De-Baghy, in the Banff Springs Hotel Lobby at 9:15 AM and drove in our "Skifari" Tilden to Sunshine Village parking lot where they had to switch to a bus for climbing the steep

TRUE GRIT. Manager John Gow of Sunshine, himself an amputee, has provided inspiration and initiative to other less fortunate lovers of the skiing experience. He has been a pacesetter for skiers like this amputee, who races through the gates at one of the events for handicapped skiers that took place at Sunshine Valley.

Marge found some nice bump runs *behind* the base lodge at Sunshine Valley, off the Wa Wa T-bar. Most of the other runs are through the terrain that is in front of the lodge.

winding one-lane road to the base lodge. No autos are permitted on this precarious road, nor, Marge observed, would any sane driver want to make the drive (up or down) in his own vehicle. The fare from the lot to the lodge was two bucks per round trip. The waiting lines were long, but they kept moving, as one bus pulled in after another. Marge commented that, unlike the lines we encountered in most European ski areas, the movement at Sunshine was orderly with no pushing, shoving or foul foreign language. Guests of the Banff Springs Hotel needn't drive. Their own bus makes the trip to the main lodge at Sunshine for four bucks a round trip. There is a steady stream of buses climbing and descending all 4 miles of the one lane access road through heavy avalanche country. It is a dirt road and all buses are equipped with chains and radios which permit passing at designated intervals. The ride to the top is beautiful, surrounded by tall dark pines which appear a lighter yellow-green when you get closer to them. The atmosphere inside the bus was jovial.

The girls left their skis outside the day lodge, convinced by Sunshine Village's PR Director Sue Yule that theft is no problem, probably because of the difficulty of escape. Sue is young, early twenties, with reddish brown hair and freckles. She invited the girls for lunch at 1:00 and introduced them to the area Manager, John Gow, who is about 30, slim and an amputee. John crashed his light plane into the spine of one of the Canadian Rockies during a sudden snow squall and miraculously survived. His walk back to civilization cost him a frostbitten leg and foot which required amputation.

Gow was now practicing for a forthcoming amputee race. Marge admired his edge control. Next, they met with Jerry Johnston, director of the Norquay and Sunshine Village Ski Schools. Jerry has a strong positive skiing style. A native of Banff, Jerry is past President of the Canadian Ski Instructors' Alliance and regularly attends international instructor conferences to keep his methodology up to date. Johnston is also well known for his work with handicapped skiers and is currently considered to be one of the foremost authorities on amputee skiing. He is President of the Alberta Amputee Ski Association.

At 10:30, the girls snapped into their bindings and rode up the Standish Chair, a double chairlift servicing a moderate 675 feet of vertical with pines on both sides and moguls beneath, which reminded Marge of a typical eastern intermediate run. The snow on Jerry's Run beneath the Standish was hard packed but not icy. Bored with that trip, the girls rode Standish again and plunged down the Headwall, marked expert. Marge was still unimpressed by the vertical drop but the panorama of the distant peaks of the Continental Divide was breathtaking, and the moguls shook up their breakfast.

The Dell Valley took them to the Angel Chairlift which brought them to the Great Divide Chairlift (Brewster) and the principal peak of Sunshine Village. The Great Divide chair rides the spine of the Continental Divide moving from Alberta to British Columbia and back to Alberta. The peak is shark fin shaped like Mt. Rundle but flatter. The snow at the top was changeable, beginning with hard packed and wind-blown new snow and a generous offering of still fresh powder on the left side of the expansive Great White Way. The powder was deep enough to leave a few nice tracks, and the sun finally peaked through a hole in the uncooperative overcast sky to throw shadows on some neat bumps. The girls liked the Great White Way so much they skied it three times. Lost in their ecstacy as the spraying snow bathed their faces on the last run, they turned well off the trail and had to hike back to the beaten path. No lift lines were an extra bonus as the girls continued to put their marks into the Great White Way. John Gow breezed past and flew through some steep moguls in flawless control. Visitors would never guess that he is an amputee. A surprise contingent of Japanese ski instructors, representing 80 of them who were visiting Sunshine to make a film on Canadian Rocky skiing, carved some beautiful turns as they flew past the girls. They all angulated Austrian style and skied with their boots tightly together. It's nice to know that I am not alone in defending this manner of skiing.

The girls did some of their own flying down Spring Hill to meet Sue Yule who guided them up to lunch at the Sunshine Inn. The Inn sleeps about 200. One night a week their bus shuttles to the Sulphur Hot Spring or to the Banff center. Other nights are serviced with a surplus of entertainment at the Inn. Three meals a day are included in packages. There is a nice bar, a huge stone fireplace, and an adequate fire burning, even at lunch time (eastern ski areas take note). The sun deck was well crowded with optimists patiently waiting for a tanning ray of sunshine to pierce the rumbling cumulus which promised new snow for tomorrow. The food at the Inn was adequate and not overpriced.

First run after lunch took the girls to the Wa Wa T-Bar where they found some neat bumps and the best snow conditions of the day. Two rides later on the Angel Chairlift, the sky broke its bladder and the pancake snow flakes that fell marked the visibility zero. The girls skied back to the Day Lodge, rummaged through the picture file for SKIER'S DIGEST, boarded the frightening bus which careened to the parking lot, drove back to the Banff Springs Hotel and brought me some black jelly beans to relieve the discomfort of my prone rendered, skiing deprived, dilemma.

Dr. Turner has diagnosed my vertebral condition to be more serious than I had estimated. This means another week of incarceration at the Mineral Springs Hospital, a postponement of our Bugaboos experience for one week and a well-deserved vacation for Marge. Oh, well, I'm getting some neat back rubs and a lot of rest. For $110 a day. Tomorrow, Marge will check out Lake Louise.

Lake Louise Ski Area

Lake Louise is world famous as a scenic summer resort. Travellers since the turn of the century have been crossing the Canadian Prairies to reach this landmark in the Rocky Mountains. In summer the Lake, 6,000 feet above sea level, is a vivid green in contrast to the white mass of the Victoria Glacier behind it.

In winter Lake Louise freezes over. And so too did life in the community that has been long sustained only by the traffic of the Trans Canada Highway and the Canadian Pacific Railway. The baronial mass of Chateau Lake Louise, built on the shores of the Lake, was literally returned to the

wilderness, with its heat shut off and its water-pipes drained, until another summer would bring its 100 days of activity and its thousands of visitors.

Skiing is now changing the scenario. This is the sport that has been growing at an average 23 percent a year since the mid 1960s. From a weekend business catering to residents of Calgary 2 hours driving time away, it has become an all-winter industry attracting skiers from eastern Canada, the United States, Japan and even from ski-sophisticated Europe. Here are some of the reasons:

- Lake Louise is the biggest ski area in the Canadian Rockies. It covers three mountain faces each in the sun at different times of the day. It has 2,600 feet of vertical drop spread over 35 miles of groomed trails. Eight lifts interlink beginner and expert runs to create all the variety of the European "Ski Circus." Except on weekends, these facilities are to be enjoyed without waiting in a lift line!
- Lake Louise adjoins the Continental Divide, the range of peaks whose snows in spring run west to the Pacific and east to the Atlantic. The water-laden clouds from the coast have turned to dry powder by the time they reach the Divide, 700 miles inland. Lake Louise at certain times every season is thus a powder skiers' paradise.
- From the 8,000-foot level of its highest lifts, skiers enjoy a spectacular view of the peaks and ice-age glaciers of the Divide and of Lake Louise itself. In short, the scenery is superb.

Compared to the hills of eastern Canada and New England, whose snows so quickly turn to ice, or compared to the wetter snows of the West Coast, Lake Louise in the Canadian Rockies offers the finest natural conditions in Canada, comparable to Aspen, Vail, Taos, Sun Valley or Snowbird to the south, and, of course to the Bugaboos, Cariboos, and Monashee wildernesses.

And until winter 1974 it has been for the most part natural conditions only. Unlike some areas, Lake Louise has been slow to develop the surrounding community atmosphere that most skiers seek at the end of the day. Visitors to Louise have had to settle either for a quiet life in one of the three comfortable hotels in the vicinity (one of which is a charming but exclusive six-bedroom log chalet at the foot of a ski slope) or drive 40 minutes back to Banff where the facilities of a tourist-oriented town are thriving.

But now the "apres-ski" atmosphere has arrived.

Chateau Lake Louise, built by the Canadian Pacific Railway, is staying open to cater to skiers. And what a place to stay. It is right on the edge of the lake with massive Victoria Glacier rising behind.

With a minimum of 250 of its rooms open for skiers, the Chateau has virtually doubled the hotel accommodations for the Lake Louise ski area. But, more than this, it has brought all the civilized amenities of an international hotel—the boutiques, taverns, night club and cuisine—that complement the wilderness and make it much more enjoyable.

Keeping pace with the growth of accommodations, the Lake Louise ski area has added again this year to its already extensive facilities. A new, high-speed double chairlift has been built on the popular Larch slope, previously served by a surface lift. Not only does the new lift carry 1,200 people an hour some 1,230 vertical feet up the mountain, but it gives access to new terrain that appeals to both intermediate and expert.

Lake Louise Ski Area, Banff, Alberta, Canada.

Time out for two skiers who have discovered that skiing is more than riding a lift just to ski back down again. Shot at Lake Louise ski area.

The Lake Louise ski area is one of the biggest in Canada. Spread over three mountain faces, with 35 miles of trails, it employs more than 120 people to operate its eight lifts, three lodges, radio-equipped safety patrols and its ski school, ski shop and ski rental services. But, all these amenities do not necessarily mean crowds. Provided you choose midweek, it is still possible to go there and not wait in a lift line! The area's capacity is designed to handle the big crowds that come 115 miles by car every weekend from Calgary. So, despite the addition of Chateau Lake Louise, it has facilities to spare, especially for those on a ski-week.

The fully licensed 250-person Sundance Cabaret offers more lively fare for the young or the young-at-heart with entertainment offered nightly except Sunday. Over at the Chateau Lake Louise the pace is not as fast, but the fun is just as great. A program of renovations designed to modernize accommodations and dining facilities at the 360-room, year-round resort hotel was carried out late this fall. Several suites and 100 rooms were redecorated, lounge facilities and meeting rooms were upgraded, the hotel's cafeteria was remodeled and alterations were carried out on the heating and plumbing facilities. Both hotels will be offering numerous winter activities in addition to the fantastic skiing.

Winter hiking and horse drawn sleigh rides will be available at both hotels as will ice skating on outdoor rinks. At the Chateau, cross-country skiing will be just outside the door with a variety of breathtaking trails readily available. A jam can curling rink will be another plus at the Chateau this season. Both hotels will have regular bus service to the three ski areas.

The Chateau Lake Louise and the Banff Springs Hotel both offer attractive ski packages. They are available through Air Canada's "Skifari" at most reasonable rates. Details concerning these packages are available from the sales offices of the airlines concerned or travel agents. *We have not found a package plan yet that provides the most pleasant accommodations, the most dependable skiing enjoyment and the least hassles as those offered by Air Canada's "Skifari."* Try them. You won't be disappointed. If you really are satisfied, drop them a complementary note and tell them we didn't "put you on." One of the advantages in having no commercial ties is that we can be completely honest in our appraisal of the areas featured in this chapter.

Marge's 45-minute drive to Lake Louise from the Banff Springs Hotel took her through spectacular scenery that is beyond description. And besides, I have run out of superlatives. Wildlife, protected by the National Park was in full view on both sides of the road. Visitors are periodically warned against feeding the bears. Mountain sheep are stocky, agile animals that occasionally descend the steep terrain into the rugged canyons to inspect the curious visitors. A mature ram can weigh over 300 pounds and stand over 40 inches high. Their ewes range about half that size. The characteristic horns of the older rams form a curl which may measure 17 inches in circumference and grow as long as 4 feet. Many of the ewes that Marge saw were pregnant. Their lambs are born between May and mid-June, with ewes and lambs roaming together while the older rams tend to move in bachelor bands, except of course at mating time in the late autumn. Marge also saw some wapiti (elk), probably the most commonly seen animal in the mountain parks of Canada. They can be seen in great numbers all along the park's highways, but their number thins out in mid-summer when the herd moves up into the high country. Just outside of Banff, strolling with confidence in the Vermilion Lakes, was a family of moose, the largest standing about 6 feet at the shoulders and weighing well over 1,000 pounds. The male proudly swung his broad, palmated antlers in protection of his waiting family. Between the Lake Louise townsite and the Chateau, well fed from the Lake Louise garbage dumping area, a family of grizzly bears with their characteristic flattened dishpan faces and voluminous withers turned shyly away and lumbered toward the back country. Although his cousin, the black bear, is generally considered more docile than the grizzly, the black is more brave and a habitual begger, frequently roaming the roadsides in search of a soft touch. More accidents occur each year involving black bears than grizzlies and visitors are constantly cautioned to view these animals from the safety of their own cars. Perhaps the most beautiful wildlife within a 10-mile radius of Banff's 1A Highway are the calcimined short black horned Rocky Mountain goats. Their virgin white coats are silhouetted quite clearly against the high rugged brown cliffs above timberline in the summer, but they are pretty hard to spot in the protection of their winter environment. Suspicious of human intruders, the Rocky Mountain goats seldom venture near the highways.

If your love for skiing extends beyond the perfunctory mechanics of riding a lift up and sliding back down to do it again, you owe it to yourself to enlarge your experience by viewing some of the nature that man has managed to protect from his own excesses and hedonistic ambitions. The best times to view wildlife in its natural habitat are during the feeding hours, early morning and late afternoon. They will be seen in greatest number along the highways and by the rivers during these periods, especially in the spring.

The most impressive mountain range on the road to Lake Louise was a cluster of ragged stone slabs called Mt. Eisenhower, spotted only with twisted dishes of snow at this late time of the season.

Parking below the Whiskeyjack Lodge, Marge rode the Olympic chair to the peak of the Grizzly Bowl, climbing the vertical drop of 2,100 feet. Beneath this chair, especially under its lower section, is a narrow swath surrounded by tall stately pines which is unnamed since only the bravest dare to challenge its perilous limitations. Lake Louise experts love it. Marge joined them.

From the top of the Olympic chair there is a magnificent view of Victoria Peak. Novices can ski off to the left down the gentle Wiwaxy Trail to the Eagle Pomalift or the Eagle chairlift if they opt to continue skiing at the higher elevations. The Wiwaxy run also continues winding all the way down to the Whiskeyjack Lodge enabling novices to enjoy

skiing the Lake Louise area from top to bottom. There are novice runs off each of the other chairlifts also.

Marge preferred to follow the experts, plunge down the Grizzly Bowl off to the right of the Olympic chair. The right side of this wide steep bump run offered some great powder speckled with pines, while the left side presented some challenging moguls. From the bottom of Grizzly Bowl, she flew over the intermediate bumps of Eagle Flight, past the Whitehorn Lodge where she had to stop to admire the spectacular panorama of Lake Louise and the glaciers of the Continental Divide. Then she skied on to the Eagle chair. From the Eagle chair novices will welcome the long gentle and winding Eagle Meadows, while intermediate skiers can bump down Eagle Flight without too much exertion. Any bun-dropper looking to exercise his avalement and wheelies can do his thing on the challenging Wapta. Wapta reminded Marge of the top of the Cliffs at Glen Ellen, Vermont.

Louise offers another peak which again provides descents for every level. The experts have their *shoot-outs* on Exhibition beneath the Ptarmigan chair. The intermediates leave their mark on the Old Ptarmigan or the Alley, and novices once again can wind their way around, wedging the Pike trail with the added bonus of viewing a magnificent bowl that is a haven for wildlife of the Continental Divide.

These trails funnel out and meet at the bottom of the Larch Poma or the Larch chairlift which embrace the Temple Chalet at 6,500 feet. Temple Chalet and Skokie Lodge are unique in the Canadian Rockies. They were built on logs more than 40 years ago and provide comfortable accommodations in the high country for those who prefer isolation. Skokie Lodge is 7 miles past Temple Chalet, deeper in the wilderness. Temple has six bedrooms with separate bathrooms and is fully modernized. Skokie accommodates 11 in five rooms and 14 people in four adjoining cabins. Their plumbing is more primitive. Both chalets include a large living room, stone fireplace and authentic log cabin atmosphere. Sure beats the plastic condominium.

Marge's favorite run off the Larch chair was the super wide, bump-nippled Bobcat headwall which probably scares the hell out of the novices who circumvent this bowl as they wind their way around the Lookout and 5 Mile Trail back to the Whiskeyjack Lodge.

Sixty- to 70-degree daytime weather during the last few weeks, and cold nights have created a variety of snow conditions over Lake Louise terrain. New snow has fallen nightly but has been quite heavy and wet. The trails are relatively desolate with most skiers consistently making the common mistake of missing the most pleasurable skiing of the year. Since the expert runs have not been skied enough, the new untracked snow is like wet cement; the kind of glue that put me into this bloody hospital. Avoid it if you can. Tomorrow, Marge will leave some tracks on Norquay.

Marge on Mt. Norquay

Mount Norquay rises to a peak of 8,275 feet, with a 3,240-foot double chairlift in the winter and a cable car lift in the summer taking skiers and sightseers through 1,300 vertical feet to the 7,000-foot level. This spectacular landscape makes the lift as popular in the summer as in the winter.

A 4-mile paved highway brings you to the expansive parking lots at the base of Mt. Norquay Ski Area which is,

Right—Mt. Norquay presents the most challenging skiing in the Banff area. Base elevation is 5,700 feet. Peak elevation is 7,000 feet. Their North American run has a much longer vertical drop, though.
Below—The Mt. Norquay Ski School is operated by Jerry Johnston's Ski Enterprises. Director is Jim Montalbetti. (Simon Hoyle photo)

also, serviced twice daily by buses from Banff. The base elevation of this area is at 5,700 feet and the longest of the six lifts rises to a 7,000-foot level. Skiing usually begins mid-November, ending in mid-April.

Mt. Norquay is an area with a slope and a tow for the learner who is on skis for the first time—novice slopes beautifully groomed on gentle, slightly rolling terrain. A challenge is also awaiting the more advanced skier at the top where he or she can choose from the famous North American, Bowl or Lone Pine.

Facilities at Mt. Norquay include two chairlifts, two T-bars and two rope tows which are servicing terrain with a minimum vertical of 200 feet and a maximum vertical of 2,400 feet, cafeteria, lunchroom, babysitting service, ski shop with full range of rentals and repairs. The Mt. Norquay Ski School is operated by the Jerry Johnston Ski Enterprises Ltd. with an office at the main base of the ski area.

A special treat awaits the keen, more advanced skier with a challenge of skiing the Big Chair for the Mt. Norquay Club 35,000 pin, which designates the number of vertical feet skied in one day. Everyone is encouraged to participate throughout the entire season. Stipulation; Skis only, no kites!!!

In the 1975-76 season, 100 gold pins were awarded, 29 silver medals and 20 bronze awards.

Today was April 18th, Easter Sunday, so Marge drifted around the Banff Springs Hotel in the morning to shoot some pics of the colored egg hunt for the kids and traditional holiday festivities. I am still supine in room 203 at the Mineral Springs Hospital watching the clouds sweep up the crest of Mt. Norquay and dump a few heavy flakes on the eastern slopes. There is a crucifix hanging on the green wall before me to remind me of the first Easter, and those somber reflections make my sacroiliac pain a bit more tolerable. Doc Turner says I will be 2 weeks on my back. A delightful nurse named Maggie has just given me a backrub but wouldn't consider rubbing the front, as she's pretty hung up on some entertainer, Al Willies, who she claims is an excellent folk singer at the Goats Eye Lounge in Sunshine Village. He read my novel, *Snowballing,* and has laid sufficient warning against dirty old men upon his Maggie, who is a real dreamboat. No need to, actually, as I can't get my mind off Marge since this therapy has separated us. She's doing a dynamite job of reporting and I know that our joint effort will bring you a little closer to the real ski scene in this great Northwest American Paradise. She also brought me a neat piece of licorice today that was 3 feet long!

Marge got her skis sharpened at Bruce Steeper's Spoke-n-Edge in Banff and took the 12:50 bus from the Banff Springs Hotel which cost two bucks for a round trip to Mt. Norquay. The bus was late, and the passengers were few. Spring is in the air and many of the locals have had it with snow. Bicycles are churning down the Banff hills and short shorts are in abundance. The bus arrived at 1:30. The view while riding up the Norquay double chair was unreal. To the left one can immediately see the precipitous Olympic inruns and jump platforms which would make even the best *gelandesprung* feel inadequate. The view of the Banff townsite in the valley between Mt. Rundle and Cascade is a storybook illustration that will rival the most beautiful of all European Tirols. One would expect to see Julie Andrews skipping over hills belting the "Sound of Music" in her inimitable sweet harmony. The difference here is that while the mountains, valleys, rivers and lakes reflect the most beautiful of European Alpine environments, the towns in the valley are decidedly American; early American in the more pleasant hand-hewn communities and practical American in the side-by-side neon merchant areas. Even Colonel Sanders has found his way to Banff. Can MacDonald's be far behind? I don't think that factory and automobile pollution will float its brown smog over Banff as it does over the town of Calgary, because of the mountain blockade. It is truly one of·the most beautiful ski areas of the world, and it will be a while before the smog reaches this elevation. They should stop the autos on their way to Banff at Canmore, though, and transport the tourists to their hotels by horse and buggy, Zermatt, Switzerland, style.

There are three expert runs off the top of the Norquay

Left—Norquay Ski School Director, "Monti," leads some of his instructors down Lone Pine with Cascade Mountain in the background. Notice Monti's classic *angulation* and compare it to the style of the last skier in the group who hasn't quite got it all together. (Simon Hoyle photo)

Above—Irwin Tonsch whistles through Lone Pine powder rotating Arlberg style to show that there is more than one way to turn a pair of skis. (Bruno Engler photo)

double chair. North American to the far left, the Bowl to the immediate left and Lone Pine to the right. All three are challenging bump runs, with North American having the steepest vertical of 2,450 feet and the longest distance of 1.6 miles which takes you all they way down to the Timberline Hotel on the edge of town. Parts of it will remind you of Al's Run at Taos if enough skiers shape the moguls, although Al's is steeper and more narrow.

Marge opted for the Bowl and had to burrow her way down as the snow was like the wet cement we had already encountered, since it hadn't been skied for so long. Then, she cut over across Lone Pine Practice to catch the Lone Pine double chairlift. There is a rope tow (come on, Norquay—rope tows went out with bear trap bindings) for real beginners on the Lone Pine Practice run, which is plenty wide, flat and gentle for learners. The Lone Pine double chair offers a super wide ballroom carpet for novices who exit at the first unloading ramp. Intermediates can ride to the top and play with a few moguls before showing off to their lesser beings.

Marge skied over to the Wishbone T-bar and tested its three novice to intermediate runs, then went over to the Stoney Squaw T-Bar where she found wide intermediate terrain. Her general opinion is that Norquay is a beginner to intermediate paradise with only three runs off the Norquay double chair offering the excitement for a vigorous skier. This kind of situation doesn't bother the seasoned skier who is into the sport for its *total* rewards. If you are a yo-yo who wants no more than to beat the lift ticket and log your vertical feet daily, you can do that at Norquay and even get a vertical-foot medal which you can shine all summer. If you dig the clean air of mountain living and want to share a little of it with roaming wildlife and if you like to remind yourself of your own insignificance when compared to the powers that have shaped these magnificent pine skirted spires, sculptured canyons and crashing waterfalls, and then reassert yourself by mastering a daring plunge down one of its

most challenging headwalls, come to Banff. Stay a week or two, but don't leave without sampling some of Canadian Mountain Holidays fantastic helicopter skiing. I will be on a chopper to Hans Gmoser's Shangri-la Lodge in the uninhabited territory of the Bugaboo Mountains next Saturday even if they have to cast this wretched hip of mine in solid iron. It is an experience I have dreamt about for 20 years. On this holy day, please save half a prayer for half a hip and I will put you right in that CMH helicopter with me, rising up to the vast tundra of untracked snowfields and glaciers hundreds of miles from civilization. I will escort you to the finest skiing anywhere, in a pure white virgin land that will not look as though it is of this world. The Western Canadian skiing that we've just enjoyed is the entrée. The Bugaboos are your dessert, and it's all on the same menu offered by Air Canada in their "Skifari" package. (P.S. Marge has not waited in a lift line once since she began skiing the Canadian Rockies this week. There are many exciting resorts in this beautiful part of the skiing world. Perhaps we will reveal more, like the super challenging Whistler Mountain in the next edition of Skier's Digest. Right now, it's lights out and more dreams about next Saturday. It is April 21st. And it's snowing!)

Discharged From Mineral Springs Hospital

It happened. I took the stretching exercises prescribed by the physio-therapist at Mineral Springs one step further and accelerated the amelioration of my sacroiliac bummer. The exercises she gave me were for 60-year-old pear shapes who haven't done a thing physical in 20 years. I took a chance, intensified the exercises and increased their frequency, and today, when Dr. Turner asked me to bend forward, I amazed him by touching my fingers to the floor. It hurt like hell, but I also have been practicing a little pain suppression. Hell, it's all mental anyway. I convinced him to release me today and promised to not ski again this season (for which I will have to compose a sincere letter of apology), packed my gear and held Marge's arm as we waddled back up to the Banff Springs Hotel, $1,200 poorer and pretty high on whatever pills those were that followed every meal. For the rest of the day I floated about 4 inches above the ground, but today, we skied Sunshine, I had to have one day on skis before flying to the lodge in the Bugaboos tomorrow morning. Fortunately, everything had held together, with the help of a constricting girdle that kept my sacrum stable. We had a marvelous day, and the area was all that Marge described. No super-expert runs, but vast above timberline terrain that is so beautiful, it gave me goose bumps.

We began by taking a few runs with the assistant director, Mike. We kicked around some technical jargon and generally agreed that all ski schools in the United States and Canada are coming closer to a consistent methodology. We disagreed, of course, on early introduction of hip angulation, but Mike agreed that it certainly is essential in the style of a more advanced skier who travels at a higher velocity. Hmmmn! We were joined, unexpectedly by Peter Honrung from the Banff Springs Hotel and Monti Montalbetti from Mt. Norquay. Then, the discussions got heavy. Another principal disagreement between us came up when one of the pros mentioned that we should pattern our recreational curriculum after the style of the racer, as racers are the finest skiers in the world. My comment was that there should be a distinction between the racer and recreational skier whose goal is control and graceful rhythm at speeds nowhere near the velocities attained by a racing specialist. A racer making a long turn at high speed can be balanced by the powerful pull of centrifugal force and can even inclinate his turn because of that tenacious pull. A recreational skier, moving at a much slower speed, is susceptible to the pull of centripetal force, and if he tries to inclinate with his skis together, we will fall on the uphill side of his skis. We also talked about a parallel traverse as opposed to a parallelogram traverse and most of the directors agreed that the uphill ski, boot, knee, hip and shoulder should lead slightly, although most of them were against a tightly juxtaposed boot relationship.

I have to tell you about one incident which occurred while we were skiing. Marge was following with our Hasselblad strapped to her chest. We had just finished discussing my theory that the torso should be perpendicular to the slope for an optimum balanced position whether crossing the slope or heading straight down. Few of the instructors with whom I discussed this theory agreed with the principle. We reached a steep pitch that we decided to traverse in order to reach some untracked powder. All six of us took off. Marge stopped me later and said, "Frank, I should have had the camera out. All but one of you traversed that steep pitch with your torsos precisely 90 degrees to the angle of the slope. The one who didn't (no need to mention his name) had a more square stance, but his skis were a foot apart." It certainly proved that hip-angulation has its place, particularly on a steep slope. Later, Peter Honrung confided to me that he essentially agreed, but that he was opposed to exposing the principle to a student at too early a stage in his learning process.

And now I will confess to you the most common reason given to me by instructors across the entire continent for: 1. Teaching you to skid your skis rather than carve your turns, as beginners 2. Teaching the wedge approach to turns rather than straight parallel turns with edge control 3. Starting you on a shorter ski 4. Teaching axial motion (propeller type) turns instead of turns by longitudinal and traverse leverage 5. Disregarding body angulation as an important assist to knee angulation, particularly for students who have wide hips. There is only one reason for the entire ATM or CSIA methodology. It is simply this—they want you to turn. Quickly. In one morning, if possible. It doesn't matter a bit if your turn is proper. Scientific analysis is in fact discouraged. If you can slip and slide around—certainly not in control, for a skidded turn is not a controlled turn—the pros feel you will be happy. You will go home from your 1 or 2-day ski vacation pleased that you have been up a lift and have chalked up mileage. And, do you know why they don't give a rap whether you have turned properly? Because they know that you probably won't be back for another year.

When I proposed my theory to Mike about teaching sideslip, edge control, turns into the hill and hockey stops and avoiding the wedge exercises entirely, can you guess what he said? "Frank, of course it is a more sensible approach, but I am afraid you will lose your student. His attention span is small. He wants to go up the lift as soon as possible and turn his way down, making *any* kind of turns. He is not a technician. He is here to play. To have fun. He wants mileage . . ."

And that's about where it is. The rationalization of ski schools across both Nations, with the exception of those teaching the Modified Austrian or the Stein Eriksen techniques, is in effect, that you, the skiing public are bumbling idiots who just want to play in the snow and get back to your beer as soon as possible. They are saying, never mind teaching your 9-year-old notes and chords on the piano, just let her bang the keys with her fist—she only wants to make noise.

One pro, Peter, with whom I really enjoyed discussing the problem, offered an interesting analogy. He said, "Frank, skiing is bending your ankles and rolling your knees to change your edges. Years ago, we all taught *down-up-down* in an effort to unweight the skis, and thousands of skiers went *down-up-down,* and made not one single turn. It is like eating. You open and close the teeth to masticate the food. But that is not eating. You must still swallow. A student must learn how to use the shape of his ski. He should learn the mechanics of a turn, or he will be chewing and not swallowing." Thank you, Peter. Right on.

Altogether we enjoyed our rap session. Oh, I am sure that many of my ideas were quickly dismissed by a few of the pros, but when we began to ski together, it became clear which principles were working and which were borderline. I haven't seen the photographs Marge took of us yet, and I don't intend to publish anywhere that these excellent skiers were a little off balance. That would be unethical. I only hope that they have liberal minds which will encourage them to at least experiment with some of my theories, as I intend to experiment with theirs. *A blending of professional minds can only lead to a more perfect form, and that which is closest to perfection is closest to efficiency and beauty.*

It was a great day. My hip held up, and I only felt imbalanced when I took off my skis. Right now, it is 1:30 AM. In 8 hours we will be riding a van to Hans Gmoser's helicopter pad. Then off to the Bugaboos. I'll talk to you more tomorrow. I'm really beat. Goodnight.

THIS IS THE GREATEST SKIING IN THE WORLD

CANADIAN
MOUNTAIN
HOLIDAYS
BUGABOOS

THIS IS THE GREATEST SKIING IN THE WORLD

It is worth repeating. This is the *greatest* skiing in the world. That's a pretty heavy statement in a book of this type, and I am sure that more than a few ski area corporations will be upset with me for having made it. Especially those areas which I have not yet visited, who have a right to demand equal time for appraisal. It is, of course, my own opinion, which is partially biased by the fact that I sit here at this moment on the sundeck of the rustic Bugaboo Lodge, looking at a wide V-shaped dark pine forest which skirts the moraines of an ancient glacier. The living glacier stretches a mile to the Snowpatch, Pigeon and Bugaboo Spires, gray granite stalagmites rising 1,000 vertical feet in the spatial cave of this wonderful winter wilderness.

Spelunkers will immediately flinch at my referral to this open territory as a *cave*, but that's the feeling I get looking out toward those massive spires and glaciers. Enclosed. Apart from the *civilized* world where the power of the dollar and pretentious propriety are king and queen. In this cave, we are free. And the remoteness of the Bugaboos will keep pollutionists from driving in to violate its natural beauty. I am not alone in this meditation. Marge sits beside me on a sawed-off pine, 4 feet in diameter, stripped of its bark and shellacked for preservation by the proprietor of the lodge, Leo Grillmair, who prefers even his benches to complement this totally natural environment. Marge is contemplative, too, as she stares beyond the chisel-faced glacier to the towering striated spires. She has just leaned over and whispered my conviction, "Frank, that had to be the greatest skiing in the world." Helicopter skiing in the Bugaboos is hard to beat. It's even more difficult to describe. Ten minutes ago we were ducking the whirling props of a settling heli that had taken us over the vast, awesome tundra of untracked snow beyond the spires and up to a lofty flat landing area called Anniversary Peak which swoops down like a gliding eagle 4,800 feet to the valley. After a thrilling skiing descent that we will never forget, the heli picked us up for lunch.

There are no words that can describe the excitement of helicopter skiing beyond the Continental Divide of the Canadian Rockies, high into the majestic peaks of this adventurous British Columbia Range. There are no lift lines. There is no boundary to the skiing area. No fences. No parking lots. Snow blanketed glaciers stretch for thousands of miles, with steep chutes and tall pine glades striping their moraines, as far as your eyes can see—in every direction. It is possible for you to ski 200,000 vertical feet in 1 week! Just for kicks, figure how long it would take you to ski that far at any ski area serviced by some form of cable lift! You have not skied, until you have dropped into one of those nearly vertical chutes and carved your turns down from one of its snow-laden rocky spines. In the winter, Bugaboo skiers push the flour-like snow ahead of them, chest high and deeper; desperately making an effort to keep from smiling and screaming in total ecstacy as the powder sprays their faces and chokes them with the ultimate thrill. They fly! In the spring, which is now, you may add to that high the delight of a baking sun that bounces off the diamond studded snow turning the daytime air to 70 degrees Fahrenheit and your skin to a golden brown.

In the spring snow variations create an added challenge which makes the Bugaboo experience even more unforgettable. Our drop-off, Anniversary Peak, began on hard steps of wind-blown, crusted snow which demanded a hard-edged short swing, until we reached the crest of a drifted wave of settled powder. We broke through the clean cornice and to our mutual delight pressed some smooth serpentine turns through a steep headwall of light powder snow which seemed to be waiting for the rhythmic flow of our ski tracks. The fluffy headwall leveled and then rose to the crest of still another white wave, changing its surface to hard and compressed, but still submissive to the sharp bite of our edges. Over the clean white ridge, we stopped and were awe-struck by the punctuation of a penetrating ice cave that ducked beneath a heavy layered cornice, appearing bluer and darker as it dug deeper into the 20-foot base of snow that will never melt. I just had to ski next to that cavern and tease the sharp ridge of snow that embraced it.

Every 500 feet of that one run presented a new challenge and an inimitable panorama that would defy a winter landscape painter's brush. Beautiful. There were times when Marge and I almost collided from admiring the view instead of watching where we were headed. To document our trip (a perfect word for the experience) we lent our Hasselblad to Leo Grillmair, who is quite an artist with a camera and a fantastic skier. He knows every nook and cranny in the Bugaboo range, and he has trained his guides to become as familiar with hidden crevasses and avalanche potential slopes. The Bugaboo slopes are steep; steep enough to remind us of their danger by rumbling every 20 minutes as a

Fig. 4W-18: Our group breaks for lunch in a valley known only to the grizzly and cougar. That's Leo Grillmair in the baseball hat.

Left—Every track you leave behind is your personal signature. You'll tend to ski better, knowing this, or you'll feel guilty of violating the virginal beauty of the Bugaboo's environment.
Below—The helicopter sure beats a chairlift. We skied 150,000 vertical feet in one week!

new rock or snow slide develops in the distance. And steep enough for Leo and his guides to ask me, as I write this, "Please don't invite any *prune-pickers* to our Paradise." "Prune-picker" is the Western Canadian equivalent to what U.S. skiers call a *turkey*. In spite of what you may have read by some author who probably stayed in the helicopter for some of the steep runs and joined the rest of the group on the flatter, lower runouts, you should be a damned good parallel skier with a fair amount of courage to ski this incredible range. Especially in the spring when the snow surface is more changeable and less forgiving. A stem-type intermediate could probably manage some of these slopes, but the time that it would take for such a skier to descend one of the hundreds of chutes and headwalls that the veterans enjoy skiing in the Bugaboos would impede the progress of the rest of the group and deprive them of their expensive enjoyment. It wouldn't make the prune-picker many friends.

Yes, heli skiing is expensive. Consider it a vital luxury. An unforgettable experience. A vivid memory. A thrill beyond description. A "happening" that will surpass any pleasurable sensation you have ever experienced. Those are commodities that *should* carry a heavy price. Don't misunderstand me. It is not a rip-off. It cost bucks to fly that helicopter. *Lots* of bucks. Leo Grillmair is not in this business to make a million dollars. He is in it for peace of mind. The Bugaboos may be the closest a real skier can come to Heaven on earth. I apologize for the inadequacy of my description. I have literally run out of superlatives. If you are a capable parallel skier and unafraid of the steep, save your pennies for a week in the Bugaboos, and I promise you that you will thank me for encouraging your adventure. I will be more specific in a moment about the cost. Some forms of happiness do, unfortunately, carry a price tag. A word of warning. Spend a week here, and you may never want to go back to a chairlift. Or a lift line. Or crowded slopes. Or greasy chow lines (Leo's wife is one of the three best cooks in the world, along with my mother and my wife).

The Bugaboos are not for skiers who get their jollies freaking out on hundreds of moguls, (I confess, I didn't miss them) or for those who like to dance on stunted skis. There are plenty of kicker cornices for heroic aerialists. The Black Forest awaits slalom buffs who can use fire charred tree trunks for their gates. The bottomless powder in winter is beyond belief and is about a foot high in spring if you want to ease into the fluff. The area is spectacular! Even our photos can't do it justice. We really hate to leave these outer limits, but, in a few days, it will be back to reality. That is the *civilized* world which its inhabitants have convinced themselves is better than the wilderness they've destroyed in building their cement forests and parking lots.

There are men who have rejected the nine-to-five, dollar-idolized imperative. Here, at the Bugaboo lodge, they are

Left—The glacier head wall makes an unusual 50-foot backdrop for Frank Covino and his wife, Marge.
Below—Endless miles of virgin snow. You'll *never* cross the same track twice!

horseback riding adventurers deep into the heart of this playland of Mother Nature. It is still far enough away from the taint of humanity to not have been destroyed by condominium villages or other apartment type ghettos and fancy restaurants. Please don't come here if you want to show off your jewels or have your boots licked. Night people are also advised to stay away. Curfew is 10 PM and the wake-up bell rings at 6:30 AM. The Bugaboos Lodge is for *skiers,* and the guides set the pace.

Pierre Lemire has the honor of being the first French Canadian to receive his guides' diploma in Canada. The next summer will be his third at the Bugaboo Lodge. After one winter of avalanche control training at Rogers Pass, about 40 miles northwest of here, he has become a fully qualified member of the guide staff at this lodge on a year-round basis. We enjoyed his leadership today through the towering spires and down the glacier. We became especially respectful of him when one of the skiers in our group did not heed Pierre's warning not to ski too far across one of the lower steep headwalls; he skied too far and touched off a minor avalanche that rumbled over the tails of my skis and scared the hell out of my wife. Marge was hit by a boulder of snow a few days ago when a skier in our helicopter group skied too closely above her, avoiding the warning of another guide, Thierry Cardon, who can also read the anatomy of a mountain like he is a part of its structure.

Thierry has an interesting sideline. During the month of June he guides mountain climbing trips deep into the Andes, a continuation of the Rocky Mountains in South America, the peaks of which rise to 20,000 feet. After a short hiatus in France, he then takes climbing groups into the Himalayas of southeast Asia and guides them up to even more incredible peaks. We appreciated Thierry as a helicopter skiing guide so much that I would like to give his private business a plug. So, if you are of the rare breed who cannot look at a rocky mountain peak without wanting to climb to the top, you can receive a brochure from Thierry, which more specifically describes his climbing tours, by writing to him at CMH Bugaboo Helicopter Skiing, Ltd., Box 1660, TOLOCO, Banff, Alberta, Canada, or by writing to one of his partners,

the *guides*. Courageous adventurers that my wife noted must be made of melanin, muscle and sperm. Like ski instructors. But ski instructors are caged in little areas that cannot compare to 1/100,000th the terrain that faces me right now. These guides are as free as the mountain lion we saw yesterday, who shared our curiosity as we glided past his territory on the Vowell glacier. We skied across his ominous tracks and prayed that he had had his dinner. The Bugaboo guides are mountain men. When the ski season is over (and it only ends because the public stops skiing, as they get into golf, sailing and other spring season diversions), most of these men teach mountain climbing or lead canoe trips and

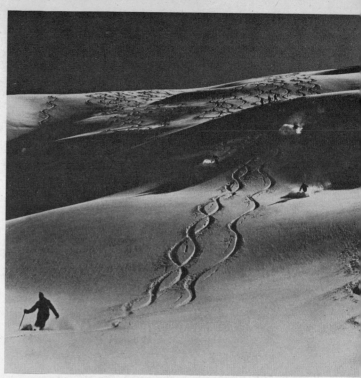

You'll find an endless variety of terrain. The crevasses and spires will blow your mind!

Late afternoon shadows made our tracks look even more impressive. *Most* of the time . . .

Henri Leblanc at 74400 Chamonix, France. Thierry is also at the latter address during the months of August to October. Climbing experience is unnecessary. All you need is a good physical condition, a tolerance for outdoor living devoid of the conveniences that have turned so many of us into vicarious adventurers and physical wrecks, and the right amount of dollars. Cardon's winters at the Bugaboo Lodge are shared by Ernst Buehler, who will have been a guide at the lodge for 5 years next summer.

In addition to his duties as an alpine skiing guide, Ernst is also assistant manager at the Bugaboo Lodge. He is the kind of man that most men hate for being incredibly handsome, masculine and, to quote one of the female guests, "super-cool." Ernst was our first guide, and I can testify that he really knows these British Columbian mountains. Hovering in our helicopter, he can spot an area of snow that he is sure will be good powder, or corn, or ice, or avalanche prone. He seldom misses. Ernst can *smell* crevasses that look like clean blankets of snow, but which would cave in under the skis of a "pilgrim" and drop him into 100 feet of dark, icy space. Relax. All Bugaboo skiers are required to wear a beeper, called a "Skadi," and all are trained thoroughly for burial location detection, primarily as a guard against avalanche. If you should be stupid enough to not heed his directions and ski into one of those crevasses, Ernst would be quick to help you. Each guide carries a 30-pound pack on his back, which holds, among other sundries, an air bag splint, a collapsible toboggan, a first-aid kit, ski equipment repair kit, (Ernst replaced a lost pole basket for me on top of Anniversary Peak in the time it took me to get into my skis!), warm-up pants and jacket, extra gloves and hat, a shovel, telescoping avalanche probe, 150 feet of rope, slings, carabiners, a compass, waterproof matches, a saw, sunglasses and other

survival equipment. The guides are ready to assist you in any emergency. In addition, the helicopter is stocked with more of each object in the guides' packs plus 20 to 39 heavier avalanche probes, oxygen, etc. They carry just about everything except "the pill." It is rumored that Ernst even has a pack of those in his pocket.

Surprisingly, the average number of fractures to skiers at the Bugaboo Lodge is only 1 or 2 per season. This is probably due to the fact that most visitors are pretty proficient skiers who are in *good* physical condition. A serendipitous plus factor is that several doctors who ski are usually in residence at the lodge. Many professional people come to Leo Grillmair's Shangri-la, because they can afford it, because it is *the best,* and because it is a grand escape from the confinement of being on constant call to the public. During high season you may feel assured that any injury you might incur will be professionally diagnosed immediately, and the helicopter at the lodge will fly you to the hospital in the town of Golden faster than you could get to one in many less remote ski areas. For a fee, of course, which is probably covered by your ambulance insurance. Incidentally, the Canadian hospitals will not accept your Blue Cross card, but they will give you a bill that you can submit to your local Blue Cross office for reimbursement. My accident in Taos cost me 11 days in the Banff Mineral Springs Hospital and $1,200, but, with the help of a corset and the generosity of Hans Gmoser and Leo Grillmair, I was able to enjoy my ski week in the Bugaboos.

The first couple of days were exasperating, though. From lying immobile on my back for so long, my balance wasn't too keen, especially in the higher elevations. It took me about 4 days to get it all together. By the fifth day, I was flying. Marge noted on the seventh day that I was skiing

Even the guide could not ski without taking a few moments to stare in awe at the breathtaking view.

Time out for a bit of contemplation. We felt so small...

faster and better than she had *ever* seen me ski, and Leo Grillmair's complement that day that I reminded him of Billy Kidd really was welcome. I hope he wasn't just referring to my cowboy hat.

The competition for King of the Mountain was heavy during our last week in April. While the professional people and the affluent come to the Bugaboos during the "high season" (January 24 through April 10), for guaranteed powder and edgeless skiing, the "off seasons" (December 20 through January 24, and April 10 through May 8) are usually attended by the hotshot skiers, the craftsmen, the rubber kneed who know how to use a ski's side camber and the racers. This is partly due to the fact that the faster knees usually belong to a younger, less solvent group who may have saved up all year for their one week *trip* to the Bugaboos. I know of at least a few who saved the fee from unemployment checks! The tariff difference is considerable between high and low season. The first week and the last week cost nearly half of what heli ski-weeks cost during the high season. The skiing during the first and last weeks also demand more precise edge control. During high season, when you are pushing snow with your chest, your velocity is considerably slower and turns are more effortless. Your stance can be square and your skis will slice through the powder more easily if they are edged less. On the harder packed surface of the "off season" though, you had better understand a little about angulation and use of your ski's side camber. You had also better be *fast*. But not too fast, or, as Nigel Woods was overheard mumbling in his sleep, you will "eat your vertical feet."

Nigel, a ski instructor from Whistler Mountain, C.S.I.A. Certified, was one of a group of ten very fast skiers who shared our week with us at the Bugaboo Lodge. On the first

day they flaunted their prowess in having skied more vertical feet than our group, but soon questioned the wisdom of that one-upmanship when they realized that they only had enough bread for 100,000, and extra verticals would cost them $4 per 1,000 feet. Nigel was justifiably concerned about "eating vertical." Their group spent Thursday in the lodge. They were an interesting rat pack who really loved helicopter skiing and had saved all year for this expensive week via dubious methods. A few of them were dropouts from responsible positions in "the establishment," who just decided that skiing is where it is happening, and responsibility be damned.

Like Coral Robinson, dropout school teacher. An incredibly beautiful, long haired blonde, whose current significant contribution to society is being caretaker for a cat whom she refers to as a lethargic "12-pound male slug." I watched her on the hill and saw the most aggressive, courageous and determined female I have ever seen turn a pair of skis. There's a touch of bitterness in that pretty little head, and she relieves her anxiety on the hill. An affinity predictably developed between Coral and Ernst. They were a picture perfect couple, and, as the week went on, a softer more pleasant Coral emerged. She even took part in the First Annual Bugaboo Lodge Snurfing Contest and *won it!* Mellowed, Coral confided that she does teach skiing part-time at a small area near Whistler called Ski Rainbow. We had an enlightening discussion about ski instructors and their peculiar mystique. Coral is an adventurous *total* skier; the kind that makes you feel like you are intruding, for taking part in *their* sport. Teaching in a regimented school system must have driven her bananas. She is one kind of skier who is lured by the refuge of the Bugaboos.

Betty Birell is different. Genuinely friendly, her affable

Above—Coral Robinson and guide Ernst Buehler rap about an exciting day of heli skiing in CMH's Bugaboos.
Right—Our guides were sufficiently impressive, like when Ernst leaped into this bowl with that 30 lb. pack on his back. Marv Parent's camera was ready.

nature has not been plasticized by her profession as a CP Air Stewardess. She could be soaking up rays on some million-aire tycoon's yacht in the Caribbean, but prefers to spend her free time skiing. Though she came to the Bugaboos with her boyfriend, Betty kept the party going for the whole week, and her gregariousness bonded the *potpourri* of per-sonalities that shared the Bugaboo Lodge that week.

They were all excellent skiers. Whistler bred, they were fearless and fast! When they pushed off the top of Anniver-sary chute and left nine pair of perfect tracks in their rhythmic wake of fresh powder, the Bugaboo Spires seemed to smile. It is not often that you get a group like that on Anniversary—Jan Tindall, a professional tennis player, Ger-hard May, a research economist at the University of British Columbia, Larry McKee and Byron Gracie, professional fishermen who were the hottest skiers of the pack, Chris Corbett, a boilermaker with iron hands, Don Biggar, a civil engineer (!) and summertime farmer, and Ray Peterson, who can boast of being certified to teach both alpine and cross-country skiing. All are *skiers,* all compromising with the establishment by making periodic contributions to society, but, all with a common end to that means—to earn enough bread to pay for their skiing. These are the tenants of the Bugaboo Lodge—in the off season.

Other paying guests (there were a few freeloaders at the lodge for commercial reasons) included interior designer Lynden Bethmuller, who traveled all the way from Australia for 1 week of Bugaboo magic, then twisted his knee on the third day and spent the rest of his time in meditation, and a delightful couple, Barb and Marv Parent. Marvin is a dedi-cated Junior College professor, who skis like an instructor and has an artistic temperment. It was comforting to have at least one other skier who took time between runs to admire the incredible scenery with me. With everyone so paranoid about chalking up vertical feet and finding new powder, I was beginning to feel like a freak for staring in awe at the environment. I used to tell my wife to bury me on Stein's Run when my time is up. I would like to be a mogul. We've

revised the plan. Now, I want to be a bump on Anniversary Peak.

The Bugaboo Lodge and helicopter skiing was the dream of Hans Gmoser, 43-year-old founder and director of Cana-dian Mountain Holidays. In his lifetime Hans has organized and led hundreds of expeditions all over the world. His lieutenants are the proprietors of the Bugaboo and Caribou Lodges, Leo Grillmair and "Kiwi" Gallagher. Sepp Renner manages the heli skiing operation in the Monashees, which I understand is the most challenging of the three areas and which will have its own lodge this winter. The Bugaboo Range is the most beautiful. The sergeants are the CMH Guides. These men are of a rare breed. They fight hard to preserve an interest in real adventure in a world that has gradually gone soft at the expense of vicarious satisfaction. They are, as I have said, mountain men, as hard as the rocks they climb, but as sensitive as the snowflakes which make their powder. They invite you to join them. They dare you to leave your plastic world for a week and get a little closer to your real self. It will cost you about a grand. That's only three bucks a day. Give up two martinis a day for one year, and you can share this paradise for a week. Eighty thousand vertical feet of skiing are guaranteed. Marge and I received pins for 150,000 vertical feet. It is possible to do 200,000 in a week, if you have the knees, and the extra 4 bills per thousand for the helicopter. Say hello to Leo for me. We are already saving for our next week at his lodge in the Buga-boos. Why Not? This is the greatest skiing in the world! Thank you CMH and Air Canada, for helping us to tell our readers about it.

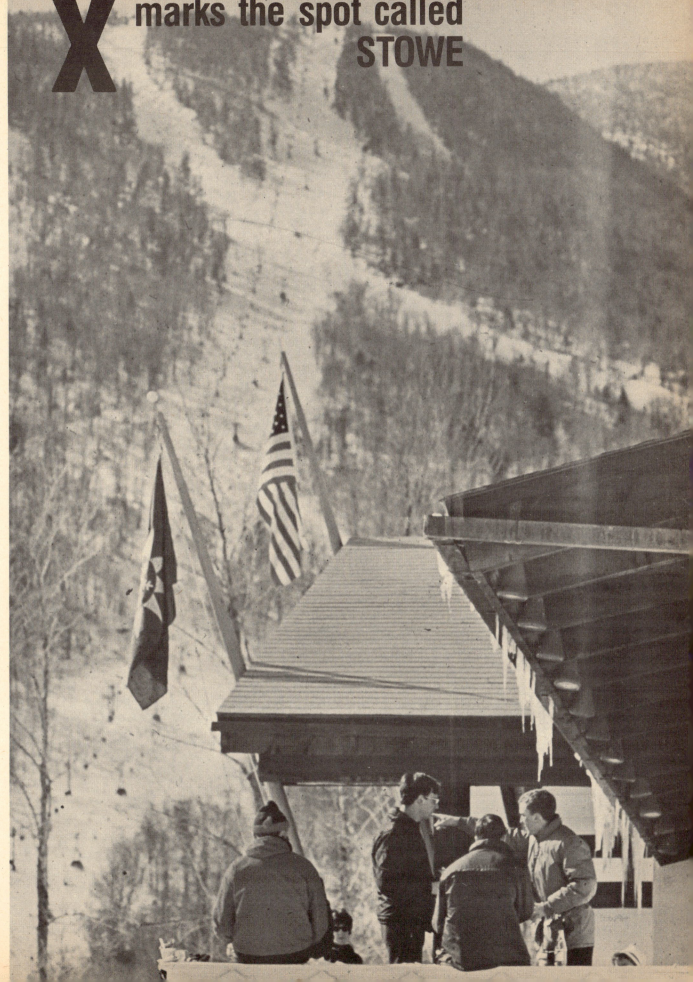

X marks the spot called STOWE

X MARKS THE SPOT CALLED STOWE

X marks the shape of the predominant trails that drop from the peak of Mt. Mansfield. The Goat, Lift Line, National and Starr trails slash the cheek of Mt. Mansfield as they drop from the Octagon, a fine peak restaurant with a panoramic view. While most ski areas have *novice, intermediate* and *expert* markings on their trails, the four heavily moguled drops I have just mentioned earn the distinction of *super-expert,* meaning super steep, meaning the mountain that is hailed by many as the Ski Capital of the East. Welcome to Stowe, Vermont.

Stowe has three distinct alpine skiing areas. The Mt. Mansfield "Nose" that I just mentioned drops its 15 ribbon trails from an elevation of 4,393 feet and varies those descents from the near vertical Starr to the 4-mile novice Toll Road. The wide western type slopes of Spruce Peak, a completely separate neighboring knoll of 3,330 feet, serviced by a double chairlift, that also has a lower level called Little Spruce which is ascended by a T-Bar and double chairlift, a ski shop, a very fine ski school, cafeteria, restaurant and lounge; and the latest addition of an enclosed four-seated Gondola lift which raises you in comfort to the "Chin," close to the highest peak of the mountain where the snow lingers on past April. Stowe designers have sensibly placed another restaurant at the Base Gondola Terminal and also provide food service at the Cliff House on top. The Mt. Mansfield Base House also has a ski shop and cafeteria, and is the terminal for three major lifts needed to disperse the anxious crowds which proliferate on the holiday weekends; the Mansfield T-Bar, 4,000 feet long provides access to six trails from novice to advanced-intermediate; the other two lifts are parallel single and double chairlifts that climb 6,400 feet to the Octagon. Unfortunately, the town of Stowe is 2 miles away from the ski area which scatters the apres ski action if that is your bag.

At Stowe you will learn how to ski through the American Teaching Method with some of the finest ski technicians supervising the staff. It surprises me that in no brochure that I have read is mention made of such respected educators as Stu Campbell, Allan Woods, Dave Stewart or Peter Duke. These are the men who are responsible for breaking down the militance of final form regimented systems of the past and who train their instructors (some of the finest in the world) in human understanding, psychological empathy and the development of basic skills which accelerate the learning process of their students at a far more rapid rate than when some of us learned to ski. The heart of the Eastern Professional Ski Instructors of America is at Stowe, Vermont, and their PR department does not even recognize the value of that asset as being significant enough to include in their brochures. Let me say it for them. If you learn to ski at Stowe, and graduate to controlled descents down the *super* steeps, you will be able to ski anywhere in the world and be looked upon as a learned professional. The Stowe Ski School was founded in 1936 by Sepp Ruschp, now President and General Manager of the Mt. Mansfield Company. Today, the School is under the direction of his son Peter Ruschp, but the names I have previously mentioned are the unsung heros in the victorious reputation of this excellent Ski School that is second to none.

I should mention that I requested a short article on ski technique authored by Stu Campbell, for whom the ski teaching profession holds the highest respect, plus some photos of ski actions at Stowe in exchange for these promotional words on what I truly feel is a most excellent ski area.

A novice skier's Paradise is the 4-mile long Toll Road trail that terminates with these gentle ballroom slopes at Stowe.

Stu was willing, but the Mt. Mansfield Company didn't feel that his feature was worth a few coins. Instead, I received the usual brochures and previously published jargon promoting restaurants, disco joints, lodges and excellent cross-country facilities that would surely satisfy any travel agent's library. Unfortunately, SKIER'S DIGEST II is a book for skiers—downhill skiers who want to improve their technical proficiency until they can really carve some turns down a chute like Stowe's Goat with the precision of a master surgeon. But, of course, ski resorts are a business, and a profitable business cannot thrive upon skiers who spend their evenings sharpening their edges and waxing their skis. We do buy lift tickets though, and we have been known to drop a few coins for a brew or two and some soothing sounds after skiing. For our modest investment, is it too much to ask for a few pointers on mastering the supreme challenges of Mt. Mansfield? And is it not high time that some of those perilous plunges down the super steep were illustrated with good action photographs? The editors of SKIER'S DIGEST sincerely hope that the photo file of the Stowe PR office shall have grown beyond the mundane motivational material available for the appetite of apres ski turkeys and include some dynamite inspirational shots for the serious skier who knows that Stowe provides the most challenging skiing in the East. When it does, we will appeal again to that office for some motivational photographs that will reveal to our readers exactly *why* the fantastic area of Stowe has earned its distinction as "Ski Capital of the East."

Left—Stowe's gondola on Mt. Mansfield affords intermediate skiers a wind protected ride *up.*
Below—Stowe's second mountain, called Spruce Peak, can be seen from the double chairlift on Mt. Mansfield. A bus ride connects the two for a minor fee.

Y

is for Youth

a report from BEECH MT., NORTH CAROLINA

BUT...WHAT DO WE DO WITH THE KIDS?

*A Report On the Kinder Klub at Beech
Mountain, North Carolina by Jean Schlichting*

Parents of young children are usually at a loss for what to do with the little skiers and still have a good day of skiing themselves. Past alternatives included putting the child in lesson after lesson; Mom supervising a while—Dad supervising a while; or just staying inside and not skiing.

But the new look at Beech Mountain has brought about innovation in the form of a creative idea of Mike Barrett, Ski School Director. It is the Kinder Klub. Most ski areas provide nursery facilities for small children, but now Beech Mountain has an all-day skiing program for primary ages (5-9). Although this is being used in other parts of the country, it is a new effort in the South.

Kinder Klub parents leave their "kinder" at the Klub at 9 AM and pick them up at 4:30 PM. The parents are free to enjoy a worry-free day.

The Kinder Klub operation is a total skiing day care center. The age bracket has been chosen to include the primary bracket. All of the children have had an introduction to school procedure and all day programming. The Kinder Klub is designed to fit into a time-block learning frame.

The day begins at 9 AM. The skiers arrive in the Kinder Klub Room, located at the end of the Ski Center. In the colorful yellow and orange room the first thing one sees is a large yellow "igloo." While waiting for all the arrivals, the new skier is given a large orange and blue Kinder Klub badge with his name and number on it. He is then fitted with skis, boots and poles, and they are numbered to match his badge. Now he is free to use any or all of the large clear plastic play areas on the floor. The toys and supplies are all chosen to help develop creative thinking, dexterity and motor patterns.

When all the "Kinders" are assembled and equipped, the day's activities are ready to begin. On a back wall is a series of motor movement posters. Everyone goes through all of the movements on the posters. This is a warm-up period. Before any strenuous exercise is begun, a warm-up should always be done, and this is a good time to begin good habits in young skiers.

After the warm-up, a short walking tour of the areas we use is given. This includes the location of bathrooms, ski patrol, dining room and Kinder Klub slope. If the child is familiar with his surroundings and can orient himself, his learning process is not blocked.

We then return to the main Kinder Klub room and each child must learn the mechanics of his skis. He must put his own skis on, take them off, and then be ready to go. The Happy Skier check begins. "Happy Skiers wear gloves,

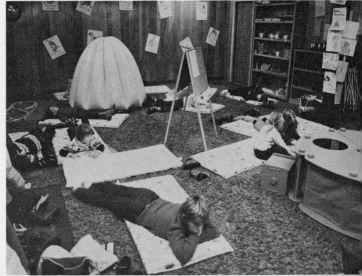

Left—Kinder Klub Director Jean Schlichting offers a word of encouragement to one of the many "Kinder" who daily take part in the ski-day care center at Beech.
Above—The main Kinder Klub play area at Beech. Children use the room to relax after the twice daily skiing lessons offered to them.

Below—The Beech Tree Inn provides a gourmet cuisine in the Beech Village Shops Area.
Right—A Beech Mountain Trademark. The 4,000-foot Italian-made, "skis on" gondola.

hats, button coats, check their badges, etc." Then en masse off to the Kinder Klub Slope.

Having an area specifically for young children is one of the best aspects of the whole program. Each child is free to express himself on skis without the distraction of adults or older family members. He is a person unto himself. The lesson block time is 1½ hours. This may seem like a long time for a small child to be held in concentration and out of doors, but it is not as intense as it appears.

The actual lesson is very brief. The American Teaching Method is used in a slightly modified manner. Walking around orients the child to the additional length on his foot. Walk and slide games elevate the stepping on skis problem, and the child becomes used to sliding. Basic ski position of bend the knees and lean forward will usually do the trick. Hands on knees holds the position. A wedge demonstration and off we go. The lessons and games exercises are taken from proven methods used through ski schools across the country. Balloons and colorful flags help to add to the fun of the first lesson.

In the event of inclement weather or fatigue, the Kinder Klub House is right on the slope. This is a small warming hut to be used by Kinder Klub badge wearers only! The outside of the building has numbers that correspond to the numbers on the skis, and so major mix-ups are avoided. The skier is free to go in and out of the Klub House as he so chooses. The many windows allow us to keep an eye on the house and slope at the same time.

A hot lunch is provided for all participants. Again, we are fortunate to have a dining area all to ourselves. The balcony of the main public dining area, the Viewhaus, is the Kinder

Klub dining room. Prearranged lunches are delivered hot to our area at a specific time, so there is no hassle about choosing food and not eating properly. The luncheon price is included in the daily fee.

After lunch everyone returns to the Klub room for a rest. This is a quiet time to "re-charge" for the afternoon activities.

Following the rest, the group has a discussion on Slope Etiquette and Rules. These are the usual National Ski Patrol System rules and common sense conduct. Hopefully, if we are able to teach our youngest skiers proper and safe conduct now, we will all have a better atmosphere in years to come. The child is encouraged to discuss slope safety with his family and fellow skiers. On the slope acknowledgement is highly praised. After such sessions, little skiers occasionally remind a reckless adult about the rules of good slope conduct.

The afternoon ski session is fun time. Games are played and creative thinking is encouraged on development of original games and races. Skiing technique is improved and corrected on a more individual basis than in the morning skiing session. Of course, all children are encouraged to participate in competitive activities, but a drop-out is not ostracized. The main objective of the second session is to see that each child is skiing safely, in good form, and enjoying the sport. Since there is a loose structure, other activities include snow games, snow hikes, feeding birds and other winter related activities.

As a child fatigues, the Kinder Klub House is available until we all go back to the Klub room. Equipment is returned to its proper place, and the play area is used until the parents arrive. This last part of the day is a good time to recap the events of the day and the reactions to the program.

The opportunity to teach little people to ski in a healthy, self-contained atmosphere is the best situation for the child. There is a great deal of difference in physical growth within the age brackets we are working with. In traditional lessons, children are grouped together at best or mixed with adults at worst. Even in an all children lesson, the short time slot does not allow for individual differences in physical growth and maturity levels. All-day care allows the child to deal with the instructor, and is therefore a more open exchange between the two. With longer times on the snow, under supervision, the frustration level is almost non-existant. Skiing becomes a fun time instead of a performance test. The slow learner can take the time to work out the mechanics of skiing at his own rate. The aggressive skier has an area to progress safely. Throughout the day, many aspects of skiing can be experienced—proper clothing, slope safety, races, turning and stopping, and outdoor adventure.

As Director of the Kinder Klub, I am excited to have been involved in the development of this program. Beech Mountain has begun a service to young skiers of the South. By maintaining such a facility staffed with qualified personnel, the Kinder Klub is likely to be a boon to children's ski programs.

(Editor's Note: Jean Schlichting, Beech Mountain Kinder Klub Director, has a B.S. degree in health & physical education and recreation from Appalachian State University, Boone, N.C.

She has been an experienced ski instructor at both Beech Mountain, and the French-Swiss Ski College, Blowing Rock, North Carolina.

Jean has taught primary level in Waterville, Maine, and has developed and supervised special education and children's skiing programs for the North Carolina School for the Deaf, and the Western Carolina Center for Retarded Children, both in Morganton, N.C.

She has received advanced training in perceptual motor development while working as an educator in Maine. SKIER'S DIGEST is pleased to herald unsung heroines like Jean Schlichting who devote their primary energies to the development of the young or the less fortunate, while the rest of us are out there enjoying ourselves.)

THE OTHER SIDE OF THE MOON is still an unexplored territory. Another curiosity is that *the highest elevation of any ski resort in the East* is boasted by an area in North Carolina! Here is a fish-eye aerial shot of the Beech Mountain summit at 5,500 feet.

Z is for zeal, and that's what you'll feel once you have skied at

SUGARBUSH VALLEY, VERMONT

Z is also for zero, and that is precisely the amount of cooperation we received from Sugarbush Valley in preparing a feature on that area for this chapter. So, we've saved it for last. We can't leave it out, for Sugarbush certainly must be among the top three greatest areas in the Northeast. I can testify to that after teaching in their ski school for almost a decade. The resort has the challenge of Stowe contrasted with excellent novice terrain, the apres ski excitement of Killington but with a broader range of cultural turn-ons. It has the powder of Glen Ellen but with more varied trail cosmetics, the beautiful women of Stratton but they are not all Fairfield County WASPs. In addition Sugarbush has a highly respected ski patrol, friendly, efficient lift attendants, and local bums who are probably the most proficient non-professional skiers in the country.

Sugarbush has magnetism. The kind that coerces its weekend regulars to think nothing of waiting 30 or 40 minutes in line for the gondola, when, just 5 minutes down German Flats Road lies Glen Ellen with empty chairs on their way to the summit. You might get more downhill skiing at Glen Ellen, but you might see Paul Newman in the Sugarbush lift line, or Joan Kennedy, or Skitch Henderson, or many of the hundreds of models, screen actresses and stewardess who come to Sugarbush because they have read somewhere that Sugarbush is where IT is happening. None of them are quite sure what IT is. Some are clever enough to realize IT is *their presence*. That is when they stop turning their heads to look for celebrities and decide to concentrate on the skiing, which happens to be sensational.

It is the variety of terrain that puts Sugarbush a step above many other eastern areas. Behind their Gatehouse cafeteria is a novice-intermediate section that is one of the finest I have seen in the East. These trails are skirted with snow-making equipment that insures good skiing—if the thermometer drops low enough. The beginner slope is as wide as a western trail and about four football fields long. It has the gentle grade of a fairway and is serviced by a double chairlift. Two recent novice-intermediate trail additions at the top are serviced by a Pomalift, but be sure to wait long enough in the season for a base to build up, as the ground there is rocky and ragged. It will chew up your skis if the snow cover is thin. The ridge next to the Gatehouse, where Stein Eriksen used to stage his full layout front flip every Sunday, has become the kicker for the free style acrobats who explode from the woods at the base of the Sleeper trail daily for impressionable spectators.

Don't pass the Gatehouse without signing up for at least one lesson with the ski school. It is run by one of the most dedicated directors in the country. Sigi Grottendorfer. Readers who may have read my novel know that there is no love lost between Sigi and me, after a conflict that ended with my separation from the Sugarbush Ski School. But that event cannot belie the fact that Mr. Grottendorfer is one of the finest skiers in the country, and he is certainly an excellent ski school director. A lesson from an instructor under Sigi's direction can be your most rewarding investment if you ski this area. Experts should ask for Pepi.

Instructor Ed Wyka splits a "Daffy" into Sugarbush's popular glade called Paradise. This steep run is not usually freestylists' territory.

Sugarbush is notorious for cliques. The first of these closed establishments was a super-rich Jet-Set group called Club Ten. They are the elite of the valley who amuse themselves with polo, tennis and the predictable martini glass. But they also ski, and, unlike their *nouveau riche* imitators, they are fairly proficient at their athletic endeavors, having spent fortunes for the best equipment and hundreds of private lessons. Their trails are not precipitous, but they can look quite respectable on intermediate terrain like the Glades of Sugarbush. Their turns are long and lazy. Their homes are miniature museums.

The post-collegiate ski bums used to pack in at the Blue Tooth after skiing, a barn for explosive rock music on the access road, but during the past season it seemed over-populated with teenagers taking advantage of the lowered drinking age law. Typical of high decible disco-joints, the Tooth is for smokers, drinkers and hip-rollers who take pride in doing their thing on the overcrowded dance floor, after a

Left—Most skiers hesitate with fear looking over the Paradise headwall. Instructor Ed Wyka likes to jump in! Here's a neat "Spread Eagle" shot of the Sugarbush flyer. Below—The Valley House at Sugarbush, above its Ski School Meeting Place and gondola terminal.

day of humiliating efforts on the ski slopes. It is good hunting grounds, if you dig young chicks. The veteran ski bums of Sugarbush take their skiing very seriously and usually use the Mall, a steep, heavily moguled narrow trail under the Valley House lift, as their arena for competition with each other every weekend. Bad runs are usually followed by more practice on neighboring Stein's Run, steeper and wider, but hidden from the critical stare of skiers on the chairlift.

From New York come other various cliques, usually separated by ethnic backgrounds, a primitive basis for friendship but one which seems to be most popular at the Bush, and they also are proficient skiers. Moving around the mountain to try and avoid the turkeys, they generally end up at the Castle Rock peak where one of the most beautiful portions of the Sugarbush bowl is to be found. The trails at Castle Rock are expert. Narrow, steep and heavily moguled, they are enough to take anyone's breath away. The narrow, twisting Rumble at Castle Rock is one of the most challenging runs in the country. It is hardly ever populated and completely hidden from view. Some parts of the Rumble are no wider than the length of a ski. It winds like a corkscrew and has a foundation of boulders and stumps which form moguls that will bounce your knees to your chin. If you ski there, take a friend, in case one of you has to summon the Ski Patrol for assistance. And a tranquilizer.

Don't miss the Paradise. It is Sugarbush's most beautiful expert run. Dropping off a short headwall at 60 degrees, it offers man size moguls and a challenging glade that dares you to "Get it on!" Two miles later, you will know you have skied one hell of a trail, and you will probably race to the gondola to try it again. The Paradise at Sugarbush is one of the most scenic and daring expert runs in the country.

Scrape off some of the condensation ice from one of the Gondola Terminal windows, and you will get a magnificent view of Lake Champlain, Canada and upper New York State if the sky is clear over Mt. Lincoln. While you snap into your bindings outside the terminal, look up to see the snow and ice capped peaks of the Presidential Range in the White Mountains of New Hampshire, or north to see the round hump of Glen Ellen just a stone's throw away and Jay Peak in the distance.

Novice-intermediate skiers are respected at Sugarbush with the accommodation of a winding road-type trail from Lincoln Peak, called the Jester. It is about 2½ miles to the bottom with enough spectacular scenery to fill a scrapbook on the way down. Halfway down the Jester, a clearing called the Ball Park gives skiers the option of skiing southeast to the tree-slalom Glade, farther south to the steep but wide Stein's Run, the challenging Mall, and the intermediate's delight, Snowball, or continuing northeast to the Downspout, Domino, Gondolier or lower Jester.

Variety is the greatest asset of this ski resort. Each trail has a personality of its own. The lift systems are sufficient to disperse the crowd during most of the season, but, consistent with all eastern resorts, even the Bush is a turkey farm at Christmas, New Years and Washington's birthday.

While this popular area has a lot going for it, it has a few defects that are surprising for a resort of such stature: 1. The lavatories stink. They are too few, too small and too unattended. 2. The Wunderbar, an apres-ski couple of over-crowded rooms with a well-stocked bar, is too small to accommodate the average crowd, and it doesn't have a fireplace. If you don't get in there at 3 o'clock with the elbow benders, you are locked out of the Wunderbar. Skiers who don't want to be choked by smoke and have drinks spilled on their parkas will consider this no great loss. 3. The peak of the mountain has no lodge for mid-day lunch, kidney relief or shelter from the sub-zero days. The hut at the top of the Castle Rock lift is not big enough or sufficiently stocked, but at least, it offers some shelter. 4. While the ski patrol is among the best in the Nation, there is no doctor in the First Aid room, and, would you believe, no transportation to the local Medical Center, although an expensive ambulance service is available from the nearby town of Waitsfield. If it doesn't happen to be in use by other unfortunate victims. At least you may have the security of knowing that the Sugarbush Ski Patrol will assist in the preparation for amelioration of your injury in the professional manner. It is curious that so few of the victims assisted by unsung heroes like the Sugarbush Ski Patrol take a few moments out of their recuperative period to at least acknowledge the samaritan effort with a note of thanks plus a contribution to the National Ski Patrol for the perpetuation of their altruistic efforts.

It has been a long time since the Sugarbush Valley Corporation has put back some of the inflationary lift ticket revenue into better services for its public. It has been too self-confident, resting on the laurels of its innovative gondola facility which is rapidly becoming commonplace at most big ski resorts, and on the Jet-Set mystique which is slowly fading, as more and more celebrities are ski vacationing at resorts where they can be pampered with more luxurious accommodations. (The men's room at Aspen has wall to wall carpeting!) An unfortunate explosion and destruction of its antiquated gondola terminal 3 years ago encouraged the Sugarbush Corporation to build a more formidable arrival building at the peak. How much more would it have cost to put a second story on that terminal to accommodate the comforts and needs of the skiing public? And, how much would it cost to keep a second-hand car parked at the First Aid hut to ferry emergency victims to the town doctor? That gesture is not even a service; it is simply humane. An area with as fine a skiing terrain as Sugarbush has to offer should complement its natural attributes by keeping up to date with its public service responsibilities. All things considered, though, Sugarbush is still my favorite eastern ski resort.

Author Frank Covino streaks his team to a second place victory in the Sugarbush Sunday Invitational. His controversial autobiographical novel, *Snowballing: The Diary of a Ski Instructor,* a Leisure Book published by Nordon Publications, New York, 1975 is available at your local paperback bookstand, or by mailing a $2 check to the author, Box 155, SD, Waitsfield, VT 05673. (Photo by Malcolm Reiss)

Chapter 5
ON TEACHING YOUR CHILD TO SKI

CHAPTER 5—ON TEACHING YOUR CHILD TO SKI

ALTHOUGH YOU HAVE read it in countless articles with similar titles, it is worth repeating that no child should be forced to participate in skiing or *any* activity, be it physical or mental. That would be the surest way to turn off a child and possibly give him a psychological scar which can have just the opposite effect than the one you intended by the coercion. On the other hand, it is your natural obligation, as an influential parent to *expose* your child to a variety of forms for creative expression. My dad used to say, "You can lead a horse to water, but you can't make him drink." The cliché has many applications. As skiers, you understandably want your offspring to enjoy skiing, in order to have a sport in which your entire family can participate for many years. Just don't rush it; and, when the child gets his first taste, don't choke him with an excess of the sport, or you may kindle a rejection that is as intense as your obsession.

Pre-school children who have not been mother-smothered will be attracted to any physical activity that is a form of *play;* particularly when other children are engaged in the same sport. This fact suggests two prerequisites for a successful introduction of your child to skiing. First, make it seem like play, and secondly, let him see other children his age playing the same "game."

Of course, if you have never stripped yourself of the plastic adult veneer and entered your child's world in other forms of play, don't expect him to suddenly accept you as a playmate on the slope. It takes months, years in some cases, of honest participation in his unpretentious world of make-believe, before a child will accept you as a friend with whom it is worth playing. We all want to take pride in our children. We are pleased when they are well-mannered in public, when they eat as fast and as thoroughly as we do, when they learn their arithmetic and spell well. We are so anxious for them to behave like adults that we frequently create little adult-like freaks who have been so brainwashed with adult rules of propriety, they have missed precious experiences of youth for which they will never again have the opportunity. Time passes quickly, and youth is so much more precious because of time's fleetingness. Enjoy the 3-year-old behavior of your 3-year-old, for soon she will be 4 and no longer interested in the things that are important to a child of 3. If your 4-year-old would rather be making a snowman or catching snowflakes in her mouth than sliding down a hill on skis, don't bury your head in your pillow and cry. That very same child could one day be a Marielle Goitschel, but her maturational level for interest in skiing may come at the age of five.

There is, in fact, no proper age to begin skiing. A fear-indoctrinated child may never overcome the phobias planted in her mind by overprotective parents who have not exposed her to activities wherein she might have chalked up

Fig. 5-2: Teach her a good traversing posture, and she'll never catch a downhill edge when she turns!

a few physical accomplishments, be they as slight as one or two good turns on skis. Some Olympic champions were strapped into the boards at the age of 2. Stein Eriksen. Jean-Claude Killy. Karli Schranz traced his first exposure back to the age of 3. Any of you who, like myself, did not begin to ski until mid-twenties, must have muttered to yourself more than once, "I wish I had started at that age . . ." every time some grade school schussboomer sprayed snow in your face. Well, we can't turn back the clock, but neither should we be so anxious to turn that clock ahead. Be honest with yourself. Is the reason why you want your child to be a precocious champion really because you feel it will benefit him; or is it to fatten your own ego?

It has been my experience after 15 years of teaching the sport, that children in this country are seldom ready for any scientific understanding of the physics of a turn before the age of 12. Few are ready for ski school type of instruction before the age of 7, and even fewer will accept the discomfort of the most basic beginning exercises before the age of 4. What we do find at the 4-year-old level is a surprising capacity for imitation, an insatiable love for play, and little feet whose toes get cold very fast. That imitative capacity can be capitalized upon. Look at the photo of my 4-year-old daughter Cameron following me in a traverse. (Fig. 5-2) She may not understand why her downhill shoulder should be the same slant as the slope but she has startled other skiers by shouting down to them from the chairlift, "Drop your downhill shoulder!" a phrase she hears from me so often. No less astounding is her conversation at the dinner table when tales of how "Daddy and me jumped over the whole mountain" are mixed with recapitulations of how she kept her "knees bent," her "skis together" and her "poles behind her." Is there any reader over 40 who will not admit to the value of rote or imitative learning? As I write this text, in the summer of 1975, Cameron has turned 5. The coming season will be only her second winter exposure to skiing. Her first season was brief, about four weekends. You may be interested in reading what we accomplished along with a few suggestions for starting your own little one on skis.

We waited for a sunny initiation. I think this is important. You will have problems enough maintaining your child's attention without having to wipe her tears over cold feet! During the long drive from Westport, Connecticut, to my chalet on Glen Ellen in Vermont, we sang a slew of songs from "Twinkle, Twinkle, Little Star" to "One Plump Robin," and when we had replayed all the songs she had learned in nursery school about ten times, we made up a few of our own. To the tune of "Swing Low, Sweet Chariot," we sang "Ski Slow, Oh, Ski Patrol," which began an enlightening conversation between us about the Ski Patrol and its function. Children like to feel protected. Cami seemed a little more secure when she learned that she would not only have her Daddy near to protect her on the slope, but even the Ski Patrol. With two Popsicle sticks, which we had to strip of their ice-cream, of course, I explained how some skiers cross their skis and fall. Keeping the sticks parallel I emphasized that she could never get hurt if both of her skis were pointed in the same direction. It wasn't long before Cameron had the sticks in hand, schussing down my chest and over my knee as my wife kept her eyes on the road. Establishing a bit of meaningful imagery is an important part of the early indoctrinational experience. Try to find a toy skier. If you can't, buy a couple of Popsicles. Drive to your ski area the night before a bright sunny day. Have a good breakfast and don't rush off to the slope. Start her on skis during the warmest part of the day, about 11AM, and plan to quit before 3. What can you do before 11? Cami and I built a snowlady with a neat carrot nose, ". . . so someone can watch the house while we go skiing . . ."

On the morning of the first day, please check the outdoor thermometer in the shade and dress your child accordingly. From the top down, make sure she has a warm hat, one that will stay down over her ears. The strap of her gogles can secure it. By all means, invest in a pair of goggles; they will protect her eyes from the direct and reflected light of the sun, and they will make her feel very professional. A long scarf will insulate the vital area of her throat and give added heat to her lungs. Get a colorful one; kids love bright things. Long underwear for children is tough to find. It is important enough for you to at least spend some time at a sewing machine recycling your husband's old longjohns; the ones that have the big tear in the crotch. You could probably make your child's bottoms out of one adult size leg. Remember that children have little tolerance for discomfort. Keep your child warm and you will have half the battle won! Make sure that you dress *together*. She will appreciate wearing the same outfit as the "big people." Silk or nylon stockings under a long pair of wool stockings is next; short socks tend to slip under the child's heels after a few runs. No holes in the stockings, please. The turtleneck shirt is here to stay. Try to find one in her size or sew a turtleneck onto one of her T-shirts. Get a neat sweater. Something with Santa's reindeer on it or snowflakes; something warm but colorful, with a crew or turtleneck. The outer skin can be a snowsuit but NOT WOOL. Snow sticks to wool and your child will

Fig. 5-3: The Jacobs Corporation, 5735 Arapahoe Ave. in Boulder, Colorado, has a fantastic line of children's clothing. They call it Hot Gear. Cami's outfit is not only cute; it's warm and comfortable.

soon be refrigerated if anything wool is on the exterior. Gloves are so important. Mittens, of course, are warmest. Get them with gauntlets and they won't fill with snow. Don't buy cheap mittens; it would not take much to freeze those tiny fingers. Fur inside is great; leather or vinyl outside. I think it is criminal the way some parents send their children out in the snow with wool gloves that soon become a cake of ice. Invariably, the same parents wear wool socks outside their ski pants. So much for clothing. (Fig. 5-3)

Boots are a separate problem. For years, children were the poorest equipped in this department, but during the past 5 or 6 years, manufacturers have been recognizing the need. It puzzles me why the more popular companies have taken the longest to provide something substantial for our little ones. Surely it is profitable; a child could outgrow her boots annually. While this should increase sales and lock in a steady customer for the dealers, it also puts a nasty dent in the consumer's pocket book. One way to get around this is to find a friendly neighbor whose child is a year older than yours. If they don't ski, lure them to the slopes for a weekend. They'll get hooked, buy their kid an outfit more expensive than the one you bought for your prodigy, and be stuck with his boots when he outgrows them in a year. You, of course, will then be quite happy to help out a neighbor and take the boots off his hands for a token figure (no more than half the original price). Children are not as hard on boots as we are; in a year, those boots will be almost like new, but better (they'll be broken in)! Another suggestion to beat the expanding size problem is to have junior try on his new boots in his sneakers; let him ski a whole season wearing his sneakers inside his boots and his boots should be just the right size next year, or perhaps a year later.

Fig. 5-4: Cami's *gators* keep the snow out and the warmth in!
Fig. 5-5: Mine are neat, too!

Fig. 5-6: Have her walk in your steps.

Fig. 5-7: "Making steps" in the snow is a great way to teach *edging*.

If his boots are not high enough to prevent snow from entering, sew up a pair of "gators" with some warm material and Velcro. Wrap it around his ankle well below the boot top and almost to his knee. Marge made a pair for Cami out of rabbit skin. (Fig. 5-4) I liked them so much that I asked for a pair for myself. Gators are a must in deep snow. (Fig. 5-5)

Off to the slope. From the chalet it is only about 300 feet to the novice area lift. The uphill walk is breathtaking, but it is a perfect warmup exercise. Kids need to "warm up" just as grownups should. Driving right to the door of the ticket booth, hopping on the lift and skiing before the body is even awake is a slothful, dangerous practice of too many skiers. You would be a lot kinder to your body if you deliberately parked your car as far away from that ticket booth as you are permitted. Walk with a brisk pace and drink up some of the clean air you have missed in the city. Your circulation will then be ready for the demands of rigorous skiing, and your joints will be well oiled. An Austrian friend of mine used to warm up his ski class for 5 minutes before every morning's session on the hill. Hartwig had his students shout cadence as they performed the exercises he prescribed. Throughout the vast acreage of Sugarbush Valley you could hear the group every morning chanting "Ski! Heil!" until some idiot with a Nazi fixation complained to the Corporation and had it stopped. Your child can't be expected to understand the value of pre-ski exercise. You, as a more enlightened parent must lead the way. The exercise may be simply a walk. The cadence can be a game of counting. (Why not train her mind along with her body?) On the way to the ticket office, point out things of visual interest. Train her to see. How many adults do you know who live their lives as if they were wearing a plow horse's blinders? Ask her how big the man was who made those tracks in the new snow. Discover a cumulus cloud and watch it boil upwards. How many New York license plates can she count in the parking lot? Show her how to carry her skis "like a big girl." At 4, she should be able to carry her own skis, if they are not taller than she is, and they *should* be no taller!

Put your own skis on first. Children get impatient fast, and you are challenging a most limited attention span if you ask her to wait for you after she has been snapped into her bindings. If you can't bend low enough to help her when you are on skis, you are in pretty bad shape and have no business skiing, let alone teaching someone else, especially a child—place her in the qualified hands of a good ski school, and find yourself an abdominal board.

You must learn how to go up, before you can come down. Cameron liked to herringbone behind me (Fig. 5-6), but soon we concentrated on the sidestep. In a traverse direction I explained to her the important principle of keeping her shoulders the same slant as the hill. I believe this little axiom to be one of the most important balance factors in the sport of skiing, so why not let it be the first thing learned. As your child's instructor, you will be doing a lot of repeating. Deliberately repeat the salient rules and you will condition your student's reflexes to act appropriately. The sidestep climbing posture is the proper traverse position. With Cami, it wasn't even too early to explain that the uphill ski should be a little bit ahead, as we proceeded to "make steps" in the snow. A child of 4 has a pretty good idea of what steps look like. By "making steps" in the snow, she was learning how to edge surreptitiously. (Fig. 5-7) The full comprehension of

Fig. 5-8: Cami's first run downhill. Her knees were too straight. She did better when I told her to try to *kneel* on her ski tips.

Fig. 5-9: A crouch will get her center of gravity closer to her skis and improve her balance.

Fig. 5-10: *Before* she falls, *you* fall, to show her that *everyone* falls, occasionally.

edge probably comes at a later age, but a simple demonstration was all that was necessary, in the case of my daughter, to show how a flat ski slides downhill while a ski that "makes steps" will not. We climbed with the sidestep in both directions, rewarding ourselves with a downhill run in between each climb. I chose a hill that went uphill again after the flat runout, in order to have her stop automatically.

The best downhill running position for children is the posture favored by many modern adult skiers whose alma mater is the school of squat. With her skis apart about hip width, Cami assumed the constipated position and pushed off with her right ski pole while her left hand held mine. One difficulty with skiing hand-in-hand is that an adult's skis will, of course, be faster. The solution is to keep your own skis in a wedge position to check your speed. It is my considered opinion, however, that the "snowplow" or wedge maneuver should *not* be taught to a child of 4 during the initial learning period, or it will become a crutch that the child will cling to tenaciously for many years. From the beginning I have instilled the awareness in my daughter that the safest way to ski is with the skis pointed in the same direction. As close to the ground as pre-school children are, there is really little need for the snowplow maneuvers. Believe that, and you won't have your heart in your mouth every time you see your little one schussing a hill with one ski pointed across the path of the other; there is no more dangerous position. While the wedge has its place (for checking speed) it should be taught at a later time, certainly after the child has made a few parallel turns. Gradually encourage your child to stand a bit taller as her downhill runs improve. We should try to save the low position for unweighting in the turns. (Fig. 5-8 and Fig. 5-9)

You may be surprised to read that "Falling" is the title of the next step in the child's learning process. It is followed, of course, by instruction for "Getting Up." Every skier falls. Some psychologists analyze our motivation for skiing as a conquest of a castration fixation—where we push ourselves to the brink of total destruction and suddenly save ourselves with a controlled turn. More often than not, we miss that saving turn and wipe out. Since falls are so common and perhaps even inevitable, learning to fall properly should be an early lesson. By falling deliberately, a thing of fear can be transformed into a kind of fun. Whether you call it a derriere, a backside, a bottom or a heinie, that round thing behind you is the most padding you have got to cushion a fall. "Watch me, Cami. I'm going to ski down and slide on my heinie . . ." I called out to my daughter as I pushed off. It is important to swing your seat to the side before you hit. Do it, and your kid will think it's pretty funny. Funny enough to try it herself, laughing all the way. (Fig. 5-10) Be sure to caution her about not trying to stop her fall with her poles!

Getting up after a fall may present some problems. Show your child the customary method illustrated in Chapter 3 but keep in mind that his little arms have not got the power of yours. If he falls on flat ground, it may be very difficult for him to rise. Most of the time I help my daughter. She will be more capable of pulling herself up next season. If your child hasn't been deprived of other self-sufficient activities to motivate independence, she will actually look forward to the day when she can rise by herself. Every time I offered to help Cameron last season she was quite adamant about my letting her do it herself, and only after four or five desperate

Fig. 5-11 (left): Three hands are better than two. At Glen Ellen the lift attendants are courteous and helpful.
Fig. 5-12 (right): Take her for a few runs like this. Give her a lot of *mileage.*

attempts did she look up and offer me her hand. If the fall takes place on a slope, gravity will assist your child. Whenever he does rise by himself, make a big fuss about it and slip him a reward.

Pavlovian as it may sound, the old reward-for-good—and-punishment-for-bad trick still is a sound system of child training, skiing not withstanding. Knowledgeable parents today have replaced the sugar reward with a chewable vitamin C tablet or fruit and nuts. The razor strap beating that conditioned many of us through our recalcitrant childhoods may have been moderated considerably, but the basic fact of a child's give-nothing-for-no-return attitude is understood by the least of armchair psychologists. If a short downhill run in good form is rewarded while a run with stiff knees or skis too wide apart brings nothing but an admonishment and another tiring climb up the hill, your child will learn her first day's lesson fast.

Sporadically, during her first day's exposure, I took Cami on the chairlift and skied down holding her between my legs. This is a most important part of your child's initial exposure in the struggle for self-sufficiency.

My wife took Cami's poles and mine after my daughter and I slid over to the lift. Riding the chairlift was one of the "rewards" I promised for good skiing. All children will be initially apprehensive about boarding the lift. Most children love to ride the swings at the local playground, though. Why not draw an analogy between the two? The idea of riding a swing together with one of her parents should appeal to any well-adjusted child. If yours is one of those blessed little creatures I have seen who scream up a tantrum at the least suggestion of trying something daring or new, don't push the child. *Forcing* him to ride the chair would be a serious mistake. Just say, "OK, Junior, you don't have to ride up. We will just keep climbing." His hedonistic instinct which seems to be a part of normal human nature will soon move him to ask *you* if, next time, you could both ride the lift.

On the way to the launching pad relieve some of the child's anxiety by taking her mind off the approaching challenge. I held Cami's hand and we both counted the number of sliding steps from our practice area to the

chairlift. I shouted the even numbers and she followed with the odds. If your child can't count past ten, think up some other diversion, and spend a little more time teaching her how to count when you get home.

At the loading spot, hold your child firmly as you both observe at least three sets of skiers board the chair and take off. If you are lucky, one of those skiers will be just a few years older than your little one. Another strange characteristic about human nature is the drive to compete, particularly in boys, who have had to lead the pack or get trampled ever since they were sperms. Rest assured, if another child rides before you, your Junior will be *anxious* to have the experience. My Cami may be only part sperm, but she is as competitive as any boy her age, so my job was easy. Slide into the takeoff track immediately after the chair in front of yours disembarks. We did it holding hands. Be sure to place your child on the same side of the track as the lift attendant. He may have to assist you when you board. You should have plenty of time to plan your next movements before your chair comes up behind you. With a firm grip under each of Junior's armpits turn to the approaching lift and get ready to lift him as you sit. Lift and slide him as far back into the seat as you can, while you sit. The lift attendant will know enough to tilt the chair back a bit so you don't get hit in the hamstrings with the seat. Tucked far back in the chair, your child's skis should now be erect, his legs almost straight. With one arm across his chest, reach up with the other and pull down the foot rest and safety bar. You're off. Please remember to say "Wheeeeeee!" or "Yahooooo!" or something to color the experience as *fun*. (Fig. 5-11)

Don't waste the ride up. It is a great opportunity to point out errors, laugh at funny falls, cheer other children skiers who seem to have it all together, and catch some snowflakes in your mouth. If is it sunny and warm, open Junior's zipper a little and loosen his scarf. Sing a few songs with him and do all you can to help him relax and enjoy the ride up. Well before the unloading platform, point to the sign that says "Approaching Unloading Platform. Raise Safety Bar." The sign should also say "Raise Your Ski Tips." Discuss its meaning with the child. Restore his confidence by telling him you will be holding him as you descend, and that the slide down the unloading hill will be just like his downhill runs on the bottom. Also instruct that when you say "Stand," he should stand up and let the skis slide. There it is. "*Stand!*" and don't be afraid to raise your voice a few decibels.

Descending from the unloading spot for the first time, I held Cami much the same as when I loaded her, pushed off with parallel skis next to hers and gradually stemmed my outside ski, gently pushing her skis into the turn at the bottom. We made it! If you do, take a moment to look back with your child, to watch other skiers descend. If some klutz should dump and get tied up like a pretzel, explain to your future skier that the demise occurred because Ms. Klutz was sitting back too far, or bending too much at the waist, or whatever. Reassure Junior that he will never fall getting off a lift because he *knows* how to ski downhill! Then slip him another C tab.

For our first day's downhill runs, I assumed a wedged position and placed Cami between my legs with my hands on her shoulders. This allowed her to ski parallel and get the thrill of skiing at a fast but controlled pace. (Fig. 5-12) Each time we traversed I mentioned the change in the slant of the

Fig. 5-13 (left): Don't waste her mileage time. Talk about "making steps," keeping her shoulders "just like the hill," etc.
Fig. 5-14 (right): If she dangles, her mileage with you will be worthless. Don't allow it!

hill, and we adjusted our shoulders accordingly. Simultaneously I recalled the ski angle for "making steps" in the snow, and Cameron began to traverse in pretty good form. We kept our traverses long, turning at the sides of the slope to temper our speed. As we approached each turning point I told Cami to sink down, applying pressure to her shoulders. This gave her skis a momentary weight release which I tried to time with my directions to "Point your skis to the *other* woods." Traversing most novice runs, there are woods in front of your skis and woods behind your skis. The word *traverse* is a bit pedantic when speaking to some 4-year-olds. Most of them know what *woods* mean, though. Try to keep your instructions within your child's vocabulary of understanding. (Fig. 5-13)

Some of you who read this may take issue with the simplicity of my directions for a parallel turn in the last paragraph. If you, like many, have spent years trying to perfect your own parallel turn, you might even take offense with my audacious insinuation that a weight release and reversed pointing of the skis is all that's necessary. Well, not *all;* remember the other axiom: "slant the shoulders the same as the hill and traverse on your uphill edges." Truthfully, that simplification is the basis of a successful parallel turn, but it especially works when the skier's height is only about a yard (and particularly when she is skiing between the legs of an advanced skier who holds on tenaciously to her shoulders). If you try to imitate the posture I have recommended when skiing with your child, be certain to hold a strongly edged lower ski in the traverses. A simple rise upward and a little back in the wedge position will effect a movement of your ski tips toward the fall line. Sink down as you direct the child to do the same and weight your outside ski as you tell her to point her skis ". . . toward the other woods." Another device that is effective is to have her point her inside finger, (the finger that is *inside* the intended turn) to the new direction along with you, just as she begins to twist her skis. This will require a kind of anticipatory movement of her upper body which will soon be followed by her lower body and her skis.

If everything is working well, and you think she can handle one more detail (it is wise not to give your child too many *rules* all at once; let her master one thing at a time), do mention that "everything uphill is ahead, the uphill ski, the uphill knee, hip and shoulder all lead us to the woods . . ." My Cameron had no difficulty with this perception, although I had to pad it with a little imagery: "Finish every turn with a *bow* to your downhill audience, Cami. Look downhill . . ." I said as we began a new traverse, "See Marge. She is our audience. Bow to her. That's it. OK. Here comes another turn. Sink DOWN and point your skis to the other woods. Neat. Now, look at Marge and BOW. GOOD TURN. Wheeeee!" She giggled all the way down and I slipped her a few raisins.

Moguls create problems, for you, not for the child between your legs. She has her skis together and can easily turn on the top of a bump if necessary, but your skis are in snowplow position. Your reflexes had better be quick. Your edging had better be positive. Even if you avoid turning in the mogul section (and you certainly *should* on the child's first day), traversing several bumps in that wedge position can be pretty tricky—particulary if the terrain is fast. My suggestion is to try to avoid the challenge, unless you are a strong and very experienced skier. If it is unavoidable, traverse the mogul field edging your downhill ski sharply and make your turn at the very edge of the slope. Above all, don't reveal any apprehension you might have to your little one. She must feel that you are the best skier in the world and fully capable of saving her should an emergency arise.

When you are 25-50 feet away from the bottom, let her try a schuss, turning by herself on the flat. She may surprise you. Cameron made a neat parallel turn, turned and giggled, "Let's do it again, Dad!" Several runs with your child between your legs will condition her to speed and the kinetic uncertainty of sliding, which can be pretty disconcerting even to a beginning adult. Only when an individual feels a certain amount of control over the sliding movement of skis will he or she be encouraged to "do it again . . ." With a child, in the between your legs position I have recommended, you represent that control.

I should emphasize that you are to thwart any attempt by the child to simply hang from your arms and dangle her skis. (Fig. 5-14) Do your best to relate her movements to correct parallel form. You are, in effect, *conditioning her reflexes* and should continue to do so until she automatically sinks down to turn (unweighting), edges her skis in the traverse (resisting centrifugal force and gravity), and angles her shoulders the same slant as the hill (to oppose centripetal force and gravity). Be firm and tell her that the slope is a skiing place not a sleeping place. If you are not forceful on this point right from the beginning, you will end up with a heavy limp weight and straying skis which could easily hook under yours and cause you both to tumble.

The second day should be much like the first, except that your child will be much steadier on her feet and probably more courageous. The trips down from the chairlift should still be wrapped in the security blanket of your skis, but on the bottom you can begin to work on the child's self-determined turn. Climb, then have her schuss, and turn to the right. Then, climb again and

Fig. 5-15 (left): Her little legs will tire. Time to play Poma-Lift!

Fig. 5-16 (right): Cami traversing in good form.

have her try a turn to the left. If she tires of the climbing steps, use your pole and play Poma lift, as in Fig.5-15, but be sure to tuck that pole shaft snugly under her bottom and tell her not to *sit*. While you sidestep, her skis should be parallel and *sliding*. Advise her not to *step*.

Here is where my philosophy differs from the American Teaching Method. While the snow plow turn or wedge position is useful in emergency situations and should be learned at a later stage, I see no reason to teach it to a child who is much closer to the ground than we are and considerably lighter on the skis. If her skis are no longer than her height, she will easily perform a parallel turn, if you can just get her to coordinate the twist of her knees and feet with an unweighting motion (preferably a *down* motion). Demonstrate a straight run down a gradual decline, then turn as you sink down by bending your knees and pushing them toward the direction of your intention. If your little one is used to being coddled, she might play games with you and refuse to follow your directions, announcing her ploy with a statement like "I can't!" Don't accept it. If she gets away with that cop-out at the age of 4, you can bet she will resort to it all through her life. Convince her that she can do anything a big person can, if she just keeps *trying*. Offer her a prize for the effort, a prize for trying, but offer her a *bigger* prize if she *succeeds*. I did notice, with Cameron, that her turns were better and quicker when an obstacle was the primary motivating factor. Thus, in a wide open nearly flat area, she often just skied straight, until her skis automatically stopped because of a subtle rise in terrain. When the speed of one of those runs took her past the subtle rise and down another decline she headed straight for the woods, and I gulped when she whipped a beautiful christie just 6 inches from the edge.

The parallel turns pre-school children perform "automatically" are skidded turns, usually on the flat bottom portion of the skis. Instructors will be quick to point out that many adults turn their skis the same way. Much of the GLM approach capitalizes upon this fact, and some schools actually applaud the uncontrolled skid turn as an effective maneuver. Well, it *is* a turn, and the beginner *does* leave his ski weekend thinking he has mastered the art of skiing. "So what, if he is confined to the flat beginner slope; at least he is outdoors doing something," many ski school directors will say, "He'll never be an athlete anyway. Look at that pot belly he's carrying around . . ."

The fact of the matter is that controlled skiing relies upon the ability to *carve* a turn, with properly edged skis. By all means, allow your child to continue his skidded turns in the early part of his learning process but bear in mind that those uncontrolled movements are *preliminary* and as soon as he is skidding when he wants to, to the right and to the left, it is time to modify his turns by introducing the proper method of edging. One of the reasons I believe in spending a good deal of time on the traverse maneuver is that it is essentially the beginning and end of every turn. A child (or beginning adult, for that matter), who has been traversing *in good form* for several days need only to be reminded of the form when he is halfway into his turn, and what was once skidded will become a *carved* turn. Don't be afraid to shout *"traverse,"* the moment your student is facing downhill, with the provision, of course, that he fully understands the meaning of the word and its preferred posture. The word *traverse* was not beyond the comprehension of my 4-year-old. Because of this importance of the traversing position, I encourage my students, young or old, to use the posture even when they *climb* with a sidestep! Points to remember about the traverse position are 1. Skis on their uphill edges, 2. Everything uphill should be slightly ahead (the uphill ski, boot, knee, hip and shoulder), 3. Tilt the shoulders to the same slant as the hill. The last point becomes

Fig. 5-17: Progress to hand-in-hand as soon as possible.

Fig. 5-18: Insist upon her good traversing posture (it's worth a few raisins) and slow your own speed with a wedge.

less imperative as the snow gets deeper, but is absolutely required for optimum balance on packed or hard terrain. (Fig. 5-16)

With the traverse reasonably under control, which should take 3 or 4 days, your child is ready to step out from in between your protective legs on all future downhill runs. I recommend the hand-in-hand method next, again, without poles. You must continue a wedged descent in order to keep up with Junior, but he is now fully capable of performing parallel turns, with your verbal directions and a sufficient amount of raisins in your pocket. From the top of the novice run, begin a traverse with your child above in good parallel form and you below in an edged snowplow position. Control your speed by releasing your edges, just enough to keep up with your student. You should be firmly grasping her downhill hand; verbally adjusting her traversing posture. As you approach the turning point near the edge of the woods, tell the child that you are both going to turn by rising UP (in preparation) and sinking DOWN to turn. Rising *up* in your wedged position will automatically cause your tips to drift downhill if you release your edge; her ski tips will follow the same gravitational pull. Shout "DOWN" at the turning point and weight your outside ski, edging it as you do so. Hand-in-hand, your child will whip around you. Remind her to point her skis to "the other woods" and slip in a TRAVERSE command. These turns, with the child on the *outside* of the turn will be easier. (Fig. 5-17)

With the child *inside* the turn while skiing hand-in-hand, you must guide her *outside ski by sliding your inside* ski right along side of it. If you fail to do this, her skis might run over your inside ski, and that could cause a tumble. At this precarious moment in the turn, I

have found it effective to tell the child to look at the other woods." (Fig. 5-18) This will prompt her to twist her upper body in the direction of the turn, and the anticipatory movement will soon be followed by a twisting of her knees, feet and skis. Be sure to shout "DOWN" at the turning phase, to effect a weight release, and "TRAVERSE" when her skis point downhill, in order to get her skis back onto their uphill edges.

While your little one may be ready to solo on the first day, I must repeat: *don't push her.* Every child has his own individual hangups and courage level. Let him tell *you* when he is ready to solo. Most children will seek that independence shortly after their first successful turn while holding your hand. Treat the poles as a *reward* for turning properly without them ("only really good skiers use their poles"). Watch your child's face during his first solo run. Does he appear to be enjoying it? Is he laughing? (Fig. 5-19) If his look is sour or frightened, he needs more training hand-in-hand. And, more raisins. Point to other children on the slope. He must not feel that he is the only little one in a grown-up world. It has got to become the child's world. You must become the intruder. And you will, soon enough. In a year or two, he will begin to wonder why *old people* ski at all, since it is obviously so much *fun!* You will have a new problem, then: trying to convince him that it can be a family sport; and, the more he improves, the harder you will have to work at keeping *yourself* in shape!

After a few solos, set up a mini-slalom course with your ski poles. Let her *watch* as *you* make a few runs through the course. Tell her that *someday* she will be able to do the same, and maybe *win a medal!* But stall her first encounter. This is the *teasing method* of child

Fig. 5-19: Her first solo will give you goose-bumps.

Fig. 5-20 (above): Upright between the turns, have her *crouch down* to turn. The drop will effect a weight release and make her axial motion easier.

Fig. 5-21 (left): Your goal is to get her to *carve* her turns on the inside edges. Tell her to show you the *bottoms* of her skis, on every turn!

Fig. 5-22 (below): Pavlov was right!

Fig. 5-23: Kids don't want to hear about ski technique. They want to have fun. Games are motivational. Slip in the instruction and physical training surreptitiously. Here, I'm developing the young thigh muscles of Tracy and Blair. I would hardly get as pleasant a response if I asked them to do deep knee bends!

motivation. It really works. He will soon be begging to try "the gates." After a couple of days of "You are not ready, yet," concede. But tell him that the medal is for skiing through *four* gates (borrow your wife's poles). Then, let him practice with two. Successful turns must be praised and rewarded. Poor form should be received with just a negative nod of your head and another demonstration by you, or your wife, or both of you. Every so often, flash the medal and shine it up.

While you are evaluating her form and demonstrating, be sure to emphasize a more erect posture *between* the turns, and a flexed posture *during* the turns. (Fig. 5-20) With her center of gravity closer to her skis, Cami's turns were effortless. I cheated a little by filling the groove down the center of her skis with hot wax. That groove is only important when a child starts jumping. You may consider yourself a success when you see your junior racer turning on *the edges* of his skis. (Fig. 5-21) Then, you will realize that all the proper traverse form practice conditioned his reflexes to oppose centrifugal force, and you won't have to worry about him catching a downhill edge! The moment you see space under his downhill edges, sigh a breath of relief, and give *yourself* a few raisins. You are both to be congratulated! Keep stoking your child with praise and rewards, and by all means try to enlist some other child to play in the same "game." A medal after a week's good effort and four successfully negotiated gates will be welcomed in awe! (Fig. 5-22)

Tears can be a sign of fatigue (if it is late in the day) or frustration at not being able to please you. Don't make it seem that important. Invent little games. Younger children will respond even more readily to games on skis, and if you are clever, you can relate the move-

ments required for the "game" to actual skiing mechanics. Whether the tears are sincere or mere ploys to test your response, *games* will effectively turn off the water. (Fig. 5-23)

Fatigue is an adversary that you should recognize and combat. There are two effective weapons, rest and nourishment. As I mentioned in a previous paragraph, don't *push* your child. You can probably use frequent rests yourself, so don't feel timid about making more than one visit to the ski lodge for some hot soup or an orange. On the other hand, don't underestimate the strength of your little one. My Cami, now 5, climbed the Burrows trail with me yesterday to the very top of Camel's Hump, a peak about 2.9 miles from the start of the trail, east of Huntington Center, Vermont. The Long Trail guidebook estimated the climbing time at 2¾ hours. We did it in 2½ hours with three rest stops. Today, I have sore knees, while Cameron is buzzing around like a roadrunner.

This chapter should give you enough guidance to get your child off to a good start. Cami is at the disadvantage of having divorced parents; consequently, she is only with me for about three weekends a ski season. If you can begin your Junior with at least one full week, there will be great value in the continuity of the experience. If you are fortunate to have him on skis for one whole season, he will probably be skiing rings around you by next spring. One final word of caution: don't attempt to teach *anyone* unless you are in top physical condition and have a clear understanding of basic ski technique. If you don't qualify, put your little one in the hands of a qualified ski instructor, but first be sure he loves kids and has a few raisins in his pocket.

Chapter 6
THE P.S.I.A. TODAY

A Round Table Discussion

PROFESSIONAL
SKI INSTRUCTOR
OF AMERICA

CHAPTER 6—THE P.S.I.A. TODAY

WHEN I TOOK MY first lesson in skydiving at the Orange airport school in Massachusetts, one of my classmates was typical of many students who have just heard a lecture on proper technique delivered by an experienced technician. She raised her hand and asked, "What if we *don't* assume a spread-eagle posture and make a vigorous exit?" The jumpmaster looked sternly at the young red-head and said quietly, "You'll die." A cowering withdrawal to the fetal position (that we all seem to take in moments of fear) would have caused her to roll and get tangled in her shrouds. She assumed the position that her jumpmaster described.

What impressed me most about the school at Orange is that the instructors have no student recalcitrance problems. New skydivers listen and do as they are told. Of course, the reason they do is that disobedience is *fatal.* There are no beginner slopes, when you dive out of an airplane. The entire classroom course, before your first jump, is only 3 hours! You *will* do as your jumpmaster advises, or you may never have to make a decision again.

Ski instructors do not have it so easy. While we know which postures will most effectively guide your descent down a graded slope, we have learned that it will take some of you years before you heed our advice. Of course, the reason is that disobedience of the ski student does not carry a fatal consequence, although, frequently the result may be harmful. Many of you begin with good intent. You push off in a flawless traverse position. You may even begin a perfect turn. Then you meet the fall line. The moment of panic! All you have just been told by your instructor is suddenly dismissed as needless rhetoric. Your ego tells you that there must be a better way. From that point on, all kinds of aberrations of proper technique take place, and you end up out of control. It gives us reason to wonder: if the alternative to following your instructor's advice was *death,* which course would you take? Many of you probably wouldn't ski at all. Recalcitrance is such a formidable characteristic of the personality of some, that they would rather not take part in any activity which requires obedience to *rules.* Unfortunately, there are many who have the same personality trait but who are also aggressive. These students will still refuse to follow directions, but they will also expend an incredible amount of energy trying to *do it another way.* They tear up their bodies unmercifully on the ski slope. They chalk up a lot of fractures, lacerations and bruises, until, one day, they concede, "Maybe that cat in the instructor's parka knows what he is talking about. I can't afford another injury. This time, I will try it *his* way." That revelation comes at different times with various individuals. For some, it takes years. How fortunate they are that recalcitrance on the ski slope does not face a fatal alternative!

There is no *one* way to make a turn on skis. Nor is there necessarily one *proper* silhouette. But there are veterans out there who are as seasoned at their craft as jumpmasters, and they know what movements are optimum for maximum efficiency and minimum physical effort. They have tried every ski technique that has emerged from schools all over the world. They keep informed about new equipment, they read *any* new literature available that concerns their sport, and they see every ski film. They have skied exotic areas all over the world and have had experience in every possible slope condition, from bottomless powder to blue ice, from slush in 60 degrees to chalk at sub-zero. They are in business not as dictators of chauvinistic dogma. They are not officious tyrants who take pleasure in toying with your inadequacy. Your ski instructor can empathize with you better than anyone, for the simple reason that he has been at your level, and he has succeeded in conquering the forces that prevent you from descending the slopes with grace and control. He has been there, and he has won. He can help you.

Why, then have so many of you rejected him? You will take lessons from your boyfriend, your husband, your sorority sisters, your cousin Alice, and some of you will spend years trying to teach yourselves. You will spend hundreds of dollars on equipment and thousands to go to ski exotic areas, but, when it comes to spending six crummy dollars on a ski school lesson, you suddenly get stingy! When you finally do enroll in a legitimate ski school eventually, you arrive in class with 6 years of bad habits that will require another 6 years to break! That is not only curious. It is downright masochistic.

Ski instructors will never be able to change the curiosities of human nature, but they have been able, at least, to oppose the pretenders, the pseudo-instructors who do more damage to their students than if they were to take no lessons at all. Instructors have organized, and, in order to qualify for admittance into their organization, they have subjected themselves to rigid examinations. They have thus weeded out the pretenders. What remains is the cream. The surgeons of the ski industry. The masters. They can be identified by the precision of their skiing and their capacity for ski school student empathy. They wear a badge that reads Professional Ski Instructors of America. It is a badge of excellence; a symbol of perfection that is welcome in an era when too many of us will settle for mediocrity.

To tell you more about the P.S.I.A., I decided to form a round table discussion with a few of its officers. My first letter went to my old friend Jimmy Johnston, former President who referred me to Werner Shuster, current President of the P.S.I.A. Mr. Shuster carboned a letter to John Heller, Executive Director and steered me to P.S.I.A. Communications Vice-President David R. Stewart, of Stowe, Vermont. I threw Dave 20 questions that I thought might have been submitted by readers of SKIER'S DIGEST:

SD: *What is P.S.I.A. and when did it begin?*

Dave: Your first question requires some reference to notes. P.S.I.A. is a national association of ski teaching professionals. Within P.S.I.A. are eight geographic divisions that enjoy some autonomy of activity, but still subscribe to the national theories of ski mechanics and instruction. The need for a national organization was first realized as a result of the confusion created by the Austrian and French approaches to skiing. A great deal of inaccurate and non-expert translation promoted this confusion. So in 1958 the East and West met in Alta, Utah, to discuss the problem. Attending this meeting were such skiing notables as Kerr Sparks, Paul Valar, Jimmy Johnston, George Bounos, Ed Heath, Dr. Chuck Hibbard, and Earl Miller. It was discovered at that meeting that technique was not the only problem confronting the national skiing scene, but certification, recruiting and training of instructors, as well as related business problems of ski teaching. Agreement to meet again prompted a gathering of over 75 instructors to discuss teaching psychology, technique, etc., at the National Ski School Meeting in Brighton, Utah in 1960. In May of 1961 the Professional Ski Instructors of America was formed at the National Ski School Meeting at Whitefish, Montana. In November, 1961, P.S.I.A. was incorporated in the State of Minnesota. P.S.I.A. became recognized and accepted by organized skiing and the ski industry. The first American clarification of skiing technique was made in the 1964 publication, *The Official American Ski Technique.*

SD: *How does the organization keep its members informed of latest developments in teaching technique and methodology?*

Dave: P.S.I.A.'s primary endeavor is education of and communication with its members and the industry. This is accomplished by many revised and up-dated, newly-generated manuals: *Ski Pro,* the newsletter and technical journal of the Association, committees in Certification, Technique, Biomechanics, Psychology, Childrens Teaching, International Relations, and the sort. Members are also able to submit their own thoughts as input to the P.S.I.A. This immense cross-communication keeps the Association informed and current with the ski teaching profession—nationally and internationally.

SD: *Of what significance is the P.S.I.A. to the average recreational skier?*

Dave: The recreational skier, to benefit most from their investment in the sport, deserves to be taught the sport according to the safest and most enjoyable means available—without gimmicks. The recreational skier benefits greatly from P.S.I.A.'s constant search for better instructional methods; be it methodology, psychology, practicality, physiology, etc. They are being taught by a PRO, not some imitation of one.

SD: *What are the prerequisite requirements of the skier who wants to become a Certified Instructor?*

Dave: This is a complex one because there is no concrete pattern to follow. The eight divisions of P.S.I.A. all subscribe to the national theory of skiing. But each division retains its own procedure for becoming certified in the American Teaching Method. The differences are mostly organizational as the final certification assures that each member has passed a grade of similar requirements and standards.

SD: *Describe briefly the events of a Certification Course.*

Dave: As I mentioned earlier there are divisional differences. Possibly I can draw an average similarity between them all. Each division requires some teaching experience and skiing skills before making application for certification. Once this has been accomplished, the candidate is subjected to several days of intense, high-level training in preparation for the Certification Test. The entire process can take as little time as 4 days or as long at 8—depending upon the division. In all divisions there is exposure to free skiing, discipline skiing, slalom, methodology, equipment, safety, teaching and the such.

SD: *Of the hundreds (thousands?) of applicants, what percentage can be expected to pass the examinations?*

Dave: There is no "expected" percentage passing the Certification Exam. The individual pits himself against the established standards and pass or fail depends upon their own knowledge and abilities. An average of 40-60 percent would appear if statistically approached.

SD: *Is a Certified Instructor required to test his skills periodically once he has acquired the badge?*

Dave: For the most part—no! Each division, though, requires of its members that they attend refresher courses periodically in order to remain current with the national and regional procedures and theories.

SD: *Are there any age boundaries for the Certification of an instructor?*

Dave: Yes and no. There is a stipulation that the candidate be at least 18-years-old when applying for Certification, but there is no age limit.

SD: *Has the P.S.I.A. ever considered the possibility of standardizing an instructor's pay and benefits structure in the manner of a union? What are the obstacles?*

Dave: Promoting the formation or establishment of a union is *not* one of P.S.I.A.'s functions. Ski teaching is a service to the recreational skier and pay would most assuredly be based on the teacher who possesses the better credentials and experience. Other variables are found in the facilities an area can provide to the recreational skier—the larger and finer resorts being able to provide the more professional service.

SD: *Has any lobbying been done to prevent ski areas from importing foreign instructors who work for "coolie" wages?*

Dave: To my knowledge there are no particular lobby group(s) who desire to keep foreign instructors from teaching in the United States. In the past *efforts have been made* to protect the employment possibilities of American instructors. The U.S. Department of Labor has said that given an equal opportunity, the American Certified instructor must be hired before a foreign Certified Instructor.

SD: *What is the ratio of women to men in the Certified ranks?*

Dave: I don't really know at the moment, but one could find out by surveying the P.S.I.A. membership list. Off-the-cuff I would estimate that women comprise 35-40 percent of the Certified members.

SD: *Are the tests for Certified women instructors any different than those designed for men?*

Dave: At different times the thought is expressed that skiing is designed as "male-specific." And that the female suffers as a result. The physical and biomechanical differences allow for a slightly different approach to a given situation, but is really of minor consequence under examination circumstances. All Certified Exams are designed as uni-sexually as possible. It is the individual who is taking the test against established standards; they are not competing against each other as if it were some sophomoric contest.

SD: *Are there any voices in the Certified ranks who are in favor of independent ski instructors? How does the P.S.I.A. feel about this?*

Dave: Most Certified professionals realize that the success of their employer and their own success is dependent upon a system of service and facilities to the customer. To work outside of such a system defeats the existence of the resort and does a great deal to create bad will between ski teaching professionals. As to how P.S.I.A. feels, may I quote from a recent issue of *Ski Pro*: ". . . our association of professionals must stay above supporting or endorsing the specific interest(s) of one member as it might cause a dispute with another. P.S.I.A. prefaced their response to (the individual) request for support by indicating that it is the purpose of an association such as P.S.I.A. to coordinate and stimulate the growth of ski instruction as a profession, as a business, and to work for the equal benefit of all its members."

SD: *How does a Certified Instructor become an Examiner?*

Dave: Once again this will vary by division. Primarily, there exists a stipulation of tenure, experience, dedication, and another examination. In some cases there is an apprentice period before becoming an Examiner.

SD: *Who establishes the standards for ski technique and teaching methodology?*

Dave: The standards are established through careful examination and coordination by the P.S.I.A. Technical Coordinating Committee. This Committee oversees the activities of its sub-committees: biomechanics, physical, psychological, technical, certification, etc.

SD: *Has there been a logical progression in ski technique and teaching methodology adopted by P.S.I.A. through the years?*

Dave: You bet there has! Skiing was introduced to the United States by Europe, and we remained under their influence for many years. P.S.I.A. was, at first, caught up in the same dogma of discipline type teaching. Fortunately the American ski teacher decided that such attitudes were not satisfactory to them and their audience. P.S.I.A. has progressed in its thinking to a point where we now are national and international leaders in skiing theory and study.

SD: *How do P.S.I.A. standards today differ from 15 years ago? 10 years ago? 5 years ago?*

Dave: Standards of what? Membership? Professionalism? Technical attitudes? Ski industry responsibilities? The original dream was to provide an association of professionals to disseminate technical and organizational information to its members and the industry, and to formulate an American attitude of ski teaching and technique. That much has not changed over the years! What P.S.I.A. has been able to prove is its existence as the bonafide leader of American skiing.

SD: *What or who do you feel is responsible for these changes?*

Dave: How can you pin the traditions and advances of two decades on any one or several people. There have been many leaders along the way and a background of supporting people who have made P.S.I.A. the success it is and will continue to be. At any given time there have been people who have seen the future and headed for it. Along the way the best have been with P.S.I.A. Much of it is now history, much of it going on presently, and only the future can tell the rest.

SD: *There is some rumbling that certain iconoclastic trade magazine writers have damaged the P.S.I.A. image. Must a wall exist between perpetrators of classical form and the radical sub-culture of freestyle skiing? Can there be peaceful coexistence?*

Dave: What can I say! You cannot be taught freestyle skiing until you know how to ski and possess skills necessary to accomplish it. Many ski writers felt that freestyle skiing was more marketable than conventional lessons; or so everyone was led to think. The recreational skier has finally seen that there is more to skiing than racing and freestyle. These are an enjoyable side benefit of the sport, but it is their own personal enjoyment and safety of the sport that they desire most. The interest is there in developing the skills of the recreational skier, and the magazine writers have only begun to notice the drift. Anyway—there *is* a "freestyle" to skiing the ATM way.

SD: *It has been said that the skiing population has leveled off among the adult contingent and continues to grow among the nation's youth. Does the P.S.I.A. recognize the responsibility toward changing this trend, or will skiing eventually join other sports in being one for spectators who marvel at the prowess of the few, rather than one for participators who prefer to join in the enjoyment of the many?*

Dave: The spectator element exists in any sport—and it is one of the finer aspects of skiing. On any given run down a mountain you can stand aside for a moment and observe the elements and enjoyments of skiing—then continue along your way. Better or worse for what you saw—but at least you were there to have witnessed it. Or you can attend any one of a number of events staged entirely for the benefit of the skiing spectator. Put all this together and you come up with the kind of sports enthusiast that is involved with the sport—having approached in their own way the limitless boundaries the "stars" seem to exceed with a greater ease than they. P.S.I.A. sees this sport-life-style type of sports enthusiast as their primary purpose for existence and as the designer of their future. So, of course, P.S.I.A. is constantly searching for methods to generate current and future business. It is the ski teaching professional's way of life.

SD: Many thanks, Dave. I think you have answered some pertinent questions that will interest our readers. Skier's Digest believes strongly in such an organization as the P.S.I.A. It is a vital protector of skiing's highest standard of values, in an era when iconoclasts have deprecated craft in their compulsive embrace of free self-expression. In the world of art, this only resulted in wasted canvasses; in skiing, the result has been unnecessary fractures. We congratulate P.S.I.A. for showing us a safer more classical way.

My next letter was directed to Horst Abraham, P.S.I.A. Vice-President and Technical Director, who is presently with the Vail Ski School in Colorado. It challenges a few of the thoughts expressed by him in one of the skiing trade magazines; in particular his encouragement of an *open stance*.

October 2, 1975

Horst Abraham, P.S.I.A. Vice-President
Vail Associates
Vail, Colorado 81657

Dear Horst:

While I must cling to my preference of the classical style of the '60's (i.e. skis together and angulation determined by slope angle) in conformance with my own kinesthetic sense and an incorrigible perfectionist personality, I applaud all your other philosophies regarding the learning experience and methods for efficacious teaching. One of the questions I must ask you, though, is whether you feel that an ice skate with a double blade should be used by ice skaters, or a tricycle by cyclists, as both devices provide "more stability." It is my contention, and the belief of many eastern instructors, that the natural (open) stance adopted so overwhelmingly by skiers who have been influenced by the work of Joubert, is, for many, a cop-out, a rationalization of technical inadequacy. While it is important for us to determine the *practical* in our analysis of methodology, there is no reason to deprecate the *beautiful*, especially when in 75 percent of the occasions, the beautiful is just as practical as that which might be more stable. You have been flexible enough, and certainly courageous, to attack the rigid final forms system of the past and enlighten your instructors with an awareness of the importance of training in the basic skills. You have restructured the entire teaching approach with great insight, to the advantage of new students and the relief of many instructors who winced at the previous rigid dogma. Will you be as open in your re-examination of the *final* final form, and admit that some consideration should be given to *form beyond the practical?* What about *grace*? The bears share the forest with the deer, Horst; we get both types in ski class. To teach a deer to run like a bear would be as fruitless as trying to get a student's skis together when his waist is 20 inches larger that his chest.

The bone in my throat is not your exposure of the open stance approach as being more stable and practical for teaching the beginner, (it is that), but your apparent rejection of "parallelity" as a final form at least worth considering by the more gracefully oriented.

In the past, every art had its "classical" form toward which artists aspired in their creations. In some cases, that perfect form was realistically unattainable but functioned as a *level of aspiration* which motivated artists to improve with each creation. It was a Platonic concept that denied men the dubious luxury of settling for the practical and mediocre. The iconoclasts of this century have almost succeeded in totally destroying that concept of motivation, and the result has been the annihilation of craft in many of the arts. It is a dangerous path that is eroding man's sensitivity, bringing him closer and closer to the personality of a "practical" machine and farther away from the natural form in which he was created. It is curious how practical radicalism has spread into every phase of our civilization, not the least of which is our skiing society. This is why I want the P.S.I.A. to survive. While it has traditionally purged itself with no reluctance to change for the benefit of the new skier's learning process, it has also represented, to many, a means of achieving an attainable goal, a near perfect form, a *final* final form that has been a source of inspiration for thousands of skiers. Please let me know your thoughts on this subject.

Sincerely
Frank Covino

October 9, 1975

Mr. Frank Covino, Editor
Skier's Digest
Waitsfield, Vermont 05673

Dear Frank:

I appreciate your comments and the offering of your opinions on our teaching scheme. Allow me to present my own thoughts on these topics, which I base upon my experience acquired from my P.E. Education, three semesters of medicine, teaching sports for three years at a Junior College level and 14 years of ski teaching, that have brought me back to the learners bench in topics like; physiology, psychology, human behavior modification and communication. While I do not wish to show my credentials to impress you (they are not impressive) I wish to express my continued concern to bring ski instruction out of its infancy with more in mind than looking glorious on skis and assuming my ability to look that way should be rubbing off on anybody else.

Our concerns and developmental schemes have to be guided by what we know about how LEARNING takes place.

In view of the above I would like to respond to the issue of widetrack:

Stability is one of the fundamental requirements in expectance of initiative on the students part. In the early stages of skiing when speed is still slow and reflex action to unbalance is not there yet, the wider track will supply a greater basis of support i.e. be stabler. We always were able to observe wide track performances by aspiring students, but found it unimportant to incorporate this feature into our own demonstrations through which we give the student a visual image of his

Author Frank Covino blasting through Loges Peak at Aspen Highlands with classic angulation.

expected performance. The recognition of the students reality and our determined effort to communicate on a level that the student can associate with, should be foremost in our mind.

Once the student has arrived at an early intermediate stage where he attempts christies, his first crude attempts at skidded turns, his wide track gains one more importance: the ability to rotate the legs. The student at that level of skiing is still apprehensive to move hastily and suddenly. The open foot relation allows him to perform a slow or fast rotation of the legs, that does not necessitate any compensatory or complimentary movement elsewhere in his body. Another advantage of this movement of braquage (Joubert) is that the movement of rotation can be interrupted and restored and requires no vertical adjustment of the body.

The rotation of the legs in a closed-foot relation is distinctly different and not as advantageous in early, slow skiing because of the movement committment that I would call large, complex, jerky (when moving slowly) weak and not endurant. You wonder what I am saying? Try it on the rug you are standing on!

Once the skier increases speed and has developed alternate and more complex means to turn, he is not obligated to remain in a wide track. Conversely we should not consider a more advanced skier in certain conditions skiing poorly just because he temporarily utilizes wide track. We much rather should see in this action a showing of versatility.

Final Form:

Gross movements precede refined stages of those same movements. Grace, economy of motion is a natural by product of improving ones efficiency of movements. The request of grace in early stages of learning is unrealistic in as much as it will be impossible for the student to emulate. Feelings of inadequacy and the probability of failure, both great barriers to learning, are created by "perfect" demonstrations. This may greatly soothe the instructor, but drastically reduces his credibility in the students eyes. If instructors allowed themselves to think of the others ego once in a while, rather than just their own, he would greatly improve his teaching effectiveness.

Besides providing to be a great ego booster for the instructor, a "perfect" demonstration has its place in showing the desired end product (visual image) to the student. Strangely enough do students seldom if ever mention in relation to what they like about their teacher, his ability to ski beautifully (Dr. F. Lighthall—Univ. Chicago), but rather mention virtues like: concern, fun, empathy, helpfulness, clarity of demonstration, explanation, etc.

Gracefulness should not be alien to skiing, but should come as a result of functionality and not as a goal precluding effectiveness.

Unfortunately we have forgotten that grace, speed, etc. are relative to the person performing, while we have come to compare a person's performance with a standard (Stein Eriksen).

Although we certainly may adore idols and take their performance as an inspiration, we should remove final forms from a working progression, since a maneuver need not be developed to a national standard (Stein) to become useful or either to build upon other skills, or show content because the students ability will not lead him any further.

While I myself groove in the esthetic realms of skiing, I feel distinctly that I am doing right when my skis are doing what I desire them to do, rather than looking a certain way (Stein). Strangely enough do I also groove if I see a good skier come down the hill but inevitably he skis efficiently. When watching Stein ski in a slalom or a real challenging situation I find him skiing like the skiers I groove with when I watch them. Conclusion: First function then style. . .

Sincerely,
VAIL ASSOCIATES, INC.

Horst Abraham
Technical Director
Vail Ski School

October 18, 1975

Horst Abraham, P.S.I.A. Vice-President
Vail Associates
Vail, Colorado 81657

Dear Horst:

Topic of concern for this letter is "Carving vs. Skidding." As a victim of ski curriculum promulgated in the '50's and early '60's, I was brainwashed into respecting *edge control* as a primary requirement of a proficient skier. My instructors, and, later, my ski school directors, not the least of whom was Stein Eriksen, felt that controlled descent was more important than the activity of merely slipping and sliding around on flat skis. *Edging* principles were taught as early as the first day on skis. The relationship between the body position of an advanced "parallel" turn and that of the "snowplow" turn was clearly demonstrated merely by sliding the non-functioning inside ski into parallel position without changing the body posture, while the outside ski remained on edge and weighted. It was assumed (by those of us who taught in that era) that that demonstration of such a close relationship between an early form like the snowplow and the ultimate or "parallel" turn would, in fact, inspire the student to master the initial skill in anticipation of one day conquering the latter. The final parallel form was administered as a high *level of aspiration* to motivate the student and had little to do with "ego," although I am fully aware of the misuse of craft mastery by braggadoccios in every field.

The popularity of the early Head Standard ski among beginners and one-weekend-a-year bashers, with its straight cut and minimum camber, only substantiated the fact that the uninformed were mistaking the sport of skiing to be one of uncontrolled skidding. The beginners' slopes began to fill with these flat ski spinners, and the Ski Patrol business boomed as they flew out of control. It was a lot easier to spin a la Joubert's "braquage" on a ski that had no side camber. There was little need for unweighting. The Head Standard might have set the pace for the whole industry if all slopes were the pitch of a beginner slope or of the generous width found in the West. But a flat ski turn didn't work on the Goat at Stowe, and if you tried it on Sugarbush's Rumble, you would soon be tasting pine. Eastern trails demand a carved turn, and it was our belief that carving was a primary skill, to be taught at the very lowest level. Thus, the traversing posture was related to the sidestep climbing movement, with emphasis upon the tenacity of the uphill edge. Skis in the snowplow position were related to *arrows,* each pointed in

Classic angulation of Stein Eriksen compared to dribbling style of champion basketball player De Busschere proves there is nothing "unnatural" about the stance. If you were to walk across a steep hill in street shoes you would *naturally* drop your downhill shoulder, as your hip would angle into the hill and your uphill shoulder and hip would probably lead your stroll. The current deprecation of this form by P.S.I.A. methodology conflicts with the opinion of the author. Supporting Frank Covino are the thoughts of Othmar Schneider, Emo Henrich, Stein and other Ski School Directors quoted elsewhere in this edition of Skier's Digest. Austrian methodology also favors this basic form.

its own direction, and the student was encouraged to edge and weight the arrow that pointed toward his desired destination. I am sure the various devices are familiar to you, Horst, as I know you have been in the business almost as long as I have. What I want to know is why should such an important control principle as *edging* be removed from the early stage of the student's learning process? Is it no longer considered to be an essential skill? Will you agree that the problems facing a skier on a slat like the Head Standard are considerably different than those experienced by a student on a slalom ski? Has the advent of "cheaters" (the short ski)

affected the opinion of the P.S.I.A. Technical Committee so greatly as to have them deprecate or tactfully eliminate the necessity of *edge control* in the primary stage of the learning process? These are questions that many of our readers, and, I suspect, many of our seasoned instructors will be interested in having us rap about. I've enclosed an editorial.

Sincerely,

Frank Covino

enc: *Three Storey Mountain:* an editorial by Frank Covino

THREE STOREY MOUNTAIN

An editorial by Frank Covino, with the first paragraph dedicated to E.P.S.I.A. examiners.

The ability to teach does not necessarily follow the mastery of a craft. The best athletes frequently are terrible teachers of their sport, and some great teachers are far behind the champions in competitive successes. Good teachers must be far more than masters of their craft. They are princes of patience, empathy, love, and charity. They have abnormal capacities of strength and endurance, and enough psychological experience to classify and identify with the variety of personalities that make up their classes. They are intelligent beyond the intellectual demands of their own profession and capable of stimulating discussion at any level of interest. They probably are in their profession because they love it, and certainly not because it is a means of earning a living. Great teachers are an esoteric breed that shares in common

the attributes I have just mentioned. The craft that each one teaches is almost irrelevant. Because of their liberal education and flexible personalities, great teachers are capable of teaching anything with but a simple redirection of their educational capacities. Even the new science of skiing can best be taught by teachers with an intellectual level of awareness. To understand the ski student, a capable instructor must first know a bit about humanity.

Behavior patterns of the individuals who comprise the vast social complex are varied. Their responses to educational stimuli of any type are dependent upon their level of awareness. The values of the uneducated human being are not unlike those of his wild animal cousins. His primary area of concentration is the preservation and survival of his self.

He respects no rules set by others, shares no food nor hedonistic pleasure save that of sex, and his motivation there is not one of mutual gratification; more than likely he is unconcerned beyond that of his *own* satisfaction. He is *selfish*, recalcitrant, iconoclastic and insensitive to the needs of others, even to a greater degree than other animals. From the moment that the uneducated human is delivered as a sperm, his foremost concern is for conquest and self preservation in his race to reach the ovum. As an infant, he will scream, cry and rage at any self-discomfort, whether it be hunger, thirst, or a dirty diaper. At a later age he will fight to satisfy his basic needs and stop at nothing to destroy any barriers that might threaten the uncontrolled exercise of his basic functions. The *uneducated* human behaves on a *mechanical* level of awareness. He represents a substantial segment of humanity. As a skier, the primitive individual will be highly competitive. He probably would have no interest in the sport if it did not present opportunities for him to beat someone. His motivation is *conquest*.

Most primitive human beings develop a curious motivation that controls their basic behavior, the phenomenon of *emotion*. This may start as early as an individual's first year, when he develops an emotion of love for the mother who dotes upon his insatiable appetite with provisions for his self-satisfaction and, occasionally, an emotion of hatred, mistrust or at least resentment toward the father, who is considered to be a rival who has the audacity to share mother's bed. Various Pavlovian responses then go on to condition other emotions in the post-primitive human. He soon learns what kind of behavior will earn praise and other rewards, and what kind of actions are followed by reprimands and expressions of displeasure. He continues to view himself as the center of the world, however, and, to the individual who functions on an emotional level of awareness, nothing significant exists beyond his own empirical varification. Sorrow, pity, hate, love, passion and other forms of mental agitation are then experienced and stockpile for reference as the individual grows and learns to relate new encounters to those of the past by *recall*. He accepts the pressures of a civilized society as necessary evils to which he must conform, in lieu of being deprived of acceptance by the group which represents his maximum security; the group which has replaced *mother*. He finds escapes from such requirements in diversions like skiing, but usually is drawn to such sports for their social aspects and emotional promise. He can be a camp follower or a loner.

Not all humans who function at an emotional level of awareness totally conform to the major control group. Some will radically reject the "establishment" and follow an iconoclastic subculture which has managed to retain some of the *primitive* character of their earlier experience. Ironically, the radical emotionalist escapes from the conformity of the majority only to find himself conforming to the contrasting pressures of the minority group, which has become his new security blanket. As a skier, he is quick to put down ski instructors and their curriculum as symbols of restriction and control over his exhibitionist nature. The radical emotionalist readily identifies with the hot doggers of today.

The common characteristic of human beings who function on both the *mechanical* and *emotional* levels of awareness is that they respond automatically to stimulus with no knowledge of the nature of their response, nor desire to analyze and understand it. The vast majority of the world's population live on one of the two levels that I have described, but contemporary civilization is a three storey mountain.

The peak of awareness is *intellectual*. It is on this level that the individual may respond to stimulus in either a mechanical or emotional manner. The difference is that he is *aware of the nature* of his response or makes a special effort to analyze and understand it. He recognizes his motivation, perceives the structure of the stimulus, anticipates his own reaction and even the reaction of others, and responds in a self-predictable manner. Aware of the nature of his own motivations, he can be more objective in his analysis of his skiing involvement. He will have less hang-ups about the necessity of competitive achievements and enjoy other aspects like the precision and grace and the beauty of its environment. Not content with the capacity to analyze his own responses, the individual who has attained the peak of intellectual awareness accepts the task of leadership in organizing various factions of the social complex in which all three types of individuals must function. He writes the books, he runs the government, he educates, he dictates, he establishes standards of propriety which combine to form the tenets of a workable civilization. The individual on this level cannot be happy with emotional or mechanical response *per se:* he must know the science behind behavior patterns. He must analyze. He must create. He must lead.

Every facet of our social complex is populated by inhabitants of each level on the three storey mountain. On the mechanical level, the skiing contingent has its competitive aggressor group, driving to conquer, to win, to get there first, *racing*, like the sperm. The exhibitionists are found on the emotional level. They dazzle us with their freestyle, wear the flashiest clothes, express contempt for formalized instruction and frequently deprecate all elements of control, whether these be prohibitions of drugs and drink or physical imperatives as basic as the laws of gravity. On this popular emotional level are the recalcitrant iconoclasts, the pot heads, the boozers, the speed freaks, still exercising their selfish drives as much as their more primitive counterparts, but under the more socially accepted disguise of a $200 psychedelic jumpsuit. The exhibitionists have learned that certain behavior patterns will reward them with the latest Chevrolet, a five-figure purse from a Freestyle contest, or at least, the adulation of adoring promiscuous groupies. While the racer's drive is to be the *fastest*, the exhibitionist's compulsion is to perform the most spectacular flip or execute the most outrageous violation of standard form and still come up on his feet. Screaming. The motivation for both is identical: to be the center of attraction; to conquer the weaker or less practical skier and win his or her applause replete with fringe benefits. The radical emotionalist has also learned that the vanquished skiers beneath him are buried in the powder, and *anonymity* is his most bitter pill. If he can't be King, he will withdraw into a deep state of depression and rise only on occasion to throw eggs at the establishment, putting down organizations like the P.S.I.A., its instructors for their controlled skiing, and any form of classical expression with which he cannot identify.

All emotionalists are not extroverted hot doggers. The stockpiling of experiences which develop the mechanically aware child into an emotionally responsive adult frequently mold an *introvert*. If the "turned on" extrovert can be classified as a *radical emotionalist,* his "downer" counterpart falls in the category of *introverted emotionalist*. The emotions of this group are self-suppressed. They speak and move quietly. They blush and embarrass easily. A Norman Rockwell painting can bring tears to their eyes. They could care less about *why* a ski is turning, but a great deal about its color. Their pain quotient is low; they will tremble when the sun goes behind a cloud. They will be more than satisfied when they achieve the dubious stature of wedge-turner and really care little about progressing any further.

Then there is the *stoic,* another type of emotionalist. Consistent with the egocentric pattern, he will accept any kind of instruction that will improve his own method of descending a hill. His recall of past experiences has taught him to reject most overt expressions of emotion; but a constant battle wages within him to be the best he can possibly be, at anything he tries. In some respects, he can be a pleasure to teach. You will never hear him complain about the cold, or his bindings, or the crowded lift line. He can also be exasperating, as he will never so much as smile, no matter how hard you have tried to teach him.

There are other types of emotionalists, like the reluctant parents who ski to keep up with the Joneses or to relate to their children's interests. Their emotion is one of anxiety to *belong;* their hangup is dependency. The instructor will find anaclitic singles also in this group, which he can capitalize upon or run away from after skiing, depending upon the vibrations they generate.

Recall plays an important part in the motivation of the skier who functions on an emotional level of awareness. Just as the essence of smell can recall a past experience and condition our response in accordance with whether the initial experience was pleasurable or disgusting, so the skiing environment can motivate a particular emotion. If early exposure to the sport was only embarrassing, frustrating and downright humiliating, a later return for another try will seldom be accompanied by enthusiasm. On the other hand, the embarrassment of the first morning on the slope may have been followed by a successful lesson in the afternoon, and the pleasure of that encounter may be recalled at every new snowfall. It is an obligation of the qualified ski instructor to see that the student's experience with him is a pleasurable one and not one of degradation.

The *qualified* ski instructor must function at the highest peak of *intellectual* awareness. He may be a racer, or even a free-stylist, but he should be aware of the nature of those interests. Only if he recognizes his own motivations can he begin to understand those of his students. He should analyze his students' anxieties, along with their physical capabilities. If the ski instructor wants his guidance to be effective, he must know at what level his instruction should be delivered. Since skiers on the mechanical and emotional levels of awareness are ego motivated, the ski instructor will most effectively communicate with them by appealing to that ego. If a student's drive is to be the fastest, the wise instructor will get rid of those ridiculous short skis and pass on to the student some basic aerodynamic principles, together with instructions for controlling his speed in the face of obstruction. He will train the aggressor to *win* the weekly NASTAR

award. He will also be well versed on the latest racing techniques and seeding of the champions, providing food for conversation with his student on the chairlift. Above all, the experienced instructor will know that the best manner of teaching skiers on this aggressive level besides providing them with sure victories is by encouraging imitation, by observation and by meaningful critique. These are the skiers who actually *prefer* a "follow me" curriculum; the *inner skier* approach.

How can we detect an emotionalist? Since the majority of skiers fall into this category, they are detected by process of elimination. The *mechanical* aggressors usually show their character in a facial and body expression of *challenge,* accompanied by a conservative but fast ski outfit; their skis are competitive. The *intellectual* stylists will pump an instructor for scientific explanations of ski methodology (feedback). They watch and listen with great patience and have a better capacity for retention of specific direction. They dress conservatively and try to ski on their edges. The group that fits neither category are those who function on an *emotional* level of awareness. It is the most difficult group to advise, because their personalities are comprised of the most variables. Their ski clothing is the brightest or most outlandish or simply a snowsuit from W.T. Grant. The pear shapes who wear wool socks outside their plaid hunting pants are in a category of their own! Mechanically or emotionally responsive students will have little patience for verbal analysis of ski technique, but they will respond favorably to imagery. The instructor can reach the intellectual by explaining that *angulation* in a turn provides resistance against centrifugal force together with counter-resistance against gravity and centripetal force, or he can just tell the racer to lean outside to avoid hitting the slalom poles. But, to the egocentric emotionalist, advice to "bow to your downhill audience" might be more effective. If angulation is not possible, as when the waist of his student is wider than his chest, the sagacious instructor will have him ski with his skis apart, but he won't tell the student it's because he is *fat*. He will say it is the latest *wide track* technique, then, pray that he doesn't hit any ice like the French demonstrators did at the Tenth Interski.

The last paragraph is written with tongue in cheek, of course. To stereotype anyone by surface manifestations alone is totally unscientific and therefore unreliable. In the final analysis, there is no one method for teaching everyone, and this fact applies to all crafts, not only to skiing. To effectively inspire and educate any individual, a teacher must first identify the personality of his student and speak to him on his particular level of awareness. The greatest difficulty arises when a teacher is faced with a class of ten individuals who differ drastically in physique and mental awareness. This is the strongest argument for smaller classes and promotion of private lessons. But, as long as ski areas are run by penurious Machiavellians who care little about the academic progress of their consumers and too much about the cash receipts, the ski instructor will have to generalize his delivery and contend with oversized classes. His students will continue to be a potpourri of skiers from every elevation of the three storey mountain of awareness. The wise instructor will do his psychological homework; it's a steep vertical drop.

October 23, 1975

Frank Covino, Editor
Skier's Digest
Waitsfield, Vermont 05673

Dear Frank:

I read your article "Three Storey Mountain" with interest and with the re-occurring need to consult my Thesaurus. . . . the subject matter dealt with in your article was well appreciated. With regard to your letter:

CARVING VERSUS SKIDDING:

The title suggest that the two words and their respective meanings are in conflict. This assumption in itself tells me that you have not thought about the mechanical aspects very thoroughly— pun intended; even Witherell in his book, *Ski as the Racers Ski* leaves himself open to this criticism.

When turning, the skis are on their edges. Even on the smoothest surface and on hardest snow "flattening the skis" is an inadequate way to describe the actual happening. Reducing the amount of edging would explain the actual happening much more accurately.

If you can agree with me on the previous paragraph, we can allow ourselves to take the controversy carving-skidding a step further.

A ski will tend to slip sideways or skid as long as the amount of edging does not match the combined forces of centrifugal and gravitational pull.

My contention is, that under natural circumstances a purely carved turn does not exist. The unevenness of terrain, coupled with the inconsistency of snow resistance and the vibrating attitude of the skis, not to mention the constant need to adjust the angle of inclination of the body and the subsequent changes in edging, make carving, as it is explained by you and other supporters of this philosophy, a desirable but elusive goal.

My contention is, for the reasons listed above, that "carving and skidding" does not refer to absolutes, but rather characterizes the intensity with which the skis become tools (helping) in the making of a turn.

For the reasons mentioned above I consider carving and skidding interchangeable. I may call a grossly skidded turn a poorly carved turn, or may call a turn done with a high degree of edge engagement and ski response, a turn with little skidding.

The issue of carving and skidding becomes to me a matter of intensity of edging and not a choice of no edging and strong edging. In my reference to the respective action that I desire to create, I will choose "skidding" when wishing to induce and suggest a less severely edged ski, and "carving" when wishing to solicit optimal ski utilization.

In our P.S.I.A. "American Teaching Method" manual we carefully weigh all pros and cons of skidding and carving. It is our contention that the average student, on average inclinations of hills offered to him, with average snow conditions to contend with, and the end goal for the average recreational skier in mind, our approach suits his development best.

ATM bases its development upon the emphasis of feebly edged skis to lead to the easy accomplishment of a reorientation of the skis. At slow speeds, a high degree of physical fear and fear of failure coupled with the resulting turn anxiety, turns are easier accomplished in a pivoting manner.

The industry (guided by Clif Taylor) supplied the skier with a tool that will respond to his initially humble pivoting skills with minimal turning resistance. The inherent problem with skidding is balance. The challenge is easily overcome by broadening the base of support—wide track. This open leg relation is further conducive to enhance the students ability to rotate the legs with a movement of *braquage* (Joubert, *Teach Yourself How To Ski*), which permits the torso and arms to remain quiet (balance). Braquage supplies the student with one more great advantage which lies in the fact, that his movements of leg rotation can be done slowly or rapidly, fluidly or in sections. The skier is thus able to perform the turn with full liberty to interrupt it, if balance should threaten to be lost.

Shorter skis and the associated methodologies have greatly speeded up skier's ability to learn. More people are enjoying more quickly the exciting joys of participating in the sport, rather than being confined to the practice slopes until their enthusiasm is drained.

As a skier improves his skills of controlling speed through turning in a skidded fashion (which is a skill he will always need and will have to further expand upon) he begins to learn, as speed increases and thus pressure on the skis, coupled with the inclination of the body towards the respective turn centers, to work on edging more strongly. This evolution should not be pushed too quickly, though awareness of more severe edge engagements and their results can be practiced much as Witherell suggests in his book *Ski As The Racers Ski*.

In the early stages of skiing we support "physical manipulation of the skis in a pivoting fashion" to control speed. Speed is slow at this stage and muscular tension tends to be high, no matter how skillfully the instructor chooses terrain. The ability to take part in the "destiny" of a given maneuver will enable the student to move, relieve some of his tension. The early skier's lack of understanding and/or trust that the equipment will do some of the work for him will be able to be dealt with as soon as he developed an option (skidded control) as a backup system for his new desires: make the ski work for you.

Degrees of skidding are present in all turns, and in steep terrain this skill is becoming very complex. *Skid to edgeset* is a needed form of moving to control speed to confine yourself to the marginal space of moving or stable obstacles. Displacement-Skidding-Edgeset is the intricate process, in varying degrees of intensity and direction, which comprises the dynamics of recreational and racing turns. The specific nature of any turn will change, if any one of those components is altered even in the minutest fashion.

In ATM we have created an environment, where these skills can be developed and gradually intermingled. The student can grow without being confined to a singular mode to operate under. A method without option is a poor one. Inexperienced instructors are uncomfortable with options and need to be educated to not only accept options, but also eloquently use them.

I hope to hear from you soon and would like very much for you to arrange to meet with Stu Campbell. Stu has been in contact with you and I regard him very highly in the field of technique and methodology. He is also more literate and at home in English than I am; I would like to continue communicating with you directly but would like to include

Stu in our dealings, since he will be able to speak with you in person, in order to clarify any misunderstandings that may develop between us.

Sincerely,
VAIL ASSOCIATES, INC.

Horst Abraham
Technical Director
Vail Ski School

November 3, 1975

Horst Abraham, P.S.I.A. Vice-President
Vail Associates
Vail, Colorado 81657

Dear Horst:

Sorry to intrude upon your understandably "loaded" work schedule, but I do feel that SKIER'S DIGEST readers will profit from reading our correspondence, and I certainly appreciate your authoritative comments.

With regard to your recent reply, I stand admittedly guilty of the pedantic rhetoric. It is a fault that I clearly recognize whenever I review one of my past books, and one I try desperately to correct with each new effort. On the other hand, words above "a simple common vocabulary" sometimes excite me in their ability to *describe* with greater efficiency, like the agile stroke of an experienced painter's brush.

Concerning your comments on Carving vs. Skidding, I could not be more in agreement with your clarification that some amount of skidding is necessarily involved in every turn. It would seem that you also agree with me that a controlled turn should always employ the inside edges to some degree. Your statement, "The issue of carving and skidding becomes to me a matter of intensity of edging and a choice of no edging and strong edging," reveals our "issue" to be a misunderstanding of semantics, one that I wanted you to clarify for the benefit of those skiers who have been advised to "skid" their turns on a flat ski and who wonder why they continue to catch their outside edges.

Topic of concern for this letter is with regard to *Ski* magazine's fall 1975 article, "The Inner Skier" by Morten Lund. Essentially, it had to do with the currently accepted psychological theory that the mind is at least divided into two halves, one which responds to mechanical or analytical stimulus such as language and one which is motivated by imagery or "holistic" perception. The article goes on to encourage the ski instructor to appeal to the latter side in lieu of confounding his experience. Thinking back to my early skiing instruction in classes conducted by European jocks whose form and accent were impressive but whose ability to instruct left something to be desired—I fear that acceptance of this philosophy may lead us back to the "bend ze knees, five dollars please" concept of ski instruction, a dangerous step backward. It is my contention, as I indicated in the editorial, "Three Storey Mountain," that such a "follow me" curriculum may satisfy the mentally incompetent or emotionally responsive skier but would seriously disappoint the skier who willingly exercises his *mind* in other pursuits and sincerely appreciates any form of scientific analysis. This later type of contemporary individual is becoming far greater in number than his ivory tower intellectual ancestors and certainly represents a substantial portion of the more educated skiing population. He pays a bundle for this ski education and wants more than a demonstration of his instructor's talents.

If I enrolled in a class for piano lessons, I would not expect the teacher to say, "Sit down and play something and I will show you what you are doing wrong." I would want her to show me where each note is on the keyboard and how specific combinations of those notes form chords. I would expect to run a few scales, before being encouraged to play Chopin. What are your vibes on this problem of motivation, Horst?

Sincerely,

Frank Covino

cc: Stu Campbell

November 3, 1975

Stu Campbell
Crossett Hill
Duxbury, Vermont

Dear Stu:

Here is a carbon of my letter to Horst plus a copy of my editorial, "Three Storey Mountain" which he appreciated but feels is too pedantic for the skiing audience. He may be right, and I will probably edit it after reading your comments. I thought you might refer to the editorial in your evaluation of The Inner Skier concept, as it will appear in the same chapter with our correspondence. Thanks.

Sincerely,

Frank Covino

November 10, 1975

Frank Covino, Editor
Skier's Digest
Waitsfield, Vermont 05673

Dear Frank:

Thanks for returning my call the other night and for including me in your correspondence with Horst Abraham. I have been following your dialogue with great interest, and am pleased to be in on the "round table discussion." I think, however, for reasons we discussed on the phone, that it would be best to avoid a critique of the "Inner Skier" by Morten Lund. [Ed.: Stu is a writer for the magazine that conceived the "Inner Skier" theory. His discussion of the concept might lead to a damaging conflict of interest.]

I have read some portions of your editorial, "Three Storey Mountain," with considerable delight, but have been a little puzzled with other sections. As a former academic teacher myself—I taught high school English for five years—I can see that you have your finger on the pulse of what it takes to be an excellent teacher in any field. And I share most of your

Stowe's brilliant technician and author of *Ski With The Big Boys*, Stu Campbell, shows the currently favored "natural stance" that the P.S.I.A. has adopted for skiing across the hill or straight down. The American Teaching Method does not presently accept *angulation of the body* as a necessary form. They prefer to limit angulation to the *knees* alone, but, of course, they are also sanctioning a wide track parallel turn, for which body angulation is indeed *not* imperative.

views on that score. I would also have to say that although your tone becomes a *little* pedantic at times, and perhaps a bit overly anthropological in spots, I don't share Horst's discomfort with the vocabulary.

As you may know, the United States, thanks largely to contributions on the part of Horst, Max Lundberg, our latest Interski coach, and Juris Vagners, author of our *Biomechanics Manual,* has suddenly been rocketed into a position of leadership in the alpine world as far as ski technique and teaching methodology is concerned. This is something that we have never enjoyed in competitive circles to any great extent, so it is a challenging new—(and somewhat frightening)—experience to have the rest of the ski-teaching nations looking to us for direction.

I guess it could be said that P.S.I.A. is trying to encourage a whole new breed of ski teachers—and the kind of instructors you describe in your editorial. The approach is far more flexible and creative than the traditional "you-will-do-it-this-way-and-you-will-like-it" methodology that was brought to this country and "popularized" by some Central European instructors. With its emphasis on "skills development" on many different levels (as opposed to a strict step-by-step teaching progression), the American Teaching Method demands a far more versatile, educated, experienced and sensitive ski teacher than we have known in the past.

The ATM "progression"—if we can call it that—is filled with *options*. This freedom of choice can be very frustrating to a new instructor who would like to be spoon-fed, and who has not yet convinced himself that there are many different ways to get to the same goal in skiing. He must convince himself, or be convinced, that his job requires him to deal with people on the three different levels (storeys?) that you so astutely list: the mechanical, the emotional, and the intellectual. Not an easy task, to be sure.

The P.S.I.A. Technical Coordinating Committee, overseen by Horst, would be the first to admit that ski technique

evolves behind the development of new ski equipment and technology, as well as behind what the racers are doing. *We do not create technique,* although we might have some influence on how technique is taught. Things are possible now—technically—that were not possible even a few years ago. It is an admitted struggle to stay abreast of all the new developments because things are happening so fast. But the basic difference between what we are doing and what some of the other nations are doing, is a difference in teaching *philosophy.*

We are trying to address ourselves to what the skiing public really wants in terms of learning to ski sooner, learning to ski better, and enjoying it more. This is an obvious departure from the attitude that suggests that skiers in lessons will do what we tell them because *we* know what is best for them. There can be no question that whatever innovations we have made in ski teaching and technique are at least partly the result of the American public's general willingness to experiment and try new things.

You come down pretty hard on ski racers and freestylers in "The Three Storey Mountain." To arbitrarily classify racers as merely "aggressive mechanics," I think, does them an injustice. I will grant that alpine ski racing involves a certain amount of chauvinistic daring, but even on a junior or collegiate level it must be considered one of the most cerebral of all sporting events. The subtleties of line and technique, the physical risks, the psychological pressures and innuendoes of strategy are unmatched in any other sport, as far as I can see. You may be revealing inexperience as a racer or coach to oversimplify, stereotype, and categorize them the way you do. [Ed.: I stand accused, and admit that my racing experience is limited. You are perceptive, Stu.]

You also seem to classify freestylers as a bunch of compulsive exhibitionists, which is not really fair either. (I hope that when you meet Robin Smith at Bromley you will feel otherwise.) Freestylers, for all their "wildness" have had the courage—and more important the technical know-how—to expand the heretofore limited horizons of skiing. If you have a chance to talk to some of the better freestyle competitors, you will find them anything but a bunch of pot heads and speed freaks. I will wager that you will find them every bit as sane and dedicated as some of the world's best nordic competitors. They exist in a colorful and somewhat whacky milieu which has been created as much by skiing publications, film makers and promoters as by themselves. Freestyle is coming of age as a legitimate aspect of the skiing scene, and it is here to stay. One of the most encouraging things is the way many of them have turned to the ski technicians for guidance. Many of them (Genia Fuller, for example) are also certified professional instructors. [Ed.: My paper states clearly that racers and freestylists can certainly have reached an intellectual level of awareness. If, in fact, they have achieved the status of champions, they certainly shall have attained that goal through an intellectual application of the knowledge of their craft. There are many others, however, who go no farther than their aggression or exhibitionism will allow.]

From your essay, it is obvious that Frank Covino, ski instructor, is someone who is extremely sensitive to the emotions, needs and abilities of the people he teaches. Obviously the ski-teaching industry needs more people like you. But it is also important to keep current on what is going on, and to develop a sensitivity to what the skis are doing on the snow. Unfortunately not all ski instructors understand all they should about how to use their skis to their best advantage.

I thought it a little unfortunate that you chose *angulation* as an example of how scientific analysis can be used to help a student with an intellectual bent. (I couldn't agree more with your basic premise regarding scientific analysis, by the way.) Modern ski design, and particularly modern boot design, has de-emphasized the importance of angulation as we used to know it (the kind of angulation that appears in the picture on your letterhead). If in fact, you are teaching people to "bow to the downhill audience"—although the imagery is great— you are teaching an awkward, contorted and outdated "pose" that has not been regarded as efficient for some time now. [Ed.: If the "bow" aligns the torso 90 degrees to the slope, it is a vital anticipatory movement that will facilitate the next turn. Consider the words of Horst Abraham, discussing Anticipation in his Ski School Vail Pointers (Italics by the editor):

> As one turn is being finished, the skis are turned away from the fall line. *The upper body does not follow the turning action of the skis, but faces in the direction of the next turn-downhill.*
>
> Angulation increases as the pole swings forward, ready to be planted. It is essential at this moment, *not to draw the downhill shoulder forward* towards the pole-plant. The down movement culminates in the setting of the edges and the planting of the pole.
>
> *Upper and lower body are at this time in a twisted relation.* This twisted tension is now released by flattening the skis while the upper body is still blocked by the pole plant. The now free skis will seek alignment with the blocked upper body and the turn is initiated. From here on stepping to the outside ski will change angulation and the skis turning is controlled by steering (turning skis with knees and feet) and leverage (forward pressure on the edged ski). THIS KIND OF TURN IS CALLED AN: "ANTICIPATED TURN."
>
> Common Mistakes:
> 1. *Planting the pole while facing the direction of the skis, rather than facing downhill.* This necessitates a hanging on to the pole as the sole turning force. It puts the skiers weight onto the inside ski and on the tail of the ski.
> 2. Some people plant the pole properly but in the extension phase *bring the hips to the outside of the turn* and end up on a flat ski and rotating."]

Edging, steering, and weight transfer are the three "primary skills" in the American Teaching Progression as outlined by Horst. Edging can be accomplished in a number of ways other than with extreme upper body or "hip" angulation. The skis operate best if someone thinks about standing *against* his outside ski, rather than *on* it. And this almost automatically implies a good deal more edging. Better edging can frequently be done— perhaps more effectively—with *inclination* rather than angulation. I think you will find inclination creeping into the skiing picture more and more as stylized angulation fades out. [Ed.: On hard packed, icy or steep terrain, inclination will cause imbalance, as proven by the French at the Tenth Interski.]

Skiing, after all, is largely a matter of changing direction. In order to build confidence in newer skiers, we try to show them how easy it is to point a ski a different direction by keeping it on a *relatively* flat plain (i.e. "feebly edged," to use Horst's words), and use the muscle groups in the legs to turn the foot. Once this is done, it is a pretty easy thing to involve some of the rest of leg muscles, as well as the knee and hip joints, to put the ski on a still higher edge and make a more rounded and complete turn. Our approach might be, "Turn the ski a little and then put it on edge." Later, when the skier becomes more proficient, we can work toward saying, "Put the ski on edge and then make it turn."

This raises the controversial question of "carving versus skidding" in a turn. And I will have to stand with Horst, even though I can do little more than try to amplify what he says. You are right that the term "flat ski" can be interpreted many different ways by different skiers. As far as the ATM is concerned, "carving" is just a matter of degree. In other words, a "carved" turn has less slippage than a previous one with a lot of lateral slide. We do not, as Horst pointed out, subscribe to Warren Witherall's initial hard-line on the "pure carved turn." *That* is an ideal, and there probably *is* a certain measure of slippage in even the most sophisticated racing turn.

Snow conditions and terrain dictate the amount of edge required more than anything else, just as you have pointed out. In the East, for example, we have more slippery conditions, but we still teach sideslipping to develop edging skills. The sideslip is not necessarily an end in itself, it simply points out the need to "release" an edge—by *decreasing* the amount of edging, but not to the point of catching an *outside* edge—so that the ski can be steered more effectively. With our icier conditions here, it is important that we teach people to reduce the amount of edging for a very brief period of time, but then teach them to get the ski *back* on a high edge again—either with or without an edge *change*. Otherwise, as you say, we would have a lot of little old ladies climbing trees on the side of the Toll House Slopes.

Best,

Stu Campbell

November 28, 1975

Frank Covino, Editor
Skier's Digest
Waitsfield, Vermont 05673

Dear Frank:

Thank you for your letter of November 3rd. Please accept my apologies for being so late with my reply. Our mountain opened, instructors needed to be trained and I did not find enough hours in a day to do everything I was supposed to do.

Having read "The Inner Skier" article, and being also aware of your correspondence with Stu Campbell, I feel it is very appropriate to qualify that article's presentation, or at least offer a humble opinion about the matter.

In recent years we have been able to read a myriad of highly stimulating books. The ones that come to my mind most rapidly are Joubert's, *Teach Yourself How To Ski*; C. Taylor's, *Ski In A Day*; W. Witherall's, *How the Racers Ski*; and most recently T. Gallwey's, *The Inner Game of Tennis*. Everyone of those books had a significant message, yet most of them promote one idea to the exclusion of all others. *The Inner Game of Tennis* and "The Inner Skier" article tend to highlight the fact that man learns from visual images. Visual "replay" greatly enhances learning, yet I would not venture to say it may become the exclusive tool of teachers of physical activities.

Language remains to be an effective tool to establish the much valued rapport and serves us well in conveying items of theoretical nature. Looking at our profession critically I must admit that we have been using language excessively and have not used images as much as we could and should have. Our current emphasis of working with visual images and with visual rehearsal is merely an attempt to bring it into perspective with other communication tools.

We realize that some students respond well to visual images, but still request and need verbal direction, encouragement and assessment of their performance.

As much as some learning theories emphasize one or the other approach, we must allow our students' learning history determine the prevailing technique we use with him. Most people of our society are conditioned to watch and listen. The arbitrary cutout of one of these stimuli would be detrimental to his learning potential.

Motor learning should use the "total picture" approach in giving a flowing image of what wants to be achieved. The learner ought to be given a chance to emulate this total picture and only when this approach fails, or you wish to solidify certain skills, will an instructor choose the "component approach." An instructor should be careful not to unnecessarily fragmentize a movement complex and must make sure that dynamic entities are practiced as such and are not taken apart. The law of specificity of movements needs close consideration. The skilled and perceptive in-structor allows learning to take place by carefully selecting the environment within which discoveries can be made by the student. Holistic and fragmentized segments of learning can complement each other wonderfully.

Summary: We tended to talk too much and show too little. Let us recognize the values of speech and visual image and practice both with consideration of what we are trying to achieve.

Sincerely,

Horst Abraham
Vail Ski School

* * *

SKIER'S DIGEST will take the summary of Horst's last letter as a cue to cut the text of this chapter short and illustrate it with an outline of the basic forms currently advocated by the American Teaching Method. It should be emphasized however that these are by no means considered to be a necessary progression of "Final Forms" in the skier's learning process. The ATM approach is full of options. What follows is merely a manual from which ATM instructors may select any form that he feels is pertinent to the particular stage of his student's ski education, guided by his analysis of the student's body type, personality, physical capacity, and, of course, slope experience. In the final analysis, his primary effort should be to teach edge control, steering, weight distribution, and balance. Illustrated here is the ATM approach to that goal.

ATM APPROACH VS PARALLELOGRAM APPROACH

Since most turns of the learner begin and end with a traverse, the posture recommended for traveling in that direction is a silhouette to consider when comparing skiing styles. The current ATM stance, as explained to me by Stu Campbell, is *square* to the direction of travel. Thus, the posture for crossing the hill at this level in the learning process is no different than the ATM recommended stance for skiing straight down the fall line. Compare it to the parallelogram stance of former years, Austrian influenced, that many of us still prefer for traversing with the feet together.

ATM: The feet should be spaced a comfortable distance apart. The body should be relaxed, with flexation in all joints. The spine should be slightly rounded. Arms relaxed, the hands should be held down, level with each other, and within the learner's field of vision. The upper body should face the direction of travel.

GLIDING WEDGE/BRAKING WEDGE

What used to be called a *snowplow* has been changed to a *straight wedge*. The reasoning behind the change in terminology is that the former adjective implied a glide on the inside edges of the skis which would eventually end with a stop, as snow would accumulate beneath the skis. ATM now lessens the accent on edging, encouraging a glide with *flat* skis in the *wedge* position, and edging inward *only* when a stop is desired.

ATM: In the straight wedge the skier's body should be symmetrical. The ski tips should remain reasonably close together. From a straight run, with the skis 3 or 4 inches apart, the skier should spread his ski tails into a gliding wedge with no appreciable down motion or braking. From a gliding wedge, the skier may assume a braking wedge by moving his pelvis down and slightly back. The stop should be gradual with little tip flutter or displacement.

WEDGE TURN

The big change in *wedge turns* today and the snowplow turns of ATM's old methodology is less emphasis upon steering with only the *outside* leg. By encouraging the learner to steer with *both* knees, the inside ski is automatically flattened to the snow surface, making a tip cross less likely. The change may seem to be minor, but I believe it to have major significance in the student's progress toward simultaneous or *parallel* skiing.

ATM: Each turn will be initiated with obvious "Foot" steering, followed by "leg" steering with both legs. Leg steering at the completion of each turn will naturally stimulate a "down" motion, which will be followed by an upward motion before the next turn. Torso faces the direction of travel.

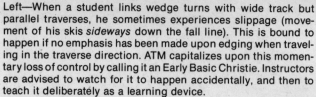

Left—When a student links wedge turns with wide track but parallel traverses, he sometimes experiences slippage (movement of his skis *sideways* down the fall line). This is bound to happen if no emphasis has been made upon edging when traveling in the traverse direction. ATM capitalizes upon this momentary loss of control by calling it an Early Basic Christie. Instructors are advised to watch for it to happen accidentally, and then to teach it deliberately as a learning device.

ATM: From a holding traverse in a relatively high stance with feet 3 to 4 inches apart, slide the tails into a wedge simultaneously. Then direct the skis toward the fall line with foot steering. Continue to turn with leg steering until the skis have passed well beyond the fall line. Then, match the skis (slide the uphill ski into a parallel but wide track relationship with the downhill ski) with a sinking motion. A short (but not rounded) sideslip will be the result. Finally, reset the edges and rise up gently to a new holding traverse. As in all other maneuvers, the upper body will always face the direction of the travel.

EARLY BASIC CHRISTIE

ELEMENTARY CHRISTIE

Above—The ATM Elementary Christie is a variation of the old Up-Stem Christie, with the exception that it is not carved on the edges. ATM designers feel that edging while turning is too sophisticated for the skier at this level; they prefer to have him skid into the final phase of the turn, eliminating body angulation altogether. Austrians disapprove. So does Stein.

ATM: From a fairly low stance in a holding traverse, (By holding traverse, they mean riding on the uphill edges.—ED.) stem the uphill ski (push its tail uphill). Direct the skis into the fall line with foot and/or leg steering. Once in the fall line, touch the inside pole to the snow and match the skis with an UP motion. Follow with a rounded sideslip and a lowering of the hips as the skis move into the new traverse. When the line of the new traverse has been reached, eliminate all slippage and begin a new holding traverse.

LONG RADIUS TURN

Left—The Long Radius Turn (which I called the "easiest turn of all") in my No Frills instruction chapter) in the present ATM curriculum, makes use of foot steering, leverage, and inclination to set the inside edges, with a bare minimum of body movement. Again, I must repeat for our readers, this turn and *any* turn which employs *inclination* as opposed to *angulation* must be executed at high speed or in deep snow. Performed at slow speed, on packed or icy terrain, inclination will most assuredly be seduced by *centripetal force,* and the unsuspecting skier will skid out and fall on the uphill side of his skis.

From a fast traverse the skier flattens his skis and initiates a forward sideslip by rising up and forward and tipping his body about one o'clock to his direction of travel. This momentary weight release and forward leverage will start the ski tips slippage downhill which the skier may assist by foot steering. The pole is touched when the skis are pointed downhill. This is followed by a down motion and progressive edging by inclining the body toward the inside of the turn. My last figure illustrates the rise up and inclination of the skier toward the next turn, tipping this time at eleven o'clock to his direction of travel.

ATM: As you begin to steer out of the fall line toward a new turn, gradually bring your skis onto a higher and higher edge. Once slippage has been eliminated altogether, rise for the next turn.

CARVED STEP CHRISTIE

This one is very similar to the old "UP-Stem Christie" except that ATM has virtually eliminated angulation in its current affinity for *inclination.* I say, OK, *for high speeds,* but please don't try to tilt your body *inside* your turn at slow speed, unless you want to finish the rest of your run on your stretch pants!

ATM: (They now call this a carved step christie.) From a holding traverse at reasonably high speed, show obvious inclination toward the turn as you make your step by lifting the uphill ski slightly and displacing its tail away from the fall line. The downhill ski should hold its original course. During the stem-step, the stepped ski should be edged sharply and your body weight should be transferred against it. As soon as the outside ski makes contact with the snow again, it should show no slippage whatsoever. (As speed increases, the stepped ski may show less displacement in the tail to demonstrate a more parallel step, but the pressure transfer must always be to the inside edge of the stepped ski.) At the completion of each turn the skis should be carving, should be together and parallel, and you should show body inclination for as long as possible throughout the remainder of the turn. (My large arrow shows how the knee drive forward and to the inside of the turn keeps the skis on edge and carving.)

The preceding sketches and comments are based upon the various *disciplines* with which I was confronted at the Instructor Certification Pre-Course. They represent the basic ATM curriculum. One exercise I have deliberately omitted is the *wide-track christie*, as I feel that it is a maneuver that will have a short life, once the powers that be realize that axial motion on a flat ski is a habit to be discouraged not encouraged, if our students are ever to learn how to control their skis and make use of their ski's side camber. For a brief description: the wide-track christie is no more than a type of wedeln (fall line turns with no traversing) that begins with the skis a hip width apart. Turning is by axial motion, with the weight on the center of the skis. Edging is not appreciable. When I asked Stu Campbell *why* such an unorthodox maneuver is included in the disciplines, he reasoned that many students are products of "shortee-ski" Ski Schools; they have learned to turn their skis like propellers, by pivoting directly under their feet. The discipline is essentially designed to enlarge the instructor's awareness of what he might encounter. Since I have already discouraged readers of SKIER'S DIGEST who opt for a ski shorter than one up to their armpits, I choose to omit the wide-track christie.

The American Teaching Method has not varied their thinking on Wedeln or Short-Swing. All schools are presently teaching these methods of descent alike. My sketches are principally of the moves that are relatively new to any instructor or skier who has had experience with traditional methodology.

Above all, it should be understood that the ATM is full of options. There is no longer the dogmatic requirement that one discipline be mastered before progressing to the next. The PSIA instructor is expected to design his teaching approach in accordance with the specific needs of his student, physical, mental or even emotional. This places instructors who wear the PSIA badge a cut above their super-jock counterparts whose extent of teaching methodology is no more than the ability to say "Follow Me!" Put your money where you'll get the most return...

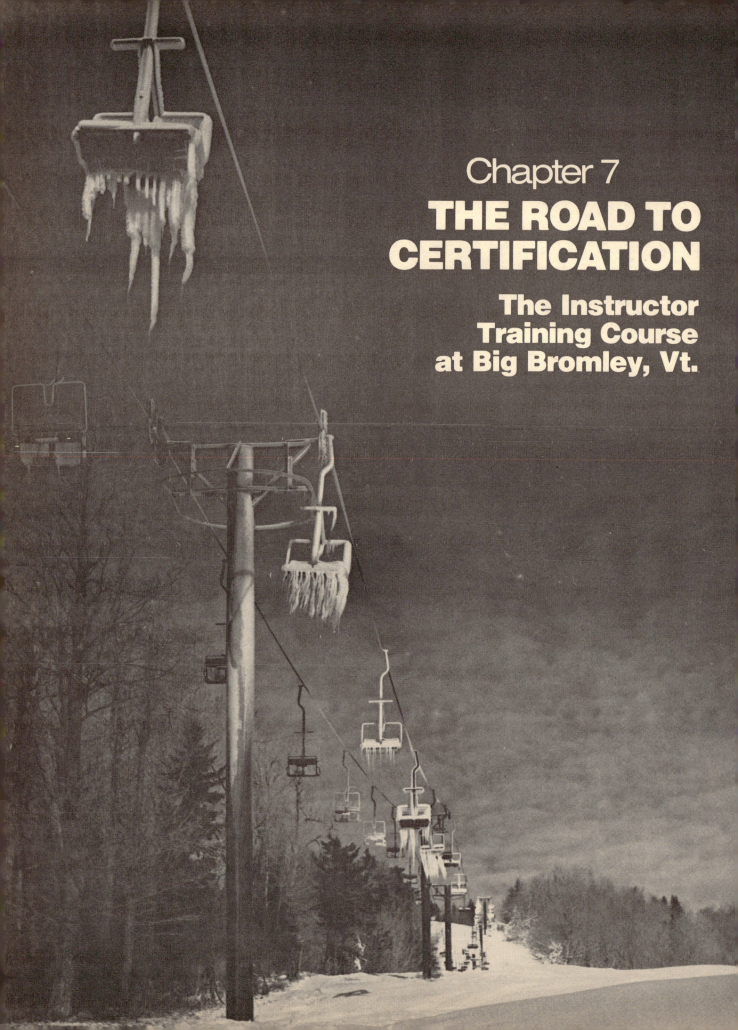

Chapter 7

THE ROAD TO CERTIFICATION

The Instructor Training Course at Big Bromley, Vt.

FAILURE. The word itself makes most of us want to bow our heads, pull up our coat collars and walk sheepishly away from the announcement. It is human nature to be ashamed of *failure*. It would appear that human nature also compels us to seek extraordinary challenges of our capacities, dangling success like a carrot before the nose of a donkey, while pebbling our path with mines of failure, as we proceed with annoying apprehension. Anxiety over the success vs. failure syndrome probably develops in childhood, when we get our first exposure to the phenomenon of *power*. First, we become dramatically aware of it as an outside force; from the moment we slip out of the security of that comforting womb into a world of giants with booming voices. We can't compete with them physically because of our size and mechanical immaturity, but we soon learn that our capacity for making sounds is reasonably competitive and that any of our personal discomforts will soon be remedied if we can just reach the right decible with our screams. Very shortly, we learn that certain behavior earns rewards, be they so minor as a kiss or pleasant smile, while other expressions result in reprimands or various forms of rejection. Successes are rewarded and failures are discouraged long before we can walk or speak, and it is not long before successes are recognized as salient ingredients of the cumulative phenomenon of power in our social structure. It is no wonder that business executives of every persuasion push themselves to the brink of self-destruction, via the popular ulcer, in their quest for success and power. A small segment of our society takes a healthier route. We call them athletes.

The drive to be successful at some form of athletics develops earlier with each decade. Many parents who suffer frustration at the lack of successes in their socially competitive lives turn to their children for aid by involving them in competitive sports and pushing them to be winners. Some children survive the ordeal of the "Little League" and go on to achieve success at some sports endeavor, despite environmental pressure. Others are psychologically scarred by a series of strikeout failures or too many years "on the bench" and are doomed to a life of inhibition and complacent dependency with a humiliating inferiority complex.

It is curious that a reversal frequently takes place in our mature years. The football hero with a long list of athletic successes who was Big Man on Campus suddenly finds himself with no more games to play after graduation. With a head full of public accolades for his physical successes and with reflexes conditioned for aggression, the power paths open for his future are few in a society that is basically programmed for mechanical or intellectual specialization and restrictive channeling of our mental and physical energies. He can become a coach, but how many athletic coaches can there possibly be? He can become a cop, or a Marine, or a student of karate. Or, the "jock" can forget about exercising his physical capacities altogether, live on the laurels of his past, get fat on the luxuries that reward his involvement in some form of "business" like his non-athletic neighbor, and die of a cardiac arrest in his forties. That scene has become too familiar.

Fortunately, there is an alternative. While the demands of our society require us to fit into its "establishment" by "getting a job" and providing some sort of social service in exchange for others that we receive, there is no reason to neglect the maintenance of our individual bodies and, indeed, our minds, by rejecting continued involvement in physical activity beyond our school years. There are sports that are available to everyone even those who never "made the team" in their youth. There are sports that ask for no physical "contact," no necessary *conquest*, no spectacular *scores* or victories. There are sports like skiing. For the majority, the rewards from involvement in the ski scene are numerous and sufficient for mental, physical, and even spiritual equilibrium. For those affected by the success-failure syndrome, who wish to go beyond those personal pleasures, there is the opportunity for conquest and score in ski racing, the opportunity for victory, exhibitionism and crowd adulation in acrobatic freestyle contests, and, for those "intellectual" sportsmen (or women) who have a capacity for *leadership* there is the opportunity for ski teaching. The ski teaching profession in this country is qualified by a hierarchy called the P.S.I.A. (Professional Ski Instructors of America). The badge of their certification is a carrot chased by many, but only a few finish the course that is heavily mined with traps of failure. That course, that road to supreme success begins annually at Bromley Mountain, just as soon as the thermometer cooperates to allow its snow guns to begin coating over 80 percent of its trails between tall, stoic Vermont evergreens. It happens every fall. I could think of no better way to tell you about it than to personally enroll in the program and have my wife Marge illustrate my report with a camera.

Sunday, November 30

After making great promises to get to bed early and take off for Bromley at the crack of dawn, a black angry cumulus crept over the peak of Glen Ellen and dropped what seemed like half of Lake Champlain on the shingled roof of our house and the sleeping forest around it! Rain washed away most of the foot of snow that had fallen a few days before and pecked at our bedroom window like a tireless woodpecker. I kissed Marge's ear and cuddled for a few more "Z's," assuming that the "free skiing day" offered by Bromley the day before the Certification Preparation program would be a washout. Any Vermonter would just smile at such an assumption. It could be pouring in Fayston and be bright and clear over Manchester just 2 hours south. It was. We goofed.

Laury Shulkin signed us in about noon. She's the right arm of the Eastern Professional Ski Instructors of America organization. More than a "girl-Friday," she makes programs like the Bromley Instructor Course work. Helping out was another unsung heroine, Diane Dearington, who was the prime mover for the Bromley event. Both girls are incredibly efficient and disturbingly beautiful. My wife quickly ushered me through registration.

We lucked out on lodging. One of my art students owns a luxurious condominium at the top of the Plaza slope and gave us a break on the rental. The Jon Ringels are like thousands of other Fairfield County affluents who have purchased a piece of weekend heaven in Vermont to make their working life in the inevitable 9 to 5 program more tolerable, and they were generous enough to allow their friends to share the comfort. The Plaza was the only trail fully covered with snow, but Karl Pfeiffer, Director of Skiing at Bromley, promised to fire the snow guns just as soon as the thermometer would cooperate.

Two hundred and twenty-six applicants later, the sun dropped behind Mt. Equinox and the mountain slept, in anticipation of the Monday morning invasion by intellectual skiers from practically every state east of the Mississippi. Some were physicians, three were psychologists. Airline pilots, attorneys, dentists, movie producers, artists and construction workers were just some of the many occupations represented. We were separated into four groups: those who had taught skiing occasionally but wanted to improve their own form; those who had taught moderately but were not interested in certification at this time; my group, those who had taught extensively and were interested in attaining the badge; and the already certified group, who attended the course to brush-up on the latest technique and methodology changes. The youngest aspirant was 16, the oldest, a man and a woman, were both born in 1915! Sixty-nine men and 33 women had had previous teaching experience; 95 men and 29 women had not taught before. Registered for the program were a total of 164 men and 62 women. One applicant came all the way from Zurich, Switzerland, where he teaches at the American International School and directs the ski instruction program. This was Big Al Willette's fourth year in attendance at this program. Typical of many participants, Al is a strong skier who braves the challenging cliffs of Stowe every winter, but is constantly seeking to perfect his style. Representing the distaff side were attractive female athletes like Jane Crowley, a 23-year-old Attitash ski instructor who swims for a water ballet show in the summer. Nancy Pottratz, from St. Louis, whose husband is P.S.I.A. certified and a teacher at Chestnut Ski Area, and Mary Sue Anter, who is a specialist in teaching the handicapped. Mary Sue took a few hours out of her training program to teach a blind student who happened to visit Bromley during the week. She will work this year at Haystack Mountain in southern Vermont. Never, in the history of skiing in this country, had so many "intellectual athletes" congregated in support of a common goal: the qualified authority to teach the science behind our captivating, adventurous and romantic sport.

Big Al Willette is a well known figure at Stowe. He skis regularly with Stu Campbell and "The Big Boys."

Mary Sue Anter gets her boards for an assignment to teach a blind skier!

Two phases of the *step-over* ballet maneuver. This was tough for those of us who had longer skis. Nancy Pottratz had no trouble at all.

Monday, December 1

I rapped with Karl Pfeiffer for a while about the need for public understanding of basic ski science and the dangers of "freestyle" misconceptions, and casually looked around, as over 200 skiers clomped into the upstairs cafeteria in half buckled boots and sat to await a screening of the P.S.I.A. sanctioned film, *A Method To The Madness*, produced by Tom Rainone and filmed by Vermont's most capable skiing cinematologist, Alan Seymour. There were a surprising amount of older instructors. One of them, Paul McBride, was a dentist from Cranmore, New Hampshire, whose 47 years made my 44 feel a bit less awkward as we talked and watched the well-muscled thighs of the predominantly more youthful contingent drape the cafeteria benches. Some of the women had that characteristic swelling just below the great trochanter that skiers facetiously label "riding breeches." All of the women were healthy and attractive. The "freestyle" experts were true to form with their psychedelic stretch suits and long hair.

At 9:15, the rain changed to snow, competing for attention with the Board of Examiners now assembled behind the movie screen, as it speckled the windows behind us. There was a rumble of grateful acknowledgement as the slopes began to turn white and Chris Rounds, course coordinator, began to introduce the officials. Karl Pfeiffer, indefatigable Director of Skiing at Bromley is most famous for his introduction of the GLM concept, the graduated length method of learning to ski which begins the student on a very short board and gradually has him progress to a standard length ski as his abilities improve. He was followed by Bob Perrin, General Manager of Bromley, who forecasted colder weather and efficient snowmaking. Pre-course examiners were then introduced: Bruce Fenn, Stu Campbell and Allan Woods from Stowe, Steve Sherlock from Cranmore, Ray Allard of Glen Ellen, Bob McDermott, Peter Palmer, John Putnam from Cannon, Cal Cantrell, the white haired veteran who has a reputation for demanding perfection from the aspirants he judges, Rudy Kirsteiner, Woody Woodward, Jim Harman, Dennis Brobst, Bill Tate and Joe Wood of the Eastern Demonstration Team, and Robin Smith from Swain,

Fig. 7-3: Karl Pfeiffer, Director of Skiing at Bromley leads some of his instructors down the fall line with some silky smooth wedeln.

who was scheduled to deliver a lecture on freestyle skiing later in the week.

The 15-minute film was both informative and motivating. Tom Rainone had managed to document the entire P.S.I.A. approach to learning in a simplified yet dynamic presentation, supported by Cal Cantrell's demanding direction and a lucid script designed by Dennis Brobst and Stu Campbell. *A Method To The Madness* was filmed by Alan Seymour at Stowe, with the purpose of showing the most logical progression of the skier's learning process, the American Teaching Method taught by P.S.I.A schools from coast to coast. The sequences range from the first straight run position on skis to an analysis of expert skiing through mogul fields. It is available from the E.P.S.I.A. for rental or purchase, and I highly recommend it as a primer for any learning skier or serious ski club.

My immediate response to the exposure of most recent methodology in the P.S.I.A. curriculum was that the emphasis is now upon limited body movement and more understanding of equipment function. This corroborated my own opinion that too much concentration in past forms of ski education has been upon body dynamics with not enough consideration taken for the ski and its realtionship to the snow and influential physical forces. My instructor for the week, Allan Woods, assistant ski school director from Stowe, soon defined the "quiet body" concept more precisely on the hill as we proceeded to loosen up with some free skiing (a decision the entire group welcomed as we had been off skis for 7 months).

On the chairlift, I first rode with Ray Allard, Glen Ellen's Ski School Director. We spoke about our mutual love for his ski area, and I asked Ray to write something for SKIER'S DIGEST that would spread the word about his quiet mountain

Chris Rounds ran a very well-organized Pre-Course. You should enroll in the Bromley program next season; you'll get a substantial return for your investment!

that towers 500 feet above Sugarbush and has one of the longest vertical drops in the East. Allard is a taciturn, lean and graceful skier who lacks the delusions of grandeur that characterize many super skiers, has an infectious smile and would probably pass unnoticed in a lift line. On the hill, he cuts a precise line with the speed and agility of a proficient athlete. The second time up, I rode with Mary Sue Anter, P.S.I.A. certification aspirant from Haystack and amputee instruction specialist, who looked like a turkey in her yellow rain outfit, but so did most of us who did not trust the dark clouds rumbling in the west and the capricious thermometer. On the next ride up, I spoke to an insurance agent who only began to ski at 34 years. Eight years later, he was vying for a shot at certification. I had a chance to rap a little with Allan Woods the fourth time up, who coincidentally had picked up my novel *Snowballing* at Kennedy Airport, announcing it with a sardonic smile. That gave me about 4 minutes to apologize for its Rabellaissian humor, rationalize my intent by explaining the prurient requirements of modern paperback publishers and plea with my examiner to not allow my exposé of life as a ski instructor to interfere with his judgement of my capabilities during the next week. Allan just smiled.

After lunch at 12, Joe Wood, an Eastern P.S.I.A. demonstrator, joined our group to demonstrate some of the new "discipline forms" that Allan described. It was emphasized that these forms were *disciplines,* the performance of which would be tested by P.S.I.A. examiners to reveal the ability of a ski instructor to demonstrate them with precision, and that these movements were not necessarily to be followed by the students we teach with an equal amount of precision. The "old school" concept of mastering one "final form" before progressing to the next is now considered to be an unnecessary regimentation that impedes the learning process. We were advised to be flexible in our teaching approach, to use less dogma and to put more fun into the educational experience. Basic skills were pointed out by Allan, like edging, up and down-unweighting, foot steering, and leverage. It was an informative first day. At 4:00, we reconvened at the main lodge for a lecture by Karl Pfeiffer on "Ski Professionalism." Here is the gist of what Karl had to say:

The dictionary describes professionalism as "Conforming to the standards of a profession. Conduct, Aim, Qualities—Characeristics of a profession."

This is not given, it is earned. The new instructor should realize what is expected of him.

I always have to smile when listing all the requirements, as probably no other profession demands such high standards:

Attitude
Appearance
Athlete (not always necessary—if to teach lower level)
Super Skier (not always necessary—if to teach lower level)
Ski Equipment knowledge
Profound knowledge of ski technique and methodology
Personality
Hard Worker
Dependable
Optimist
Public Relation sense
Cooperative and helpful to everyone

Let's analyze each standard.

Some of the Pre-Course applicants had picture perfect style.

ATTITUDE

Probably the key to becoming a successful pro. Friendly, positive, willingness to learn, a feeling of care for people. I personally feel that I can teach most instructors to ski and how to teach skiing, but I never succeeded in changing anyone's attitude. A ski pro with three national certifications but with a poor attitude probably is not the greatest ski teacher.

APPEARANCE

We have to present a group feeling with responsible leadership to the public. If we are to be successful, we have to put our best foot forward. We should also look like a pro.

ATHLETE

To teach the higher levels of skiing, it is necessary to be able to perform all the maneuvers in splendid manner. I am not saying that every ski teacher has to be a super skier; it all depends upon what type of skier he teaches. A racing coach for junior racers has to be a good example so the little ones can imitate him. If a student desires to learn mogul skiing, then I would assume he would prefer an instructor who truly skis the moguls in an excellent manner.

SUPER SKIER

A ski pro must understand why a ski turns, the basic science of controlled descent, etc. He must be able to ski most slopes in acceptable form. The fastest skier again is not always the best skier, falling three or four times in each run.

EQUIPMENT KNOWLEDGE

That was easy 30 years ago when we all used wood skis, 210cm long. Today, equipment knowledge is a most important part in successful teaching. It would seem impossible to ski a parallel skier into a carved turn on an icy slope when his skis have not been tuned well or when he used a recreational ski with wrong performance characteristics.

SKI TECHNIQUE AND METHODOLOGY

Naturally, the new instructor does not know much, but he had better realize that he must make a great effort to learn as much as possible. To open the lock (to help the student), the more keys (technique and methods) the instructor can employ, the easier he will succeed. Dialogue with the student is a must. Why is the student in ski school, what is his goal, etc? This will take time, and only years of teaching and learning will provide the basic knowledge of ski technique and methodology. We have a long way to go in ski teaching. . . .

PERSONALITY

A ski teacher has to be able to converse and deal with every segment of the skiing market. Skiing should be fun.

Is it fun? Sometimes it is 30 degrees below zero, or it is raining, etc. A good teacher will make the best of it and will create an atmosphere of enjoyment and learning. He must be able to get along with 50 to 200 other instructors. Not easy. The director may not be such a dear guy, either.

HARD WORKER

After teaching 6 days in sub-zero weather, three classes per day, taking part in social programs, etc., ski teaching suddenly can become a gruelling profession and some of the glamour can be lost.

DEPENDABLE

For a ski school to function well, the instructor corps must be dependable and have a great interest in the success of the school. If one fouls up, the public does not say this was Karl, no, they say it was the Bromley Ski School!

OPTIMIST

Every student can be taught something. Be optimistic in helping all students. A successful instructor will help all eight students in his class, and not push three students very hard, while neglecting the five others who may drop out and most likely will never attend another ski school class. Neither should the instructor give up easily. Some people will take a long time to learn. A lot of patience and optimism is needed. Always be positive. Never say to the student that his movements were BAD; rather, say the movements weren't very good, but point out some aspect of their maneuver that was successful.

PUBLIC RELATIONS

The ski instructor has a glamour reputation. The skiers know him, the other workers on the mountain know him. Every time a newspaper writes an article on a ski area or takes pictures, ski instructors are always participating. A friendly, public relations-oriented ski pro can be a great asset to a ski area. It does not take much. Friendly, helpful, gracious, in other words, the ski pro should be a lady or a gentlemen.

COOPERATIVE

Not only to the skiers, but also to his fellow instructors and the ski school management. Assignments, sometimes are mixed up. A ski pro may have to teach the same level three times in a row. The Ski Patrol may need help for the sweep. Most of all, he must cooperate with other area personnel, from the lift operator to the rental shop people.

After Pfeiffer's talk, which turned out to be one of the better efforts of the course coordinators, we were herded into a long narrow section of the lodge for a "get acquainted party," compliments of Karl and Bromley Mountain. The fried chicken was delicious and the beer flowed from a bottomless barrel. Outside, the mercury dropped. We hit the sack early and prayed for snow.

Tuesday, December 2

My first run from the Ringel condo to the base lodge at Bromley was shin bruising. Snowcats had chopped up the artificial snow on the Plaza, but the freezing temperature had just turned their efforts into ice cubes. The rising sun promised to corn up the slope, but its rays were too weak at 8:30; it cost me a layer of blue wax and an arduous hour of bottom preparation. Slalom gates were set up for fall line practice. Many of the skiers revealed racing experience in their form, but Allan emphasized that no clock would be watched when we would be tested on the slalom course. All the examiners wanted to see was controlled carved turns and quick reflexes. After several practice runs on the single-pole course, our examiner cleverly moved one pole 3 feet out of the fall line without informing us. It was an unexpected ploy that did challenge our reflexes, and he pointed out those of us who met the obstacle without breaking our rhythm. The sun began to blaze and fulfill its promise of corn snow.

From slalom practice we were briefed on current P.S.I.A. methodology. I have already spoken of the suppression of body movement and accent upon ski function and physical forces. Another notable trend is emphasis upon skidding rather than carving in the early maneuvers. There was, in fact, no mention of carving at all, and even the traditional "snowplow" exercise has been changed to a "gliding wedge;" the principle difference being one of severe edging

Al Woods showing our group that the basics have not changed much, except for the elimination of *angulation*. I think it's an important posture. It will return. Here, Al demonstrates the *gliding wedge*.

vs. minimal edging. From what I could gather in Allan's defense, a skidded turn, on skis almost flat to the snow surface, encourages the new skier to initiate and effect his turn by "foot steering," then, "leg steering," and, only when he has reached his new traverse direction, by "aggressive leg steering," which employs the skis' edges. I was criticized for "unnecessary angulation" which, it was explained, although functional at a later level, would only confuse the new skier and give him more to think about. In an effort to simplify the whole procedure of turning, no mention is made of upper body counterpoint. In fact, the upper body is kept facing the direction of travel in the early exercises, and only in the advanced parallel stage is the skier encouraged to "face the fall line in anticipation of the turn." The new methodology also stresses a natural athletic posture for straight running: feet apart by 4 to 6 inches, all joints flexed, a slight crouch with rounded shoulders, eyes ahead toward the direction of travel, and arms forward and away from the body.

After lunch we watched video playbacks of our class in action. I was very impressed by the quality of the TV setup at Bromley. Almost all the video efforts I have seen at other ski areas are so primitive that the skiers are no more than black silhouettes against flat white snow. For the P.S.I.A. Training course the video program is produced by Herbert Hammett, who is as professional as his product. There is a full tonal range in the playback pictures, and the camera is guided by a steady hand. I was amazed that he uses no tripod!

More methodology after noon. I rode the lift with Tom Rainone who produced the P.S.I.A. film *A Method To The Madness*, and we rapped about politics within the organization. Tom had produced the film on speculation without official sanction from the Board of Directors, and the P.S.I.A. hierarchy gave him a little static about chain-of-command. Only the quality of the film finally encouraged the powers that be to finally give it their stamp of approval. Rainone's defense is that there were no dollars in the P.S.I.A. bankbook to finance the effort, so he went ahead and produced it with his own scratch. Protocol notwithstanding, the film is excellent and will survive as a fine example of the P.S.I.A. curriculum in 1975-6.

On the next ride up, I rode with certification aspirant Bill Peck, who had a significant idea that the Board of Directors should consider. In the final examinations, when the aspirant's teaching capabilities are being tested, why not have him teach an actual class of volunteer students, rather than a mock class of other proficient skiers who are also vying for the badge? Low level skiers would jump at the chance for free lessons, and the examiners' evaluation of the aspirant's teaching effectiveness would be far more valid. I agree. When our own class was used to test each of us in our teaching abilities, the use of proficient skiers as a mock class became clearly invalid. A prime standard for the evaluation of a teacher should be his ability to recognize and correct student errors; these mistakes should not have to be faked. I can think of no more valid estimation of a teacher's capabilities than that which would be marked as he directly influences a student's progress.

Big Al Willette was my next partner on the chairlift. Al has the dubious distinction of being a "close friend and drinking buddy" of several P.S.I.A. examiners. For this

Herb Hammett runs a very professional TV camera that allowed us to view ourselves in action. An amazing way to detect your flaws and correct them.

reason, he has never taken the final examination for certification, although he has attended four preparation courses. Al just likes to ski, and he wants to be more than a "hacker." With a chalet "just a snowball's throw" from Mt. Mansfield, Willette knows Stowe like the back of his hand. By profession, he's a commodity broker.

We broke at 3PM for a lecture in the base lodge by Bruce Gavett on Handicapped Instruction. He was followed by Gwen Bevier, Supervisor of the Handicapped Program, Gore Mountain Ski School. Her outline is a paper worth reproducing for your perusal:

TEACHING SKIING TO THE PERCEPTUALLY HANDICAPPED

by Gwen Bevier

A perceptually handicapped person is one whose understanding of his internal and external world about him is markedly less than his potential.

1. Due to physiological limitations, this person has great difficulty achieving success which has been established as today's standards. The perceptually handicapped person has a confused or limited concept of his internal body relationships. Also his gravitational understandings and his external physical relationships to space or distances are sometimes clouded. He has difficulty in combining these judgements to achieve a specific task or movement. Movement patterns develop from gross movements, such are found in the startle reaction of an infant, to specialized movements, (moving both arms together), to refined movements such as eye-foot coordination. All the above require the monitoring of the perceptual processes. If these perceptual processes are limited or undeveloped, the end results can be and often are inadequate or below the established

performance standards.

The repetition of below standard achievements quickly establishes a pattern. This is a pattern of failure, inadequacy and personal defeat. When a person cannot perform due to movement pattern limitation, he often interprets this defeat as being dumb, slow or retarded. He often feels rejected which certainly may be correct. Soon this failure pattern is so firmly established that it encompasses the total person and becomes a permanent element of his development and life.

The ability to learn requires many factors. The ability to perceive is one. For the person with perceptual disabilities, the constant and conscious monitoring of these perceptual processes is a must. This monitoring cannot be done alone. Additional assistance must be given this individual to aid in the development and reinforcement of these systems. QUESTIONS, QUESTIONS, QUESTIONS relating to these processes are a form of reinforcement and should be asked. Examples of such questions are: "Can you FEEL the difference between skiing on ice and powder? can you HEAR the difference? and can you SEE the difference by looking at the snow and your tracks?" The judgement of distance relationships is exemplified by such questions as: "How many climbing sidesteps are there to the patch of ice?, can you stop in a wedge *before* the ice?, *after* the ice?" These questions demonstrate the tactile, visual and auditory processes, the body's relationship to the surrounding world, and the combining of all these factors to perform an established task or goal. The end result or goal is the ability to coordinate the ski, the leg and body to the visual and auditory command of stopping before/after the ice patch. This is a refinement of many movement patterns.

"Recognizing the different goals and needs of the students and then solving these needs is an important quality in ski instruction."

2. Needless to say, a perceptually handicapped person needs a good guide or instructor. He needs someone who is aware of both the specific task and concept of the task or goal. The instructor must be aware of each individual student's needs and must also be an excellent observer. The instructor thinks positively, encourages, is patient, and asks QUESTIONS. If skiing is going to be fun and a successful experience, negative comments such as "that wasn't right, try again, or you goofed" are *not* to be made. QUESTIONS, such as, "did you *feel* the foot turning the ski?, let's do it right here, standing still to get this feeling," are less defeating for the student.

The awareness of perceptual problems and the incorporation of these teaching suggestions will further aid our educational system's approach to learning disabilities. Old fashion recess and gym classes have acquired a new identity. New games are introduced to help define a student's body image, body coordination, space definitions, and gravitational relationships. In other words, the up's, down's, right's, left's, before's, after's, etc. are all learned concepts with which may be difficult for the perceptually handicapped individual to deal. Remedial reading and resource teaching are other examples of educational programs dealing with learning disabilities.

The uniqueness of our program is that we are applying this knowledge to the recreational and fun sport of skiing. Using these teaching suggestions in skiing will introduce and allow success to another group of individuals—the perceptually handicapped. It will also expand our own awareness of individual needs, each individual's goals in addition to broadening our own skiing and teaching abilities.

Sources
1. Dr. J. Baxter Swartout, F.A.A.O., F.C.C.V.D., Gesell Optometrist Graduate, Consultant and Lecturer
2. "Educational Psychology as Applied to Skiing" by J. William Younce.

Ms. Bevier's contribution was followed by a talk on Bio-Mechanics by Serge Duvillard. With limited time, Duvillard could offer no more than a list of definitions for meaningful phrases like *sagittal plane* and *axial motion*. To this he added very basic explanations like "the lower your center of gravity, the more stable you will feel." The general consensus of the audience was a wish that he had gone further and showed more specific relationships of the terms he defined with skiing movements and, in particular, with ski *instruction*. My personal opinion, after speaking with Serge when his lecture was over, was that he is a brilliant scholar who, unfortunately, lowered the level of his delivery in lieu of confusing a less educated audience. What he may not have realized is that his "less educated" listeners included physicians, psychologists, dentists, attorneys, airline pilots and several Ph.D's! Many instructors looked forward to the talk on Bio-Mechanics with great anticipation and were disappointed at this cursory presentation. We finished Tuesday with a great steak at the Sirloin Saloon in Manchester and 2 hours of filing edges and waxing blue.

Wednesday, December 3

Today's early morning slalom practice was again through single pole courses. Some of the aspirants rumbled about the absence of open and closed gates, but at least there were a few moguls on the course which broke up the boredom of wedeln turns. Allen then skied us over to the Lord's Prayer, another novice slope where the Bromley guns had made tons of snow. There, he evaluated our teaching abilities. My assignment: "Your class can only make early basic christies. You have reached a steep drop of 50 feet. How do you get them down?"

An early "basic christie" is similar to what we used to call a stem turn. It begins with a high holding traverse. The skier then stems his ski tails into a wedge. Gravity automatically begins to pull his ski tips toward the fall line. He assists this turn initiation by steering, first with his feet, then with his legs, and finally with an aggressive movement of his outside knee forward. When his skis have passed well beyond the fall line, they are "matched" or brought together with a sinking motion, resulting in a brief sideslip. The skier then resumes a new "holding traverse" with a gentle motion, resetting his edges. Most learning skiers blow this maneuver when they reach the fall line. It is well known that *fear* is the primary deterrent to progress in the skier's learning process. The "moment of truth" is when the fall line is met face to face. It is then that most learners panic. Their eyes dilate, their skin blanches, their mouths open and their knees shake when they are facing *downhill*. That momentary freeze, that trembling shock is the cause of most unsuccessful turns and wipe-outs than any other phase of all turning maneuvers. It has been my experience that any effort made by an instructor to divert the low-level skier's attention from the fall line can only result in more rapid progress in his mastering a turn. A most effective suggestion is to encourage the learner to *look only in the traverse direction.* If his initial traverse is west, I like to stand on the east side of the slope, below the learner. I advise him to look ahead while traversing. Once he has stemmed the tail of his upper ski and gravity begins to pull his ski tips into the fall line, I immediately call out a command to "look at me!" Turning his head to the new traverse direction is a mild form of anticipation that almost always is followed by the necessary foot and leg steering that completes his turn. By this ploy, the learner never "faces" the frightening fall line and thus avoids the stimulus of his *fear.*

Allan scored me high on that theory and added that other solutions, like having the whole class sidestep down the steep portion of the hill would also be valid. The refreshing attitude embraced by the modern P.S.I.A. is one of flexibility with three guideposts: "safety, fun and learning," each of which was extemporized in Karl Pfeiffer's welcome speech.

After lunch, Woods offered a lucid explanation and demonstration of the avalement maneuver. Throughout the week he proved to be a brilliant teacher and authoritative examiner. Our entire group considered ourselves fortunate to be under the wing of such a professional.

An unusual experience followed. Gwen Bevier took us for a run on one ski with outrigger pole units used by amputees. She must have legs of iron. The J-Bar trip to the top was especially tiring. Turning was not difficult when the ski was on the outside leg, as that usually bears the most weight in normal parallel skiing, but difficulty was annoyingly experienced when the ski was on the *inside* leg of the turn. Freestyle experts who are used to skiing on either leg experienced no difficulty at all. Most of us agreed that we could master the handicapped apparatus after four or five runs.

The thermometer continued to drop and Bromley's snow guns began to blast the Boulevard and Twister trails from just below the peak of the mountain to the base lodge. Some of those bursts hit the chairs and created an almost surrealistic setting as giant man-made icicles sparkled against a deep indigo ski. I looked at Marge, skiing with a Hasselblad strapped to her waist and whispered, "Get *that*!" What a picture. It introduces this chapter.

Robin Smith, Ski School Director at Swain Ski Area in western New York and member of the E.P.S.I.A. Pre-Course Team, then presented an excellent lecture on free style skiing, supported by good video analysis. He had this to say in his *Guide to Teaching Free Style* outline:

"Freestyle is the fastest growing aspect of skiing. It offers both the aspiring competitor and the recreational practitioner a challenge and an unlimited opportunity for creativity and freedom. The teaching of freestyle offers the ski school and the instructor an opportunity to regain their credibility with the advanced student and to make money.

The coaching of competitive freestyle demands extensive training, knowledge and specialized equipment, and it is beyond the intent and scope of this outline. We instead direct ourselves to the teaching of the recreational skier and the junior competitor just starting the sport.

Teaching freestyle is not anymore difficult than teaching any other level of proficiency in the sport. Good teaching principles apply. The instructor must provide safety, enjoyment and learning, in that order. A basic format of teaching any new freestyle maneuver should be:

1. Analyze the maneuver to be learned, separating known skills from skills which must be developed to insure success.
2. Develop the new skills involved in isolation.
3. Recombine new skills with known skills such that the skier's first attempt is a safe and successful one.

This is no different than teaching wedge turns. The freestyle teacher must just be more analytical in observing the new maneuvers and highly creative in developing an approach to teaching them.

Smith emphasized science and logical progression, promising to prove his point on the hill the next day, when all 226 aspirants would have a chance to try some basic ballet maneuvers, restricted by the length of our skis.

Thursday, December 4

Robin Smith was assisted by Tommy O'Connor, freestyle expert from Kissing Bridge Ski Area and a few other E.P.S.I.A. D-Team members, in schooling us on modern ballet techniques. It was surprising to many veterans like myself that it is possible to teach an old dog new tricks, even on 190cm skis! We toyed with outriggers, royal christies, cross-overs, 360's and tip drags and spent most of the day flirting with the ever-present danger of torn ligaments. But there were no casualties, and the program was exceptionally well organized.

At 4:00 PM, Frank Johnson, Director of the Bromley Mountain Ski Patrol, gave an interesting lecture of the role of a ski

Tommy O'Connor, ballet expert from Kissing Bridge was an excellent demonstrator.

Many of us found skiing on the uphill ski a bit awkward, but it's so necessary in most ballet maneuvers.

PSYCHOLOGY OF LEARNING AS APPLIED TO SKI INSTRUCTING

by Cionia Lanza

INTRODUCTION

One cannot make pupils learn any subject by simply demonstrating and lecturing. In dealing with people and not objects, one should consider the differences in people and their emotional states.

Concepts from the "Psychology of Learning" will be used here for analysis purpose, but as psychological considerations are offered, they will appear like simple, common sense suggestions.

Motivation, lack of fear, intellectual understanding and good motor coordination are qualities needed in learning to perform a sport.

In this paper, ways to deal with inadequate amounts of these qualities will be explored.

instructor in an accident. He read the National Skiers' Courtesy Code and encouraged ski instructors to learn basic procedures for ameliorating life endangering situations. These were the steps he recommended in the event of an accident:

1. Mark the trail and report the accident to the Ski Patrol.
2. Calm the injured and keep him warm.
3. Leave his boots on if the injury is to the ankle or leg; it functions as a splint.
4. Cross the skis of the injured above him to prevent collision from other skiers.

Answering the question of liability, Johnson quoted Vermont's "Good Samaritan Law:" If you *can* help and *don't* help, you can be fined for evasion of responsibility!

Friday, December 5

The sun shone gloriously on the last day of the course and a welcome gift from Bromley Mountain was over a foot of man-made snow covering the Twister and Boulevard trails. Reluctantly, we filed into the base lodge at 9:00 AM for a lecture by Cionia Lanza on the psychology of ski teaching. Chained to novice terrain for 4 days, we were all chomping at the bit to do some *real* skiing. Mrs. Lanza prefaced her speech by saying that she, too, would rather be on the hill and that she would make her talk as painless as possible. It was not only painless, her thoughts were stimulating, informative and inspirational. It took the attractive blonde psychologist about 10 minutes to mesmerize our group and make us forget about the untracked snow in front of the base lodge.

Cionia began to ski at the age of 33. She could easily identify with the agony and fear of adult beginners. She pointed to the virtual lack of fear in child beginners: "They are freer to imitate . . . they are learning all the time . . . " She explained that the cognitive, chain-learning principle is more applicable to the adult who appreciates the science behind the effect. She believes that fear is inherent in all intelligent adults, although it might be subconscious. Here is the fascinating paper composed by Cionia.

Cionia Lanza

TEACHING CHILDREN AND ADULTS

Ordinarily teaching approaches should vary according to the age of the pupils. Children learn differently from adults, and, in a way the most important consideration in ski instructing is to give children's classes to instructors who like children, since they most of the time like the instructors in return, and usually few problems occur. Children spend a great deal of their time learning, in school and everywhere, so they simply accept learning to ski as the way things are for them and for a change as something that at least is a lot more fun than regular school.

The picture of an adult who goes to ski school is different and generally more complex. As a rule there are more problems, at times they are psychological, at times physical. Physical problems, such as age, lack of coordination, overweight, poor physical fitness or others, are complicated in a person who is also anxious or afraid. He may then think badly, perceive badly or not at all, and may react with poor body movement.

The way children learn depends very much on the stage of their development. Often the most visible characteristic in young pupils is the lack of fear, combined with poorly developed motor coordination and no intellectual understanding of the movements involved. They take off, skiing downhill without any consideration for good form or style. Imitation is often the only thing they use to learn; they imitate the movements of the instructor or of other children. There is not much thinking or talking going on.

Instead, we assume that adults have reached the highest level of their development, so a more complex set of conditions exists. For adults, the cognitive part of learning has become usually very important; for some it seems indispensible. Adults like to talk about the techniques of skiing, while they are on skis and afterwards. Therefore, they usually need to have a description in great detail of the movements and their sequence involved in each maneuver. In the psychology of learning, this type of learning is called "chain" learning, where each step (link of a chain) has to be very clearly thought out first, and tried out to be mastered later.

Each psychological view on how pupils learn has some application to ski instruction. We will review some here.

The *Behavioristic* view puts an emphasis on the observable part of the learning, and as far as skiing is concerned they would only care about the final performance.

The *Cognitive* view gives importance only to the intellectual work that precedes or is happening during the movement. Instructors who would fit in the first approach will ask the pupils to follow them and do as they do; and this at times works very well. In the second approach there is an awareness that imitation is not working for many adults, since they need to think the movements over, sometimes overnight. Then they also might find some practice on their own to be very useful, as well as thinking about the exercise.

The *Motivational* view will consider the fact that skiing is fun, and the pupils will want to learn just to enjoy the sport more. This also works very well in some cases.

The *Stimulus-Response* view will explain why students will try to stay on their skis, as a natural reaction to avoiding a fall. And one can easily have seen this happen in many cases.

From the above theories, it seems logical then that one should have a multiform approach in instructing, by using different methods for different cases. Not a very simple thing indeed, but one that will differentiate the better instructor from the mediocre one.

THE MOST IMPORTANT CONDITIONS OF LEARNING

All pupils, children and adults need to satisfy three conditions, at least to some degree, to practice a sport. They must have:

Motivation, to do it.
No fear, to try it.
Good, natural *Motor Coordination.*

In the sport of skiing, where the element of risk of personal injuries is present and much publicized, the need to learn to do it properly is rather obvious, and the presence of the three conditions above become rather critical.

One can use a "continuum line" on a graph to illustrate the extreme outcomes of success in correlation to the existence and the amounts of the three conditions.

| High Motivation | (Intermediate Conditions) | No Motivation |
| No fear | | Fear |
Good Motor Coordination		Poor Motor Coordination
Most successful learning (Easier to instruct)	(More typical situation)	Least successful learning (Most Difficult to instruct)

We will examine these and other related conditions in some detail.

In all learning motivation is essential. Motivation is the reason one wants to do something. It reduces some personal needs in the learner; for instance: one is motivated to eat because he is hungry and will feel better afterwards, or he desires to taste good food. In skiing the social need to be where the action is, be part of the crowd or be admired, motivates people to learn to ski. Once in ski school, the need to succeed and be promoted to a higher class motivates the pupils to master his level.

A factor that affects the motivation and usually makes for better learning is to have a moderate amount of stimulation, so the interest is aroused. The novelty of the subject, the glamour or excitement provided by the environment, usually provides this. At times the instructor has to add his personal touch to the class atmosphere to make it fun, exciting and interesting.

Another factor that improves motivation is a sense of competence; competence gives people a feeling of control. Competence can be felt privately or "internally" and makes skiing fun to do; it feels good to be able to ski. Thus a person is motivated to do it better to have more fun. On the other hand, when competence in a sport is directed outwardly or "externally," one seeks the approval of other people, their admiration or their acceptance of him in their group. This is a highly motivating factor.

There is no need to explain fear and its effects on all human actions. In skiing it has definitely a negative effect.

Motor coordination is needed in learning situations, where more than intellectual or verbal skills are required. It is used in all types of crafts and sports. Good motor coordination is the result of a well developed "chain" type of action, where all the steps involved have been mastered.

A ski instructor will frequently be faced with a teaching situation that could be placed graphically (in our graph presented earlier) on the end of the "continuum line:" not much motivation, a lot of fear and poor coordination. How can a pupil be helped to "move" his position toward the left side of the line? One has to improve somewhat all the three conditions of learning: motivation, less fear and motor coordination.

To *improve motivation,* the pupil has to get in return for his efforts some pleasurable thing. Skiing is very hard work at the beginning, and some instructor might not have that always in mind, since he might never have experienced it. In psychological terms the pleasurable things are called "reinforcements," and they are dispensed by the teacher or by the pupil to himself. In ski instructing these reinforcements could be:

• a good comment from the instructor
• A word of encouragement
• less effort in moving about with skis

Silhouetted against the coruscating rays of a welcome sun, Pre-Course candidate takes the last lift ride for one final run at Big Bromley.

- be with friend or family "up on the mountain," when proficiency is reached
- be less anxious and have more fun.

As mentioned earlier, a stimulating experience makes for excitement, and with a moderate amount of excitement the learning improves. Vivid, vital, pleasurable experiences are the easiest to remember and make for better learning. As excitement increases though, the learning decreases; so one has to be aware, as an instructor, not to allow an excessive amount to occur.

Since gaining *competence* in a sport is very important to increase motivation and therefore learning, we should now see how it could be increased. "Nothing succeeds like success," said a wise man once. Storing success in one's mind and heart gives self-confidence, which could be called "having competence." A pupil feels competent if he can make sense out of things; if he can find out how things work or how they are done; if he can do what others are doing; or if he gains control over himself and the environment. By following the rules, one is rewarded. It is similar to other situations of learning, such as social skills: the reward is to belong to the group. This reward, as noted earlier usually motivates a person to become competent. Competence, or

we could call it better fitness and ability, is built up gradually. In higher level classes, the intermediate or advanced skier will be able to recognize when to use different skills. For example: the person who had earlier learned the snowplow will decide to use it if he needs to slow down.

Considerable amount of effort on the part of the instructor seems to be needed in dealing with *fear* in his students. Frequently women display fear, but men experience it too. There are ways to reduce or minimize fear: if a person knows what to do if he is about to fall, in the way that it will not cause an injury, falling down will be considered less of a catastrophe. Or if a person can rehearse in his mind what sequence of movements should be followed when losing one's own balance, the reaction will be predictable and controlled. Fear is the result of not knowing what to do if something unexpected happened or if one does not know what lays ahead. In the case of a particularly complicated maneuver, it is more comfortable and less fearsome to know intellectually at least how to execute all the steps. A general rule the instructor should follow if a student is afraid, is, never ask too much of him and never mention the words: "fear" or "scared." A sense of comfort, relaxation and confidence in students is the result of the feeling that the instructor has a human and personal relationship to each of them.

Poor motor coordination and lack of physical fitness is very common in adult Americans, it is the result of our socio-economic development. At times one feels that there is not a great deal one can do about it. Motor coordination can improve (to reach the best personal level), if motivation and the level of competence are improved and anxiety is reduced. These two conditions are not always apparent and the instructor should be aware that merely asking to do something once more, there and then, might not work at all. Probably a "homework" (borrowing the term from regular school) assignment, is a better suggestion. "Homework," mentioned here has a purpose in learning: it is a form of self-instruction on a prescribed exercise, and it is an opportunity to practice what has just been learned, so as to make it an effortless, almost natural movement.

CONCLUSIONS

It is desirable to have a sense of the state of mind of each pupil. Ideally, a one to one ratio of instructors to pupils, such as in "private" lessons, would make this easier to achieve. But if this is not realistic at all times and a larger group is to be instructed, one has to remember that there are as many states of minds as there are people. Then the instructor has to generalize more his approach, to take care of many personal situations: one has to make a common denominator for all, with fun, comfort and an opportunity for achievement for all.

One final point: while skiing or making love, one should let the Ego out. It should be just fun. There should be nothing to prove. People should ski and enjoy it, without the pressure of the working world, like it is "back home." But as instructors you should know that this is not always so. Many people, while they ski, put their "image" at stake: it is directly tied in with their skiing performance. Sometimes one feels like one could see their Ego worn on the sleeves of their fashionable ski outfits.

So try to be aware of these points, take a tip from psychology and use common sense.

It was a pleasure to take a few free runs and get my feet back together. An occasional bump even inspired some avalement.

Paul McBride follows with ATM *open stance.*

After the talk, we snapped into our bindings and looked mournfully at the long trail of new snow that wound up Bromley Mountain, anticipating another training period on the novice slope. Allan looked at us, looked up toward the peak, and said, "Today, we will take a look at your free skiing form. Let's Ski!" With that, we all bolted toward the chairlift like a bunch of kids who had just been offered an ice cream cone! For three runs, no one spoke. The snow was like velvet. Its brilliance against the deep blue sky was only rivaled by over 200 smiles that bounced back the sunlight like icicles dripping off the pines. "I didn't know you guys had teeth!" laughed Allan as he beamed with pride at the progress of his class in less than a week.

Can you imagine giving up those perfect conditions for one last lecture? For some reason, the course coordinators scheduled a talk on Bindings by Carl Ettlinger for *noon* on Friday! "This guy had better be good!" I overheard one aspirant grumbling, as the thermometer rose and presented perfect snow conditions. Ettlinger *had* to be good. He held the group spellbound as he proceeded from notes on the evolution of the boot top fracture and supported his claims with slide projections. We got a look at spiral fractures (excessive twist), communuted fractures (many fracture sites) and compound fractures (bone through the skin). The high top boot has been instrumental in the decline of ankle injuries. Overall ski injuries are down over 50 percent in the past decade; ankle injuries are down over 70 percent! Two-thirds of all ski injuries are reportedly connected with *equipment,* notably from poorly adjusted bindings or from bindings that are incompatible with the boots of the skier! Ettlinger conducts his tests and surveys at Glen Ellen

Candidate Jeff O'Brien in a moment of serious contemplation. He scored well.

Mountain. While he did mention brand names in his talk, no part of it was with commercial intent. I thought it commendable that he didn't even mention which binding he personally uses. They are Burts. Ettlinger's talk and my discussions with another authority, Gordon Lipe have convinced me that plate bindings like the Burts are by far the safest and most dependable. One correlation that Carl did reveal is between high cost bindings and the lack of injuries. They are your legs; if you value them, don't spare the investment!

An afternoon of boogying down the Boulevard and Twister trails created moguls like those on Sun Valley's Exhibition. It was a truly inspiring and aesthetic experience to watch so many proficient skiers flying down one trail. A neat treat. At 3:30 we reported to the base lodge for our evaluation sheets and course completion certificates. Those who had achieved scores above 3 were encouraged to apply for one of the full certification exams during the season. We were graded for: A. *Free skiing,* with evaluation based upon: 1. Body Positioning, 2. Control, 3. Adaptability of Terrain; B. *Teaching,* with evaluation based upon: 1. Class handling, 2. Demonstration. 3. Correction of errors, 4. Presentation; C. *Slalom,* with evaluation based upon: 1. Stability, 2. Control, 3. Stance and body position; D. *Teaching Forms,* with evaluation based on preformance of maneuvers as described. My "report card" showed a perfect score. I am proud of it, but my satisfaction extends beyond that pride, as I feel that the entire course at Bromley enriched my awareness of the problems and answers peculiar to the ski teaching profession. I plan to take the final exam in March. Al Woods thinks that I'm a cinch for the badge, but then, that's only one man's opinion.

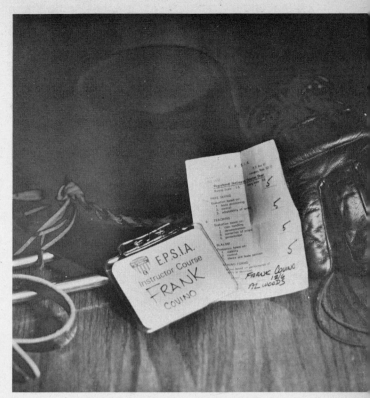

One man's opinion. Thank you, Al.

"I think you're a cinch for the badge," confided Al Woods, my Pre-Course conductor. He backed up his statement by giving me a perfect score on my evaluation sheet.

Chapter 8
MODERN SKIING
Is Stein Still King?

Chapter 8—MODERN SKIING WHAT IS NEW AND WHAT ISN'T

MY FIRST SKI LESSON was in the Arlberg tradition at Mont Tremblant in Quebec. Instructing for the Ernie McCullough Ski School, a ruddy faced bon vivant named Robert (pronounced Ro-Bayr) taught the class to wind up our upper bodies like corkscrews and follow through, powering each turn with a rotation of our torsos. For many years, this counter-rotation and rotation of the upper body was considered essential for positive steering at all levels of skiing proficiency.

Stein Eriksen came onto the ski scene from Norway with an innovative suggestion, borrowed from Isaac Newton's action-reaction principle. He eliminated the rotation and reasoned that the upper body working in opposition to the lower body is a natural movement. Thus, a twist of the torso uphill will naturally be countered by a twist of the hips, legs and skis in the opposing direction. *Reverse shoulder* was a term on the lips of every skier in the early fifties. Stein explained that a restriction of shoulder rotation would also keep the outside hip back and prevent overturning. His turns looked so graceful, we all tried to imitate them.

The Austrians agreed with the reverse shoulder principle but attacked the "windup" or counter-rotation of the

"The way we ski has been *modern* for 20 years . . ." Stein Eriksen, Park City, Utah, Ski School Director.

shoulders as an unnecessary motion. Their variation kept the skier's torso facing downhill at all times. Their economy of motion allowed for longer runs with less fatigue. Once again we modified our style.

Ski technique might have remained right there, were it not for drastic equipment changes. French racing analysts, obsessed with the compulsive drive to be the fastest in the world, noted that skis would accelerate if they were thrust forward by "jetting" the feet. To enable their racers to recover from this moment of speed and imbalance they demanded from boot manufacturers a high-backed boot. In addition, they advised ski manufacturers to move back the side camber or waist of their skis, which facilitated turning from a "sitting-back" position. Our speed increased and once again we modified our skiing posture.

Avalement and *anticipation* became the watchwords on the lips of skiers from the mid '60s to the present day, but these two movements are not necessarily new. While he may not have used the terms, Stein Eriksen was employing both movements in his skiing over 20 years ago. In his book, *Come Ski With Me,* four pages of illustrations clearly illustrate both "new" concepts. On pages 136 and 137, the movement of *anticipation* could not be more clearly demonstrated. To quote Stein: "The pole change must be quick, in a pendulum action alongside the body. One pole replaces the other as you prepare for the next turn." (Fig. 8-4) You will notice in Stein's third position, when his uphill pole basket begins to move forward, that his torso begins to dive toward the fall line *anticipating* his new direction. By retracting his heels, changing his leading ski and rolling his ski tips onto their inside edges, his turn carves automatically, with the help of that anticipatory movement. Position 5 shows the classic angulation popularized by Stein and currently under attack by *modern* ski schools which advocate skiing with the feet apart. With the feet together, centripetal force (the physical force that pulls toward the center of the turn, in opposition to centrifugal force which pulls outside the arc) would cause him to spill uphill if he did not keep his torso *perpendicular to the slope,* especially on steep, icy terrain. Another device cleverly employed by Stein on steep hard packed terrain is what the Austrians called *schrittbogen,* lifting the tail of the inside ski to insure body weight pressure against the inside edge of his outside ski, shown clearly in position 4.

Turning to pages 138 and 139 in Stein's book, we see a perfect demonstration of the "modern" avalement maneuver for skiing the bumps. (Fig. 8-5) Stein was *swallowing* the moguls by retracting his knees before Patrick Russel, the model for Joubert's book on the *new* French technique, was even born! The third and fourth positions here are the noteworthy ones. In position 3, we see Stein's knees retracting simultaneously as his outside pole basket begins to

Fig. 8-4: Illustrations from *Come Ski With Me* by Stein Eriksen, pgs. 136 and 137. From the bottom, clockwise: Figure 1) Stein checks hard, using HIP power, to create a PLATFORM of snow. 2) He bounces off the platform. Tails are airborne as he begins to retract his knees. 3) Full retraction. Inside ski tail is lifted higher to insure weighting of his outside ski when he regains contact with the snow. He changes his leading ski! 4) Look at the ANTICIPATION as he punches his uphill fist toward the fall line. His outside ski is set hard onto its inside edge. 5) Classic displacement of his lower body marks Stein's ANGULATION. He rides his inside edges. 6) Still on his inside edges, Stein begins to advance his pole for the next turn. 7) Pole ready. Watch his hip . . . 8) Pow! The PLATFORM. Stein's is the only turn that features a momentary swing of the hip *downhill* in preparation. This creates a more formidable platform of snow than mere feel thrust. 9) The bounce. Tails are displaced to the outside of the turn. 10) Knee retraction. A little less this time keeps his skis on the snow. His inside ski moves ahead. 11) The inimitable Stein Eriksen ANGULATION. It is my contention that there is no more beautiful way to ski. Advocates of the "modern" style, with their training wheels stance, frequently ski that way as a cop-out for technical inadequacy. Don't let them snow you. You can ski with as much stability and look a lot more graceful with your feet together.

7

8

9

10

11

3

2

1

2   1

Fig. 8-5: Illustrations from *Come Ski With Me* by Stein Eriksen, pgs. 138 and 139. The arrows are mine. Counter-clockwise: Figure 1) Stein prepares for his turn by sinking DOWN with a hard edge set. Skis bend into reverse camber. 2) Stein springs UP. Camber snaps back. There is air under his skis. His boots JET forward. 3) Stein RETRACTS his knees to "swallow" the bump. His torso is beginning to move

DOWNHILL. *Pure avalement*! 4) Look at Stein's outside arm. His fist punches downhill as he advances his outside pole. *Anticipation!* 5) Both hands forward to weight the ski tips and thus keep them in contact with the snow. Note change of his leading ski! 6) Pure *angulation*! On his inside edges, Stein carves the finish of his turn with his torso 90 degrees to the angle of the slope.

pendulum forward. In position 4, the pole basket continues to swing forward as he punches his torso toward the new direction (anticipation). Look also at his boots, they are jetting forward to keep his skis in contact with the snow. You will also notice a barely perceptible lift of his inside ski tail as he changes his leading ski. In position 5, Stein is on his inside edges *before* he has even reached the fall line! In the final illustration of this sequence, the inclination of Stein's lower body is greater than 45 degrees. If his torso was not perpendicular to the angle of the slope, he would be chewing snow flakes!

Well, if *anticipation* and *avalement* are not really *new* techniques, what exactly *is* new about modern skiing? My opinion is this:

1. The adoption of a shorter ski for learning (GLM)
2. Equipment modifications:
   a. high-backed boots with high heels
   b. stiffer tailed skis
   c. retarded side cambers on skis
   d. shallow grooves down the middle of skis
   e. turned up tails on skis
3. Acrobats joining the sport
4. Outrageous colors and fits in ski clothing
5. Beards, long-haired men, and no brassieres.

The shorter ski concept, more than any other innovation, has changed the face of skiing. Important contributors to ski education like Clif Taylor and Karl Pfeiffer showed us that skis can be turned by axial motion along with little unweighting if: 1) the skis are short, 2) the side camber (if any) is moved farther back, 3) the skier is in a crouched *athletic* position with all joints flexed, 4) the new direction is anticipated by a movement of the torso in that direction, 5) the skis are *skidded* rather than carved, 6) the slope is not much of a grade.

The high-backed boot was a blessing. It not only prevented the most common beginner error of *sitting back* but also kept his knees in a plumb line with his toes, where they must be for optimum control.

Hotshots soon learned that they could *jet* their boots forward and allow gravity to begin the pull of their ski tips downhill. The new "retarded" side camber allows a neat turn to be carved on the stiffer tails of modern skis, and the curved-up tails even allow for controlled "wheelies." Moreover, when the fall line has been reached in this type of modern turn, the new high-backed, high-heeled boots allow for easy resumption of tip pressure to keep the skier in balance during the last part of his turn.

Acrobats on the scene have certainly changed the face of

our sport. Excessively, I might add. The inherent dangers of applauding their heroics and allowing them to dominate the skiing trade magazines is that they are scaring away many potential participants in the sport by providing an inconceivable level of aspiration. It is one thing to try to convince an unathletic individual that he has the ability to ski with safe, controlled turns, and quite another to try to convince him that he is capable of performing a moebius flip. The real danger is that excessive fanfare for the flipping freaks might change our sport into another spectator sport rather than one whose pleasures are available to all. Don't get me wrong. Some of the aerial and ballet boys are my very good friends. I respect their achievements and envy their daring, but as an old adventurous veteran who still gets a thrill out of linking figure-eights in the shadow of the Matterhorn, I can't look at any of the various aerial or ground contortions and say to myself honestly: This is skiing. For many of us, that's not "where it's at." If that's your bag, by all means, go for it. *Just don't tell me that "this is skiing." Its so much more.*

For many of us, skiing represents healthy escape, from a white collar and tie society bent so avariciously into the power syndrome that it is choked with various forms of pollution and overpopulation. Skiing is a flight away from the 9-to-5 program. It is clean air and blue skies, diamond sparkled snow that invites the caressing strokes of finely tuned skis. It is a wind that bites your cheeks; a challenge to

Stein doesn't always ANGULATE. Here, he *banks* an inclinated turn in deep Park City powder. Centrifugal force holds him secure against a platform of snow that props his outside ski *higher* than his inside ski, like the banked track of a cyclist. Don't try it on an icy slope!

your romantic spirit; an invitation to your explorative curiosity. There is always another mountain to ski, another country that beckons. Skiing is a challenge that offers an attainable goal, and that proficiency must be earned, it cannot be bought. Skiing is a man and a woman, blending as one in the pleasure of an intangible sensation. Skiing is a man, alone. It is a high, a rush, a comfort, a peace. This is modern skiing, but it is also antique skiing. While techniques may change and pseudo-technicians who claim their methods as the only way to ski will come and go, and even after some ski gymnast does 83 back flips from a low flying plane, skiing will remain an invitation to exotic adventure extended to *anyone* who only dares to participate.

Let's get an authoritative point of view from Stein Eriksen. He was the first professional to do a full layout front flip on skis. (Fig. 8-6) Few of the modern aerialists can perform that trick as flawlessly as Stein Eriksen. Today, the former Olympic champion and first winner of three gold medals directs the ski school at Park City, Utah, one of the most complete ski complexes in the world. If I occasionally sound biased in my affection for the man, it is because I was fortunate enough to have taught skiing under his direction for 3 years. We also traveled with the International Ski Show circuit for 4 years performing what came to be known as a "chalk-talk," a visually aided instructional program wherein Stein did the talking and I did the chalking. If there has to be a King of the Mountain in our sport, one who has contributed more to our understanding and enjoyment of it, and one who can still show up the best of modern skiers boogying down a bump run, it must be Stein. He has mastered the total science of skiing. His skiing style is precise, dynamic and inimitable. Here is what Stein had to say to SKIER'S DIGEST about modern skiing:

"Modern skiing . . . Old fashioned skiing . . . Arlberg . . . Reverse shoulder . . . Avalement . . . Anticipation . . . Jet-turns . . . Put it all together. We do it. All of it; sometime or another during our skiing years. Looking back at what we used to teach 20 years ago or at what was taught even before that time, it all links together. Read an instructional book of today, the American Teaching Method, for instance, and compare it to what has been written during the past 20 years, with regard to "methodology." Many of the "old" exercises have merely been adapted in the "new" methods of today and have been given new names. In a nutshell, we have skied the "modern" way for many, many years, as far as I am concerned. The vocabulary has changed. So have the ways of explaining basic maneuvers, but the way good skiers ski has been modern for 20 years."

SKIER'S DIGEST appreciates your statement, Stein. All things considered, we give you our vote for King of the Mountain, in sincere appreciation for the example of perfection of form that you have set, which is an inspiration to anyone who has ever seen you ski. You are a valuable asset to the Park City ski resort in Utah and reason enough to lure any serious skier to that exciting part of the country. If you can't take a run with Stein, at least take a lesson from an instructor who is under his direction. You may learn a few new things. You may also learn that those new things are 20-years-old.

Fig. 8-6: Stein flips!

Chapter 9
FREESTYLE GENESIS
Where It All Began

Eddie Wyka Free-Dogging on St. Mary's Glacier, Colorado.

CHAPTER 9—FREESTYLE GENESIS: WHERE IT ALL BEGAN

IT WAS ABOUT the mid '60s. For two decades, skiers of the United States had been subjected to conjecture from evey nation on how to ski, via hordes of European instructors who were imported by hungry ski resorts because of their skiing proficiency, their accents and their glamorous image. What was more exasperating than their inability to speak English was their chauvinistic rejection of skiing methods developed in other countries. Ethnic factions sprung up within our skiing cities that expanded the list of prejudiced groups then prevalent in our society. Over the din of garbled voices at cocktail parties and in the smoke-filled ski buses, you could occasionally hear the admonitions: "Oh, he skis *Austrian*"; ". . . Are you still skiing *Arlberg*?"; ". . . Don't you know how to ski *French*, man?" American instructors were trying hard to compete with the European giants by organizing and developing our own national system. American recreational skiers were confused.

At that time, I was teaching the Stein Eriksen Ski School technique at Sugarbush Valley, Vermont, which bore some resemblance to the American technique, but which incorporated some characteristics that were diametrically opposed to the American system. Stein had a few ideas of his own that made his style for most, inimitable. One Saturday morning, a sudden spring rain sent thousands of weekend skiers scurrying to their cars. "What can we do?" asked Stein, certain that the rain would turn to snow in an hour or two. "If we could just hold them . . ." I suggested holding a "chalk-talk" in the Gatehouse cafeteria. Together, we devised a teaching method that saved the day for Sugarbush and gave us material for a successful road show during the following fall. Stein "talked" ski instruction while I "chalked" on an overhead projector. We were both amazed at the enthusiastic audience response. It made me realize that, in this country, at least skiers appreciated knowing some of the science behind their movements on skis. Thousands of skiers let us know how much they appreciated our logical explanations of why a ski turns and how to best turn it. Collectively, our audiences convinced us that they wanted more than the "Follow Me" approach currently advocated by some trade journalists under the disguise of the "Inner Skier" method. The response to our newspaper column, "Ski Tips" corroborated that need for scientific analysis before practical application.

Our "Chalk-Talk" traveled from coast to coast as a feature attraction of the Leonard-Simons International Ski and Winter Sports Fair. These "Ski Shows" quickly became a vital part of the recreational skier's programming in preparation for the approaching season. At the shows winter friends are reunited annually, new skis and bindings are exposed for promotion, ski resorts build lavish displays to lure consumers to their areas, new ski movies compete with each other for the admiration of their impatient-to-ski audiences, and, sporadically, during each weekend of the 3- or 4-day conventions, all eyes stop wandering to fix in amazement on the various stunts performed on the Ski-Dek, a moving carpet that spins upward over rollers like a conveyor belt, simulating downhill movements of performing skiers above it.

While the Ski-Dek was used by ski racing champions like Stein Eriksen, Anderl Molterer, Tony Sailer and others to demonstrate their form and teach basic ski technique, it never was used more efficiently than by its inventor, Phil Gerard, in the production of a spectacular musical extravaganza, during one of the years that Stein and I toured with the shows. On the Dek, as its principal performer, was a wide-eyed, touseled haired young boy named John, whose tight-fitting stretch pants revealed a pair of stone hard legs that could turn a pair of skis faster and in more directions than anyone had ever seen. His partner was a pretty blonde delight named Tara (whatever happened to you) who followed John's movements and literally danced with him while skiing on the moving carpet! I can still hear the background music of "Up, Up and Away" as a hundred balloons were released amidst colored lights that made John and Tara's beautiful skiing ballet psychedelic. This was years before anyone had heard the word psychedelic. It was also over a decade before ballet and stunt skiing became a part of our sport. John's last name is Clendenin. You may have seen him in the memorable K2 ski film that blew everone's mind. He went on to become a freestyle champion. John can turn 'em both ways! He's dynamite! Outta sight!

But John might be no more than a Malibu beachcomber today, were it not for the efforts of the teacher behind him, Phil Gerard. Curiously, Gerard is responsible for many of the best "talents" of the freestylists including those of the number one queen of our sport, Suzy Chaffee, Bill O'Leary, Bob Salerno, Jim Rollins and many others. That could be because Phil is a true Renaissance man who believes that *talent* is a phenomenon composed of very human traits, not the least of which is intelligence. About 500 years ago Benedetto Croce said, "There are no born cooks, and no born poets." Gerard would add that there are no born skiers. His approach to the mastery of the sport is wholly intellectual. The brochure that advertises his ski school called "Ski World" (17815 Ventura Boulevard in Encino, California) boasts: "You can be an expert skier this season AND WE GUARANTEE IT! The only physical requirement is the ability to walk into our shop." The flyer should add, "You do need a brain," for that is the principal part of the body to which Phil's instruction appeals. Phil says, "Learn the physical rules of skiing before going on the ski slopes!" To help you he has devised his own system, called "The Method" which

Poetry in motion. Beautiful Suzy Chaffee swings a little wedeln with technician Phil Gerard, who has trained the best of skiing's freestylists off season on his magical moving carpet.

guarantees that he will make you a better skier or give you your money (a modest fee) back at the end of the course. Needless to say, he hasn't had to do that yet. He "sells" nothing but guidance that will improve your form on skis after it defines absolute physical principles that work together to produce that good form. Helping this goal is a larger version of the Ski-Dek used on the Ski Show Circuit which makes use of a horizontal bar to help new skiers (or new freestylists) balance themselves until they master their particular exercise. (Fig. 9-2) Phil proves that advanced freestyle forms are merely extensions of basic moves taught to the beginning recreational skier on his Ski-Dek.

He is as opposed to the reckless, uncontrolled form of the "Go for it!" skier—who pulls out all the corks as he skids from bump to bump on a flat ski, praying for a safe finish—as many ski educators who fear that such radical aberrations are scaring away potential participators from the sport of skiing. On the other hand, Phil recognizes freestyle as an important extension of what was once a relatively conservative sport. By analyzing freestyle movements, on the snow or in the air, Gerard has devised a logical progression toward their mastery that defends these movements as credible inclusions in the ski educational curriculum. I personally can't wait until I visit Encino for my first freestyle lesson on the Ski-Dek.

Here is Phil Gerard to tell SKIER'S DIGEST readers a little about himself and his opinions of the modern ski scene:

PHIL GERARD ON TODAY'S SKIING

I was asked to wite an article about myself. That is a very difficult thing to do. To require a person to point out the virtuous aspects of his past and present endeavors is akin to asking him to thrust his head into a hole in a canvas wall that suddenly becomes the target of abuse for the waiting audience, the mildly curious, and the disinterested as well as the interested. The present controversy raging over freestyle skiing easily converts my pie to poison for others—as I consider freestyle an amelioration, or betterment, of our sport. Many more conservatives are of the opposite opinion. Ironically, this conservative faction of our sport has been and is now a major asset to freestyle in the form of opposite polar energy. Without this form of energy freestyle skiing would have taken a fragmented direction. As it stands, freestyle is required to qualify its departures in a classical, timeless fashion. Its movements are required to reflect primary constants that allow no margin for error or dispute. In a sport that has displayed as many technical approaches as there are people involved in it, this requirement is a decided advancement that will ultimately inure to the benefit of all concerned; therefore, the conservatives are as important as the innovators. They impose a pensiveness on those of us who are not pensive by nature. Freestyle has become the natural outgrowth of the normal human inclination to polish a discovered diamond . . . skiing is the diamond and freestyle is now

It takes an alert mind and acute balance to perform some free-style stunts. Ed Wyka shows he has both at Sugarbush Valley, Vermont.

Suzy Chaffee, once an Olympic contender, has traded in her racing skis for ballet boards. Here she practices a classic Reuel with the help of the Ski-Dek's balance beam.

the burnished gleam of that diamond. It has reached this elevation, by the combined energy, direction and dedication of not only those that are in it but those who brought skiing to where it could be fashioned in this way.

The people who actually put the physical elements together, combined the elements in other closely enough related sports to be applicable to skiing, and produced freestyle skiing are many. In short, nobody brought skiing to ballet, skiing to gymnastics and acrobatics or skiing to skating. All these sports were brought to skiing in the same manner ballet was brought to skating or diving, and acrobatics and gymnastics were brought to the trampoline. So the creation of freestyle skiing is once again, like any other creation, the combination of elements that already exist. The credibility or validity of these combinations is directly commensurate with the familiarity and depth of understanding of those elements that are being combined. The only critics of freestyle skiing are other skiers who lay claim to a purity that exists only in their imaginations. The only real challenge the creators of freestyle had—and still have to quite a considerable degree—is the lack of an indisputable, mechanically optimum, basic technique to apply these other sports to. This missing element is now surfacing, thru necessity, and will present skiing in a more acceptable light to that segment of the public who would like to try skiing but requires more comprehensive information to try it than is currently available.

The sensitivity surface of our sport has been extended by the addition of feminity, with its attendant subtle aspects of music, supple motion, responsiveness and emotional capacities. This has contributed effectively to the submerging of the image held by the general public that skiers were an obvious manifestation of the death wish, and those who supplied them with the fiendish instruments of demise a blight in the advancement of our civilization. I cannot lay enough stress on the necessity of this change. For those of us professionally involved in this sport, this change will attract the more cautious, a group never before available to the ski industry. The prudent utilization and exploitation of this recent trend in the general public's hide is paramount and will determine the timely advance of our income that should be commensurate with the energy requirements and an awareness of our endeavors in this direction. The general public's acceptance of our sport and its participation will provide the "big corporate brother" that Beconta's Jim Woolner tells us we require for survival.

The attempts to present freestyle in the same reckless abandon manner that racing was presented to the public is a tendency that has to be subdued if the professionals in our sport are to experience more than the meager existence the former negative publicity of personal jeopardy provided. The ballet discipline of freestyle is the positive force that will captivate and lure the potential skier to active financial participation. The ballet discipline has made every slope, no matter how small it is, a place of satisfactory participation. The challenge is no longer the mountain but the skiers themselves. Graceful kinesthetics appeal and encourage participation. Physical risk interests the curious but repels and inhibits their participation.

In this manner freestyle in general, and ballet skiing in particular, has been and is now an extreme departure from

Al Tweeter and Rick Bates carve perfect outriggers on the Lone Pine Practice slope, Mt. Norquay, Alberta, Canada. This popular ballet stunt, and most others currently in vogue, were the inventions of ballet technician Phil Gerard and date back all the way to the early 1960's!

Unidentified skier pulls off a spectacular *helicopter turn* with the Victoria Glacier as a backdrop, Lake Louise Ski Area, Alberta, Canada. Phil Gerard was doing spins like this on his rolling carpet Ski-Dek in 1965. His aerial and ballet moves have been the inspiration for the whole current freestyle movement.

the esoteric sport from which it was derived. It is making a positive impact in that sport financially as well as esthetically. To know that myself and some of the people I have trained and helped train have had a major influence in fashioning and initiating this sport is extremely satisfying to me. This is a great deal more compensation than is generally available to anyone in a lifetime. Internal recognition of your efforts in this world has a higher value than external recognition, once your understanding of the scheme of things increases.

Some of the freestyle competitors I have had the pleasure of offering my ideas and facilities to and exchanging information with are: John Clendenin, Bill O'Leary, Suzy Chaffee, Jim Rollins, Dianne Beard, Bob Salerno, Mike Williams, Peter Johnson, Mike Lund and others. My ski school in Encino, California, includes a revolving Ski-Dek, trampoline, ballet school and a rather unique ski jump. It is in the middle of the huge Los Angeles metropolis. The Freestyle School is located behind the regular school that is geared solely for recrea-

tional skiers. The moment any information surfaces that can be used to more easily communicate to recreational skiers how to turn right and left, it is immediately included in their regular training practice—because freestyle, to me, is research and development for recreational skiing."

Thank you, Phil. SKIER'S DIGEST salutes your efforts as an asset to the industry and your school as a vital source of information to the uninformed skier at all levels.

While we consider you to be one of the most influential sources of the freestyle movement, we must also acknowledge the following precursors without whom the sport of skiing would not enjoy its present breadth. SKIER'S DIGEST recognizes:

1. Dr. Fritz Reuel's book in 1929, entitled *New Possibilities in Skiing* wherein he correlated skiing with the art of figure skating. The cover of this book illustrated the "Royal Christy," a decidedly unconventional turn on one ski which is now a common movement in the classic freestylist's repertoire.

2. Emile Allais's free and flowing "mambo" turn of 1951, which employed Issac Newton's physical principle of action followed by reaction, in relation to twists of the torso effecting turns to the opposite direction.

3. The mambo was popularized in this country by another freestyle contributor, Olympic champion Stein Eriksen, who was also first to amaze the skiing public with full layout back and front somersaults off man-made kickers. I helped build some of those kickers at Sugarbush Valley, when I was an instuctor in Stein's Ski School, and can testify that never have the two flip variations been more perfectly performed. Would you believe—on 210cm skis!

4. Hermann Goellner and Tom Le Roi for shocking the world and even Stein with their *multiple* flips, seen by the masses at the Fall Ski Shows in the first of the great ski films sponsored by Hart, *The Incredible Skis,* and then again in the *Moebius Flip,* in 1965 by Summit Films, Roger Brown and Barry Corbett's new company which took the

documentary character out of ski films and created visually stimulating works of art for their skiing audience.

5. Art Furrer, probably the first real acrobat on skis to put together a continous ballet routine that included the Javelin turn, the Stepover, 360 degree turns and the Charleston. And the late Roger Staub, who clowned with Furrer on Phil Gerard's Ski-Dek in 1965 to give the public the first glimpse of the limitless possibilities of freestyle skiing, all dependent upon the mastery of edge control. I took Roger's place as Furrer's clown in a demonstration on a small Ski-Dek at the Newark, New Jersey, Shopping Mall several years ago, and can tell you personally that there is a good deal of science involved in the ballet and stunts you see performed on the Dek. I took a spill the first time, but was reassured by Art when he said that Tony Sailer had done the same his first time on the Dek.

6. *Ski* Magazine and their contributing editor Doug Pfeiffer who took a hard whack at the regimented final forms of ski schools of the '60s and motivated the recalcitrant iconoclasm that was welcomed by the drug oriented youth of that era. While they paid the hard way for their "free" expression (many fractures and at least three paralyses that I know of), they did loosen up the classical academic dogma of the ski schools and showed us that there truly is more than "vun vay to schki!" At the same time, their bruises taught them that even freestyle maneuvers demand disciplines which have scientific bases that could easily be related to the basic disciplines of modern ski schools. Pfeiffer's rat pack was like the discordant noise of modern art. Radical and diametrically opposed to classical form, it was initially welcomed by an equally recalcitrant and iconoclastic society. But society has a way of choking itself with hedonistic excesses that oppose academic principles and then, just before it is extinguished in the chaos of wild disunity, it recognizes the necessity of a return to a classical mean. In other words, Pfeiffer and his "hot-dogs" have cleaned up their act. They may not have gotten haircuts yet, but their overalls have been replaced with psychedelic stretch suits, and they look a lot cleaner. What is of greater significance though, is that they have analyzed their "free" forms of expression on skis and discovered that they could *control* their aberrated movements with logical extensions of the basic skill of edge control. Even the aerialists at the freestyle camps are startled to hear officious directions from their instructors like "Get your hips high!" or "Keep your eyes on that spot" as they spin, instead of just "Go for it!" As sure as the art appreciators of our era are getting tired of pseudo-critics equating outrageous innovations with *quality,* at the expense of craft, so the skiing public has recognized the difference between a mogul run in good form and an uncontrolled suicidal free fall that rides the thin line between victory and serious disaster.

7. The P.S.I.A. for recognizing that the stunts of ballet and freestyle are merely extensions of basic skills which are taught in the American Teaching Method curriculum, and for including these movements as optional post-graduate work in their training program.

Freestyle is here to stay, and the sport of skiing is all the better for it. If I wasn't over forty, I would *"go upside down,"* myself. I just don't heal as quickly as I used to. Now, tell us, Phil, whatever became of Tara?

Freestylist Buck Duncan in a 360 outrigger. (Photo by Greg Albracht)

Chapter 10
A PRIVATE LESSON WITH JEAN-CLAUDE KILLY

CHAPTER 10—A PRIVATE LESSON WITH JEAN-CLAUDE KILLY

IN 1975 I EDITED a book called *133 Ski Lessons* by Jean-Claude Killy. The publisher was DBI Books Inc. Basically, it was a compilation of newspaper columns written by the triple gold medal Olympic champion, with the help of Doug Pfeiffer. If you haven't seen it, find it, as you will welcome its addition to your skiing library. Well illustrated by Tony Ravielli, the Killy columns provide useful advice for the beginner, the intermediate and the advanced skier.

I was one of the first skiers to resent the first Killy manuscripts published in one of the popular ski magazines. At that time, the magazine felt that a description of Killy's unorthodox *rucklage* manner of accelerating his skis would make stimulating if not controversial copy that would elicit good reader response. I don't know how many readers responded, but my letter of deprecation appeared in their "Letters to the Editor" column, and I soon regretted it. In my letter, I said something about questioning the validity of a racer giving advice to a recreational skier. I also put down the "sitting back" posture as dangerous and practical only to the professional whose oak tree thighs are strong enough to help him recover from that precariously unbalanced position. My final *faux pas* was to ridicule Killy's wide track stance and put him down for encouraging the skier to employ a similar posture when skiing for recreation. One week after my letter was published, I found myself sharing the bill on the International Ski Show circuit with, you guessed it, Jean-Claude Killy. We had to perform in six major cities from coast to coast with about four shows a day and three or four shows on weekends. My gig was an audio-visual ski instruction presentation called a "Chalk-Talk" which was partially sponsored by Kneissl Skis. Killy performed under a special tent sponsored by Head and Chevrolet. Some M.C. pumped Jean-Claude with tacky questions in between films and slide shows of his racing accomplishments. The crowd loved it. We played to over half a million skiers that year, and I got to know Jean-Claude a little better. I was embarassed for having written that letter.

Lots of snow has fallen since then. Recently, a P.S.I.A. examiner put me down for "sitting back" on my skis! On the slopes today, there appear to be more skiers using the wide stance than those who keep their feet together! Styles have changed along with equipment and perhaps the greatest awareness that has developed among ski writers is that there are indeed *many* ways to descend a slope. It is the wise skier who listens to all new theories and tests each for himself. How else can we arrive at a style that suits our *particular* personalities, our individual physical and mental capacities, our singular emotional needs?

Jean-Claude Killy could be skiing's greatest hero; certainly, he has proven to be one of its greatest racers. The columns he has written are authoritative, meaningful manuscripts that may be added to any file on classical technique. They imply authorship by the unknown Killy—the technician, the scientist, the academician. Although he admits to never having attended a typical ski class, his words indicate a profound awareness of methodology that may astound you.

In this chapter, we have borrowed the question and answer segment of *133 Ski Lessons* by Jean-Claude Killy to tease you into purchasing his book. Fifty Questions, with the champion's answers. Your private lesson with Jean-Claude. *A votre sant*é.

QUESTIONS AND ANSWERS

Following is a compilation of questions most frequently asked of Olympic World Champion, Jean-Claude Killy. Like most great athletes, his answers to such purging are brief, thorough and authoritative. Slightly chauvinistic, Killy strongly defends French systems, products, etc., but at no time has he deprecated any other product nor put down any other skier for differences in style, theory or technique. He is a true champion in every sense of the word.

Weight Distribution

Q. Is it true that you ski with your weight distribution on both skis equally, rather than mostly on the downhill ski?

A. Yes, most of the time my weight is on both skis, but there are many exceptions. Sometimes my weight is on the uphill ski, as for example when I come out of a gate too low and must skate up. When I sit back, often my weight will be on the downhill ski.

The point is, I don't decide in advance where my weight is going to be. I adapt myself to the terrain. I weight the skis equally, or I weight the uphill or downhill ski, or I sit back or go forward—all as needed. Versatility is what makes the great skier.

Are Arms Important?

Q. What part do the arms play in competition skiing?

A. The arms are quite important. On icy slopes, you frequently need to dig in with your poles. And in downhill, how you carry your arms is important to your speed. Wind tunnel experiments have shown you can lose seconds by holding the arms too far from the body. We sewed our bibs (racing numbers) to our jackets and wore tighter clothing after we saw the results of those tests.

But you can't always ski in an optimum aerodynamic position. The arms are needed for balance, and they must be ready for poling. That's why strengthening the arms must not be neglected in any conditioning program.

Choice of Ski Length

Q. In a film I saw of you skiing, I noticed you used two different ski lengths. What are the different conditions that determine your choice?

A. I use different lengths according to the different events, the different kinds of races, not for different kinds of snow conditions. For slalom, I always use 207 cm. For GS, I've used 212 or 215 cm. And for downhill, I've used everything from 219 to 230 cm, though I've found 220 cm to be best for me. For recreational skiing, I generally use something around 210 cm. As you might guess, the general rule should be, the faster you ski, the longer the ski should be; the more turns you make, the shorter it should be—provided it is long enough to give you stability at the speed you want to go.

Are Wood Skis Competitive?

Q. Would a racer today stand any chance of winning an event if he were using one of the topnotch wood skis that racers used a decade ago?

A. Provided he were racing against others of roughly the same ability, he would stand no chance of scoring a good time.

Relaxation

Q. How do you relax before a race?

A. Relaxing before a race is simply a matter of knowing you have done everything you could to prepare properly for the race.

Philosophy of a Skier

Q. Andre Maurois wrote, "The body of an athlete and the soul of a wise man—this is what is needed to be happy." Is skiing a source of wisdom in itself—a world or the world in miniature—or is it an escape from the demands of life?

A. For me, skiing is a world in itself. It's close to nature—but there's nothing miniature about it. Everyone must find his own answer, but for me, I enjoy skiing for its own sake, not as an escape from anything.

Why Haven't U.S. Skiers Done Well?

Q. Why do you think U.S. men skiers have not done so well in international competition?

A. Back in 1964, when Bill Kidd and Jim Heuga won their Olympic silver and bronze medals at Innsbruck, I thought the U.S. team really had it made. All the guys were going to college, and still they were in the top of the international class racing brackets. Well, now I'm not sure. It's a big handicap not to ski all of the time. Maybe it's better that the Americans do go to school, but I think that is why they are not able to beat the Europeans who ski 100 percent of the time.

Fastest Speed

Q. What's the fastest you ever skied?

A. I went to Cortina one summer to compete in the speed trials. But I had the wrong equipment, so I didn't do very well. The fastest I reached was 160 kilometers an hour (just under 100 mph).

Extra Speed

Q. In a number of your races in the Killy Challenge, you seemed to be even with your opponent up to the last gate and then managed to get an extra burst of speed to beat him. How did you do that?

A. Though it may seem that a race is won between the last gate and the finish line, that is rarely the case. The momentum builds up for several gates beforehand. In the Killy Challenge, it is possible the camera angle created the illusion that I was winning with a sudden burst of speed.

Of course, there are things a racer can do to pick up fractions of seconds at the finish line. I always study where the electric eye is to see whether it will help to jet my skis out in front at the finish. I also check to see whether the finish line is parallel to the last gate. If not, I might shave a hundredth of a second off my time by coming out of that gate close to the pole that is nearest the finish line.

The Biggest Threat

Q. In the Killy Challenge, who posed the biggest threat?

A. Because of the handicap system, all were threats. But Pepi Stiegler was the one who came closest to beating me. First of all, he was familiar with racing over parallel courses. Secondly, he was in good shape. And finally, he is still a very strong, very dangerous skier.

Memorize the Course?

Q. Must a racer memorize a slalom course?

A. Though you don't have to memorize a whole course, it is necessary to memorize the traps and places where you have to change rhythm. Otherwise you may not know where you have to slow down, where it would be suicidal to go all out. But in practicing slalom, it's best not to memorize a course so that you can develop your instincts and reflexes.

Boots—Rigid or Not?

Q. On a downhill course, should your boots give some play to the ankles, or is it best to have complete rigidity?

A. Personally, I like my boots to be unyielding. But I know some very good racers who never fasten the top buckle when they run downhill so they'll have some play. It's whatever gives you the best control that counts.

Racing Head-to-Head

Q. Do you prefer racing head-to-head, as the pros do, and as you did on the Killy Challenge, to racing the clock as the amateurs do?

A. I like them both. I like being alone on the course, going all out for the best time. But I also like the excitement of the man-to-man event. In any case, I think the future belongs to the parallel courses because it is so much more interesting for the TV viewer.

Is Skier's Height Important?

Q. Do you have to be tall to be a good downhiller?

A. No. Karl Schranz, one of the world's greatest downhillers, is not tall. Neither is Henri Duvillard nor Leo Lacroix nor any number of other fine downhillers. Technique, not height, is what counts. Some people say that if you are heavier, you have an advantage in acceleration, but on the other hand, your skis might sink into the snow more.

There are many theories on the subject, but I've never seen any proofs. All I know is that both small men and big men have won downhill races.

Obsession With Speed

Q. When did you decide to be a ski racer?

A. There was no particular moment when I decided upon that direction. I received my first skis when I was five and have spent most of my life on them. My obsession with speed on skis prompted my parents to nickname me *Toutoune,* for I have always attacked the sport like a wild dog.

First Victory

Q. Where and when was your first skiing victory?

A. There were many unofficial contests, between myself and the other children of Val d'Isere, but my first competition *avec dossard* was for a cup presented by Holland's Queen Juliana. The event was slalom. I was eight.

Form is Not as Important as Speed

Q. You have been criticized for your lack of form and seeming awkwardness racing through the gates. Do you deprecate the final forms employed by ski instructors?

A. I have the ability to imitate anyone's ski form. If I choose to stray from picture perfect style for a moment in lieu of losing my spontaneity and speed, it is because I race to win. The clock is the final arbiter in any racing event, not the camera.

Injuries

Q. Have you ever broken a leg?

A. In my early teens, when ski boots were too soft to offer my ankle protection, and bindings were still primitive, I competed for the Ilio Colli Cup at Cortina d'Ampezzo in Italy and suffered a minor fracture. My three months of recuperation only stoked the coals of competition which burned inside me. In less than half a year I was racing again. Ironically, I broke my leg again at the Ilio Colli in early 1962, which prevented me from competing for the World Championships at Chamonix that year.

First International Win

Q. When did you win your first international competition and in what event?

A. That was a slalom contest, the Grand Prix de Morzine, in 1961. It was a memorable occasion, culminating in a much more prized award: that of the rooster, official emblem of the French team.

Most Forgettable Performance

Q. Have you ever felt discouraged with any of your performances?

A. I would like to erase the memory of the 1964 Olympics at Innsbruck. Placing only fifth in the GS event, I was eliminated in the Slalom and Downhill contest. It may sound like sour grapes, but I honestly feel that inferior equipment and its maintenance were partly to blame. I was also racing against an amebic dysentery affliction which really sapped me.

Most Exciting Race

Q. What was your most exciting race?

A. That would have to be the second run at Kitzbuhel in 1965. Karl Schranz took the first race by 1.38 seconds, but he was 3 full seconds behind me in the second event. I also took the Combined Medal that year. This is to say nothing of my World Champion victory at Portillo, Chile in 1966, which of course, I shall never forget. The French team was awarded sixteen of twenty-four medals. It took a long time for someone to depose the formidable Austrians.

Staying in Shape

Q. What do you advise for staying in shape off season?

A. For most racing champions, there is no "off season." Somewhere in the world there is still snow, and that is where we go to train. Should this be impractical for you, try bicycling or just plain running. Don't avoid the hills while biking; there's always a downhill "reward," if you're patient. And, try running off the track, where various obstacles will train your reflexes along with your legs. Progressive weight lifting is also good for any athlete, for non-athletes, too, I might add. There is a popular misconception that exercises which involve weights are just for mesomorphic Mr. Universe types. A logical progressive system of weight lifting will not only improve your appearance beyond that of the common man, it will develop the muscles you need to ski more proficiently than him also.

The Right Wax

Q. How important is wax?

A. Champions are well tuned machines whose victorious performances are dependent upon every detail of preparation. Often, only hundredths of a second separate a World Champion from second place. The right wax can make the difference. For a recreational skier, too, the right wax can mean the difference between a smooth graceful descent and a choppy staccato run. Vary your wax with the temperature and with the condition of the snow, as described on the box in which it is packaged. My good friend and coach Michel Arpin conditions my skis with wax and proper sharpening before every race. I share my victories with him.

Recommends Instruction

Q. Were you ever enrolled in a ski school class?

A. While I have never had that experience, I highly recommend it for anyone who begins to ski at a later age. I started before school age, skied every day and had masters like Henri Oreiller around to guide me. You will progress faster and more safely if you take a steady diet of competent ski instruction.

Skis and Boots

Q. Which is more important, skis or boots?

A. The best tuned skis in existence must still be guided, first by your eyes, then your brain, then your thighs and knees and finally, by your boots. If your goal is to be "the best," let each of these items be "the best" you can acquire.

Best Brand

Q. Which brand is best?

A. As a Frenchman, I am naturally in favor of French products, although we did not have a strong contender for the best ski until 1966, after I proved to my country's ski manufacturers that the French could win with the right skis; I raced on Austrian skis at the Megeve downhill and won. Since the development of fibreglass technology and the improvement of French equipment which helped me win the World Championship downhill, many brands have changed their ski construction for your advantage. Unfortunately the price of the equipment is usually commensurate with its performance, whether you are considering boots or skis. As far as boots are concerned, function and form run a close race for major concern. A good performing boot is of little use to you if it does not fit properly. I suppose your American expression "try, before you buy" is the most sensible answer I can give to your question.

Skis Together or Apart?

Q. My ski instructor keeps his skis tightly together, yet almost every photo I've seen of you shows your skis apart. Which is right?

A. What is "right" for me might not be right for your ski instructor. He is paid to look elegant, poised and graceful. I am paid to win races. At the speeds with which I travel independent leg action is absolutely essential. I find a stance with the skis apart most effective for me, although I keep them close together in deep powder.

Unweighting

Q. Which is better, to unweight with a down motion or with an up motion?

A. Unweighting is an important element of every turn, but whether you choose up or down is arbitrary and entirely dependent upon the particular situation. For example, a bump or rise in the surface will automatically cause what appears to be a moment of down unweighting, if your knees are flexible. What actually happens is that your knees are forced upward towards your chest; your *derriere* appears to drop. We call this movement *avalement,* referring to the "swallow" of the mogul by the knees. Another method of turning over the bumps is to first check the edges sharply and then bounce the tails upward to allow the ski tips to carve the turn; this is a form of unweighting with an up motion, more popular in the fifties. One thing remains constant: the skis are turned when they are in an unweighted state. Up or down is your choice.

Glissement

Q. Georges Joubert has written that "the art of skiing resides in the sliding of the skis—what in France we call glissement." Do you agree?

A. Sliding the skis requires little skill, as gravity is the prime mover. To be able to *carve* a turn with the skis on their edges is the "art" of skiing.

Angulation

Q. Is angulation necessary?

A. Fail to angulate on an icy steep slope and you'll soon know the answer. In deep "bottomless" powder you may bank your turns because the pull of gravity downhill is not as great, but as that pull increases with faster packed terrain, you had better drop your downhill shoulder. A good general rule is to keep your shoulders about the same slant as the hill, especially if you ski with your skis close together.

Face Direction of Travel

Q. Should I face in the direction my skis are pointed, at all times?

A. A good skier looks toward the direction in which he is traveling, downhill and well ahead of his next turn. Your skis are often not pointed in that direction.

Skiing New Powder

Q. Should I sit back when skiing through new powder snow?

A. If the depth of the new snow is a foot or under, your technique need not be modified, but if the powder is waist deep or more, it is important to plane the tips of your skis upward or they will dive and bury you. Above all, keep your body weight equally distributed and turn both skis as a single unit in deep powder.

Weight on Downhill Ski

Q. Should my weight always be on my downhill ski?

A. To get a higher faster line into a gate I frequently step uphill weighting my uphill ski for a moment. There are other times when it may be practical to stray from tradition, as in powder snow, when you had better keep your weight equal on both skis.

Avalement

Q. Is avalement the best method of skiing a mogul run?

A. If your thighs are strong and your knees are flexible. It also takes an exceptionally strong stomach. Should your knees and footwork be fast, try what you Americans call "running the river," checking your speed against the uphill side of the mogul and sliding through the groove between it and the next bump, but be sure to keep your hips and shoulders perpendicular to the fall line at all times. Variation of methods will enhance your style and make your skiing more enjoyable. There is nothing more insipid than a skier making the same kind of turn from the top of the trail to the bottom.

The Most Common Error

Q. What is the most common error you have detected among tyro racers?

A. Entering a gate too low. This forces the racer to check his speed with a traverse that practically has him starting the next turn with no momentum at all. Watch how often a pro scissors his ski tips for a moment, stepping uphill to get a faster line, a *higher* line to enter the next gate at maximum velocity.

The Reverse Shoulder

Q. Whatever happened to "reverse shoulder"?

A. Reverse shoulder is alive and well and evident in every racing turn that brings the skier close to the inside gate. If the inside shoulder does not lead, it will smash into the pole and cost you some time. Extreme exaggeration of the position led to the mannerist Austrian and Stein Eriksen variation for recreational skiing, very popular in the fifties and early sixties. Since then, ski schools all over the world have adopted a less extreme counterpoint of the upper body, with the shoulders reversed only as much as the skis. To be more explicit, as the uphill or inside ski leads the downhill or outside ski by a few inches, so also does the inside boot, knee, hip and shoulder follow the same length of lead, for recreational skiing today.

Anticipation

Q. What is meant by "anticipation"?

A. It is basically an initiation of the turn by a movement of the upper body toward the fall line, coupled with either an up or down motion to release bodyweight from the skis. Since I believe in always facing the fall line I am in constant anticipation each time I plant my pole and attack my turn. Anticipation is perhaps the formost characteristic of modern skiing.

Turning on Ice

Q. Whenever I turn on ice or boilerplate my skis slide wide apart and I skid for yards before catching my new traverse. What am I doing wrong?

A. You probably are throwing your hip to the outside of the turn, *mon ami*. Touch your downhill pole as you anticipate your new direction but lead the turn with your inside hip once you reach the fall line and begin to angulate strongly with your bodyweight mostly on the center of your downhill ski. Also, you should reduce your down-up motion when preparing for a turn on the ice; rely more upon your knees and your feet to turn the skis.

Skiing on "Crud"

Q. What about skiing "crud"? We get a lot of garbage conditions in the east; you know: ice cubes, breakable crust.

A. Stay on both feet and jump your turns around. This may not be a graceful maneuver, but it is the safest way to handle such *conditions mal*.

To Start Racing

Q. How can I begin racing?

A. Most ski schools terminate their ski week programs with a race between students. This is a great way to improve your skiing with qualified instruction and get the feel of competition and perhaps victory at the end of your effort. Beyond this, look into organizations such as the Canadian Ski Instructors Alliance, if you live in Canada, or the various Ski Instructors Associations of the United States, like the Unites States Eastern Amateur Ski Association, the Central U.S. Ski Instructors Association, the Rocky Mountain Ski Instructors Association or the Far West Ski Instructors Association. Your local ski school director can guide you.

Effortless Mogul Skiing

Q. What is the most effortless way to ski over a mogul?

A. Probably using the turn called *le serpent* by Georges Joubert. Assume a balanced upright position between the moguls. When your ski tips reach the top of the bump, plant your inside pole on the downhill side of the mogul facing your upper body to the fall line. Then, relax allowing your upper body to tip forward between your skis and your planted pole. Bend your knees to absorb the bump and your skis will slide effortlessly into the turn. This turn is very effective in rutted slalom runs also, in case you should get a late starting number.

Sliding on the Edges

Q. I have heard it said that you are a master of glissement. Can you translate?

A. *Glissement* refers to the sliding of the skis, but not necessarily on their bottoms. A good racer has mastered *glissement* on the edges of his skis, remaining in continuous contact with the snow. Get into the air and you will lose vital seconds.

Stiffness on Turns

Q. What can I do to correct a stiffness I experience just before every turn? I am just beginning to parallel.

A. Try to loosen up by bouncing your ski tails off the snow as you traverse. Add an anticipatory movement of your upper body to the last bounce and your skis will automatically turn.

Too Old to Start?

Q. Am I too old to ski? (This question is frequently asked by men and women from teens to over-forties. Ed.)

A. If you can see, if you can think, and if you can run, you are capable of learning how to ski; add to those requirements the important prerequisite of desire, and you will learn very quickly.

Proper Camber

Q. How much camber should my skis have?

A. Skis with too much camber will be difficult to turn in most good snow conditions. Place your skis together, bottom to bottom, and measure the space between. An inch to one and a half inches is sufficient.

Old Skis

Q. My skis get worse every year. They don't seem to slide into the turns. They want to go straight all the time. Should I put them out to pasture?

A. All that may be necessary is a good flat filing. The bottoms of skis will sometimes cave-in, allowing the edges to ride lower. I think you Americans call this "railing." A railed ski will track straight unless it is powered by a great effort. Flat-file the bottoms and keep them that way.

Goggles Are Important

Q. How important are goggles?

A. As important as your eyes, they can even affect your race. A dark lens will protect your eyes from sunburn on a very bright day, while yellow lenses will cheer up a foggy day by bathing it with simulated sunshine. Yellow goggles will also darken the mogul shadows. Goggles also have a tunneled vision effect that will help keep your eyes on the course and away from the *jeune filles* on the sidelines.

French Dominance

Q. How do you account for the sudden emergence of France as a major skiing power?

A. It would have happened before, had we had better equipment and more informative ski racing technology. Now that we have, France will continue to be a *formidable* contender.

A Final Word

Q. Do you ever get sick of skiing?

A. *Alors!* Do you ever get sick of breathing?

Marge carves her way down Katchina, Taos Ski Valley, New Mexico

500

Chapter 11
SKI AREA DIRECTORY USA
Ski Areas in the United States Which Have a Vertical Drop of Over 500 ft.

CHAPTER 11—SKI AREA DIRECTORY USA

EVERY SKI AREA in the United States was contacted for inclusion in this listing. If any were overlooked, it is because their state Chamber of Commerce was unaware of their existence at the time this list was compiled. Others may simply have failed to answer our request. Any changes completed after April, 1976 have not been included as they took place after SKIER'S DIGEST went to press. For the most part, though, we feel that this index is complete and sincerely hope that you will find it helpful in planning your next ski season.

NAME OF RESORT	ADDRESS	No. Trails			No. Lifts				VERTICAL IN FEET	longest run (mi.)	NEAREST AIRPORT	MILES FROM AREA
		beginner	inter	expert	T-bar	chair	gondola	other				
ALASKA												
Arctic Valley	Anchorage				1	1		3	1,000			
Cleary Summit	Fairbanks	3	11	2	2				1,200			
Mt. Alyeska	Girdwood	9	12	8		3		5	2,500	2.5		1
ARIZONA												
Arizona Snow Bowl	Flagstaff					1		4	2,100			
Sunrise	McNary	4	4	4		2		1	1,400	2	Springerville	23
CALIFORNIA												
Alpine Meadows of Tahoe	Tahoe City	25%	45%	35%	1	9		3	1,700	1.5	Reno	45
Badger Pass	Yosemite National Park	2	5	2	2	3		1	560	2		
Bear Valley	Bear Valley	18	15	22		6			2,100	3	Columbia	45
Blue Ridge Ski Area	Wrightwood					2		1	1,100	.9		
China Peak	Lakeshore	3	4	8	2	2		1	1,500	3	Fresno	62
Dodge Ridge	Long Barn	40%	40%	20%		6		6	1,050			
Donner Ski Ranch	Norden					1		2	826	.8	Truckee	17
Goldmine	Big Bear Lake					1		7	1,500			
Heavenly Valley	S. Lake Tahoe	30%	50%	20%	1	15	1	4	4,017	7.3	Reno	
Holiday Hill	Wrightwood	30%	40%	30%	1	3		3	1,600	1.5	Ontario	40
Homewood	Homewood	3	5	1	1	2		5	1,800			
June Mountain	June Lake	3	8	10	1	4			2,562	2	Bishop	54
Kirkwood Meadows	Kirkwood	4	10	4		4			2,000			
Mammoth	Mammoth Lakes				3	14	2		2,153	2		
Mt. Baldy	Mt. Baldy	3	4	6	1	4	1		2,300	1.5	Los Angeles	49
Mt. Waterman	LaCanada	2	3	5		2		1	1,200	.5	Burbank	40
Northstar-At-Tahoe	Truckee	20%	60%	20%		6			2,200	2.5	Truckee	3
Peddler Hill	Jackson				1			3	700	1		
Sierra Ski Ranch	Twin Bridges	20%	60%	20%	2	3			1,570	2		
Ski Shasta	Mt. Shasta	4	10	12	1	2		1	1,600	2	Weed	23
Ski Sunrise	Wrightwood	8	7	4				6	800	1	Ontario	60
Snow Summit	Big Bear Lake	30%	50%	20%		3		6	1,200	1.3		
Snow Valley	Running Springs	40%	40%	20%		4		4	1,121	1		
Soda Springs	Soda Springs	10	6	4	2	1			650	.8	Truckee	12
Squaw Valley	Olympic Valley	33%	33%	33%	5	17	2		2,700	4	Reno	
Sugar Bowl	Norden	9	5	19		7		2	1,500	2	Truckee	15
Table Mountain	Wrightwood							8	750	.8		
Tahoe Donner	Truckee	6	4	2	1	2			1,000	1	Truckee	5
Tahoe Ski Bowl	Homewood	40%	50%	10%	1	1		2	750	1.5	Truckee	21
COLORADO												
Arapahoe Basin	Dillon	5	10	6		4		2	1,700			
Arapahoe East	Golden	3	3	3		1		2	550			
Berthoud Pass	Berthoud								973		Denver	
Breckenridge	Breckenridge	17	14	23	2	8		2	2,223	2.6	Denver	70
Copper Mountain	Copper Mountain	9	20	9		6		1	2,450	2	Denver	75
Crested Butte	Crested Butte	4	13	12	1	6	1		2,150	3	Gunnison	
Fun Valley	Littleton				1	2		1	550			
Geneva Basin	Grant	30%	30%	40%		3	1		1,200			
Hidden Valley	Estes Park	3	3	2	2	1		2	1,800	1.5	Denver	78
Lake Eldora	Nederland	5	12	8	3	2			1,400	2		
Loveland Basin & Valley	Georgetown	7	14	4	1	5		4	1,430	1.5	Denver	60
Monarch	Garfield	6	10	4	1	2			1,000	1.5		
Pikes Peak	Colorado Springs								1,000			
Powderhorn Ski Area	Grand Junction	2	5	10		2		1	1,700	2		40

NAME OF RESORT	ADDRESS	beginner	inter	expert	T-bar	chair	gondola	other	VERTICAL IN FEET	longest run (mi.)	NEAREST AIRPORT	MILES FROM AREA
COLORADO (cont.)												
Purgatory	Durango	25%	50%	25%		3		2	1,600	2.5	LaPlata	44
Ski Broadmoor	Colorado Springs	1	1	2		1			600		Colo. Spr.	10
Squaw Pass	Golden								700			
Stagecoach	Steamboat Springs	3	6	3		3			1,700			
Steamboat Ski Area	Steamboat Springs	28%	49%	23%	1	9	1	2	3,600	2.5	Steamboat	5
Sunlight Ski Area	Glenwood Springs	10	8	5	1	2		1	1,800	3.5	Glenwood	10
Telluride	Telluride	20%	50%	30%		6			3,200	2.5	Montrose	62
Vail	Vail	9	23	19		9	2	5	3,050		Eagle	30
Winter Park	Winter Park	14	18	20	2	11			2,100	2	Granby	20
Wolf Creek	South Fork	6	8	5		1		2	1,125	1.3	Alamosa	45
CONNECTICUT												
Mohawk Mountain	Cornwall	4	6	4		3		1	640	1.5	Bradley	38
Ski Sundown	New Hartford	1	2	1	1	1		3	550		Bradley	20
IDAHO												
Bald Mountain	Pierce								670	1		
Bear Gulch	St. Anthony	2	2	1	1	1		2	765	1		
Bogus Basin	Boise	6	13	12		5		5	1,500		Boise	18
Brundage Mountain	McCall	3	5	3	1	1		1	1,600		Boise	100
Caribou	Pocatello					1		1	700	.7		
Cottonwood Butte	Cottonwood	1	3	1	1			1	845	.7	Grangeville	20
Lookout Pass	Wallace							3	700	1		
Magic Mountain	Twin Falls				1	1		2	740	2		
Pomerelle	Albion	1	3	1		1		2	400	2		
Rupert	Albion		5	3	1	1		3	1,000			
Schweitzer Ski Area	Sandpoint	4	35	30	1	7		1	1,800	2.3	Spokane	75
Silverhorn	Kellogg	4	1	10				1	1,922	1.2	Shoshone	12
Skyline Ski Areas	Pocatello		5			1		3	1,650	1	Pocatello	23
Soldier Mountain	Fairfield	8	10	8	1	2		2	1,400	3	Twin Falls	70
Sun Valley	Sun Valley	18	24	13		15			3,400	2.5	Hailey	12
Taylor Mountain	Idaho Falls					1		4	800	.7		
MAINE												
Agamenticus Mountain	York	2	3	3	1	1		1	500	1		
Camden Snow Bowl	Camden	1	5	1	2	1			900	1.3	Rockland	10
Eaton Mountain	Skowhegan	2	3	4		1		1	750	.8		
Enchanted	Jackman				1	1			1,200	1.5		
Evergreen	Stoneham City	3	3	1		3			1,050	1.5		
Moosehead	Moosehead Lake	2	4	4	2	1			1,700			
Mt. Abram	Locke Mills	4	8	2	3	1			1,035	1.5		
Pleasant Mountain	Bridgton	10	3	9	3	3			1,200	1		
Saddleback Mountain	Rangeley	9	5	4	2	2			1,700	2.5	Rangeley	8
Ski Way of Arrostock	Mars Hill								900			
Squaw	Greenville	2	6	3	2	1			1,800	2.5		
Sugarloaf/USA	Kingfield	8	10	10	5	4	1		2,600	2.5	Waterville	56
Sunday River	Bethel	2	6	6	3	1			1,500	3.5	Portland	
MARYLAND												
Wisp	Oakland	4	8	5	1	1		2	610	2	McHenry	3
MASSACHUSETTS												
Berkshire East Ski Area	Charlemont	7	4	8	1	2		1	1,180	1.9		
Berkshire Snow Basin	West Cummington	3	4	4	1			1	550	1	Bradley	60
Bousquet	Pittsfield	5	5	4	1	1		2	750	1.2	Pittsfield	1
Butternut Basin	Great Barrington	3	2	3	1	4		1	1,000	.9	Gt. Bar'ton	7
Jiminy Peak	Hancock	6	4	11	2	2		1	1,120	2	Pittsfield	14
Mt. Mohawk	Shelburne				2			1	500	.9		
Mt. Tom	Holyoke	3	5	2	2	2		2	840	1.1	Bradley	20
Mt. Watatic	Ashby	2	4		4			2	550	.7		
Wachusett Mountain	Princeton	3	3	1	2			1	650	.8	Fitchburg	10
MICHIGAN												
Big Powderhorn	Bessemer	5	6	3		4		2		1		
Boyne Highlands	Harbor Springs	5	7	5	1	6		2	625	1	Harbor Spr.	4
Boyne Mountain Lodge	Boyne Mountain	5	7	6		8		1	600	1.5	Boyne Mtn.	0
Cliffs Ridge	Marquette	3	7	3	2	1		2	600	1.3		8
Porcupine Mountains	Ontonagon	1	3	5	1	1		2	600	1.5	Ironwood	50
Sugarloaf Mountain	Traverse City	5	9	6	1	5			600	1		
MINNESOTA												
Lutsen Ski Area	Lutsen	2	9	3	1	3		1	630	1.5	Duluth	90
MONTANA												
Bear Paw Ski Bowl	Havre							3	800	.5		
Beef Trail	Butte				1			3	800	.5		
Belmont	Helena				1			4	1,500	2.3		
Big Mountain	Whitefish	3	12	8	2	2		2	2,200	2.5	Whitefish	8
Big Sky of Montana	Big Sky	3	7	8		3	1	1	2,275	2.3	Gallatin	43
Bridger Bowl	Bozeman	10	24	15	1	3		2	2,000	2.8		25
Corona Lake	Plains							1	700	.5		
Deep Creek	Wise River				1			1	900	1		
Grass Mountain	Townsend							2	700	.5		
Jack Creek	Ennis				1			1	1,500	1.1		
Kings Hill	Neihart				1	1		3	1,400	1.3		
Lakeview Mountain	Monida							2	1,050	1.2		

NAME OF RESORT	ADDRESS	No. Trails			No. Lifts				VERTICAL IN FEET	longest run (mi.)	NEAREST AIRPORT	MILES FROM AREA
		beginner	inter	expert	T-bar	chair	gondola	other				
MONTANA (con't.)												
Lost Trail	Hamilton							3	650	1.3		
Marshall Mountain	Missoula	2	5	3	1	1		5	1,500			
Maverick Mountain	Polaris	2	3	2		1		1	1,450	2.5		
Rainy Mountain	Elkhorn Hot Springs					1		5	1,650	1.7	Butte	100
Red Lodge	Red Lodge	3	6	4		3		2	2,000		Billings	65
Sundance	Red Lodge					1		1	700	.8		
Teton Pass	Choteau					1		3	1,300			
Turner Mountain	Libby				1			1	2,200	2		
Wraith Hill	Anaconda							3	600	.3		
Z-Bar-T	Butte				1			2	1,000	.6		
NEVADA												
Lee Canyon	Las Vegas				2	2			970	.9	Las Vegas	45
Mt. Rose	Reno	6	8	6	1	2		1	1,450	1	Reno	20
Ski Incline	Incline Village	4	7	9	1	5			800	.8	Reno	35
Slide Mountain	Reno	4	11	2		3		2	1,450		Reno	22
Tannenbaum	Reno				1			3	550	.5	Reno	18
NEW HAMPSHIRE												
Attitash	Bartlett	8	17	8		4			1,525	2		
Black Mountain	Jackson	4	6	4	2	1		1	1,100	1.3	Portland	60
Bretton Woods	Bretton Woods				1	2			1,100			
Cannon	Franconia	8	15	7	3	3	1		2,200	2.3		
Dartmouth Skiway	Hanover				1	1		1	900	1.1		
Dundee	Center Conway								700			
Gunstock	Laconia	4	10	8	3	3		2	1,400	2		2
Highlands	Northfield	4	4	2	2			1	700	1.3		
King Ridge	New London	9	4	3	2	2		2	800	.9	Lebanon	30
Loon Mountain	Lincoln	6	7	4		3	1		1,850	2.5	Manchester	68
Mittersill	Franconia				2	1			1,700	1		
Moose Mountain	Brookfield				2	1			1,000	.8		
Mt. Cranmore	North Conway	3	10	3	1	3	2		1,500	2		
Mt. Rowe	Gilford				2	1			500			
Mt. Sunapee	Sunapee	8	10	1	2	5		1	1,500	1.8		
Mt. Whittier	W. Osipee				3	1	1	1	1,600	1.3		
Onset Ski Area	Bennington	3	3	4	1	2			650	1	Manchester	25
Ragged Mountain	Danbury	4	6	3	1	1			1,125	1.5	Boston	100
Tenney Mountain	Plymouth	3	2	3		2			1,300	1.5	Laconia	40
Tyrol Ski Area	Jackson	4	6	4	1	1		1	1,000	1.3	N. Conway	10
Waterville Valley	Waterville Valley	5	8	5	2	7			2,150	2		
Whaleback	Lebanon				1	1			640	1.3		
Wildcat Mountain	Jackson	7	7	8	1	3	1		2,100	2.8	Berlin	18
Wilderness at Balsams	Dixville Notch	3	6	3	2	1			1,000	2	Portland	120
NEW JERSEY												
Vernon Valley/Gr. Gorge	McAfee	5	17	16		13		5	1,080	2.5	Sussex	5
NEW MEXICO												
Angel Fire	Angel Fire					3			2,180	3.5	Angel Fire	1.5
Pajarito	Los Alamos	2	8	6	1	1		2	1,100			
Red River Ski Area	Red River	35%	40%	25%		2		2	1,537	2.5	Albuquerque	167
Sandia Peak	Albuquerque					2	1	3	1,750	2.3	Albuquerque	
Santa Fe	Santa Fe	7	10	12					1,660	2		
Sierra Blanca	Ruidosa	5	8	8	3	1	1	3	1,700	2.5		
Sipapu Lodge	Vadito	3	3	5				3	800	1	Albuquerque	
Ski Cloudcraft	Cloudcraft				2			2	1,250	1.4		
Taos	Taos Ski Valley	8	11	19		5			2,655	5.3	Albuquerque	
NEW YORK												
Addison Pinnacle	Addison					3		1	723	.8		
Adirondack	Corinth					3			1,000	2.2		
Belleayre Mountain	Pine Hill	7	13	11	2	4		1	1,265	1.5	Kingston	40
Bluemont	Yorkshire	4	2	1	1	1		2	800			
Catamount	Hillsdale	6	6	6	3	3			1,000	1.4		
Catskill	Andes	2	9	4	2				1,050	1.8	Oneonta	45
Dutchess	Beacon					3			1,020	.8		
Glenwood Acre	Glenwood	2	7	5	2	1		2	510	.9		
Gore Mountain	North Creek	5	12	8	2	5	1		2,100	3.5		
Greek Peak	Cortland	8	7	5	2	4		1	790	1.5		
Hickory Hill	Warrensburg	1	3	3	2			1	600	.7		
Highmont	Highmont	3	3	3	3			5	825	1.3		
Hillside Inn	Narrowsburg							2	550	.4		
Holiday Valley	Ellicottville				3	2		2	750		Buffalo	50
Hunter Mountain	Hunter	7	16	12	1	9		5	1,600	2.5	Maben	10
Innsbruck, U.S.A.	Binghamton	3	5	2	2			2	500	1	Broome	10
Intermont	Solon	3	10	4	2	1		1	820	1		
Ironwood Ridge	Cazenovia	4	3	1	3			1	518	1		
Kissing Bridge	Glenwood	10	8	2	5	3		4	500	.7	Buffalo	30
Moon Valley	Chasm Falls				1	1			600	.7		
Mount Cathalia	Ellenville				1	1		1	525	.9		
Mount Storm	Stormville				1			4	600	.6		
Mystic Mountain	New Woodstock	5	5	3	2	1			600	1		
North Creek Ski Bowl	North Creek				2				1,000	.9		
Oak Mountain	Speculator	3	5	3	3	1		1	650	1.1		
Paleface	Jay	4	7	4	1	1			730	.8	Plattsburgh	35
Plattekill	Roxbury	2	4	4	2	1		1	990	1.4	Oneonta	35
Royal Mountain	Johnstown				1			1	550	.9		

NAME OF RESORT	ADDRESS	beginner	inter	expert	T-bar	chair	gondola	other	VERTICAL IN FEET	longest run (mi.)	NEAREST AIRPORT	MILES FROM AREA
NEW YORK (con't.)												
Scotch Valley	Stamford	4	4	5	1	3		1	750	1		
Shu-Maker Mountain	Little Falls	1	4	1	1	1		1	760			
Ski Wing	Allegany	3	7	5	2	1			813	1.3		
Snow Ridge	Turin	3	4	4	3	3		2	500	1	Utica-Rome	40
Song Mountain	Tully	9	5	4	4	1			750			
Sterling Forest	Tuxedo	4	5	6		5		2	450	.6		
Swain	Nunda	6	12	6	4	1			600	1.3		
Toggenburg	Fabius	4	6	2	3	1			600	1	Syracuse	30
West Mountain	Glens Falls	3	8	1		3		1	1,010	1.5	Glens Falls	8
Whiteface Mountain	Wilmington	7	7	10	1	4		1	3,119	2.4	Saranac Lake	25
Windham Mountain Club	Windham	2	5	5		4			1,500			
NORTH CAROLINA												
Beech Mountain	Banner Elk	4	5	2	2	4	1	1	796	1.5	Beech Mtn.	4
Catalooche	Maggie Valley	3	2	2	1	1		2	750	2.5	Asheville	45
Seven Devils	Boone	1	3	2		2		1	600	.6		
Sugar Mountain	Banner Elk	5	5	2	1	3		1	1,200	1.5	Tricities	55
Wolf Laurel	Mars Hill	1	3	2	1	1		1	700	.7	Asheville	45
OREGON												
Anthony Lakes	Baker	1	4	4		1		1	900	1.5	Baker	34
Hoodoo Ski Bowl	Sisters	6	11	9		3		3	1,000	1.1		
Mt. Ashland	Ashland	3	10	6	1	1		2	1,500	.8	Medford	22
Mt. Bachelor	Bend	6	10	3		4		1	1,400	1.2	Bend	22
Mt. Hood Meadows	Mt. Hood	40%	30%	30%		4		1	1,161	1.8		
Multorpor Ski Bowl	Government Camp					4		7	1,400		Portland	53
Spout Springs	Elgin	5	4	3	2	2		2	550	.8		
Timberline Lodge	Government Camp	8	10	5		3		2	1,900	3	Portland	60
Tomahawk Ski Bowl	Klamath Falls							3	650	1.4		
PENNSYLVANIA												
Big Valley	Kempton				1	1			512			
Blue Knob	Claysburg				2	2		2	1,000	2		
Camelback	Tannersville	8	5	3	2	3		2	780	1	Allentown	30
Charnita	Fairfield	5	2	1		2		1	600	.8		
Denton Hill	Coudersport	3	5	3		1		3	570	.9	Bradford	58
Elk Mountain	Union Dale	7	4	6		4			1,000	2	Wilkes-Barre	35
Jack Frost	White Haven	3	5	2		5		1	500	.5	Wilkes-Barre	19
Laurel Mountain	Ligonier	3	6	1	2	1		3	900			
Oregon Hill	English Center				3			1	520			
Peek'n Mountain	Youngsville	4	5	5	2	1		1	579	1	Jamestown	25
Seven Springs	Champion	5	8	2		7		7	870	1.3	Somerset	18
Wonderview	Bloomsburg	3	2	1		2		3	540			
SOUTH DAKOTA												
Terry Peak	Lead					1		3	1,200	1.5		
TENNESSEE												
Gatlinburg	Gatlinburg					2		3	800	.9	Knoxville	48
Renegade	Crossville	2	2	1	1	1		2	500			
UTAH												
Alta	Alta	11	21	9		6		4	2,000	3	Salt Lake	25
Beaver Mountain	Logan	4	7	12	1	3			1,600	2		
Brianhead	Cedar City	4	8	4	1	2			1,200	1.8	Parowan	13
Brighton Ski Bowl	Salt Lake City	9	18	8	1	4			1,250	1.2		
Nordic Valley	Eden	1	4	3		2			1,000			
Park City	Park City	12	17	15	2	8	1		2,400	3.5	Salt Lake	
Park City West	Park City	4	7	8		4		3	1,800	2	Salt Lake	
Powder Mountain	Eden	2	7	5		2			1,000			
Snow Basin	Ogden	6	24	14	1	4			2,200	2.5		
Snowbird	Snowbird	5	11	19		4	1		3,100			
Solitude	Brighton	5	13	6		3		1	2,000	.7		
Sundance	Provo	4	9	10		3			1,700	4	Salt Lake	50
VERMONT												
Bolton Valley	Bolton	10	7	4		4			1,100	1.5	Burlington	20
Bromley	Manchester Center	6	11	5		5		1	1,334	2	Rutland	25
Burke Mountain	East Burke	6	9	8	1	1		2	1,800	2.5	Lyndonville	6
Carinthia	West Dover	2	4	2	1			1	800	.8		
Dutch Hill	Readsboro	3	3	2	2			1	570			
Glen Ellen	Waitsfield				1	4			2,645	1.7	Montpelier	30
Haystack	Wilmington	5	9	6	3	2		1	1,400	2	Mt. Snow	5
Hogback	Marlboro	4	6	2	4				500	.7	Keene	35
Jay Peak	Jay Peak	3	7	10	3	3	1		2,100	3		
Killington	Killington	12	22	18		8	1	2	3,060	5	Rutland	20
Madonna	Madonna	6	10	11	3				2,100	3		
Mad River Glen	Waitsfield	7	8	7		4			2,000	3	Montpelier	30
Magic Mountain	Londonderry	30%	50%	20%		4			1,600	2.3		
Maple Valley	West Dummerston	1	3	1	1	2			850	.9		
Middlebury College	Middlebury				1	1		3	1,200			
Mt. Ascutney	Brownsville	9	8	7	3	2			1,470	1.8	West Lebanon	18
Mt. Snow	Mt. Snow	8	24	6		12	2	1	1,850	3.5		
Mt. Tom	Woodstock	5	5	5	4				500	1.1		
Norwich University	Northfield	5	3	6		1		2	902			
Okemo Mountain	Ludlow	8	7	7		3		6	2,150	4.5	Rutland	20

NAME OF RESORT	ADDRESS	No. Trails			No. Lifts				VERTICAL IN FEET	longest run (mi.)	NEAREST AIRPORT	MILES FROM AREA
		beginner	inter	expert	T-bar	chair	gondola	other				
VERMONT (con't.)												
Pico	Rutland	20%	60%	20%	2	5			1,967	2.5	Rutland	9
Pinnacle Ski-Ways	Randolph							2	640	1.2		
Prospect Mountain	Bennington				2			1	650			
Round Top	Plymouth Union	2	5	3	1	2		1	1,250	1.5	Rutland	20
Snow Valley	Landgrove	1	6	2	1	1		2	700	1	Manchester	6
Sonnenberg	Barnard							2	500	1		
Stowe	Stowe	4	20	5	3	4	1		2,150	3.5	Burlington	42
Stratton	Stratton Mountain	17	21	10	3	4		2	1,946		Albany	95
Sugarbush	Warren	6	10	17	2	6	1	1	2,400	2.5		
Suicide Six	Woodstock	6	3	6	2	4		1	600	1.1		
Timber Ridge	Windham	3	3	4	1	1			800	1.5	Springfield	19
VIRGINIA												
Bryce Mountain	Basye	1	1	1		2		2	550	.7	Bryce	0
Homestead Ski Area	Hot Springs	1	1	1	1			3	550	.8	Ingalls	15
Massanutten	Harrisonberg	3	3	3		4		1	795	1.1	Shenandoah	20
Wintergreen	Wintergreen	1	2	3		3			525	.5		
WASHINGTON												
Alpental	Snoqualmie	3	5	7		4		5	2,400			
Crystal Mountain	Crystal Mountain	10	15	10	1	6		9	2,430	3.5	Seattle	67
Hurricane Ridge	Port Angeles					3			500			
Mission Ridge	Wenatchee	3	20	7		4		1	2,140	5		12
Mt. Baker	Bellingham	10	15	15		5		4	1,500	2	Bellingham	
Mt. Spokane	Spokane	8	12	10	1	4		5	2,200	1		52
Satus Pass	Goldendale	5	5	1	1			1	500			
Ski Acres	Seattle	11	3	3		6		17	900	1		
Skyline Basin	Dayton				1	2			1,500			
Snoqualmie Summit	Snoqualmie Pass	25%	55%	20%		8		9	900	.8	Seattle	48
Stevens Pass	Leavenworth		15	10		6		3	1,800			
White Pass Village	Yakima		8	6		3		2	1,500	1.3	Yakima	52
WEST VIRGINIA												
Canaan Valley	Davis	5	6	3		2		1	850	1	Elkins	30
Snowshoe	Slatyfork	5	4	2		3			1,500		Elkins	43
WISCONSIN												
Hiawatha Hills	Alma	3	1	2	1	1		1	600			
Mt. LaCrosse	LaCrosse					2		3	516	1	LaCrosse	10
Rib Mountain	Wausau	4	4	2	2	1		4	680	.8	Central Wis.	12
WYOMING												
Antelope Butte	Grayball	1	1	2	2				600			
Grand Targhee	Alta	6	17	6	1	2		1	2,200	3.5		
Hogadon Basin	Casper				1			1	650	.8		
Jackson Hole	Teton Village	3	11	10	3	4	1		4,100	5		
Meadowlark	Worland	1	2	1		2			600			
Medicine Bow	Centennial	4	4	3	2	1		1	600	1.4		
Sinks Canyon	Lander				1			2	780	.8		
Snow King	Jackson	2	2	4		2		2	1,571	.9	Jackson	6

Vail, Colorado. Photo by Peter Runyon)

Chapter 12
BEYOND SKIING
The Hang Gliding Experience

CHAPTER 12—BEYOND SKIING: THE HANG GLIDING EXPERIENCE

Hang gliding skier soars toward Spar Peak, having taken off from the top of the Great Divide Chairlift at 9,000 feet, Sunshine Village, Banff, Alberta, Canada. (Simon Hoyle photo)

SINCE THE ANCIENT tale of Icarus first planted the seed of hope in man's heart, he has persisted in his struggle to conquer gravity, that formidable force that shackles us to tenacious *terra firma*. This century has certainly seen the conquest of gravity by motor power, and even the wonders of space travel as we know it today will probably seem primitive to the man of the next century. But, for every motorboat on the water, there is at least one sailing ship, for every snowmobile, there are probably ten skiers, and for every motor driven aircraft there is probably some dreamer who still would rather fly like a bird and not have to depend upon *combustion*. Many of these dreamers are skiers. You have felt it, if you have ever sprung off the lip of a cornice and drifted 20, 30, maybe 50 feet to the slope. You have surely felt it if you have ever crouched down the chute of a Nordic jump and dove into the sky and its air currents. You may even have felt something of the freedom of flight just lifting off a mogul and sailing 10 or 15 feet. Dan Poynter has gone a step further. A big step. We at SKIER'S DIGEST are impressed. We are not telling you to try Hang Gliding; we are not even sure that *we* might. We are simply . . . *impressed*. We think it looks like a far out experience; we empathize with the thrill! We recognize its kinship to the sport of skiing. We also are congnizant of the dangers. We want only to tell you a little about it, to have you see some fantastic photographs, to have you consider Hang Gliding or "Skysurfing" as a possible ultimate thrill beyond the rush of skiing. For an authoritative report, we have chosen Dan Poynter. He is the guy who has had that ad for Hang Gliding information in the Classified section of the skiing magazines for so many years. He is the author of two important books on the subject which are respected as bibles by the new breed of skysurfers and which should be in your library if you have any inclination at all toward this fast-growing sport and its outer limits. They are: *Hang Gliding, The Basic Handbook of Skysurfing*, and *Manned Kiting, The Basic Handbook of Tow Launched Hang Gliding*, both of which you can get in your local bookstore or by writing to Dan Poynter, Post Office Box 4232-73, Santa Barbara, California, 93103. For SKIER'S DIGEST, I have asked Dan to write an article of particular interest to skiers and to discuss the relationship between the two sports, along with including some basic technical data that you may find useful. Skiers, here is Dan Poynter:

HANG GLIDING—AN ALTERNATIVE

by Dan Poynter

It is only natural that hang gliding and skiing should both appear in these pages since they can be found on or above the same terrain, and they appeal to the same active,

Launching on skis is probably the easiest way. Level the glider, slide forward to pick up speed, raise the nose and you're airborne!

outdoors people. Man was not meant to fly or to slide down snow covered mountains on boards, yet millions have accepted the challenge to not only succeed but to excel. Like learning to swim or ride a bicycle, there is a tremendous sense of self-satisfaction as you master the techniques of foot launched ultra-light flight.

It is awkward moving from the lift to the launch area. The wind is blowing, and you are carrying not only your skis but a 40-pound hang glider which is bundled up into a package some 8 inches in diameter and over 18 feet long. Your unstrapped helmet seems gimbaled on top of your head, and it alternately slips over your eyes or falls to the ground. Erecting the kite takes longer than it did last summer. The snow is slippery, the wind wants to play games and some adjustments may necessitate the momentary removal of a warming glove. But finally the glider is ready; it is up and has undergone a thorough pre-flight check. Skis on, helmet cinched, you pick up the kite, steady yourself and begin to slide forward gathering speed and momentum. The sail flaps louder and louder as you pick up speed holding the wing parallel with the ground. At a little over 20mph, you ease the control bar forward to lift the nose of the kite, the seat straps tighten as the sail fills with air and you LIFT OFF breaking away from the steep hillside. Lifting over the heads of the other skiers, over the tree tops, ever higher and higher into the smooth, crisp, clear upper air. You can hear every sound from below: the hum of the lift, the cars in the parking lot and the gasps of the upward-looking crowd. The only sound from above is that of the wind as the kite passes through the air at some 20mph producing a hum in the wires. The view is

The prone position gives one the feeling of flying like Superman. One may launch on foot or with short skis.

The pilot is suspended from the center of the glider. Steering is accomplished by moving the bar in front which is tightly connected to the frame with cables.

incredible and almost personal as few others have lifted themselves to such a lofty position; hundreds, perhaps thousands of feet in the air. Over the trees, out over the valley, you can see for miles as you fly in a manner that until now was available only to Icarus, Superman and the birds! Now a series of turns faces the sail of the glider alternately into and out of the sun adding a bright dash of color to the black and white of winter. Descending to the landing area, you set up your approach, hoping the crowd will stay back long enough for you to come to a complete stop before their arrival. You glide to the snow-covered ground near 25mph, the skis slap down and you slide forward. A push on the control bar raises the nose, filling the sail like a parachute braking you to a halt. It is time to break down the glider and head indoors for something warm but here comes the crowd.

The easiest, fastest and safest way to learn hang gliding is in school. You didn't ski from the mid-station the first day out, and you won't fly from there either. In both sports, one must start from the smaller slopes to master the basic skills before progressing ever higher.

Basically, there are three ways to launch a hang glider; on foot, on water skis and on snow skis. The water ski method is usually employed by flat landers. They enjoy ultra-light flight by towing themselves to altitude and releasing to glide back to terra firma (or the water). Foot launched hang gliding is practiced on hills and requires one to run with the kite until an airspeed of 15mph is reached and liftoff can be accomplished. Note that was "airspeed" not "ground speed."

One must have 15mph of air passing over the glider's surface to create enough lift to fly. Now if the wind is blowing up the slope at 10mph, one need run only 5. The snow ski launch offers one great advantage: you can ski far faster than you can run. On skis, you can take off easily in a no-wind condition and even with a slight downhill or "tail wind."

Ground winds are not always smooth; the trees and other obstacles make a smooth wind turbulent. During takeoff, the glider may drift to one side, and it is imperative that the pilot follow the kite with the skis, not attempt the opposite. One should try to turn the kite and to fly it straight down the hill but if it should veer to one side, follow with the skis. This is an umbrella in a wind storm. You can't muscle it around, it's stronger than you are. Attempting to pull the kite along the track of the skis will only result in an aborted takeoff.

Once airborne, all hang gliding is alike. Turns are made by banking the glider in the direction you wish to go. This is done by moving the control bar in the OPPOSITE direction. The pilot is suspended from the center portion of the craft, and the control bar is tightly wired to the framework. Moving the bar tilts the kite banking it to one side.

A 2,000-foot drop may give you a flight of 2 to 4 minutes and much more if the air is rising. This happens when a wind strikes the side of a hill and deflects upwards (ridge lift) and when sun-heated air ascends (thermal lift). Typically, a glider will have a sink rate of 4 to 8 feet per second (depending on the model); if the air is rising faster than your descent, you can stay up as long as you like. Now you can follow the soaring birds; those who fly all day with rarely a flap of their wings.

Landings, like takeoffs, are made into the wind to minimize ground speed, and once the skis touch down, the bar is pushed way forward to pitch the nose of the craft up changing this sleek flying machine into a parachute type drag device as it fills with air and minimizes the landing roll. Landing on skis is not only easy but a lot of fun as you can approach the ground at a higher rate of speed and plane along lightly on the snow for some distance, if desired.

Site selection for hang gliding requires a number of considerations. In foot-launched flight, one becomes quite concerned about access to the launch area and landing areas; usually a road from bottom to top. In ski launching, the lift supplies the access but since the area is highly developed, there are other considerations such as the location of power lines, lifts and trees. Trees make a smooth wind turbulent in the launch area, and they may surround the landing site making a steep descent necessary. Wires often cross the trails and the landing area to provide lighting for night skiing. One must never fly near the lift, as knocking one out for even a few minutes is not only dangerous, it is very poor P.R. for the sport! One can become most unwelcome by both skiers and the management. The landing area must be away from the skiing crowd; out of the line of traffic since novice skiers cannot always move off your runaway as easily as the foot borne.

The Alps of Europe offer not only some of the world's best skiing but some of the best hang gliding as well. The mountain slopes are very steep, the lifts are swift and the support facilities are excellent. Often there are restaurants at both the top and the bottom. In Europe, the gliders break down to 3 meters (10 feet) so they can be carried easily on the lifts. Many ski areas have not only accommodated the kite flyer, they have established schools to teach the new sport.

Close to the German border in the Austrian Tirol not far from the legendary ski areas of Innsbruck and Kitzbühel lies a sleepy little ski village named Kössen. The snow here is good, the mountain is steep and the night life is memorable, but it isn't as well known as its bigger neighbors. The little town of 2,000 has some far-sighted leadership, however. In March of 1975, they staged the first large international hang

Setting up in the snow at Sugarloaf, Maine.

Bruno Engler's camera catches Willi Muller of Muller Kites in Calgary flying off the peak of Mt. Norquay. That's Rundle Mountain just beyond the Banff townsite, Alberta, Canada.

gliding competition and pulled off an outstanding event through hard work and typical Germanic efficiency. Their promotion attracted some 300 kite flyers, not the 100 they expected, and 50 came from the U.S. While they spent over $18,000 hosting the event, they realized over $1,000,000 worth of advertising in German magazines and on television; this sleepy little Austrian ski village suddenly became the hang gliding capital of the world. All summer long the hang gliding school was at capacity, the air was filled with kites while the parking lot and restaurants were overflowing with camera-toting German tourists. That winter, people came to Kössen not only to fly but to watch the flying and to ski. Kössen was on the map!

With the formation of the Commission Internationale de Vol Libre (Hang Gliding) of the World body Federation Aeronautique Internationale, Kössen was accorded the honor of hosting the First World Hang Gliding Championships in September 1976. The Kössen story is being repeated in numerous ski areas across the U.S. and Canada, as ski area management and whole towns realize the potential of this new and attractive, exciting aviation sport.

Typically, hang gliders measure between 16 feet and 20 feet along the leading edges and keel and weigh around 40 pounds. They glide at 4:1 or better (depending on the model), i.e., they fly forward 4 feet for every foot of descent. Some of the newer craft may glide twice as far providing a much greater range.

You may build your kite or purchase it ready made, but the factory built models prevail today. There was a time when kits were good enough; it only had to fly. Now, however, the demand is for the performance and quality that only a professionally designed and manufactured model can supply. You might have started your skiing career on re-worked Army surplus skis (I did) but you wouldn't consider them now. (Come to think of it, my first glider was of the primitive home-designed, home-built variety). Sources can best be found in the pages of *Ground Skimmer* Magazine, the official publication of the United States Hang Gliding Association; the address follows this article.

This is not to say, however, that you shouldn't understand the construction of your glider. One should be able to make repairs and must be able to competently assess damage after a hard landing.

The word "kite" came from water skiing where flat kites were towed aloft or "kited" above the water behind boats. Later, they switched to the familiar two-lobed Rogallo design, and it was found that this new "kite" could be released at altitude for a "gliding" return back to earth. Then a foot launch was tried, and an exciting new aviation sport was reborn. We say "reborn" because the Wright Brothers were hang gliding in all their early testing at Kitty Hawk. They made numerous soaring flights over the dunes

The hang glider flies between 15 and 30 mph, is highly maneuverable and may be landed almost anywhere. In good lift conditions, fliers have ridden the wind to remain aloft more than 13 hours. Some have gained several thousand feet altitude and others have flown more than 50 miles.

when the wind was right. But when they strapped on an engine and captured the imagination of the world, hang gliding was pushed into a closet for more than half a century. After the foot launch came the snow ski launch, but the hang glider was still often referred to as a "kite." Interestingly enough, the term "hang glider' came from the German "Hangëgleiter" coined by the early pioneer of flight Otto Lillienthal in the late 1800s. But more recently, the Germans have used the word "drachen" or "dragon." After all, every one knows that kites came from China and in China all kites resemble dragons. So much for today's language lesson.

Very short skis are best for the ski launch. Long ones are awkward both to carry and to fly, and length offers no advantage to kite flying. Very short skis are necessary if you wish to fly in the prone position. [Plate bindings like the Burt will prevent you from losing a ski, should it release inadvertently.—Ed.]

Safety is another important consideration. Man must accept certain risks whenever he ventures beyond his element in the quest of the enjoyment in conquering new frontiers. Proper training, a dose of common sense and a dash of fear will go a long way toward producing a lengthy and happy flight career. One should never fly alone or in areas inaccessible by rescue vehicles. Flight should never be attempted in winds above 20mph particulary in the learning stages and in tree-studded ski areas where the wind is liable

to be turbulent. Hang gliding is a clear weather sport. Flying in falling snow may lead to loss of sight with the ground and serious disorientation.

Hang Gliding offers the skier an alternative on the slopes as well as a challenge. Those clear, sunny, no-wind days when the snow is just a bit too icy are just ideal for ultra-light flight. Now you can take part in two exhilarating outdoor winter sports on the same ski slope, and you may return again later in the year to fly over the warm summer countryside.

For more information on hang gliding, send to the United States Hang Gliding Association (P.O. Box 66306-P, Los Angeles, California 90066) for a free information kit. They will provide you with a list of dealers and schools in your area.

The author's book, *HANG GLIDING, The Basic Handbook of Skysurfing,* may be purchased from him (P.O. Box 4232-73, Santa Barbara, California 93103) for $5.95 postpaid.

(Editor's note: Dan Poynter not only "wrote the book;" he is President of the International Hang Gliding Commission and serves on the boards of both the United States Hang Gliding Association and the U.S. Parachute Association. SKIER'S DIGEST is pleased to end its second edition with his seductive invitation to take a step beyond skiing in our quest for the ultimate kinesthetic adventure.)

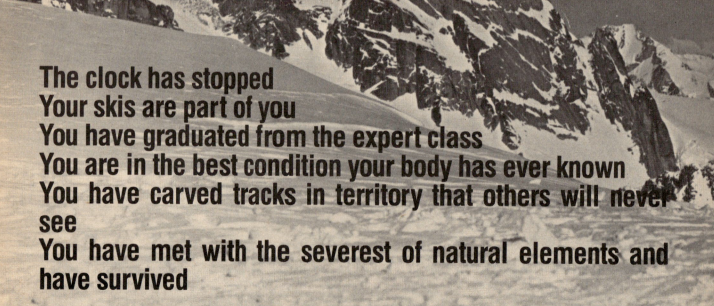

The clock has stopped
Your skis are part of you
You have graduated from the expert class
You are in the best condition your body has ever known
You have carved tracks in territory that others will never see
You have met with the severest of natural elements and have survived

You are a **SKIER.**

Acknowledgements

FIRST and foremost, my appreciation is for Marge, my incredible wife, who took most of the photos for this book, developed them in a closet and printed them in a damp basement. She did all the typing, some editing and even some ski reporting while I healed in the Mineral Springs Hospital, Banff. In addition, she has been a fantastic wife, cooking, sewing, chauffeuring while I wrote—the outrageous silver parka that I wore for most of the photos is the work of her needle.

Thanks also, Stu Campbell, Dave Stewart and Horst Abraham for telling our readers a little about current P.S.I.A. methodology; and appreciation to Certification Pre-Course Conductor, Allan Woods, for giving me a perfect score. Gratitude to the Lange USA family for allowing us to visit their plant. Thank you, Jean-Claude, for permitting us to use the wisdom of Killy in SKIER'S DIGEST. Thanks, Stein Eriksen, for letting us prove that you were ten years ahead in your style of skiing. *Ein Prosit,* Othmar Schneider, for keeping good form alive in America, along with men like Emo Henrich, Réal Charette and Sigi Grottendorfer. Thank you, Tom Corcoran, for preparing such an informative manuscript about Waterville Valley; you, Sara Widness for the Killington report; and you, Phil Gerard, for your Freestyle contribution. Thanks, Dan Poynter, for turning us on to Hang Gliding. A big hug for Cameron, my daughter, for your patience with me in developing Chapter 5. Thanks Ed Wyka for the use your enlarger and the Glen Ellen photos.

Special thanks are extended to the affable Ernie Blake for treating us like close relatives at Taos Ski Valley, our favorite American resort; to Hans Gmoser for hosting us in his Bugaboo Lodge, where we were treated royally by Leo Grillmair and his wife and were guided down 150,000 vertical feet of the "greatest skiing in the world"; and to Air Canada for their exceptional generosity. Finally, I would like to thank the 8,000 plus students whom I have taught on the mountain, as your particular needs and responses to my instruction have been the major motivation behind this creative effort.

Frank Covino